Archaeologies of Rules and Regulation

Archaeologies of Rules and Regulation

Between Text and Practice

Edited by
Barbara Hausmair, Ben Jervis, Ruth Nugent and
Eleanor Williams

berghahn
NEW YORK • OXFORD
www.berghahnbooks.com

First published in 2018 by
Berghahn Books
www.berghahnbooks.com

© 2018, 2025 Barbara Hausmair, Ben Jervis, Ruth Nugent and Eleanor Williams
First paperback edition published in 2025

All rights reserved. Except for the quotation of short passages
for the purposes of criticism and review, no part of this book
may be reproduced in any form or by any means, electronic or
mechanical, including photocopying, recording, or any information
storage and retrieval system now known or to be invented,
without written permission of the publisher.

Library of Congress Cataloging-in-Publication Data
A C.I.P. cataloging record is available from the Library of Congress

British Library Cataloguing in Publication Data
A catalogue record for this book is available from the British Library

ISBN 978-1-78533-765-9 hardback
ISBN 978-1-83695-051-6 paperback
ISBN 978-1-83695-184-1 epub
ISBN 978-1-78533-766-6 web pdf

https://doi.org/10.3167/9781785337659

Contents

List of Illustrations viii
Acknowledgements xii

Archaeologies of Rules and Regulation: An Introduction 1
Barbara Hausmair, Ben Jervis, Ruth Nugent and Eleanor Williams

Part I. Networks

Introduction: Rules, Networks and Different Kinds of Sources 21
Natascha Mehler

Chapter 1
Rules, Identity and a Sense of Place in a Medieval Town: The Case of Southampton's *Oak Book* 25
Ben Jervis

Chapter 2
Meat for the Market: The Butchers' Guild Rules from 1267 and Urban Archaeology in Tulln, Lower Austria 43
Ute Scholz

Chapter 3
Rubbish and Regulations in the Middle Ages: A Comparison of Urban and Rural Disposal Practices 61
Greta Civis

Chapter 4
How to Plant a Colony in the New World: Rules and Practices in
New Sweden and the Seventeenth-Century Delaware Valley   83
Magdalena Naum

Part II. Space and Power

Introduction: Rules and the Built Environment   105
Harold Mytum

Chapter 5
Embodied Regulations: Searching for Boundaries in the Viking Age   109
Marianne Hem Eriksen

Chapter 6
What Law Says That There Has to Be a Castle? The Castle
Landscape of Frodsham, Cheshire   127
Rachel Swallow

Chapter 7
Shakespearian Space-Men: Spatial Rules in London's Early
Playhouses   148
Ruth Nugent

Chapter 8
US Army Regulations and Spatial Tactics: The Archaeology of
Indulgence Consumption at Fort Yamhill, Oregon, United States,
1856–66   168
Justin E. Eichelberger

Chapter 9
Religion in the Asylum: Lunatic Asylum Chapels and Religious
Provision in Nineteenth-Century Ireland   192
Katherine Fennelly

Chapter 10
Prison-Issue Artefacts, Documentary Insights and the Negotiated
Realities of Political Imprisonment: The Case of Long Kesh/Maze,
Northern Ireland   212
Laura McAtackney

Part III. Corporeality

Introduction: *Maleficium* and Mortuary Archaeology: Rules and
Regulations in the Negotiation of Identities   233
Duncan Sayer

Chapter 11
Gone to the Dogs? Negotiating the Human-Animal Boundary in
Anglo-Saxon England   238
Kristopher Poole

Chapter 12
Adherence to Islamic Tradition and the Formation of Iberian Islam
in Early Medieval Al-Andalus   254
Sarah Inskip

Chapter 13
Break a Rule But Save a Soul: Unbaptized Children and Medieval
Burial Regulation   273
Barbara Hausmair

Chapter 14
Medieval Monastic Text and the Treatment of the Dead: An
Archaeothanatological Perspective on Adherence to the Cluniac
Customaries   291
Eleanor Williams

Chapter 15
'With as Much Secresy and Delicacy as Possible': Nineteenth-
Century Burial Practices at the London Hospital   311
Louise Fowler and Natasha Powers

The Archaeology of Rules and Regulation: Closing Remarks   329
Duncan H. Brown

Index   333

Illustrations

Figures

1.1	Map showing the extent of the Guild Merchant's control	34
1.2	58 French Street, Southampton	37
2.1	Map of Tulln in the thirteenth century with excavated areas	44
2.2	Excavation plan of the main market (*Breiter Markt*) in Tulln in the thirteenth century	49
2.3	Distribution of animal species according to absolute quantities in percentages	53
3.1	Excavation plan of Diepensee. Archaeological features mentioned in the text are marked: circle = well; square = pit; black line = ditch	66
3.2	Excavation plan of Diepensee. Relative amount of animal bones per area (TF)	69
4.1	Geography of New Sweden. Map drawn by P. Lindström in 1644/55	85
4.2	Gloria Dei (Old Swedes') Church in Philadelphia, serving a Swedish-speaking Lutheran congregation throughout the late seventeenth and eighteenth centuries	89
4.3	Lower Swedish Cabin in Drexel Hill, Pennsylvania	90
5.1	The doorway of the reconstructed Iron Age longhouse of Ullandhaug, Stavanger, Norway	115
5.2	The hall building at Borg in Lofoten, northern Norway	116

5.3	The Forsa ring from Hälsingland, Sweden, with its runic inscription	116
6.1	Location of Frodsham Castle within (a) England, (b) Cheshire and (c) its immediate landscape	130
6.2	Tithe Map with field name annotations	135
6.3	Earthwork remains running north of Dig Lane, to the west of Castle Park, Frodsham	136
6.4	Mound in Castle Park, view to south	136
6.5	Ground and magnetometry geophysics surveys at Castle Park, Frodsham	137
7.1	The Rose Playhouse: phases 1 and 2	154
7.2	Buchelius' copy of DeWitt's sketch of the Swan c. 1596	156
7.3	'The Wits, or Sport upon Sport' frontispiece, 1662	156
7.4	Surviving box-pews in Worthenbury church	159
8.1	Northwest Oregon Territory c. 1856, showing the location of Forts Yamhill, Hoskins, and Umpqua, and the Coastal Indian Reservation	174
8.2	Map of Fort Yamhill c. 1864, showing the fort layout and the location of company kitchen in relation to the parade ground and the officers' quarters	175
8.3	Feature map and schematic drawing of the company kitchen	176
8.4 and 8.5	Sample of alcohol bottles and tobacco pipes recovered from the company kitchen	178
8.6	Spatial contexts at the company kitchen	179
8.7	Kernel density distributions of alcohol and tobacco-related artefacts	182
9.1	Stanley Royd Hospital Church, Wakefield, nine months after its destruction by fire	193
9.2	The grounds of the former Maryborough District Lunatic Asylum chapel site, with the Roman Catholic church in centre middle-ground and the Anglican church in left middle-ground	193
9.3	The interior of Maryborough Asylum Roman Catholic church (now St Fintan's Church)	194
9.4	Plan of the Maryborough Asylum site as it stood in 2014, with significant features labelled	199
9.5	Plan of the Maryborough Asylum churches	202
9.6	Rear elevation of the Maryborough Asylum churches	203
10.1	Front entrance of an H Block	218
10.2	A Nissen hut contained within a wired compound	219
10.3	Loyalist banner used for marching in the Compounds. Confiscated and held in the Northern Ireland Prison Service Museum, Millisle	221

10.4	Metal household bin being used to distill alcohol in the Compounds. Confiscated and held in the storage room of the Northern Ireland Prison Service Museum, Millisle	222
10.5	Photograph taken by prison officers of debris after prisoners had broken all the windows of their non-complying H Block wing. Northern Ireland Prison Service Museum, Millisle	226
12.1	Map of Spain with major Islamic sites: 1) Huelva, 2) Cadiz, 3) Seville, 4) Écija, 5) Córdoba, 6) Malaga, 7) Granada, 8) Almeria, 9) Murcia and 10) Alicante	258
12.2	Islamic right-side burial at Çatalhöyük with face and body orientated towards Mecca	264
13.1	Map of Mount Göttweig	280
13.2	Age distribution within the sample of infant inhumations from the church of St George	281
13.3	Excavation plan of the church of St George and the surrounding infant cemetery	282
13.4	Overlapping infant burials in the southern area of the cemetery	283
13.5	Mount Göttweig with the Benedictine Abbey on its northern plateau. St George is located on its southern peak, visible in the left part of the photo	284
14.1–14.3	Individuals from La Charité's thirteenth-century gallery possibly exhibiting skeletal evidence for preparation in line with the *Bern*	297
14.4	Individuals from pre-gallery cemetery possibly exhibiting skeletal evidence for preparation in line with the *Bern*	298
14.5–14.7	Individuals from Bermondsey Abbey exhibiting no clear skeletal evidence for preparation in line with the *Bern*	300
14.8–14.10	Individuals from Bermondsey Abbey exhibiting varied forearm positions	302
14.11–14.13	Examples of lower limb positioning in individuals from La Charité and Bermondsey Abbey	303
15.1	Plan of the excavated burial ground	317
15.2	J.G. Oatley's (?1907) reconstructed plan of the hospital buildings in c. 1830	318
15.3	Copper-alloy wire <86> and a rib and vertebra with drilled holes from [23401], found in association	319
15.4	Context [52203] showing standardized portions reunited for burial	323

Tables

3.1	Chronological development of find spectrum in Diepensee. n: Sum=75,265. Phase 1=713; Phase 2=9,047; Phase 3=19,429; Phase 3–4=6,280; Phase 4=11,991; Phase 2–3=8,456; Unphased=19,349. Cadaver-pits are not included	70
3.2	Animal species as represented in selected features: (a) well no. 6459; (b) ditch surrounding the village	71
3.3	General find spectrum in Diepensee	72
4.1	Criminal cases reviewed by the Court of Upland between 1676 and 1681. Approximately 60–66 per cent of the residents under the Court's jurisdiction were Swedes; Englishmen were the second largest group	93
8.1	Alcohol and tobacco artefacts recovered from the company kitchen	177
8.2	Artefact, weight and MNV counts for alcohol-related artefacts recovered from the company kitchen by spatial context	181
8.3	Artefact, weight and MNV counts for tobacco-related artefacts recovered from the company kitchen by spatial context	181
8.4	Percentages of indulgence-related artefacts by spatial context	181
8.5	Results of Pearson's chi-square statistical analysis for alcohol-related artefacts	184
8.6	Results of Pearson's chi-square statistical analysis for tobacco-related artefacts	185
11.1	Frequency with which dogs are identified with Anglo-Saxon bone assemblages	240
12.1	Number of statistically significant sex differences in the Coracho pre-Islamic and Écija Islamic skeletal material	259
12.2	Chi-squared test results on joint modifications in the knee and ankle for pre-Islamic Coracho and Islamic Écija	261
12.3	Prevalence of tibial squatting facets in various Iberian sites	262

Acknowledgements

As with any project of this type, this volume has taken a long time to produce and would not have been possible without the support of a number of colleagues. We would like to thank all of the contributors for both their stimulating contributions and their patience. We would also like to extend our thanks to Natascha Mehler, Harold Mytum, Duncan Sayer and Duncan Brown for their summary chapters that have excellently drawn common themes from the chapters, and to all the reviewers who have so kindly given their time and expertise.

For their support and advice throughout the project, we are particularly grateful to Howard Williams and Duncan Sayer. We would also like to extend our thanks to the staff of Berghahn Books, in particular Caryn Berg and Caroline Kuhtz, for their help and encouragement in the final stages of production.

The Zukunftskolleg/University of Konstanz kindly provided financial support for the preparation of the volume's index, which was compiled with a lot of effort by Michele Hughes (Glen Dore Indexing).

Archaeologies of Rules and Regulation
An Introduction

Barbara Hausmair, Ben Jervis, Ruth Nugent and Eleanor Williams

Rules are central to how we negotiate and experience the world. They structure social practice; if followed, they inhibit social action and if transgressed, then there are consequences for individuals and society as a whole. Archaeologists have long recognized the importance of rules, but, with the exception of studies of 'ritual' behaviour, their influence on past societies, and our understanding of them, has not been theorized. The aim of this volume, is to explore the relationship between written and unwritten rules and the archaeological record.

Our contributors explore the complexity of rules by comparing the physical evidence of everyday practice with documented directives, examining discrepancy and divergence, manipulation, reinforcement and varying interpretations of rules. In so doing, they have tried to avoid a naive dichotomy of domination versus submission or the tracing of acts of rebellion. Instead, the chapters collected here explore the rich interplay between rules structuring and being structured by society. The volume as a whole approaches rules (the terms upon which regulation is practised) as a spectrum of behaviour, expectations and punishments, and discusses how responses to regulation could strengthen or dilute existing rules and practices. Crucially, the archaeological perspective is uniquely capable of addressing intersections between text and practice by harnessing both material evidence and written sources.

The interdisciplinary nature of the volume is matched by its chronological and geographical scope. It surveys past societies from the United Kingdom, Ireland, France, Spain, Austria, Germany, Scandinavia and the United States, from the fifth century AD to the 1970s. The volume is divided into three parts, each centred on burgeoning themes in archaeology and the humanities and social sciences: 'Networks', 'Space and Power' and 'Corporeality'. This broad span of time and space, orchestrated by three specific themes, is vital for what is a groundbreaking introduction to an overlooked area of archaeological and historical research.

Theorizing Human Behaviour

One only has to look at a map of prehistoric cultures, or the distribution of different styles of material culture, to appreciate that archaeologists are excellent at identifying difference between and amongst past societies (e.g. Myres 1969). The application of social theory has allowed us to examine why these variations occur, but has also led to questions of sameness, coherence and normative behaviour surfacing as areas of archaeological enquiry. It is the mechanisms through which behaviour becomes normative, and social norms are challenged or transgressed, which form the focus of this book. Rules are mechanisms used by societies to regulate behaviour, to reinforce or forcefully change social norms and structures, and that act as mediators of continuity by bringing stability to communities.

There is a growing interest in the archaeology of legal culture; however, studies principally focus on the administration of law, for example, through the study of places of justice (e.g. Buckberry and Hadley 2007; Auler 2008, 2010, 2013) or the ways in which landscapes of administration develop (Baker et al. 2011; Reynolds 2012; Baker and Brookes 2013; Brookes 2013; Oosthuizen 2013; Smith and Reynolds 2013), with a particular emphasis on the early medieval period. Some archaeologists have sought to identify evidence for the adherence to known rules in the archaeological record, for example, in relation to waste management, the subject of several case studies in this volume (e.g. Rathje and Murphy 1992; Brown 1999; Jervis 2013). However, studies often employ textually transmitted regulations solely as sources for explaining patterns in the archaeological record, negating the possibility that the material remains may also embody actions of nonconformance, resistance or simply adaptions of normative behaviour that developed and changed over time. Examinations of the relationships between legal, regulatory or normative texts of various kinds and the archaeological record that pay specific attention to this complex reciprocity of regulation and action have, until now, remained underdeveloped. By making this relationship the central focus of study, the chapters in this volume offer various methods and frameworks for the exploration of how behaviour is managed, how rules serve to bring stability to communities or create tensions negotiated through the use of material culture and, more generally, in relating written texts to human practice. In this introduction we briefly outline some of the approaches taken in these chapters, their relationship to different theoretical perspectives on human behaviour and practice, and their implications for the integrated study of documents and archaeological material.

Cultural Knowledge and Habitus: What is it to Act Normally?

Across archaeological scholarship, Pierre Bourdieu's (1977) concept of habitus has been particularly influential. This theory – that we subconsciously reproduce normative behaviour as a form of cultural knowledge – has been particularly used to explain how people relate to built spaces and items of portable material culture (e.g. Blinkhorn 1997; Giles 2000). Sameness and continuity are explained as the reproduction of habitus; the way things always were. Within historical archaeology, this has been most evident in the study of buildings, with scholars such as Kate Giles (2000) and Roberta Gilchrist (1994) emphasizing the presence of spatial logics that transcend different types of space, for example. Some archaeologists have critiqued the application of habitus, arguing that rather than identifying habitual behaviour, it is more pertinent to examine how such behaviour emerges and its effects on people, specifically in relation to identity creation (e.g. Chapman and Gaydarska 2011: 37).

Such a challenge is taken on here by Marianne Hem Eriksen (Chapter 5), who uses the idea that habitus is reflected in the layout of built spaces as a starting point for a discussion that focuses on what it was that became habitual, and why it came to be reflected in buildings. Behaviour was not just normalized through a passive reproduction of habitus, but rather through the effects of this cultural knowledge, or ontology, being active in determining how people conceived and perceived of spaces. Whilst buildings might act as theatres for the reproduction of cultural memory, they also become media through which knowledge is not just reproduced but also applied to make spaces that may seem alien to us, but entirely logical within their context.

The concept of habitus has a difficult relationship to regulated behaviour. By its very nature, habitus is subconscious behaviour, consisting of deeply ingrained ways of doing. By implication, therefore, habitual practices should not need to be regulated. Yet there are contexts in which such habitual behaviour might be challenged, in which spaces of ambiguity open up, and it is in these spaces that we can see rules playing a role in seeking to maintain the status quo rather than allowing social order to be challenged. In her study, Greta Civis (Chapter 3) works towards a similar conclusion with regard to waste management, drawing on the writing of Mary Douglas to argue that people may categorize waste in ways they are not necessarily consciously aware of, with normative behaviour emerging within a context as this knowledge is reproduced and applied. She argues that this knowledge surfaces in contentious moments, when it is not possible to reproduce this behaviour, for example, as rural attitudes to waste are unable to be reproduced in the town, leading to the emergence of civic regulations.

A further such context, the Elizabethan theatre, is discussed by Ruth Nugent (Chapter 7). Theatres can be viewed as transgressive spaces, where rich and poor might mingle, where men take on the persona of women and where, generally, things need not be as they seem. Nugent, drawing on an established body of scholarship, demonstrates that it is the contentious and challenging nature of these spaces that caused them to be situated in marginal locations within London and that led to a range of regulations being developed to control theatrical performances. However, rather than focusing on these written rules, Nugent studies the use of space within the theatres, finding parallels between the spatial organization of these public structures with more familiar buildings – churches and elite houses. The reproduction of habitus through spatial grammar is a familiar trope in the study of medieval and early modern buildings, for example, in Giles' (2000) study of the relationship between guildhalls and churches in York. However, Nugent sees this spatial grammar not as a simple reproduction of habitus, but rather as a concept abducted and put to work in the theatrical setting; by being translated into these socially liminal buildings, the use of space could be employed to temper the disruptive and socially jarring nature of the activities that went on within them. This brought a sense of order and regulation that countered the potentially transgressive nature of the theatrical environment.

The colonial context discussed by Magdalena Naum (Chapter 4) is a similarly contested environment. Settlement in new places is a severely disruptive process, which causes habitual behaviour to surface, perhaps as it becomes impossible to re-create it. Whereas in Nugent's study habitual understandings of space were put to work to calm tensions, in Naum's study we see rules being developed to create circumstances in which habitual behaviour can be reproduced, a similar process to that identified by Civis. Rules can therefore be seen, in this context, as a conscious tool used to re-create particular social conditions in which traditional behaviour and attitudes could persist; in Naum's words, they were a means through which familiarity and constancy could be introduced. If, as Naum argues, the North American colonies were shaped by their

European roots, rules were, perhaps, less an instrument of domination and subjugation and more a tool for closing off spaces of contention and ambiguity, designed to mitigate against the effects of re-adjustment.

We see here several different sets of relationships between habitual or normative behaviour and regulatory action emerging. For Eriksen, cultural knowledge, manifesting in habitual behaviour, acts itself as a regulatory mechanism. For Nugent, in the context of the Elizabethan theatre, habitus can be seen as being abducted, becoming a regulatory mechanism in a contentious environment, whilst for Civis and Naum, rules become a conscious tool used to create an environment in which normative behaviour and attitudes can persist. A further perspective is advanced by Eleanor Williams' study of medieval Cluniac burial practices (Chapter 14) and Louise Fowler and Natasha Powers' study of the reburial of dissected individuals used in the teaching of anatomy (Chapter 15). In both cases, rules can be seen as emerging from behaviour that was already practised. The 1832 Anatomy Act appears to have legitimized existing practices for the exhumation and reburial of corpses for scientific study, whilst Cluniac customaries record specific elements of a wide spectrum of behaviour practised at the motherhouse, Cluny, and variously across its network of religious houses. Williams' study in particular raises interesting questions about the relationship between normative behaviour and regulated behaviour. Cluniac customaries apply to a range of different behaviours, viewed, at the scale of the individual house, as normative, but, at the scale of the Cluniac Order, potentially as nonstandard. Burial is an area that lends itself to explicit regulation because of the transformative and symbolically loaded nature of death. Here rules seem to emerge as a mechanism for dealing with necessary divergence from accepted practice, creating enough freedom for practices to adapt to specific circumstances, but also defining the limits of what is considered acceptable.

In all of these examples, therefore, we can see the relationship between habitual (or normative) and regulated behaviour being negotiated in different ways. Using the archaeological evidence in isolation limits us only to identifying patterns of similarity and difference (what we might interpret as different regulatory regimes or sets of cultural knowledge). Similarly, in isolation, rules themselves appear prescriptive. The strength of the interdisciplinary approach taken in these studies is to demonstrate that the processes through which rules develop vary contextually and have a complex relationship with how people act, in some cases legitimizing behaviour, in others explaining it and in further contexts becoming a tool in which social tensions can be diffused, thus becoming a medium for persistence.

Processes and Biographies

By seeking to restrict behaviour, regulatory regimes are fundamentally about managing processes. A key metaphor for understanding processes within the archaeological literature is that of biography. As people, places and things pass through time, they can be seen to gain and shed meanings, with their role in past events having implications for their future one. Principally developing from the writing of Igor Kopytoff (1986), ideas of cultural biography have been applied to a range of archaeological materials from Iron Age mirrors to Anglo-Saxon brooches and also to archaeological deposits (Joy 2010; Morris 2011; Martin 2012; see also Gosden and Marshall 1999; Mytum 2010). Allied to the concept of biography is that of the *chaîne opératoire*, a reconstruction of processes (typically in relation to the production of objects) with a focus on the ways in which these processes are socially situated (Lemmonier 1993). Within these related schemes of thinking about the temporality of people, places and things, it is clear that social actors, be they human or nonhuman, exist in a social context, which has implications for them. These implications may be iterative (that is, certain behaviours may be reproduced) or episodic (that is, relating to a particular process of transformation or stage in the 'life course' of a person or thing).

In the most literal terms, these ideas relate to the way in which people operate within a social context. Sarah Inskip's examination of skeletal remains from medieval al-Andalus (Chapter 12) provides an example of the implications for rules within iterative action. Inskip demonstrates that by participating in rituals of prayer and gendered division of labour as prescribed by Islamic law, rules might be seen as becoming embodied, indicated by the presence of particular skeletal modifications related to kneeling (prayer) and manual labour. Here we can see a clear indication that rules are more than texts; they are bundles of ideas that, if enacted in social processes, have wide implications for human experience. These rules do more than lock people into iterative processes of prayer, for example – they also physically affect people, potentially impacting the ways in which they are able to experience the world. Therefore, on the one hand, the enacting of rules limits behaviour in a regulatory way and, on the other hand, these regulated performances can have further, unintended consequences for how the biography of an individual might be able to develop, even within the spectrum of permitted courses of action. An example of the role of rules in processes of transition is provided by Fowler and Powers, who demonstrate that the biography of a person does not end at death, but that burial, excavation and re-interment is a process through which personhood is renegotiated. By being exhumed and enrolled in a process of scientific study, bodies can be seen as developing new meaning as scientific objects (see Richards 2001; Robb and Harris 2013). It is the transformative and dangerous nature of this activity that stimulated the development of specific regulations that, as described above, served to legitimize these practices. The 1832 Anatomy Act can therefore be seen as opening up possibilities for bodily biographies to be extended into death, with rules becoming a means through which this transformation was intended to be managed safely for the medical sector, while simultaneously, the very same rules conflicted with the understanding of the "Christian body", further reinforcing social class divides. Furthermore, the regulation imbued certain people with the ability to exhume these bodies, creating new forms of specialist employment, which would have broader implications for how they sat, as potentially marginal figures, within the communities in which they lived and worked. Within these two studies, therefore, we see rules as having different implications for people; on the one hand, they regulate behaviour explicitly, but also impact the body and the range of human experience, while on the other hand, rules provide a framework in which processes of transition can occur.

It is not only for people that rules could have implications; they can also mediate the ways in which places and things could become meaningful. In her study of the medieval castle at Frodsham, Rachel Swallow (Chapter 6) demonstrates that the development of the site is closely bound up with its legal status. Legal status gave the castle, as a place, particular official power over a region, allowing it to develop along a specific trajectory not open to other places. Crucially for Swallow, this legal status does not need to equate to any specific architectural form, but rather to a set of associations that imbue significance. It might be considered that for this reason, sites of significance in the early medieval period retain their significance in the later medieval period, with these processes of persistence being less about the taking over of existing places of power by incoming elites and more about places continuing along a trajectory through which they had acquired and continued to maintain specific associations, mediated through their legal status, from which their significance was derived.

However, as Katherine Fennelly (Chapter 9) demonstrates in her study of nineteenth-century asylum chapels, this can also be true in relation to the marginalization of places and the people who occupy them. Through the study of the development of asylum buildings, Fennelly demonstrates that the biographies of these buildings are closely related to how outsiders perceive of the care offered inside. This perception is bidirectional, with a desire to be perceived of as offering appropriate care influencing the form of buildings, and structural forms impacting upon these perceptions. It was, Fennelly argues, this preoccupation with perception that resulted in these communities becoming increasingly marginalized and the development of distinctive forms of asylum architecture within the legal structures associated with care. A similar link between architecture and behaviour can be seen in Laura McAtackney's study of twentieth-century internment in Northern Ireland (Chapter 10), with changes in the form of buildings taking place in response to unrest and riots. McAtackney's chapter also makes a profound point about the temporality of biographies. Portable material culture can be seen as having a biography that runs more quickly than those of the buildings. For example, the appropriation of objects for disruptive purposes (for example, as weapons) played a role in determining the development of the prison architecture. Furthermore, this portable material culture was situated within the wider power structures of the prison, with the maintenance and availability of objects being controlled by prison authorities. We can therefore see how the decision to transgress regulatory structures within the prison, and the performance of the structures themselves, had material implications, entangling the biographies of the prison buildings, staff, prisoners and portable objects. Therefore, by tracing the biographies of buildings and objects, as well as of the people occupying these institutions, we can understand how regulatory structures had implications for how institutions, as bundles of all of these human and nonhuman actors, developed – for example, asylums came to be marginalized from society and prisons were continuously contested spaces.

We have thus seen how people, institutions and buildings were all shaped by rules, which limited how their biographies could develop, with both intended and unintended consequences. In her study of medieval waste deposition, Civis develops a specific framework for articulating this social embeddedness of behaviour, coining the term *chaîne éliminatoire* to describe the biography of waste and rubbish deposits. This framework offers a way of both reconstructing streams of waste within settlements, but also of understanding these in relation to cultural knowledge about how substances might contaminate spaces. As discussed above, it is when this cultural knowledge surfaces due to the inability to reproduce these practices that rules develop. Ute Scholz (Chapter 2), in her study of waste deposition in the medieval town of Tulln, also demonstrates this embeddedness, seeing deposition, and its regulation, as a medium through which consumption, religion and power are all performed, exemplifying that cultural knowledge and rules relate to different stages in the process of food consumption and preparation.

Amongst these diverse case studies, therefore, general points emerge about the relationship between rules and biographies. The first of these is that rules, if enacted, have a cumulative impact, as iterative behaviour causes particular effects. This is most vividly apparent in Inskip's study, but is also evidenced in the discussions of waste management and deposition by Scholz and Civis, in which an emphasis on the social embeddedness of processes sees the reproduction of cultural knowledge. Similarly, Swallow shows how the biographies of places emerge out of, and reproduce and strengthen, regulatory systems. As Civis demonstrates, a further intersection occurs at points of transition, when existing practices cannot be performed. This is also evident in Fowler and Powers' study of the transition of corpses into scientific bodies, and Fennelly's considerations on the development of asylum buildings. Indeed, both Fennelly and McAtackney's studies show that the iterative and episodic relationships between actors and rules are not distinct from one another, but that changing attitudes or transgressions of rules can culminate in processes of transition, which may have the effect of changing power dynamics, or the relationship of a community or institution to the outside world. A useful means of conceptualizing this relationship can be seen in Gilles Deleuze and Félix Guattari's (1987: 47) concept of the 'coding' of social action, with iterative behaviour serving to restrict social action within a particular spectrum of behaviour. Particular actions serve to reinforce the code or channel biographies along particular trajectories or 'lines of becoming'. The episodic events can be seen as processes of 'over-coding', in which existing codes become submerged beneath new structures, which emerge from their weakening through social interaction, leading in turn to new coding structures (Deleuze and Guattari 1984: 288–89). With this in mind, it becomes clear that rules and regulatory frameworks are a vital, but understudied, element of biographical perspectives on archaeological material.

The Ontological and Material Turns

A key transition has occurred in archaeological theory in recent years. Two separate but connected intellectual 'turns' are evident. The material turn (Hicks and Beaudry 2010) sees archaeologists paying more attention to the active role of objects and materials in the lives of past societies, developing out of perspectives on the nature of material agency (Gell 1998; Latour 2005; Robb 2010). The second is the ontological turn, which has emphasized the importance of appreciating that societies develop ontologies that differ from the modern Western worldview. This has, for example, led to discussions of animism and active materials, which provide further frameworks for understanding the power of the material. Indeed, Hodder (2012: 86) has even suggested that regulations emerge to allow us to harness the power of the material and to stop us getting into trouble with things. The implications of this are twofold. First, archaeologists might be encouraged to identify and discuss the ontologies of past communities (e.g. Jones 2005) and, second, alternative ontologies might be used as a tool to view archaeological problems from alternative perspectives (Harris 2014). In doing so, the ontological turn has forced archaeologists to question the nature of knowledge and cast a newly critical eye on our understanding of the past.

The influence of the material turn is evident in Ben Jervis' contribution (Chapter 1), which considers the agency of medieval guild rules. Jervis, following Bruno Latour's (2010) ethnography of the French legal system, argues that rules should be considered participants in social action. As discussed above, rules limit social behaviour as long as they are enrolled within performances of social action. However, Jervis argues that rules do not possess agency, but rather contribute to the emergence of particular forms of agency that prompt certain actions and limit others within the context of the town. The agency of material culture is also demonstrated well by McAtackney's discussion of the appropriation of material culture in a prison environment. In a discussion, which is analogous with Bruno Latour's (1993) classic discussion of how neither guns nor people kill people, but rather that a shooting is the result of an assemblage of the two, so too might we see unrest as emerging from the joining of people and objects within an oppressive regulatory environment.

Several studies reflect more explicitly on the relationship between rules and past ontologies, or ways of knowing the world. Civis, for example, highlights elemental theory as a dominant medieval ontology that contributed to cultural understandings of how types of waste should be treated. The other dominant ontology in medieval Europe was Christianity. However, Barbara Hausmair's study of the treatment of unbaptized children in medieval Austria (Chapter 13) highlights the dangers of imposing an idealized version of such ontologies on the past. It is clear from Hausmair's chapter that documents reveal an idealized, or perhaps scholarly, ontology, but also that people may mistrust this top-down orthodoxy as a result of their living in the world. She suggests that the illicit burial of unbaptized children on consecrated ground is indicative of this process, with knowledge emerging through social experience and practice and what is written down being only one part of knowledge. A further perspective is provided by Justin Eichelberger's study of a US military camp (Chapter 8). Eichelberger highlights how the use of space within the camp is codified in military rules and regulation. However, the process of dwelling in, and inhabiting, this space caused it to be experienced and thought about in different ways. Focusing on the evidence for illicit drinking, Eichelberger shows how surveillance and regulations caused new spatial understandings to emerge as hidden spaces became locations for the performance of transgression and resistance. Therefore, as in Hausmair's study, the archaeological record betrays the messiness of social realities and the ways in which top-down frameworks may be treated with ambivalence in order to open up spaces for the performance of necessary but culturally undesirable acts to occur. These studies offer an interesting contrast to Fowler and Powers' study of the treatment of corpses in medical study, in which rules were developed in order to legitimize what was initially illicit and questionable behaviour. Therefore, we can think about how rules may be based upon such idealized norms, but that behaviour takes place in a more complex world in which the ambivalence towards rules may not be conscious dissent, but rather a means of adapting to the harsh realities of life.

For the early medieval period, attitudes are less clear, due to the patchy nature of the historical record. Kristopher Poole (Chapter 11) focuses on attitudes towards animals, specifically dogs, in Anglo-Saxon England. His discussion questions whether the clear modern ontological divide between humans and animals existed in the Anglo-Saxon mind. This discussion demonstrates how dogs can be active agents and highlights how a tension may have arisen between rules intended for a category of people that may have been broader than that which exists in the modern world. Furthermore, through analysis of the archaeological record, it is suggested that attitudes towards dogs differed between contexts (for example, between town and country). Thus, it is clear from this study that an anthropocentric view of agency and regulatory frameworks may not be appropriate in all instances, and that when we examine the evidence of past behaviour, we should contextualize this behaviour in a manner that is not beholden to a modern perspective on relations between people and the natural world. Eriksen's study also highlights the importance of contextual ontologies, arguing that boundaries in Viking houses and settlements were determined by understandings of the world that differ from our own. This is more than habitus, being instead a conscious and rational scheme based on a particular understanding of the world.

The issue of alternative perspectives and categories is also highlighted by Swallow in her study of the medieval castle. Swallow uses the term 'black boxes' to describe the term 'castle', arguing that it potentially had different meanings in the medieval period, depending upon the nature of discourse. This discussion finds parallels in Fowler's (2013) discussion of circulating references in prehistoric burial archaeology and Jervis' (2016) discussion of medieval towns. Swallow's study is important in this regard because it demonstrates how we must take care in adopting legal terms and applying them directly to categories of archaeological material. A similar point can perhaps be transferred to Poole's study of dogs, in which the dog circulates as a loaded term in archaeological literature, with sets of associations which they may not have held in the past.

Contemporary theoretical perspectives, focusing on the diversity of ways of knowing the world and the active role of the material, have thus offered fertile ground for exploring the archaeology of rules and regulation. On the one hand, we can see written rules as a powerful form of material culture in themselves, enrolled in performances of life with other objects and materials. On the other hand, we can use the archaeological record to reconstruct past ontologies, to question processes of categorization based upon legal terminology and to understand how, as Poole and Eriksen seek to do, cultural knowledge was articulated through practice. However, as Hausmair and Eichelberger demonstrate, the archaeological record may provide evidence of transgressions, which do more than show disobedience or deviation from normative behaviour. Rather, these can be used to illustrate a complex relationship between people and regulatory frameworks, in which ambivalence may be a necessary tool for dealing with the realities of a messy social existence.

Text and Practice

The problem of how to integrate archaeological evidence and historical documents is a persistent one in archaeological practice. Nancy Wicker (1999) outlined a tripartite scheme for characterizing this relationship: seeing approaches as either crossdisciplinary (combining historical and archaeological sources to a common end), multidisciplinary (using these approaches separately to address the same question) or interdisciplinary (exploring the links between text and the material record). Scholars such as Anders Andrén (1998) and John Moreland (2006) have all emphasized the need to move towards approaches equivalent to Wicker's interdisciplinary approach by considering the active nature of documents as forming a part of, and finding meaning through, social processes. The chapters presented in this volume form a contribution to achieving this goal, through addressing the relationship between text and practice in a variety of ways.

The most explicit attempt to achieve this aim is Jervis' study, which uses the writing of Bruno Latour to provide a framework for understanding how rules both emerge from, and contribute to, social practice. Other contributions also demonstrate this point by working through specific examples. For Williams, Cluniac customaries find meaning through enrolment in practice, with a dialogue existing between the circumstances and materiality of burial, and the ideals recorded in these documents. In Eichelberger's study, it is in the performance of ambivalence that we can see tensions emerging between authority and rank-and-file soldiers; here we see the potency of rules in bringing about alternative ways of thinking about, and experiencing, space. Scholz demonstrates how the writing down of rules is an important component of the mediation of power, whilst Naum clearly illuminates the active role of texts in practice, both by limiting behaviour and also by opening up areas of ambiguity in which new transgressions might occur (for example, the selling of weapons to Native Americans). That rules also open up spaces of ambiguity is exemplified by Fowler and Powers, who highlight variability in the treatment of interred human remains as the Anatomy Act does not specify what decent re-interment is.

Studies by Eichelberger, Williams, Inskip and Hausmair all consider the malleability of rules. If documents are seen as repositories of knowledge of how to behave, it is clear from the variations presented in each of these studies that people know the world through other mediums too. Knowledge and ideas are all negotiated through behaviour. As Inskip shows, the same meaning was not understood by everyone reading a document and, as Hausmair argues, knowledge also emerges from living in the world. It is then in the dialogue between archaeology and texts that we can reveal how texts, such as rules and directives, mediated understandings of the world.

By emphasizing processes of writing down rules and by seeing them as a form of material culture, it is also possible to gain deeper insights into the social dynamics and areas of tension within communities. This can work in a variety of ways. In Nugent's study, texts did more than document the socially dangerous nature of theatres; they also served to reify their potency as the recorded attitudes were played out. Similarly, in Fennelly's study, buildings come to materialize social attitudes from which the regulatory framework in which these buildings existed emerged with the institutions themselves. In Civis' study, we see a different type of tension, with rules emerging as a process of managing new kinds of space, with texts emerging from practices, as an urban translation of rural ways of living with each other and the environment.

However, it is not only regulatory documents that detail rules and regulation. Working in the early medieval period, both Poole and Eriksen demonstrate how a range of documents and literary traditions reveal attitudes. Folklore emerges out of real situations and is grounded in contemporary knowledge. As such, it not only provides insights into what was regulated, but it also highlights where areas of tension may emerge and therefore where regulation might have been required, for example, in the maintenance of real and cosmological barriers in the case of Eriksen's study.

A key point arising from Swallow's study is that within crossdisciplinary or multidisciplinary approaches, treatment of the historical record as fact can have implications for archaeological interpretations. Swallow makes one of the strongest cases for interdisciplinary study by highlighting how legal terms and archaeological sites find meaning in relation to one another, meaning that we cannot fully understand one without the other, not because of the incompleteness of either record, but because of their inherent relatedness. This is a point made in a different way in McAtackney's chapter, which highlights how the biographies of prisoners, prison artefacts and prison buildings are indivisible from regulatory developments, highlighting the potency of documents as part of the material world.

Although highly varied, the studies presented here all make contributions to the development of an interdisciplinary approach in which the relationships between documentary and archaeological evidence take centre stage. These chapters demonstrate that rules have implications that extend beyond simple regulation. Rather, they are central components of social interactions that must be taken seriously, whether we are considering the biographies of objects, narratives of continuity and change, or seeking to discover how people understood the world around them.

Barbara Hausmair is a post-doctoral researcher at the Freie Universität Berlin, Germany and previously held a Marie-Skłodowska-Curie-Fellowship at the Zukunftskolleg, University of Konstanz, Germany. She gained her Ph.D. from the University of Vienna, Austria where she was also a research associate and site supervisor in international excavation projects in France, Austria and Italy. She is the author of *Am Rande des Grabs: Todeskonzepte und Bestattungsritual in der frühmittelalterlichen Alamannia* (Sidestone Press, 2015), co-editor of *Spruch von den sibnen* (Thorbecke, 2016) and has published several articles on medieval mortuary practices and social dynamics as well as the archaeology of twentieth-century internment.

Ben Jervis is Lecturer in Medieval Archaeology at Cardiff University, United Kingdom, having gained his Ph.D. from the University of Southampton in 2011. He is the author of *Pottery and Social Life in Medieval England: Towards a Relational Approach* (Oxbow, 2014) and has published widely on topics including medieval urbanism and the application of archaeological theory to the study of medieval objects in journals such as the *Journal of Social Archaeology* and *Early Medieval Europe and Medieval Archaeology*. He is also the co-editor of *Objects, Environment and Everyday Life in Medieval Europe* (Brepols, 2016) and *Insight from Innovation: New Light on Archaeological Ceramics* (Highfield Press, 2016).

Ruth Nugent completed her doctoral thesis on mortuary culture in English cathedrals in the Department of History and Archaeology at the University of Chester, United Kingdom, where she is also a visiting lecturer. She has previously published on early Anglo-Saxon mortuary practices and perceptions of bodies, material culture and their spatial arrangement, e.g. in 'Medieval Archaeology'. Her research interests include interactions between bodies (living or dead) and physical/conceptual spaces, and the role of touch in navigating this intersection.

Eleanor Williams is Lecturer in Archaeology at Canterbury Christ Church University, United Kingdom, specializing in human osteology, zooarchaeology, and medieval archaeology. She gained her Ph.D. from the University of Southampton, United Kingdom, on burial practices in Cluniac monasteries in England and France, with a particular focus on the relationship between practice and the Cluniac customaries. She has presented and published on different aspects of her research, including with the Centre d'Archéologie et d'Histoire Médiévales des Etablissements Religieux. She is currently collaborating at CCCU on the HLF sponsored community project 'Finding Eanswythe: the Life and Afterlife of an Anglo-Saxon Saint'.

References

Andrén, A. 1998. *Between Artifacts and Texts: Historical Archaeology in Global Perspective*. Philadelphia, PA: Plenum Press.
Auler, J. (ed.). 2008. *Richtstättenarchäologie, Vol. 1*. Dormagen: Archaeotopos-Verlag.
———. 2010. *Richtstättenarchäologie, Vol. 2*. Dormagen: Archaeotopos-Verlag.
———. (ed.). 2013. *Richtstättenarchäologie, Vol. 3*. Dormagen: Archaeotopos-Verlag.
Baker, J., and S. Brookes. 2013. 'Governance at the Anglo-Scandinavian Interface: Hundredal Organization in the Southern Danelaw', *Journal of the North Atlantic* 5: 76–95.
Baker, J., S. Brookes and A. Reynolds. 2011. 'Landscapes of Governance: Assembly Sites in England from the Fifth to the Eleventh Centuries', *Post-Classical Archaeologies* 1: 499–502.

Blinkhorn, P. 1997. 'Habitus, Social Identity and Anglo-Saxon Pottery', in P. Blinkhorn and C. Cumberpatch (eds), *Not So Much a Pot, More a Way of Life*. Oxford: Oxbow, pp. 113–24.

Bourdieu, P. 1977. *Outline of a Theory of Practice*, trans. R. Nice. Cambridge: Cambridge University Press.

Brookes, S. 2013. 'Outside the Gate: Sub-urban Legal Practices in Early Medieval England', *World Archaeology* 45(5): 747–61.

Brown, D. 1999. 'Class and Rubbish', in P. Funari, M. Hall and S. Jones (eds), *Historical Archaeology Back from the Edge*. London: Routledge, pp. 150–63.

Buckberry, J., and D. Hadley. 2007. 'An Anglo-Saxon Execution Cemetery at Walkington Wold, Yorkshire', *Oxford Journal of Archaeology* 26(3): 209–39.

Chapman, J., and B. Gaydarska. 2011. 'Can We Reconcile Individualisation with Relational Personhood? A Case Study from the Early Neolithic', *Documenta Praehistorica* 38: 21–44.

Deleuze, G., and F. Guattari. 1984. *Anti-Oedipus: Capitalism and Schizophrenia*, trans. R. Hurley, M. Seem and H.R. Lane. London: Bloomsbury.

———. 1987. *A Thousand Plateaus: Capitalism and Schizophrenia*, trans. B. Massumi. London: Bloomsbury.

Fowler, C. 2013. *The Emergent Past: A Relational Realist Archaeology of Early Bronze Age Mortuary Practices*. Oxford: Oxford University Press.

Gell, A. 1998. *Art and Agency: An Anthropological Theory*. Oxford: Oxford University Press.

Gilchrist, R. 1994. *Gender and Material Culture: The Archaeology of Religious Women*. London: Routledge.

Giles, K. 2000. *An Archaeology of Social Identity: Guildhalls in York, c.1350–1630*, BAR British Series 315. Oxford: Archaeopress.

Gosden, C., and Marshall, Y. 1999. 'The Cultural Biography of Objects', *World Archaeology* 31(2): 169–78.

Harris, O. 2014. '(Re)assembling Communities', *Journal of Archaeological Method and Theory* 21: 76–97.

Hicks, D., and M. Beaudry. 2010. 'The Material-Culture Turn: Event and Effect', in D. Hicks and M. Beaudry (eds), *The Oxford Handbook of Material Culture Studies*. Oxford: Oxford University Press, pp. 25–98.

Hodder, I. 2012. *Entangled: An Archaeology of the Relationships between Humans and Things*. Oxford: Blackwell.

Jervis, B. 2013. 'Rubbish and the Creation of Urban Landscape: A Case Study from Medieval Southampton, UK', in J. Bintliff and M. Caroscio (eds), *Pottery and Social Dynamics in the Mediterranean and beyond in Medieval and Post-Medieval Times*, BAR International Series 2557. Oxford: Archaeopress, pp. 57–73.

———. 2016. 'Assemblage Theory and Town Foundation in Medieval England', *Cambridge Archaeological Journal* 26(3): 381–395.

Jones, A. 2005. 'Lives in Fragments? Personhood and the European Neolithic', *Journal of Social Archaeology* 5(2): 193–224.

Joy, J. 2010. *Iron Age Mirrors*, BAR Series 518. Oxford: Archaeopress.

Kopytoff, I. 1986. 'The Cultural Biography of Things: Commodization as Process', in A. Appadurai (ed.), *The Social Life of Things*. Cambridge: Cambridge University Press, pp. 64–91.

Latour, B. 1993. *We Have Never Been Modern*, trans. C. Porter. Cambridge, MA: Harvard University Press.
———. 2005. *Reassembling the Social: An Introduction to Actor-Network-Theory*. Oxford: Oxford University Press.
———. 2010. *The Making of Law: An Ethnography of the Conseil d'Etat*, trans. M. Brilman. London: Polity Press.
Lemmonier, P. 1993. 'Introduction', in P. Lemmonier (ed.), *Technological Choices*. London: Routledge, pp. 1–35.
Martin, T. 2012. 'Riveting Biographies: The Theoretical Implications of Early Anglo-Saxon Brooch Repair, Customisation and Use-Adaptation', in B. Jervis and A. Kyle (eds), *Make-do and Mend*, BAR International Series 2408. Oxford: Archaeopress, pp. 53–66.
Moreland, J. 2006. 'Archaeology and Texts: Subservience or Enlightenment', *Annual Review of Anthropology* 35: 135–51.
Morris, J. 2011. *Investigating Animal Burials: Ritual, Mundane and Beyond*, BAR British Series 535. Oxford: Archaeopress.
Myres, J.N.L. 1969. *Anglo-Saxon Pottery and the Settlement of England*. Oxford: Oxford University Press.
Mytum, H. 2010. 'Ways of Writing in Post-Medieval and Historical Archaeology: Introducing Biography', *Post Medieval Archaeology* 44(2): 237–54.
Oosthuizen, S. 2013. *Tradition and Transformation in Anglo-Saxon England: Archaeology, Common Rights and Landscape*. London: Bloomsbury Academic.
Rathje, W., and C. Murphy. 1992. *Rubbish! The Archaeology of Garbage*. New York: HarperCollins.
Reynolds, A. 2012. 'Crime and Punishment', in S. Crawford, H. Hamerow and D. Hinton (eds), *Oxford Handbook of Anglo-Saxon Archaeology*. Oxford: Oxford University Press, pp. 910–31.
Richards, R. 2001. *Death, Dissection and the Destitute*. Cambridge: Cambridge University Press.
Robb, J. 2010. 'Beyond Agency', *World Archaeology* 42: 493–520.
Robb, J., and O. Harris. 2013. *The Body in History: Europe from Palaeolithic to the Future*. Cambridge: Cambridge University Press.
Smith, K., and Reynolds, A. 2013. 'Introduction: The Archaeology of Legal Culture', *World Archaeology* 45(5): 687–98.
Wicker, N. 1999. 'Archaeology and Art History: Common Ground for the New Millennium', *Medieval Archaeology* 43: 161–71.

Part I

Networks

Introduction
Rules, Networks and Different Kinds of Sources

Natascha Mehler

The chapters presented in Part I analyse and discuss some of the rules and regulations that linked people with other people, and with institutions and homelands during the later medieval and early post-medieval period in parts of Central and Northern Europe and beyond. The interpretations are guided by, and embedded in, a firm body of social theory, predominantly drawing on concepts from Pierre Bourdieu (1977) and Bruno Latour (2010). The approaches presented here are both fascinating and inspiring. Ben Jervis engages with the agency of rules by means of a late medieval merchant's guild book from Southampton, United Kingdom, and by presenting these rules within the framework of Latour's approach to law and regulation. Beyond that, and in the context of this late medieval document, he reflects critically on the relationship between archaeological and historical sources, herewith providing a methodological umbrella for Part I as a whole. Ute Scholz draws on sociological consumer research, predominantly using concepts of systematic food consumption, in her analysis of the late medieval archaeological material discovered at Tulln, Austria. Greta Civis, in her analysis of rubbish management in the medieval settlement of Diepensee, Germany, applies the concept of habitus for her discussion on how refuse can help to study regulation by means of archaeology. Furthermore, she offers a persuasive methodology for the interpretation of rubbish in the archaeological record, based on the concept of socially embedded material culture. Civis and Scholz both discuss regulations concerned with hygienic matters. But while Scholz presents her material from a consumer perspective, Civis does this from the point of view of disposal. Finally, Magdalena Naum gives an understanding of how the lives of the settlers of New Sweden, United States during the seventeenth century and later were guided and influenced by regulations from their motherland of Sweden. It should be pointed out that her discussion, based almost exclusively on written sources, allows us also a rare insight into disobedience and the defiance of rules, a theme that reappears throughout this volume.

The case studies presented here stem from a period that is characterized by a steady increase in literacy, recording and the creation of private documents, which accrued and transmitted the many aspects and expectations of previous generations. Indeed, our knowledge about how trade, waste management, consumption, and religious and moral interactions were regulated and connected through networks stems largely from written sources that require critical consideration regarding the extent of their implementation, and it seems to be straightforward to transfer our knowledge from these. Consequently, all the authors in Part I embed their discussions within this context. Jervis particularly moves beyond a multidisciplinary approach that is historical and archaeological into an interdisciplinary reflection about the meaning of textualization for social dynamics, and how inherited written regulations evolve within, and are influenced by, networks. Considering Part I from a methodological point of view, all the chapters are characterized by a confrontation of the archaeological record with written sources that convey the regulation of social interactions. Archaeological findings of, for example, food waste are contrasted with textual directives for waste management; something that is only rarely possible. Jervis particularly stresses that such a contrast of the archaeological with the written record is more than an attempt to provide explanations for patterns observed in the archaeological material, and he calls into question the nature of the reality or truth that archaeologists and historians often believe they encounter in their evidence. Anders Andrén has reminded us that such a contrast between the archaeological and historical source material is deeply rooted in the research traditions of the specific academic disciplines (Andrén 1998: 172). Indeed, all the authors – being archaeologists – share the standpoint that archaeological material can reveal past realities not presented in the written record. While some documented regulations seem to express an ideal condition that may never have been enacted, the archaeological material is viewed as a unique source that may tell us how things were handled in reality, even more so when the archaeological record tells a different story from the written documents. In fact, such a contrast makes evident yet again that one source group cannot be understood without the other, and this also stresses the need to critically reflect on investigations that provide a larger set of particular evidence (e.g. written sources) and very little of another (e.g. archaeological sources). The latter is the case with Naum's study, where archaeological evidence is sparse. Her critical comparison of the rich body of written regulations with other accounts of the colonists' engagement with their material environment enables Naum to trace the dynamics that underlie the relationship of governance and identity creation in colonial contexts. What we need to keep in mind here is that the description of people's interaction with material culture is in itself a representation that needs to be handled with caution, especially when the scarcity of contemporary archaeological material and contexts does not allow for further scrutiny of past practice.

What the chapters, and the contrast and tension evident between the different kinds of sources, leave us with is a challenge to think about the many facets of the relationship between regulation and reality. Historical reality is at the centre of the research of both historians and archaeologists. Still, we are unable to fully know and understand past realities (Goertz 2004: esp. 11): no matter how many types of evidence we investigate and methodologies we apply, we only find fragments of past realities. Is it that rules, as Jervis has suggested, present an idealized state and hence only suggest how things could have been handled in reality? Moreover, what does it mean when our sources at hand do not give us any indication about regulation at all? By engaging with questions such as these, the studies in this part outline what different kinds of sources may tell us about rules, regulation and disobedience, and how we can move beyond the dichotomy of the different and sometimes even contrary evidence at hand to get a step nearer to past realities.

Natascha Mehler is a historical archaeologist, with a Ph.D. from Kiel University, Germany. She has published widely on the development of the discipline and on material culture and is especially interested in interdisciplinary work. She is Senior Researcher at the German Maritime Museum in Bremerhaven, Germany, Docent at the Department of Prehistory and Historical Archaeology at the University of Vienna, Austria and Honorary Reader at the Centre for Nordic Studies at the University of the Highlands and Islands.

References

Andrén, A. 1998. *Between Artifacts and Texts: Historical Archaeology in Global Perspective*. Philadelphia, PA: Plenum Press.

Bourdieu, P. 1977. *Outline of a Theory of Practice*, trans. R. Nice. Cambridge: Cambridge University Press.
Goertz, H.-J. 2004. 'Abschied von "historischer Wirklichkeit": Das Realismusproblem in der Geschichtswissenschaft', in J. Schröter and A. Eddelbüttel (eds), *Konstruktion von Wirklichkeit*. Berlin: De Gruyter, pp. 1–19.
Latour, B. 2010. *The Making of Law: An Ethnography of the Conseil d'Etat*, trans. M. Brilman. London: Polity Press.

Chapter 1

Rules, Identity and a Sense of Place in a Medieval Town
The Case of Southampton's *Oak Book*

Ben Jervis

Introduction

A key feature of medieval towns is their heterogeneity. Urban settlements vary in terms of size, economy and, most importantly for the purposes of this chapter, custom. Municipal rules, on the one hand, can be considered to reflect customs, whilst on the other hand, adherence to regulations served to maintain the character of a place and community. Therefore, rules do not simply reflect a social context. By regulating practices, they contribute to the emergence and, particularly, the maintenance of the relationships, which underpin social life as a web of entangled connections between a variety of human and nonhuman actors. Archaeologists and historians have struggled to develop methods and interpretive frameworks in which it becomes possible to explore this relatedness. Rather than being truly interdisciplinary, in the sense that it is these relationships that are the subject of study, examinations are generally cross-disciplinary, in the sense that one source of evidence is taken to support the other (Wicker 1999: 169). Such an approach has dominated attempts to integrate medieval history and archaeology, with one often being used to account for the other's deficiencies, rather than exploring the common ground and related nature of these sources (Tabaczynski 1993: 3; Andrén 1998: 32). Rather than seeing either the textual or archaeological record as reflecting the 'way things were' in the past, we can alter our perspective to see texts as a form of material culture, formed through and active in social relationships, albeit with particular properties that differentiate them from the structures and portable objects that are the focus of the archaeologist's attention (Driscoll 1988: 167; Moreland 2006: 137). The aim of this chapter is therefore not to simply trace the adherence to rules in medieval England, but rather to explore the effect of rules in the development of a particular social context: that of medieval Southampton.

Medieval Municipal Rules and the Southampton *Oak Book*

From the reign of Henry I (1100–35), established towns in England increasingly sought to gain varying degrees of independent rule by means of the granting of charters that bestowed rights and privileges upon town burgesses (Campbell 2000: 60). In the context of Southampton, which forms the subject of this chapter, a charter of 1249 sanctioned 'that the alderman of the guild merchant shall be chief both of the Guild and of the town' (Studer 1910: xx). Therefore, Southampton was one of only a small number of towns to achieve a high degree of autonomy in its governance, where the burgesses of the town could elect officials (Rigby and Ewan 2000: 292). In the context of Southampton, the Guild refers to the Guild Merchant, an association of townsmen that existed for commercial and social purposes, with a defined membership and particular privileges, principally relating to trade.[1] Such guilds were common features of towns across northern Europe and are likely to have exhibited a high degree of variability in their origins, character and administration (Gross 1927: 20). However, a unifying theme of these organizations was the protection of the mutual interests of their members (Reynolds 1997: 71–73; Campbell 2000: 64). The rights granted in charters, including the right to form a Guild Merchant, were largely confirmatory in character and there were a number of motives behind their granting. Chief amongst these were the securing of lines of credit between merchants and the king, and the need to secure the support of the towns for military service and, more generally, political stability, as well as the generation of income in exchange for the granting of these rights and privileges (Reynolds 1997: 182; Campbell 2000: 66–70). In the case of Southampton, an urban settlement since the mid-Saxon period (see Jervis 2011 and references therein), it is likely that the medieval Guild Merchant had pre-Conquest origins. The first written reference to the Guild Merchant in Southampton is in a charter of 1154, but it was considered by Studer (1910) that within Southampton it is possible that the Guild Merchant was founded by immigrant merchants to cement their position in the developing port, with local merchants and others gradually joining the group as barriers broke down. Chief amongst the concerns of the Guild Merchant was the securing of the right to buy and sell within the borough market without paying the tolls or customs levelled at non-members (Hilton 1995: 92). Certainly there is evidence for the presence of continental traders in Southampton in the mid and later Anglo-Saxon periods, and it is likely that the Guild Merchant, or its predecessor, became a means by which a cosmopolitan community of merchants, which did not just include those from England and Normandy, but probably also individuals from Flanders and elsewhere in France, could construct communal links and maintain power over commerce within the port (Platt 1973: 19; Reynolds 1997: 167). Southampton therefore stands in contrast to the new towns of post-Conquest England, in that it was an established centre of trade with customs that likely stretched back some way in time. However, it is important to stress that in the twelfth and thirteenth centuries, the Guild Merchant, although influential within the town, was quite distinct from the municipal authorities (Gross 1927: 62). The granting of charters most probably formalized existing customs and it is common amongst medieval towns that those that had long been established exhibit the most individuality of character in terms of their civic organization and regulation (Campbell 2000: 78).

Guilds of all kinds existed principally for the protection of the mutual interests of their members. One way in which this could be achieved was through the establishment of rules and regulations, which were intended to prevent the development of individual monopolies, ensure fair and low prices, and secure the good character of a town (Britnell 1996: 92). The *Oak Book* contains the guild ordinances of Southampton and is believed to date from around 1300. The writing down of rules was one way in which customs could be formalized, in particular, perhaps, in response to the inward migration, which towns experienced throughout the Middle Ages (Reynolds 1997: 185). This not only protected the essence of the place and the position of its inhabitants, but also provided a basis upon which new social and economic relationships could be founded on a foundation of trust (Blockmans 2010: 579–80). For a port such as Southampton, the wealth of which was reliant upon international networks of trade and credit, and therefore trust, rules were essential for maintaining the reputation of the port as a credible place to do business and defining the community as good and trustworthy (Rosser 1984: 112; Casson 2012: 398). Furthermore, it was essential that towns exhibited evidence of being trustworthy and just places in order to receive further grants and liberties from the king, and to ensure that those that had been received were not rescinded (Casson 2012: 405). Rules were therefore a mechanism through which the goal of the Guild Merchant could be achieved and through which the status and identity of the town and its population could be maintained; indeed, they can be considered to have been produced as much for those outside of the guild as for those within it (Gerchow 1996: 140).

The *Oak Book* itself is preserved in Southampton's city archives and consists of sixty vellum leaves bound in hard oak covers. The section that is the subject of this chapter dates from around 1300 and consists of the ordinances of the Guild Merchant. In the medieval period, the book appears to have been known as the 'Paxbread', as the Southampton court was held at Easter (the pasche) (Studer 1910; Barron 2012). Later, probably fifteenth-century, alterations to the original text are present on the document. These are principally minor changes of procedure that do not fundamentally alter the spirit or substance of these ordinances (Studer 1910: xxxvii). The document consists of seventy-seven ordinances relating to a range of activities. They begin with the rules surrounding the administration of the Guild Merchant, including the electing of officials and the arrangements for meeting. Also addressed early on in the ordinances are the charitable and welfare functions of the guild, including provisions covering the illness or death of a guild member. The majority of the ordinances relate to the regulation of economic activity in Southampton, including detailing regulations to control trading activity and the regulation of activities such as baking and butchery within the town. The document goes on to outline some procedures relating to the organization of the town watches, the procedures for those who witnessed a breach of the rules and rules surrounding the management and organization of the quayside, including the loading and unloading of ships. The earliest surviving legal records date from the fifteenth century and relate to the common court, which was concerned with the upkeep of English common law (Olding 2011). The Court Leet met to pass judgment in relation to the upkeep of local laws; however, the earliest surviving records date from 1550 (*Court Leet Records*). The 1550 records show the addition of new rules (such as those preventing the milking of cows in the streets), as well as the upkeep of existing rules – for example, Thomas Casberd was fined for 'polluting the street'. These records show that the rules were regularly updated to adjust to new problems and also that they were upheld. Future study of the *Court Leet Records* may allow the identification of new rules developed between the writing of the *Oak Book* and 1550 through the records of punishments; however, this is beyond the scope of the current chapter.

The granting of freedoms to Southampton and the conflation of the Guild Merchant and the town administration poses an important question regarding who these rules were for and the extent of their effect. Only a limited number of trades or crafts are referenced in the document – bakers, brewers, butchers, victuallers, innkeepers, brokers and porters – and of these, all but the last two can be considered forms of public servant (Studer 1910: xxviiii). For example, ordinance 29 relates to the calculation of the assize of bread and ale. This was a means through which the price of bread was fixed in relation to the price of grain in order to secure the supply of food to towns. One function of this was to limit the profit of bakers, who, in accordance with contemporary social theory, were seen as operating for the common good of the town (Davis 2004: 485). Furthermore, by regulating profit and wages in this way, the assize became an instrument for bringing about social stability (Britnell 1996: 92; Davis 2004: 404–5). Butchers too were essential to providing sustenance for the urban population. However, the regulation of their activity principally relates to the treatment of their waste and can be seen to relate chiefly to a concern on the part of the Guild Merchant in relation to the spread of disease through 'miasma' (bad smells) and the need to project an image of being a 'respectable' town (Carr 2008; see also Chapters 2 and 3 in this volume). The rules can be considered to have been administered to by the burgesses of Southampton and it was they who took an oath, to be found at the beginning of the ordinances, to uphold these rules. The burgesses, however, did not account for the whole population of the town and therefore the community defined through adherence to these rules was limited to the population of burgesses (Reynolds 1997: 184). Many of the rules, particularly those relating to the control of trade and market activity, refer to burgesses and grant them privileges. These rules had the effect of both excluding those from outside of the town and those who were not members of the guild from participating in these activities. This was a useful instrument for maintaining a degree of social and economic hierarchy, essential to the running of the town. Certain rules, for example:

> That no man have before his house muck or dung, or pigs about. No man shall have any pigs going about in the street or have before his door, or in the street, muck or dung beyond two nights; and if any one has, let whoever will take it away; and he who shall have acted contrary to this statute shall be grievously fined (*Oak Book*: ord. 43)

as well as those relating to the arrangements for keeping the town watch, appear to relate to the whole population of the town. Here, perhaps, we see some clues to the development of the document as the writing down of a disparate set of customs, some relating to the wider management of the town when it was administered by royal officials and some derived from previous ordinances of the guild, defined when it was concerned only with the activities of its members and not of the management of the town as a whole. The rules then appear to derive from Southampton's history both as a cosmopolitan port and as a royal town (Gross 1927: 159).

With the conflating of the Guild Merchant and the town administration, we see the guild hierarchy becoming the urban hierarchy. To some extent, therefore, the guild ordinances can be considered to exist to further and protect the interests of the guild members, who constituted the legal, if not the actual, population of the borough. The extent to which this can be considered a form of urban oligarchy is a matter of debate (Rigby and Ewan 2000: 291). Whilst only a small proportion of the urban population were involved in the municipal authorities (Hilton 1995: 100), a simplistic view is problematic. There is, however, inevitably a certain degree of protectionism inherent in the formation of guilds and the ordinances that they created. Within the medieval mindset, the 'worthiest' men, considered the most well-qualified to speak on behalf of the townspeople, were also the wealthiest (which perhaps was considered to relate to class and status, given moralistic concerns regarding the corrupting influence of money) and most-established burgesses (Thrupp 1948: 15; Reynolds 1982: 15; Hilton 1995: 114–17). Furthermore, a degree of literacy was required to execute official roles, and this was a skill limited to a few within the context of a medieval town (Hilton 1995: 60). We cannot necessarily think of the guild, and particularly its officers, as a closed clique amongst the urban community (Kowaleski 2003: 114). In reality, they are likely to have only met a few times a year and, furthermore, the self-interest of individuals was intrinsically linked with other burgesses, with whom lines of credit may have been extended and with the success of the town as a whole (Rigby and Ewan 2000: 311; Goddard 2013: 19). Furthermore, in order for the pool of potential officials to be refreshed, it was necessary to recruit new members into the higher ranks of officialdom, for example, through the sponsorship of applications by individuals to become a burgess (Kermode 2002: 45–46; Kowaleski 2003: 114). Indeed, Susan Reynolds (1997: 73) has gone as far as to argue that the development of guilds and ordinances was an extension of the rural manor where the lord had a duty to protect his tenants. The rules then were more than simply a tool that could be used by a mercantile elite to suppress the urban population and preserve their own self-interest. Whilst this was one effect, they also played a crucial role in underpinning trust networks and the towns reputation and bringing a degree of socioeconomic continuity that was central to the success and prosperity of the town and its population.

The Agency of Rules

The guild ordinances present in the *Oak Book* have not been subject to major recent study. Archaeologists have seen the document as a useful resource to explain certain patterning in the archaeological record; principally ordinance 43 (quoted above) has been used to explain the management of waste in the town (Brown 2002: 157–58; Jervis 2013a). Whilst such an approach is useful to a degree, it equates to a cross-disciplinary approach where historical evidence is used to corroborate or explain archaeological patterning, rather than a truly interdisciplinary approach through which we can explore more closely the links between the ordinances and the archaeological record. In order to achieve this, we need to develop an interpretive framework in which the *Oak Book* can be considered an effective form of material culture, which was actively enrolled in the creation of the social context of medieval Southampton rather than being considered as prescribing or reflecting the way things were in the town. In order to develop such an approach, I wish to consider a study by Bruno Latour entitled *The Making of Law*. In the late 1990s, Latour (2010) set about studying the workings of the Conseil d'Etat, the body concerned with French administrative law, in Paris. His study considered not only the human discussions behind law making, but also the documents and places central to this process. Whilst clearly relating to a different context from our medieval guild ordinances, there are some general points that can be applied to our interpretation of the *Oak Book* and other similar documents that can allow us to integrate them more fully into social discourse, and therefore to examine their relationship with the remains we encounter in the archaeological record.

Latour sees the 'social' as composed of an entangled set of relationships between humans and nonhumans. As such, it is dynamic and ever-changing, requiring anchoring points, with which social interactions are repeated, to mediate continuity. Latour formulates the law in a similar way, seeing it not as a prescribed entity, but as an ever-changing and debated set of relationships between law makers, documents and the outside world. Within such a formulation of the law, documents have a very specific function. In the case of twentieth-century France, these are diverse, including written judgments, but also evidence such as maps or newspaper articles. It is considered that no document is inherently legal; rather, it *becomes* legal by being enacted through legal engagements (Latour 2010: 77). Once enacted as such, it is able to have 'legal' effects (Latour 2010: 80). A map then can be enacted as a legal document, but also as a navigational aid or even as an artwork, for example. These documents are not the law; rather, the law is considered as intangible, it is a bundle of referential associations between people, documents, things and places that emerges through what we might term legal action and is sustained through the replication of chains of reference. The role of written documents such as judgments or rules is to provide a point of reference. As they are continually re-enacted, they bring durability and stability to the law and thus to the wider 'social'. This process of creating a referential starting point to ensure that the law does not need to be reformulated in relation to every event is referred to by Latour as 'blackboxing'. To follow Latour, then, the efficacy of these documents must be constantly refreshed through the re-enacting of these rules and of their meaning through legal reasoning (Latour 2010: 160). The law is not rules, but these rules are powerful texts that contribute, through being enacted in legal courses of action, as stabilizing influences in the making durable of a social context. It therefore follows that the law is impermanent; if documents fail to be enacted, they lose their legal meaning (Latour 2010: 163). They can therefore be forgotten or applied flexibly. Rules are not set in stone; rather, the legal reasoning that underpins their application unfolds as these documents are enacted in different courses of action and create social effects that may be multiple and far-reaching. The *Oak Book* can therefore be considered a potentially powerful document that was central to bringing social stability and durability to Southampton, which can be considered as a 'social' made up of a myriad of ever-changing human–nonhuman relationships, including those formed directly and indirectly with this document.

As discussed above, the guild ordinances were closely related to the fortunes of those who produced and enforced them. It must be remembered that the law relates to the relationships between these people, documents and the rest of the world. Latour argues that the law cannot be separated from the career and life trajectories of the lawyers who produce it, with their identities being forged through the making of law; documents, people and the law are mutually constitutive. Such an approach provides a useful lens through which to consider the emergence of identities in the medieval town. The *Oak Book* records, one assumes, decisions made by the guild merchant when presented with particular problems and ensures fairness and consistency in the administration of punishment. It therefore 'blackboxes' these considerations, providing a reference that, when enacted as a legal document, affords durability and continuity within the order of the town. Through producing this document and by continually re-enacting it through practice, the identities of virtue and trustworthiness discussed above, which were so crucial to the success of the community, could be re-formed. The rules developed through the need to forge such identities in order to secure trade and privileges at both the individual and communal scale and, through being re-enacted, allowed these identities to be reinforced, bringing durability to the 'social' of medieval Southampton. Following Latour, in isolation the *Oak Book* is simply a record of the guild ordinances; it is not an inherently legal (or perhaps more accurately regulatory) document, but becomes enacted as such through its use, with varying implications for the everyday lives of Southampton's residents.

However, my concern in this chapter is not with the nature of rules, but rather with their effect. It is now widely acknowledged that things can have agency (see Robb (2010) for a summary of recent debates), which could perhaps be defined as the potential to cause an effect. This might be broken into two strands: the first being that an object (or document) may have human agency deferred upon it and the second being that a thing's material properties may guide or restrain human action. Here, though, I wish to conceptualize agency in a relational manner. We can consider that nothing and no one can act alone and therefore agency cannot be seen as inherent within a person, thing or document. Rather, the ability to cause effect – agency – is constructed through processes of assembly, of the coming together of people, things and spaces (Whatmore 1999: 27). Furthermore, the effects of assembly can be multiple and diverse, intentional and unintentional. Indeed, the intentionality that we can read into the *Oak Book* can be seen as only being there because the agency for it to emerge was spun in the varying processes of assembly and courses of action behind its formation – chiefly the coming together of people and things through economic exchange in a particular place at a particular time. To talk then of rules having agency is something of a misnomer. I am not arguing that they act on behalf of people or that they have an intrinsic agency of their own. Rather, through being entangled in action and therefore being enacted, the capacity for them to have effect, or for them to afford particular things, emerges. We can therefore begin to explore the relationship between written rules and the archaeological record by considering how rules developed agency as they were put into practice, using the archaeological evidence to consider the effect of the regulation of the interactions people could have with each other and their material surroundings.

Rules, Identity and Sense of Place

Medieval towns can be considered 'social assemblages', formed of connections between humans and nonhumans, which might include portable material culture, buildings and documents (see Jervis 2011, 2013b). In turn, these were connected to other places and people, forming the larger 'social assemblage' of medieval society, whilst they are also divisible into assemblages such as households and even individuals, whose identities may be constructed of wide-reaching associations with places, people and things.

Figure 1.1 Map showing the extent of the Guild Merchant's control (shaded area). (Illustration by Ben Jervis)

One of the documents that was enrolled in the emergence and durability of Southampton as a social assemblage was the charter of 1249, which acted as a legal judgment. In practice, the document was continually re-enacted, making durable the authority of the Guild Merchant over the stretch of coast from Langstone in the east to Hurst in the west (Figure 1.1) (including the member ports of Lymington, Hamble and Portsmouth; see *Local Port Book 1439–40*), providing a basis upon which the interactions and connections from which Southampton was formed could be sustained, as trade was focused on Southampton, remaking the agency for Southampton to continually become a port through ongoing economic engagements.

As discussed above, the making and re-enacting of regulations was central to the establishment and maintenance of the town, and its burgesses building a sense of trustworthiness to secure trade. This can be considered a key function of the *Oak Book*. A number of ordinances regulate the way that trade may be undertaken and stipulate punishments if they are broken, for example:

That no man of the town sell merchandise of a merchant bought under pretence. No one of the town shall under pretence of buying or under any other kind of pretence, sell to others the goods of a merchant stranger, whereby the merchandise would be sold for more than the merchant could have sold it by his own hand, and the townspeople would lose their profit; but the merchants who bring their goods for sale shall sell them by their own hand. And he who shall do this and be thereof attained shall lose his guildship if he be a guildsman,[2] and if he be of the franchise he shall lose his franchise, until he has made amends for his offence. (*Oak Book*: ord. 30)

Once trade had been secured, the re-enacting of the ordinances also served to develop the agency for the establishment and maintenance of identities within Southampton through the limiting and focusing of economic activities. For example: 'No one except a guildsman, shall buy honey, salt, seim [grease or fat] salt, herring, oil, millstones, hides except on market day or fair day' (*Oak Book*: ord. 20) and 'No ... stranger[3] shall sell or buy merchandise before a burgess' (*Oak Book*: ord. 23).

It can be debated whether such rules led to the development of an oligarchic mercantile elite. What they certainly did do was create a situation where, as long as the rules were adhered to and reproduced in practice, the agency to develop a mercantile identity was limited to a few and a hierarchical social system with limited social mobility could be retained (see also Kermode 2002: 29). A similar effect was achieved through the rules surrounding the assize of bread and ale (discussed above). The exact circumstances surrounding the writing of these rules remain a mystery, but they would appear to be the product of insecurity and the need to regulate practice so as to bring about social stability and ensure the social order was maintained. Identity can be defined as the way in which humans define themselves in relation to human and nonhuman others (Jervis 2013b: 453), and therefore the effect of the re-enacting of these rules was to limit the relationships people could form and thus regulate the processes through which identities, or perhaps more accurately categories of people, could emerge.

Engagement in urban trading activity allowed for particular forms of identity to emerge. On the one hand, the rules regulated the ability to develop a 'professional' mercantile identity, but in reality, by limiting the ability to generate wealth and thus acquire property or prestige goods, they also regulated the ability to develop a 'cultural' mercantile identity. Analysis of the distribution of imported pottery in Southampton (Brown 1997; Jervis 2008), for example, shows the area around the waterfront, believed on the basis of both archaeological and historical research to have been the merchants' quarter, to have consumed the most varied and exotic forms of pottery. Whilst certain imports (particularly those from the Saintonge region of France, imported on the back of the wine trade) were exchanged in the marketplace almost as local products, others may have been brought back as souvenirs or purchased as items to display cosmopolitan taste and wealth (and therefore virtue). There is no specific fixed guildhall mentioned in the *Oak Book* and it is possible that guild members hosted meetings and feasts in some instances, and these may have provided a setting in which to demonstrate these traits.[4] The same can perhaps be said of the Italian glass and other exotic products found in excavations in the waterfront area of Southampton (Platt and Coleman-Smith 1975). The recently excavated merchant houses in Southampton's French Quarter (Brown and Hardy 2011), as well as those excavated in earlier campaigns of excavation (Platt and Coleman-Smith 1975), show how a mercantile identity was manifest in domestic life, with houses typically containing cellars or ground-floor spaces for use either as warehouses or shops, as, for example, at 58 French Street, a merchant's house believed to date from the fourteenth century (Figure 1.2). The wealth accumulated through economic transactions allowed these houses to be built of stone. Little is known of lower-status houses in Southampton, but the limited evidence suggests them to have been smaller and lacking in the architectural features associated with the mercantile class. The effect of the enacting of these rules was far-reaching, expanding from the regulation of market interactions to spill over into the domestic sphere, playing a part in the formation of the agency for interactions with particular forms of portable material culture, as well as for the development of the fabric of the town.

It may seem logical to conclude that the rules had the effect of marginalizing those who were not members of the guild and who lacked the privileges surrounding trade and economic activity in particular. However, following Reynolds (1997: 165), we can question whether this was the case. Whilst the rules surrounding trade clearly served the interests of the mercantile elite (see Kermode 2002: 38–39), they also secured Southampton as a prosperous place in which a variety of craftsmen and labourers could earn a living. Whilst excluded from the legally defined burgess community, the rules can be considered to have potentially allowed a sense of community to develop. The rules perhaps fostered a sense of communal responsibility; certainly, we see in the deposition of waste in backyards across the town an adherence to rules surrounding waste (Jervis 2013a). These, and rules surrounding the sale of foodstuffs, can also be shown as evidence for the elite taking responsibility and care for the non-burgess population of the town (although a further effect of these rules was to suppress profit and the ability to generate wealth, thus limiting the potential for social mobility). By building a sense of community,

Figure 1.2 58 French Street, Southampton (photograph by Ben Jervis)

a stable and durable 'social' could be formed, which allowed mercantile activity to continue and lowered the likelihood of revolt. Therefore, whilst archaeological evidence alone may indicate clear socioeconomic divides within the town, on the basis of architecture and material culture, consideration of the rules provides a more nuanced picture, in which a distinctively hierarchical urban community developed and was underpinned by regulation. The rules also united the community, creating the basis for the town to prosper and creating a united urban identity where one might feel a member of Southampton, even if not legally a burgess.

Amongst this community, the writing and referencing of rules can also be considered to have a mnemonic element, which further contributed to the development of a sense of place and communal memory. Certain rules reference particular places and individuals – for example, 'this shore extends in English Street to the lane that was Walter the Flemeng's, and in French Street to the house where Jack le Wyte used to live' (*Oak Book*: ord. 71).

The use of notable people from the mercantile past of Southampton can be seen as having a specific effect upon those members of the merchant class familiar with the book, in infusing the urban landscape with connections to the Guild Merchant and its rules, serving as a reminder of the history of the guild and the longevity of the trust networks that it maintained. It can be considered that through this familiarity and this constant referencing of places and people, members of the Guild Merchant and, potentially, the wider population of Southampton, developed a unique understanding and appreciation of Southampton's landscape, which contributed to their own sense of identity and also to the emergence of collective memory. The book then not only regulated the guild but also functioned in the building of cohesion amongst the Guild Merchant and in conditioning the ways in which its members perceived both the town around them and their own place within it.

Conclusion: The Effect of Rules

Following Latour's insights into the 'making of law', it is argued here that medieval guild ordinances were both a product of social interaction and also an actor in the making of the medieval 'social'. The granting of power to the Guild Merchant and the subsequent formalization of their customs played a clear role in the making of Southampton as the pre-eminent town in its region. Any site along the coast with the right physical setting had the potential to develop into a cosmopolitan market, but the focusing of mercantile activity through the enacting of the charter and the *Oak Book* rules limited this potential to the town and contributed to its durability as a distinctive place. The rules themselves could easily be seen as a proxy for the hierarchical society of Southampton, with them underpinning the position of a ruling mercantile elite and the marginalization of the remainder of the urban population. Rules create an illusion of permanency; however, as Latour argues, they must be continually re-enacted to maintain their power. In being re-enacted, they were enrolled in the making of varying forms of identity at a range of scales. As can be seen from the archaeological material culture, the rules played a role in the emergence and maintenance of the urban elites, but we can also question the archaeological evidence for inequality by seeing adherence to the rules as producing a cohesive rather than a fractured sense of urban identity in Southampton. As social actors, rules are complex. The ordinances found in the *Oak Book* were formed as urban life developed customs and, as they were enacted and re-formed through practice, played a role in the constitution of identities, a sense of place and the meanings of the objects that people were able to come into contact with, maintaining a social hierarchy and creating circumstances in which certain objects, which could only be acquired by the connected and wealthy, could become exclusive in the context of this medieval port. By being enacted in practice, the *Oak Book* became a medium through which the Guild Merchant could realize authority as it became a political document, develop professional identities as it became an economic document and maintain hierarchy whilst fostering a sense of communal identity as it became a social document. These rules did not determine the 'social' of Southampton, nor do they reflect it. As customs, they were formed within it and played a role in making it durable, but a role that should not be privileged or demeaned in relation to that of the people, objects and spaces that were equally entangled in the processes in which these rules were made, enacted and effective.

Ben Jervis is Lecturer in Medieval Archaeology at Cardiff University, United Kingdom, having gained his Ph.D. from the University of Southampton in 2011. He is the author of *Pottery and Social Life in Medieval England: Towards a Relational Approach* (Oxbow, 2014) and has published widely on topics including medieval urbanism and the application of archaeological theory to the study of medieval objects in journals such as the *Journal of Social Archaeology* and *Early Medieval Europe and Medieval Archaeology*. He is also the co-editor of *Objects, Environment and Everyday Life in Medieval Europe* (Brepols, 2016) and *Insight from Innovation: New Light on Archaeological Ceramics* (Highfield Press, 2016).

Notes

1. The Guild Merchant should not be confused with craft guilds. For Southampton, the earliest record of the incorporation of a craft guild relates to the Tailor's Guild (1468), with the majority of records dating to the sixteenth and seventeenth centuries (Southampton Corporation 1964: 11).
2. 'Guildsman' refers to a member of the guild, who did not need to be resident within the town. A burgess held property in the town and had sworn an oath to uphold the responsibilities associated with this status (Gross 1927: 72).
3. A 'stranger' refers to an individual who is not a member of the guild, most commonly in this context a merchant from overseas or elsewhere in England.
4. Although it is known that the guild held a feast in the Bargate (the main gateway into Southampton) in 1434.

References

Primary Sources

Court Leet Records Vol. 1 Part 1, A.D. 1550–1577, ed. F. Hearnshaw and D. Hearnshaw. 1905. Southampton: Southampton Record Society.
The Local Port Book of Southampton for 1439–40, ed. H. Cobb. 1961. Southampton: Southampton Record Series.
The Oak Book of Southampton of c. AD1300, Volume 1, ed. P. Studer. 1910. Southampton: Southampton Record Society.

Secondary Literature

Andrén, A. 1998. *Between Artifacts and Texts: Historical Archaeology in Global Perspective*. New York: Plenum Press.
Barron, C. 2012. 'Sources for Medieval Urban History', in J. Rosenthal (ed.), *Understanding Medieval Primary Sources*. London: Routledge, pp. 163–76.
Blockmans, W. 2010. 'Constructing a Sense of Community in Rapidly Growing European Cities in the Eleventh to Thirteenth Centuries', *Historical Research* 83(222): 575–87.
Britnell, R. 1996. *The Commercialisation of English Society 1000–1500*. Cambridge: Cambridge University Press.
Brown, D. 1997. 'The Social Significance of Imported Medieval Pottery', in P. Blinkhorn and C. Cumberpatch (eds), *Not So Much a Pot, More a Way of Life*. Oxford: Oxbow, pp. 95–112.
———. 2002. *Pottery in Medieval Southampton: c 1066–1510*, CBA Research Report 137. York: Council for British Archaeology.
Brown, R., and A. Hardy. 2011. *Trade and Prosperity, War and Poverty: An Archaeological and Historical Investigation into Southampton's French Quarter*, Oxford Archaeology Monograph 15. Oxford: Oxford Archaeology.
Campbell, J. 2000. 'Power and Authority 600–1300', in D. Palliser (ed.), *The Cambridge Urban History of Britain. Vol. 1: 600–1540*. Cambridge: Cambridge University Press, pp. 51–78.

Carr, D. 2008. 'Controlling the Butchers in Late Medieval English Towns', *The Historian* 70: 450–61.
Casson, C. 2012. 'Reputation and Responsibility in Medieval English Towns: Civic Concerns with the Regulation of Trade', *Urban History* 39(3): 387–408.
Davis, J. 2004. 'Baking for the Common Good: A Reassessment of the Assize of Bread in Medieval England', *Economic History Review* 57(3): 465–502.
Driscoll, S. 1988. 'The Relationship between History and Archaeology: Artefacts, Documents and Power', in S. Driscoll and M. Nieke (eds), *Power and Politics in Early Medieval Britain and Ireland*. Edinburgh: Edinburgh University Press, pp. 162–87.
Gerchow, J. 1996. 'Gilds and Fourteenth Century Bureaucracy: The Case of 1388–9', *Nottingham Medieval Studies* 40: 109–48.
Goddard, R. 2013. 'Medieval Business Networks: St Mary's Guild and the Borough Court in Later Medieval Nottingham', *Urban History* 40(1): 3–27.
Gross, C. 1927. *The Gild Merchant, Vol. 1*. Oxford: Oxford University Press.
Hilton, R. 1995. *English and French Towns in Feudal Society: A Comparative Study*. Cambridge: Cambridge University Press.
Jervis, B. 2008. 'For Richer, for Poorer: A Synthesis and Discussion of Medieval Pottery in Eastern Southampton in the Context of the High and Late Medieval Towns', *Medieval Ceramics* 30: 73–94.
———. 2011. 'A Patchwork of People, Pots and Places: Material Engagements and the Construction of "the Social" in Hamwic (Anglo-Saxon Southampton), UK', *Journal of Social Archaeology* 11(3): 239–65.
———. 2013a. 'Rubbish and the Creation of Urban Landscape', in J. Bintliff and M. Carcoscio (eds), *Pottery and Social Dynamics in the Mediterranean and beyond in Medieval and Post-medieval Times*, British Archaeological Reports International Series 2557. Oxford: Archaeopress, pp. 57–72.
———. 2013b. 'Cuisine and Urban Identities in Medieval England: Objects, Foodstuffs and Urban Life in 13th–14th Century Hampshire', *Archaeological Journal* 169: 453–79.
Kermode, J. 2002. *Medieval Merchants: York, Beverley and Hull in the Later Middle Ages*. Cambridge: Cambridge University Press.
Kowaleski, M. 2003. *Local Markets and Regional Trade in Medieval Exeter*. Cambridge: Cambridge University Press.
Latour, B. 2010. *The Making of Law: An Ethnography of the Conseil D'État*, trans. M. Brilman. London: Polity Press.
Moreland, J. 2006. 'Archaeology and Texts: Subservience or Enlightenment', *Annual Review of Anthropology* 35: 135–51.
Olding, T. (ed.). 2011. *The Common and Piepowder Courts of Southampton, 1426–1483*. Southampton: Southampton Record Series.
Platt, C. 1973. *Medieval Southampton: The Port and Trading Community, A.D.1000–1600*. London: Routledge and Keegan.
Platt, C., and R. Coleman-Smith. 1975. *Excavations in Medieval Southampton 1953–69, Vol. 1: The Sites*. Leicester: University of Leicester Press.
Reynolds, S. 1982. 'Medieval Urban History and the History of Political Thought', *Urban History* 9: 14–23.

———. 1997. *Kingdoms and Communities in Western Europe, 900–1300*. Oxford: Oxford University Press.

Rigby, S., and Ewan, E. 2000. 'Government, Power and Authority 1300–1540', in D. Palliser (ed.), *The Cambridge Urban History of Britain. Vol. 1: 600–1540*. Cambridge: Cambridge University Press, pp. 291–312.

Robb, J. 2010. 'Beyond Agency', *World Archaeology* 42(4): 493–520.

Rosser, G. 1984. 'The Essence of Medieval Communities: The Vill of Westminster 1200–1540', *Transactions of the Royal Historical Society* 34: 91–112.

Southampton Corporation. 1964. *Southampton Records 1: Guide to the Records of the Corporation and Absorbed Authorities in the Civic Record Office*. Southampton: Southampton Corporation.

Studer, P. (ed.). 1910. *The Oak Book of Southampton of c. AD 1300, Vol. 1*. Southampton: Southampton Records Society.

Tabaczynski, S. 1993. 'The Relationship between History and Archaeology: Elements of the Present Debate', *Medieval Archaeology* 37: 1–14.

Thrupp, S. 1948. *The Merchant Class of Medieval London*. Chicago, IL: University of Chicago Press.

Whatmore, S. 1999. 'Hybrid Geographies: Rethinking the "Human" in Human Geography', in D. Massey, J. Allen and P. Sarre (eds), *Human Geography Today*. London: Polity Press, pp. 22–39.

Wicker, N. 1999. 'Archaeology and Art History: Common Ground for the New Millennium', *Medieval Archaeology* 43: 161–71.

Chapter 2

Meat for the Market
The Butchers' Guild Rules from 1267 and Urban Archaeology in Tulln, Lower Austria

Ute Scholz

Introduction

Tulln an der Donau, a town in Lower Austria (situated about 30 km upstream of Vienna) was subject to widespread excavations from the 1970s until 2012. It is considered to be one of the best-excavated cities in Austria (Scholz and Krenn 2010). Medieval occupation is traceable from the eighth century onwards, starting in the area of the former Roman camp and spreading out to the south and west by the eleventh century. At this time, the town developed into a centre for the surrounding rural area, being located on the Danube River, a key trading route (Csendes 2002). From the beginning of the thirteenth century, the town expanded. A huge market place (*Breiter Markt*, today *Hauptplatz*/main square) was established in the centre of newly built town plots in the western part of the city, which was subsequently surrounded by a city wall (Scholz et al. 2007; see Figure 2.1).

Dating from the period of urban expansion is one of the earliest sets of guild rules from Austria, Tulln's Butchers' Guild Rules from 1267 (*Tullner Fleischhauerordnung*). The rules were divided into five chapters, which were intended to regulate the butchers' attitudes towards sanitary and trading behaviour (Eggendorfer 1980a). Fixed with the seals of the magistrate and the judge of the town, the *Fleischhauerordnung* can be seen as a council order to manipulate the handling of meat and to regulate commercial competition.

Chapter 1 of the *Fleischhauerordnung* deals with the competition between master butchers and journeymen: the latter were not allowed

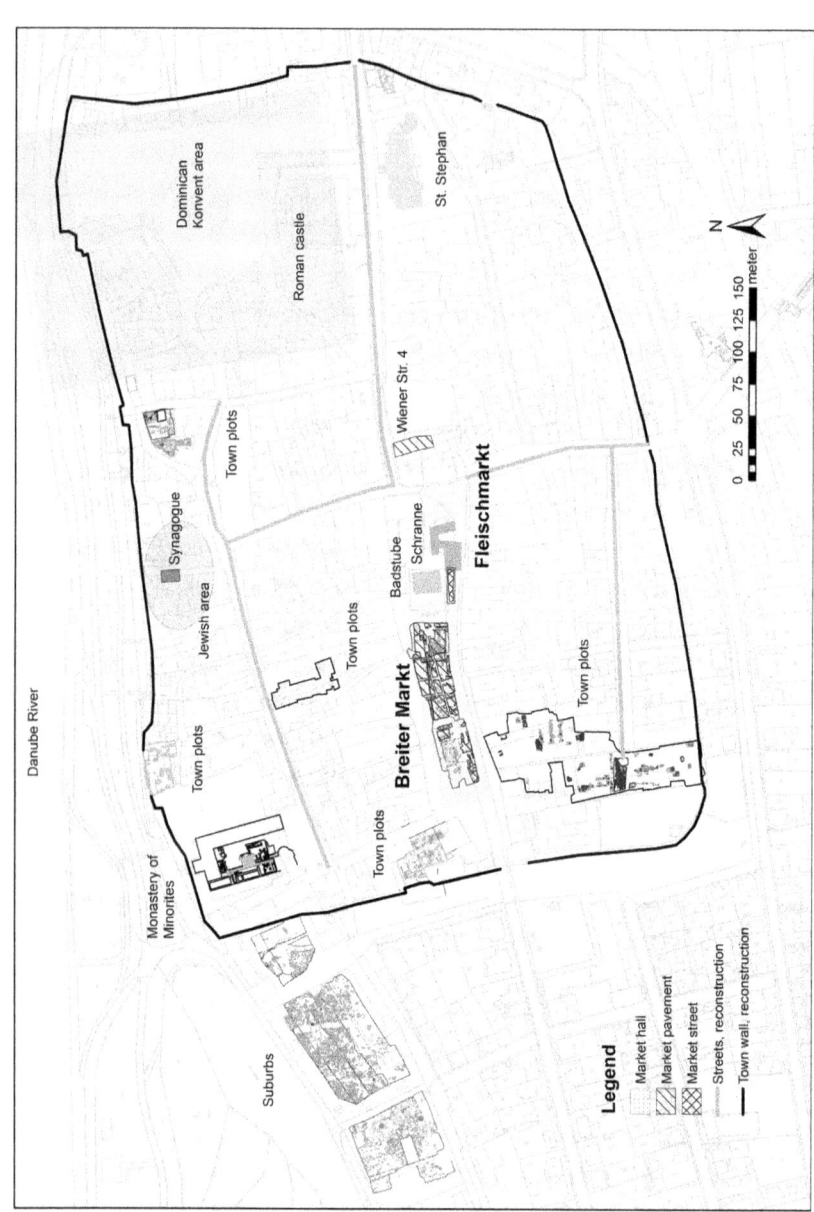

Figure 2.1 Map of Tulln in the thirteenth century with excavated areas (illustration by Ute Scholz)

to buy and sell meat, either in the city or in the countryside. Chapter 3 forbids the master butchers from buying meat from external butchers on market days. Two chapters refer to sanitary regulations: Chapter 2 prohibits selling meat on the same day that it was slaughtered and Chapter 5 decrees that guild members who sell impure meat will be detained and sent to court. Scholars refer mostly to Chapter 4, which deals with the regulation of the Jewish meat trade (Lohrmann 1990: 100–1; Wiedl 2009: 297). Christian butchers were allowed to add a 10 per cent surcharge on cattle, sheep and goats when selling to Jewish butchers, who slaughtered and sold the meat themselves. This is interpreted as a compensation payment for the lost profits of the Christian master butchers (Eggendorfer 1980b: 13).

The main topics covered in this document touch on several issues relevant to different groups of the town community. They reveal diverse regulations regarding the functions and organization of, and access to, a market. The necessity for regulations emerged with hygienic requirements and commercial competition that were related to two religious groups, Jews and Christians, but also the growing differences between urban and rural areas and the hierarchical system of professionalization between masters and journeymen.

In relation to the surviving written record, this chapter seeks to discuss whether these attitudes towards meat consumption can be traced in the material record or show asymmetries between imposed regulations and actual practice. In order to address these issues, it is necessary to consider the rules of consumption in medieval towns, especially in relation to the importance of food and the power of religion for the organization of everyday life or exceptional events. Based on models drawn from consumer research, the archaeology of the Tulln market will be explored, focusing on traces of everyday religious practice outside of explicitly religious environments, such as churches or graveyards, and evidence for meat consumption in the urban community.

Consumption and Food in the Medieval Town

Since the 1980s, consumer research has become an established area of investigation within the social sciences. It deals with the organization and mechanisms of consumption in different social environments (for an overview, see de Grazia 2001). Mechanisms of consumption have been characterized by terms such as commodification (Kopytoff 1986), conspicuous consumption (Veblen 2007), spaces of consumption (Goodman, Goodman and Redcliff 2010) and the changes in consumption leading up to the history of globalization (Trentmann 2009). Due to a rather thin evidence base, studies of consumption during the medieval period largely deal with topics related to clothing and food (Scholz 2012: 8–10). Since food is our point of interest, we need to look at mechanisms of food handling in society. George Gumerman (1997) suggested an approach towards food as a socially determined category. He identified different stages of a society's engagement with food and classified them as the production, preparation, distribution, consumption and disposal of food (Gumerman 1997: 107). The Tulln Butchers' Rules mainly concern the production and distribution of meat. Gumerman argues that the production of food involves categories such as ethnicity, social status and gender relations, and therefore food is a tool for constructing and maintaining power relations (Gumerman 1997: 114).

Food, Consumption, Religion

Caroline Walker Bynum's (2008) study of gender and Christian practices of food consumption shows that religious power is a relevant factor as well. Religious ontology also structures the attitude towards food and gender in Jewish practice (Eidelman 2000). Obvious differences between Christian and Jewish food preparation practices become apparent when looking at slaughter methods and food consumption, for example, Jewish rules regarding the separation of dairy and meat dishes. Alongside fixed dietary rules, the practice of using different cooking tools for separating specific kinds of food mainly developed from the eleventh century onwards. It can be seen as a hygienic measure for avoiding the same utensils for preparing *milchig* (milky) and *fleishig* (meaty) food (Kraemer 2009: 99–107). Kraemer points out that in the mid thirteenth century, regulations were not as strict as later ones – for example, one pot could be used for cooking milk, followed by vegetables. After this intermediate step, it was even considered acceptable to prepare meat in this pot (Kraemer 2009: 104).

Christian regulations principally consist of directives for fasting and feasting (Henisch 1978: 2). Restrictions mentioned in the thirteenth-century sermons of Berthold of Regensburg warn against gluttony (Cormeau 1990) and contain statements about moral standards for businesses and reflections on fraud and the manipulation of goods and food. They deal with topics of, for example, falsely declaring meat of grown animals as meat from young ones or selling rotten meat (Cormeau 1990: 80–81).

The German historians Ulf Dirlmeier and Gerhard Fouquet (1993) analysed eating habits and practices in late medieval Germany, concluding that nutrition with grain dishes was the most important way of supplying calories until the beginning of industrialization in the eighteenth century. Meals containing meat were controlled through fasting and feasting; meat was consumed on reserved days, while on other days its consumption was prohibited by religious rules (Dirlmeier and Fouquet 1993: 511–12).

Food, Consumption, Power

Medieval urban households were provisioned through a combination of self-supply and the market, which is considered as a core element of the medieval town (Baeriswyl 2003: 23–34). Town and market were also entangled in a direct relationship with the countryside that can be described through a centre/periphery model or a network model (Müller 2010). The commercial relationship between urban and rural partners, which occurs as a consequence of food production, trade and consumption, creates dependencies and requires a mutual relationship of trust.

Questions about the regulation of food supplies are therefore questions about power: what kind of control did town inhabitants have over the variety of cattle they were offered from the countryside (Sykes 2009: 64)? Different sorts of meat were classified and only consumed in certain social environments. Poultry and venison were reserved for the nobility, while beef and pork in particular were consumed by the majority of town inhabitants (Grieco 2003). Meat consumption in the thirteenth century can thus be described as elitist and was arranged along socially determined lines.

Consumption also has a spatial aspect: where do we distribute, prepare, cook and eat food? The market has to be conceptualized as a place of consumption and distribution. As a place of distribution, there must therefore exist a functional infrastructure that provides a suitable environment for the delivery and sale of goods, as well as the disposal of waste. As a place of consumption, the market operates as a space for assembly, feasting and the consumption of market-specific food (Scholz 2013). Furthermore, the market embodies a space where the various interests of different groups of the town meet and possibly also collide. Therefore, the market is a space where power relations and interests are constantly negotiated.

The Market and the Town

Following Douglas (2008), we can consider that when, where and with whom we eat relates to particular types of meal and categories of time and space. Daily, weekly or extraordinary meals relate to different forms of distribution at daily and weekly markets or annual fairs. The organization of a medieval market was related to the seasons and the festive calendar of the town (Opll 1996). Different types of market, which occurred at different frequencies, served different needs. Daily and weekly markets offered everyday goods and provided a platform for selling agricultural produce from the countryside. Markets that lasted a week or longer were often connected to religious feasts, for example, the feast of the patron of the main church. In the thirteenth century, fairs had developed in the south and west of Germany as an advanced trade system. The main function of a fair was to distribute nonregional products and to connect long-distance merchants, who offered special goods to a regional market (Irsigler 2007: 1–6).

The existence of a fair system in mid thirteenth-century Austria is not recorded in written sources (Opll 1996). The archaeological evidence indicates that a huge market square was built in Tulln (*Breiter Markt*) around the beginning of the thirteenth century – almost a hundred years earlier than any written documents refer to market activities (the earliest recorded fair in Tulln at *Breiter Markt* was documented as occurring in 1317) (Kerschbaumer 1902: 349 CLXXX). The archaeological evidence thus indicates the establishment of larger market events significantly earlier than the introduction of market-related regulations that are evidenced by the surviving written sources.

Excavations at *Breiter Markt*, where the annual fair took place, revealed the basic shape of a rectangular marketplace with an open space at its centre, where no traces of market installations were found (Figure 2.2). The square was paved with gravel extracted from the Danube. At the eastern end, a street connected the *Breiter Markt* square with the neighbouring meat market (*Fleischmarkt*).

The main buildings of the thirteenth-century market square were constructed of wood on a gravel pavement. These were replaced by an open walled wooden hall at the end of the century. There is evidence for a thirteenth-century wooden market hall at St Pölten, another Austrian town, some 40 km southeast of Tulln (Scherrer 2009: 148–50). But what were the halls used for? The St Pölten hall was interpreted as a 'Schranne', which means it served as a market hall and a place for the city council. In the mid fourteenth century, a stone walled town hall, also referred to as 'Schranne', was built in Tulln in the eastern part of the marketplace, situated between *Breiter Markt* and *Fleischmarkt*, at the eastern end of the excavated street (see Figure 2.2).

In the northeastern part of the square, rows of postholes were interpreted as relating to stalls or racks for sales purposes. It should be kept

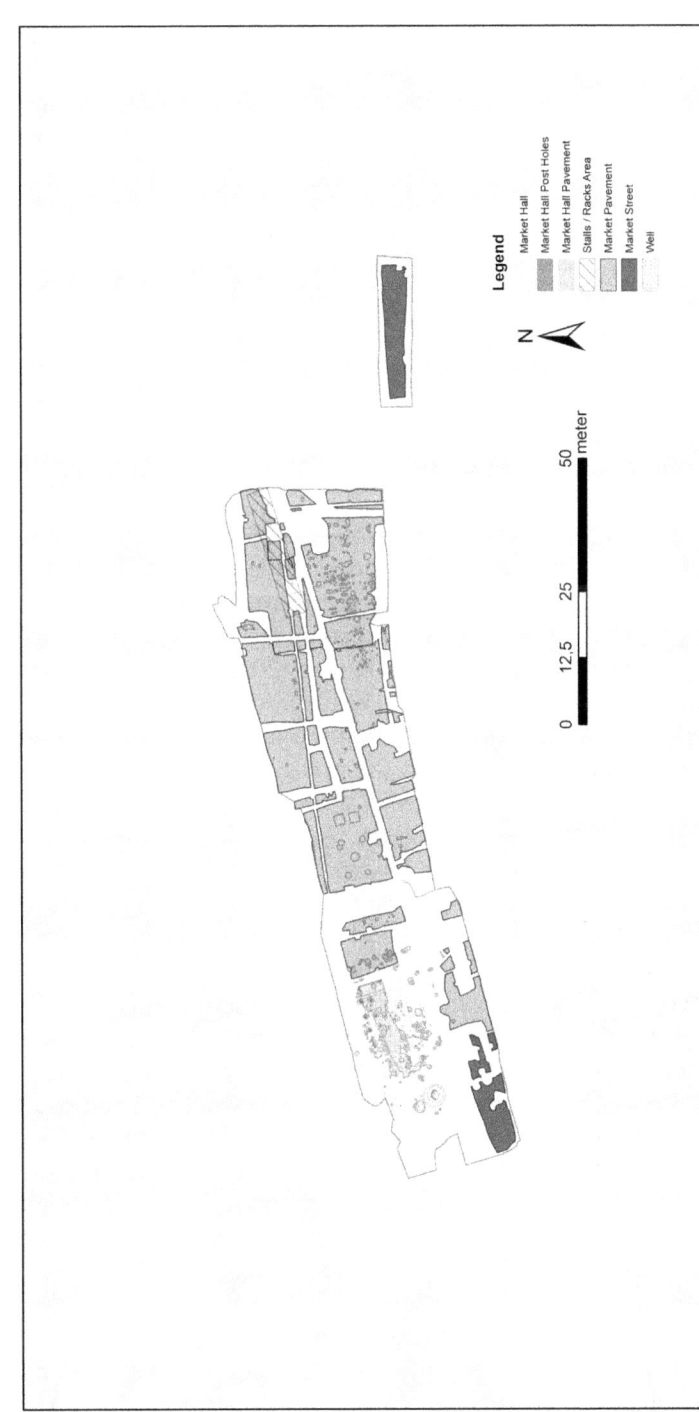

Figure 2.2 Excavation plan of the main market (*Breiter Markt*) in Tulln in the thirteenth century (illustration by Ute Scholz)

in mind that equipment such as folding tables, sheets or canvases left no archaeological trace. A stone-walled well was situated in the western part of the square, near the market hall; however, no evidence was found for rubbish pits, latrines or municipal elements such as a market clock, a pillory or a mint.

Indications of market activities can be drawn from written sources: the annual fair is reported to have taken place at *Breiter Markt* (Biack 1982: 356–66). In the fourteenth century, there is further evidence for a fish market, a weekly market in *Milchgasse*, a crop market (Biack 1982: 336, 368) and for the meat market at *Fleischmarkt*, which today is called *Rathausplatz* (Biack and Köstlbauer 1991: 78–79, 124).

Religion and Urban Archaeology

It is important to ask whether there were specific areas in the town associated with the trade between Jews and Christians, or whether the entire community used the same merchandising areas. One building in the northern part of the town was identified as a synagogue through building archaeological analyses. Simon Paulus (2003) dated the complex to before the beginning of the fifteenth century. After recording all available written sources, Paulus concluded that the Jewish settlement areas had been located in close proximity to the synagogue since the beginning of the thirteenth century. This study is the only archaeological investigation in Tulln's former Jewish quarter. Substantial excavations of urban building plots belonging to the Jewish community were conducted in Vienna (Mitchell 2004) and Regensburg (Codreanu-Windauer 2004). In both cases the synagogues and several residential buildings were identified. In Vienna there are indications that the Jewish living quarters were surrounded by a separate wall, which included approximately ten gates, which presumably regulated passage at night. For Tulln, we can follow the medieval city wall in several places (Hirsch 1996; Scholz et al. 2007); however, near the assumed Jewish areas, there is no evidence for an additional wall. Furthermore, no structures have been identified that would indicate specific Jewish trade or market areas. Several archaeological studies of the material culture related to medieval Jewish communities clearly indicate that it is largely the same as the material culture of Christian households, except for finds that show religious symbols, Hebrew characters or ritual objects themselves (Harck 2004: 25–27).

In the northwestern part of the town, another religious community was located that is archaeologically traceable through the construction of the monastery of the Conventual Franciscans (*Minoriten*), founded in 1258 (see

Figure 2.1), where some thirteenth-century stone walls of the monastery building survived (Tuzar 1997). The area is located only some 200 metres westwards of the supposed Jewish area. But one plot of land near the city wall, located between both areas, was excavated without providing any information about a specific religious identity (Hirsch 2003). Close to the former city centre, however, religious power was represented through the presence of St Stephan's church, which was established around 1014 and still stands (Csendes 2002: 5). In the charnel house attached to the southwestern part of the church, the butchers' guild donated an altar dedicated to St John the Evangelist (Biack 1982: 338). There might have been preparations for the installation of another religious centre in the former town centre, because in 1280 the Tulln Dominican Convent was founded (Hofer 2001: 202).

In the mid thirteenth century, we can therefore distinguish two religious groups in the city. Whereas the Christian majority was evenly spread over the entire medieval town, the Jewish minority clustered around the northern part near the city wall and the River Danube, bordered by a Christian religious house to the west, the former town centre and market area to the east and a newly established market and town plots in the south. Municipal areas have not yet been excavated. The 'Schranne', which was the official town hall, is only known from written sources, which date the building to around 1350 (Biack 1982: 246; Biack and Köstlbauer 1991: 120–23). Most of the excavated areas of medieval Tulln which revealed archaeological material and contexts dating to the mid thirteenth century were connected to households of the Christian majority and provided information about their lifestyle as well as areas of production and consumption within the town.

Meat and the Town

Research on meat consumption in the medieval town is reliant upon a combination of archaeological and archaeozoological sources. Monika Doll (2003) collected data from Germany, Austria and Switzerland and her interpretation also refers to written sources and imagery. In the context of the preparation and distribution of meat the spatial and legal considerations are important. Doll talks about medieval slaughterhouses (Doll 2003: 173), which were usually situated in close proximity to running water, for example the archaeological evidence for a late medieval/early modern slaughterhouse (*Schlachthaus*) in Linz, Upper Austria on the Danube (Knecht 1966). Regarding the purchase of meat, Doll refers to medieval images that show meat products for sale, hanging down from wooden structures or lying on wooden tables (Doll 2003: 214–20; Schubert 2006: 99–101). In written sources 'butcher stalls' (*Fleischbänke*) are often mentioned as places for selling meat at the market, but in some cases they also appear to have been used for chopping and butchering (Doll 2003: 175–76).

Written sources from Tulln situate the butcher stalls (*Fleischbänke*) 'opposite to', 'alongside of the corner' and 'near' the meat market (Biack 1982: 337–41; Biack and Köstlbauer 1991: 15, 77–78, 123–24). Some stalls were registered in the cadastre as early as 1301 (Kerschbaumer 1902: 344 CXXXVII), thus indicating the selling of meat at the meat market or at least close by. These stalls were, presumably, permanent installations occupying a designated space composed of several buildings. It is very likely that huts or tables for sales purposes were rigged up in the open space at the meat market (*Fleischmarkt*), which was bounded on the western side by the 'Schranne' and to the south and east by houses (Figure 2.1). Due to a lack of excavations in this area, we cannot make any statement about the market installations. The archaeological excavation closest to the meat market took place in Wiener Str. 4 (Figure 2.1), but only resulted in a poorly defined sequence of settlement features. Predominantly, pits and two wells dating to the thirteenth century were recorded, though without any evidence pointing towards meat processing in this area (Krenn and Singer 2007).

Although the written records indicate that from the beginning of the fourteenth century onwards meat commerce mainly took place at the meat market (*Fleischmarkt*), it is not clear whether such activities were already taking place in the thirteenth century. The wooden structures of the first phases of market buildings (Figure 2.2) at *Breiter Markt* date to that period and could provide some indications. They were built solely with postholes, which contained very little archaeological material. Evidence is better preserved, and present in higher quantities, in associated pavements and levelling layers. The pavements contained a ceramic assemblage, consisting of a large quantity of storage pots and various metal finds, including an abundance of horseshoes and iron nails. Most striking, however, is the majority of the material: the pavements were littered with highly fragmented animal bones, raising the question of whether meat sales or processing took place directly in the market square at that time. The Butchers' Guild Rules, dating to the mid thirteenth century, indicate the need of a regulation for the purchase of meat in the town. But are we able to find any spatial relationship to that in the archaeological record?

Evidence for a medieval meat market exists from the German town of Lübeck, where the butchers' stalls were situated in the southern part of

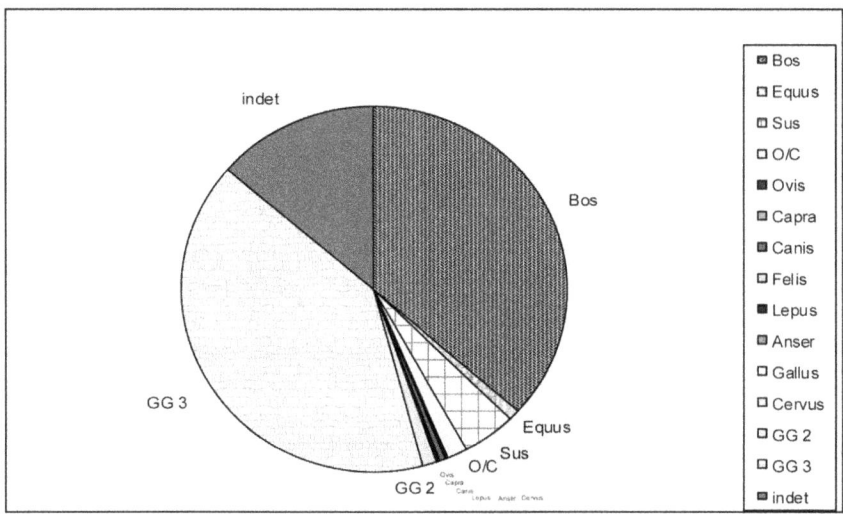

Figure 2.3 Distribution of animal species according to absolute quantities in percentages (illustration by Herbert Böhm/VIAS)

the main market square (*Schrangen*) (Mührenberg 1996). Traces of stalls (*Litten*) were excavated, consisting of rows of postholes. The features, however, did not provide enough data for a reconstruction. A layer containing a noticeable assemblage of animal bones was recorded just next to the posthole structures. The wooden structures fit very well with the information given by the excavation of the butchers' stalls in Lübeck. Mührenberg interprets the rows of postholes surrounding a pavement containing gravel and crushed bones as tables, stalls or arcades used by the butchers (Mührenberg 1996: 26).

A quite similar situation is apparent at *Breiter Markt* in Tulln and, additionally, numerous fragmented animal bones were found in the thirteenth-century pavements of the entire main market square. But in Tulln the material suggests that activities other than the selling of meat were being undertaken. The animal bones from Tulln are currently being examined by archaeozoologists from the Vienna Institute for Archaeological Research (University of Vienna/Herbert Böhm). Though the analyses have not yet been completed, initial results relevant to the market square pavement allow for some general observations regarding the animal waste. The overwhelming majority of the bones are long bones from cattle (Figure 2.3) in a highly fragmented condition, which seems to be the result of deliberate crushing. Additionally, there are sheep, goat and pig bones in the same fragmented state. Generally, the bones had characteristic signs of processing, though originating from very diverse processing activities: observable cutting or chopping marks can be interpreted as the result of meat processing, both slaughtering and meat preparation, but there were also hints of bone handicraft, e.g. cutting marks on horn cores. Moreover, the rare horse and dog bones are, by far, not as fragmented as the other pieces. The spectrum of animals and processing traces points towards highly mixed utilization and disposal processes. We can define the bones as recycled material deriving from different stages in the consumption process that was reused as building material in the market square. The condition and various marks on the bones are evidence for slaughtering, meat preparation and handicraft, while on the other hand, the archaeological context in which the bones were found relates to disposal and building practices. The context and composition of these finds makes it difficult to interpret the bone assemblage as an indicator of meat processing or merchandising at the market itself, since it is not clear where the bones actually came from. Although the analysis of the pavements belonging to the stalls or table structures has not yet been completed, new information regarding the time when the Butchers' Guild Rules were published can be expected in due course. The spectrum of species represented in the sample provides an insight into the consumption habits of the Tulln population. A similar situation is documented in Bremen, where the market pavement, also dating from the thirteenth century, was mixed with handicraft waste, especially cattle bones (Bischop 2006). However, the distribution of the species is not as extreme as in Tulln (50 per cent cattle, 20 per cent pig and horse, 13 per cent goat and sheep), thus pointing towards varying consumption habits among the urban population.

Most archaeozoological material from medieval urban contexts is dominated by cattle bones (Doll 2003: 274). This is not only a result of a dominant meat production based on cattle, but also of manufacturing dairy products and the use of cattle as working animals (Sykes 2009: 57–60). Therefore, the argument put forward by some for the superiority of cattle bones as an indicator for the existence of a Jewish settlement becomes doubtful, especially as Ole Harck has shown that pig bones were often disposed of in Jewish contexts as well (Harck 2004: 27–28). Even if there are contexts that have a secure relation to a Jewish settlement horizon (Daróczi-Szabó 2004), it is necessary to base the interpretation on a combination of written sources and archaeological evidence that represents special relationships to the Jewish community, such as decoration with distinct religious symbols. In the case of a well in Budapest that was filled with disposal from first a Jewish and later a Christian community in the fourteenth century, there are finds with a carved Star of David and Hebrew inscriptions. Animal bones show a minimum range of pig bones in the assumed Jewish backfill and an expectable increase of this animal species in the Christian levels above. László Daróczi-Szabó (2004: 257) also points out that Jewish dietary laws exclude the use of hind legs of cattle because of ritual practices and thus postulates a prevalence of front legs in Jewish material. These examples show that although using solely animal bones as an indicator for Jewish consumption rules is mostly inconclusive, a combination with additional information through small finds or written sources can lead to relevant results.

Rules of Consumption in the Town: Meat and Power: Final Conclusions

When critically reviewing the evidence on medieval meat consumption provided by written sources on the one hand and archaeological finds and features on the other, it has to be concluded that extractable information, even when deriving from the same kind of source, is often contradictory. Consumer research terms help to systematize some facts. The five stages of food consumption listed by George Gumerman (1997) can be applied to the archaeological record: there is data for the *production* of food traceable in some levels of the market square provided by animal bones that show cutting and chopping marks. The pending analysis of the stalls' pavements might reveal additional information belonging to butchery or meat processing. For the *preparation* of food, there are hints given by the objects associated with food handling at the market like storage vessels or pots. The *distribution* of food is indicated by wooden buildings at the market place, for example, the postholes for the market hall and stalls or racks in the northeast. In addition, the evaluation of the material from the stalls can provide further information. Meat *consumption* can be reconstructed partially from the archaeozoological assemblage present in the occupation layers of the market, although problems arise regarding the provenance of the material. As indicated before, the bones could have been collected from different parts of the town and then brought intentionally to the market square for reuse as building material. Therefore, it is problematic to make substantial statements about the reference of the material to one specific social or religious group of the town's population. The variety of species present amongst the animal bone assemblage appears to be 'typical' for medieval society, with a high percentage of cattle bones, followed by pig bones. *Disposal* of commodities or unusable parts of consumer goods is only known from the different levelling or occupation layers, but not in special contexts like latrines or waste pits. This fact indicates an organized waste disposal system for the market, leading to questions of organization and power.

Social and religious relations are the main topics in the Butchers' Guild Rules. For instance, fees for Jewish butchers were increased, matching regulations introduced by the Fourth Lateran Council in 1215 (Wiedl 2009: 275), which involved several restrictions for the everyday life of the Jewish communities. The *Tullner Fleischhauerordnung* dates back to the same year as the provincial synods of Wroclaw/Breslau and Vienna in 1267, which prohibited Christian consumers from buying meat from Jewish butchers (Wiedl 2009: 297). The rules are currently the earliest known regulations of the medieval period regarding meat consumption, but they were followed by numerous similar orders in Austria and Germany (Eggendorfer 1980a: 16–22). This is a noticeable indication for regulations of the commercial dominance of Christian butchers through magistrates, landlords and, equally importantly, the Church as religious institutions influenced the spatial appearance of the town, for example, in town planning (separated living areas delimited by walls, as recorded in Vienna), or through the presumably strategically placing of official Christian buildings around the whole town. The posthole structures on the main market that date to the same period as the Butchers' Guild Rules perhaps represent a place of sale belonging to a strengthened guild, claiming their rights over one of the most important areas of the town.

Small finds in the archaeological record are much harder to interpret. The existing dietary rules, for both Christian and Jewish community members, can only be connected to the material record after thoroughly investigating the space and stage of consumption. The presence of animal bones in backfills or levelling deposits has to be linked to these categories to make any secure interpretation. Though the information transmitted by written sources is very important in interpreting the archaeology of a market, circumstances like those in Tulln demand a reconsideration of the relationship between official rules and actual daily practice. The directives of the *Tullner Fleischhauerordnung* can only partly be observed in the archaeological record, thus revealing an asymmetry between institutional regulations and trading realities of the medieval urban community. Professional competition, urban–rural relations and hygienic standards could not be illustrated in detail at this stage of data analyses. But altogether, it seems likely that there were changes in the spatial distribution of meat purchasing in the town: from the beginning of the thirteenth century up to the date of the Butchers' Guild Rules, there are hints of an existing sales space for meat at the main market. But changes occur around the fourteenth century, when meat sales in Tulln happened not at the big fair (*Breiter Markt*), but at weekly or daily markets held at the smaller *Fleischmarkt* square.

Ute Scholz is a researcher at the Institute of Prehistory and Historical Archaeology, University of Vienna, Austria. The focus of her work is on urban archaeology, historical archaeology and archaeological theories (consumer research, sociology of space and architecture). As a fellow of the research project 'Space and Material Culture of a Medieval Town: Archaeological Research in Tulln', she conducted her Ph.D. thesis on space and place of the market.

References

Baeriswyl, A. 2003. *Stadt, Vorstadt und Stadterweiterung im Mittelalter: Archäologische und historische Studien zum Wachstum der drei Zähringerstädte Burgdorf, Bern und Freiburg im Breisgau*, Schweizer Beiträge zur Kulturgeschichte und Archäologie des Mittelalters 30. Basel: Schweizerischer Burgenverein.

Biack, O. 1982. *Geschichte der Stadt Tulln*. Tulln: Eigenverlag der Stadt Tulln.

Biack, O., and J. Köstlbauer. 1991. *Tullner Häuserchronik*. Tulln: Eigenverlag der Stadt Tulln.

Bischop, D. 2006. 'Mit Knochen gepflastert: Die archäologischen Beobachtungen und Grabungen am historischen Bremer Markt', *Zeitschrift für Archäologie des Mittelalters* 34: 215–30.

Bynum, C. 2008. 'Fast, Feast and Flesh: The Religious Significance of Food to Medieval Women', in C. Counihan and P. van Esterick (eds), *Food and Culture*. London: Routledge, pp. 138–58.

Codreanu-Windauer, S. 2004. 'Regensburg: Archäologie des mittelalterlichen Judenviertels', in C. Cluse (ed.), *Europas Juden im Mittelalter*. Trier: Kliomedia, pp. 465–78.

Cormeau, C. 1990. 'Essen und Trinken in den deutschen Predigten Bertholds von Regensburg', in I. Bitsch, T. Ehlert and X. von Ertzdorff (eds), *Essen und Trinken in Mittelalter und Neuzeit*. Sigmaringen: Thorbecke, pp. 77–83.

Csendes, P. 2002. *Tulln: Kommentar zur Siedlungsgeschichte, Tulln a. d. Donau. Österreichischer Städteatlas*. Vienna: Wiener Stadt- und Landesarchiv.

Daróczi-Szabó, L. 2004. 'Animal Bones as Indicators of Kosher Food Refuse from 14th Century AD Buda, Hungary', in S. O'Day, W. van Neer and A. Ervynck (eds), *Behaviour behind Bones*. Oxford: Oxbow, pp. 252–61.

De Grazia, V. 2001. 'History of Consumption', in N.J. Smesler and P.B. Baltes (eds), *International Encyclopedia of the Social & Behavioral Sciences Vol. 4*. Amsterdam: Elsevier, pp. 2682–87.

Dirlmeier, U., and G. Fouquet. 1993. 'Ernährung und Konsumgewohnheiten im spätmittelalterlichen Deutschland', *Geschichte in Wissenschaft und Unterricht* 44: 504–25.

Doll, M. 2003. *Haustierhaltung und Schlachtsitten des Mittelalters und der Neuzeit: Eine Synthese aus archäozoologischen, bildlichen und schriftlichen*

Quellen Mitteleuropas, Internationale Archäologie 78. Rahden/Westfahlen: VML.
Douglas, M. 2008. 'Deciphering a Meal', in C. Counihan and P. van Esterik (eds), *Food and Culture*. London: Routledge, pp. 36–54.
Eggendorfer, A. 1980a. 'Die Tullner Fleischhauerordnung von 1267', *Nöla: Mitteilungen aus dem niederösterreichischen Landesarchiv* 4: 12–24.
———. 1980b. 'Studien zu den Frühen Tullner Urkunden (1261–1365)', M.A. dissertation. Vienna: Institut für Österreichische Geschichtsforschung.
Eidelman, J.M. 2000. 'Be Holy for I am Holy: Food, Politics, and the Teaching of Judaism', *Journal of Ritual Studies* 14(1): 45–51.
Goodman, M.K., D. Goodman and M. Redcliff. 2010. *Consuming Space: Placing Consumption in Perspective*. Farnham: Ashgate.
Grieco, A. 2003. 'Lebensmittel und soziale Hierarchien im spätmittelalterlichen und frühneuzeitlichen Europa', in M. Prinz (ed.), *Der lange Weg in den Überfluss*. Paderborn: Schöningh, pp. 37–46.
Gumerman, G. 1997. 'Food and Complex Societies', *Journal of Archaeological Method and Theory* 4(2): 105–39.
Harck, O. 2004. 'Die archäologischen Funde zur jüdischen Geschichte in Mitteleuropa', in E. Wamers and F. Backhaus (eds), *Synagogen, Mikwen, Siedlungen*. Frankfurt am Main: Archäologisches Museum, pp. 25–40.
Henisch, B.A. 1978. *Fast and Feast: Food in Medieval Society*. London: Pennsylvania State University Press.
Hirsch, N. 1996. 'Die Grabungen im Bereich Roter Turm, Stadtgemeinde Tulln', *Fundberichte aus Österreich* 34: 377–84.
———. 2003. 'Rettungsgrabung im Altstadgebiet von Tulln', *Fundberichte aus Österreich* 41: 388–94.
Hofer, N. 2001. 'Von Comagenis zu Tulln: Neue archäologische Erkenntnisse zur Stadtwerdung Tullns', in S. Felgenhauer-Schmiedt, A. Eibner and H. Knittler (eds), *Zwischen Römersiedlung und mittelalterlicher Stadt*, Beiträge zur Mittelalterarchäologie in Österreich 17. Vienna: ÖGM, pp. 195–204.
Irsigler, F. 2007. 'Messen, Jahrmärkte und Stadtentwicklung in Europa: Mittelalter und frühe Neuzeit', in F. Irsigler and M. Pauly (eds), *Messen, Jahrmärkte und Stadtentwicklung in Europa*. Trier: Porta-Alba-Verlag, pp. 1–24.
Kerschbaumer, A. 1902. 'Regesten zur Geschichte der Stadt Tulln', in A. Kerschbaumer (ed.), *Geschichte der Stadt Tulln*. Krems: Verlag der Stadtgemeinde Tulln, pp. 311–471.
Knecht, G. 1966. 'Mittelalterlich-frühneuzeitliche Tierknochenfunde aus Oberösterreich (Linz und Enns)', *Naturkundliches Jahrbuch der Stadt Linz* 12: 11–72.
Kopytoff, I. 1986. 'The Cultural Biography of Things: Commoditization as Process', in A. Appadurai (ed.), *The Social Life of Things*. Cambridge: Cambridge University Press, pp. 64–91.
Kraemer, D. 2009. *Jewish Eating and Identity through the Ages*. London: Routledge.
Krenn, M., and M. Singer. 2007. 'KG Tulln, SG Tulln an der Donau, VB Tulln', *Fundberichte aus Österreich* 45: 41–42.

Lohrmann, K. 1990. *Judenrecht und Judenpolitik im mittelalterlichen Österreich*. Vienna: Böhlau.

Mitchell, P. 2004. 'Synagoge und jüdisches Viertel im mittelalterlichen Wien', in F. Backhaus and E. Wamers (eds), *Synagogen, Mikwen, Siedlungen*. Frankfurt am Main: Archäologisches Museum, pp. 139–50.

Mührenberg, D. 1996. 'Der Schrangen zu Lübeck: Fronerei und Fleischmarkt', in *Archäologische und baugeschichtliche Untersuchungen auf dem Lübecker Stadthügel*, Lübecker Schriften zur Archäologie und Kulturgeschichte 24. Bonn: Habelt, pp. 7–52.

Müller, U. 2010. 'Zentrale Orte und Netzwerke: Zwei Konzepte zur Beschreibung von Zentralität', in C. Theune, F. Biermann, R. Struwe and G.H. Jeute (eds), *Zwischen Fjorden und Steppe*. Rahden/Westfahlen: VML, pp. 57–67.

Opll, F. 1996. 'Jahrmarkt oder Messe? Überlegungen zur spätmittelalterlichen Handelsgeschichte Wiens', in P. Johanek and H. Stoob (eds), *Europäische Messen und Märktesysteme in Mittelalter und Neuzeit*, Städteforschung A 39. Vienna: Böhlau, pp. 189–204.

Paulus, S. 2003. '"... in der Judenschuell" – Neue Befunde zur mittelalterlichen Synagoge in Tulln', in *David: Jüdische Kulturzeitschrift* 58. Retrieved 11 May 2017 from http://david.juden.at/kulturzeitschrift/57-60/58-Paulus.htm

Scherrer, P. 2009. 'Vom Breiten Markt zum Rathausplatz', in W. Huber and R. Risy (eds), *Sant Ypoelten*. St Pölten: Diözesanmuseum St Pölten, pp. 145–52.

Scholz, U. 2012. 'Konsum und Archäologie: Zur Anwendung von Theorien der Konsumforschung in der Historischen Archäologie', *Historische Archäologie* 1: 1–18.

———. 2013. 'Jahrmarkt und Johannisfeier: Kulturelle Perspektiven und Archäologie der spätmittelalterlichen Öfen am Breiten Markt von Tulln. Ein Werkstattbericht', in F.X. Eder, O. Kühschelm, B. Schmidt-Lauber, P. Ther and C. Theune (eds), *Kulturen des Ökonomischen*. Vienna: Verlag des Instituts für Europäische Ethnologie, pp. 141–66.

Scholz, U., and M. Krenn. 2010, 'Stadtarchäologie in Tulln: Die Großgrabungen 2005-2009', in *Proceedings of the 15th International Conference on Cultural Heritage and New Technologies*. Vienna: Stadtarchäologie Wien, pp. 51–66.

Scholz, U., A. Steinegger, M. Singer and M. Krenn. 2007. 'Stadtkernarchäologie: Vom antiken Comagenis zum heutigen Tulln', *Archäologie Österreichs* 18(2): 4–18.

Schubert, E. 2006. *Essen und Trinken im Mittelalter*. Darmstadt: Primus.

Sykes, N. 2009. 'From *Cu* and *Sceap* to *Beffe* and *Motton*: The Management, Distribution, and Consumption of Cattle and Sheep in Medieval England', in C.M. Woolgar, D. Serjeantson and T. Waldron (eds), *Food in Medieval England*. Oxford: Oxford University Press, pp. 56–71.

Trentmann, F. 2009. 'Crossing Divides: Consumption and Globalization in History', *Journal of Consumer Culture* 9: 187–220.

Tuzar, J.M. 1997. 'Minoritenkloster, Tullner Stadtarchäologie II: Neue Ergebnisse zur Stadtarchäologie in Tulln. Grabungen des Vereins ASINOE der Jahre 1991–1997', *Mitteilungen des heimatkundlichen Arbeitskreises für die Stadt und den Bezirk Tulln* 11: 38–54.

Veblen, T. 2007. *Theorie der feinen Leute*. Frankfurt am Main: Fischer.
Wiedl, B. 2009. 'Jews and the City: Parameters of Jewish Urban Life in Late Medieval Austria', in A. Classen (ed.), *Urban Space in the Middle Ages and the Early Modern Age*. Berlin: De Gruyter, pp. 273–308.

Chapter 3

Rubbish and Regulations in the Middle Ages
A Comparison of Urban and Rural Disposal Practices

Greta Civis

Introduction

History, and our understanding of past thought, is usually based on written sources. But the majority of the medieval population, those living in the countryside, left very few written sources behind. From other medieval contexts, such as monasteries and towns, a variety of written records survive, which shape our ideas of the medieval mind. It is, however, questionable whether rules established within an urban context can be assumed to apply to contemporary villages or, indeed, whether all rules were adhered to in the city at all, and what implications the acknowledgement of rules might have for our understanding of the medieval conception of the world.

Especially in settlement contexts, nearly every find excavated is, in one way or another, refuse (for terms and definitions, see below). Refuse has been repeatedly addressed by archaeologists over the decades, be it from taphonomic (Schiffer 1987: 47–49; for an overview on taphonomic works, see e.g. Sommer 1991: 58–60; Blum 2002: 123–26), sociological (e.g. Rathje and Murphy 1994; Zimring and Rathje 2012) or historical perspectives (e.g. Thüry 2001). In the following chapter I will test if and how far it is possible to interpret a society's rules about disposing of its waste, and what wider interpretations can be derived from such analysis. The example of a medieval village in Brandenburg, Germany, is used to explore this question. After introducing rubbish as an archaeological concept, the methods, methodology and theory underlying my work will be briefly outlined.

The archaeological data is then presented and interpreted. Finally, I will compare a selection of written laws and regulations with the interpretation of the archaeological data and will discuss their acceptance, use and applicability in a medieval rural society in the framework of Pierre Bourdieu's concept of habitus (1982).[1]

From Rubbish to *Chaîne Éliminatoire*: Terms and Methodology

I chose the term *rubbish* as analogous to the German term *Müll*, which carries with it a strong vilifying connotation, and also relates to Michael Thompson's 'Rubbish Theory' (1979), which contains many of the ideas underlying my work. *Refuse* is my translation for *Abfall*, which in German literally means 'something that fell off' and can, in the first instance, be described as less emotive than rubbish. Rubbish causes reactions like disgust and demands action; nondirty refuse can be ignored.

In this terminology most archaeological findings are *refuse*, while a study about rules and regulations on refuse tries to identify *rubbish* and reconstructs actions of disposal to discuss the past mental structures of those who disposed of it.

Methodology: Chaîne Éliminatoire

The first formulation of the idea of an amalgamation of mental as well as social structure and material treatment basically goes back to André Leroi-Gourhan (1980: 190f.). This *chaîne opératoire* (or *operational sequence*) is based on the idea that single steps of the production of, for example, a stone tool can be reconstructed by certain steps of analysis (refitting, experimental archaeology, etc.). These reconstructed steps and materials can also provide insights to the cognitive and/or social capacities of a group. The regular use of material that was not at hand in the area where the tool was found, for example, demands the transport of a material or tool, knowledge of a certain material's quality, and accessibility to the material. The combination of two materials shows cognitive capacity. The techniques and the knowledge also needed to be passed on to form stable archaeological evidence. Recently Ofer Bar-Yosef and Philip van Peer stated: 'Technological classification is not considered anymore as simply a heuristic device but as a system that reflects emic cognitive standards' (2009: 114). The basic idea to reconstruct *chaînes*, or sequences, of material treatment as a pathway to understanding past mental structures has a lot to offer to a study on rubbish in the sense defined above. Therefore, I offer the *chaîne éliminatoire* as a reformulation of *chaîne opératoire*, as a way to interpret rubbish in the archaeological record. The following is more of an outline than a complete methodology. *Chaîne éliminatoire* is based on the concept of socially embedded objects, especially object biographies (e.g. Appadurai 1986; Kopytoff 1986. Mytum 2010 proposed the writing of biographies for historical archaeologies). As Chris Gosden and Yvonne Marshall (1999: 172) put it, a biographical viewpoint offers a lot to debate: 'Questions about the links between people and things; about the ways meanings and values are accumulated and transformed.' James Morris (2011: 167–68) successfully used a biographical approach to investigate the deposition of animal bones and Hill's (1995) work followed the idea of reconstructing the 'afterlife' of animal bones as part of society.

Confrontation and Contamination

Chaîne éliminatoire is basically founded on two terms: *confrontation* and *contamination*. *Contamination* describes a concept of pollution that Thompson (2003: 24) connects with negative (economic) value. Apart from positive value (which one desires and which can be compared with other things of value) and absent value (which has no effect on its environment), there is a negative value, which one rejects, and which has the potency to devalue a context. The connection and comparison of value and contamination seems likely because most of what can be said about traded goods can also be said about rubbish, conversely including the fact that someone has to be paid when the material changes its owner. Contamination describes the danger that is felt to be caused by rubbish, be it social, aesthetically or in terms of health. Contamination is, therefore, what transforms harmless refuse into dangerous rubbish. So a *confrontation* with contaminant classes of refuse (that is, rubbish) should be avoided. To avoid this confrontation, actions have to be taken and practices need to be established. In the archaeological record, attempts at avoiding confrontation, or of there being no interest to avoid confrontation with a certain material or of a material with a certain environment, can be interpreted.

The Social Dimension

The *chaîne éliminatoire* has strong social implications. Disposal is a socially anchored expression of categorizing and ordering processes. Rubbish is not just a necessary (useful) element of consumption and production, but also an autonomous process that works according to rules and patterns that express the categories working in a society.

It is not necessary for those who dispose to be consciously aware of their rules and categories. It is much more likely that naturalizing explanations are given (see Douglas (1986: 48) on naturalizing defence of social arrangements), which describe the management at work as the only way that makes sense. Processes of disposal and the understanding of rubbish is a distinct process working according to inherent patterns, structures and rules that are embedded in the structures and classifications used and working in a society. A *chaîne éliminatoire* describes mental structures, because the boundaries of these structures become visible. But disposal also raises social questions: who disposes what in which way is also prescribed by social roles and social context. Therefore, social roles (and also status) can be negotiated in relation to who disposes what and in which way.

Concept Violation as Showing Structure

In her widely known work *Purity and Danger* (2002), Mary Douglas focused on the concept of impurity and dirt as a violation of the concepts, classes and the categories that a group applies to its world. If the borders between separated spheres are violated, certain action has to be taken, whether to re-establish and strengthen the boundaries between the spheres (Douglas 2002: 48–49), to control, rescue or punish, or to maintain an awareness of the boundaries. Douglas' work is based on a concept of classification and is of enormous fertility for a study about the cultural impact of disposal and the rules surrounding it. Rules and regulations are part of a classification system that defines correct and incorrect behaviour, and demands the need for certain actions to correct the incorrect. 'The prohibitions trace the cosmic outlines and the ideal social order' (Douglas 2002: 90). According to Douglas (2002: 44), the appearance of dirt always indicates a system: 'Dirt is the by-product of a systematic ordering and classification of matter, in so far as ordering involves rejecting inappropriate elements.' So rubbish as material dirt is also a central feature of ordering and classifying. According to cognitive and social studies, I will use the term 'categorizing' in the following way. In recent years, categorizing has been widely described as a central feature of human cognition (Berlin and Kay 1969; Rosch 1978; see also, among many others, Lakoff and Johnson 2003) and social life (Jenkins 2000). Patterning and categorizing seem to be widely applied practices by humans to orientate in their world. The material world is perceived in categories, too, and these categories experience violations (see also Thompson (1979), especially Chapter 5 for a debate of this issue). Douglas (2002: 197) showed that the main role of rubbish is to threaten and offend the existing order and normality. Judith Butler (1990) and Michel Foucault (1969) are just two of the theorists who showed that focusing on the threatening and violation of concepts is a fruitful way to elucidate the norm itself. In an archaeological context, it makes sense to view rubbish as a central feature and permanent violation of processes of ordering and categorizing the world. A society without rubbish would thereby mean a society that does not violate its own classification of the material world or does not classify its (material) world.

So far, we have no hints for such a society in medieval villages (for example, Morsel (2006: 222) can indicate a strong bipolar structure in the medieval mentality). Rubbish is therefore also a promising field to be studied in a medieval village in Brandenburg. Practices of disposal are shaped by cosmological ideas. Corbin (1984) illustrates impressively how pervasive the idea of smell as dangerous was in seventeenth to nineteenth-century society, and how this shaped private as well as public (re)actions and attitudes. It is of course unlikely that these modern scenarios can be directly adopted for a medieval village in Brandenburg, but Corbin's study is a great example of a society dealing with a different concept of hygiene from bacteriology. Hygienic concepts are rather unconsciously incorporated than reflected. We can also assume that different parts of medieval society felt different practices to be correct, e.g. according to their gender, status, age. Dangerous influences demand a certain way of reacting, which can be described with Bourdieu's concept of habitus (1982: 277–78). Habitus is a set or pattern of dispositions that is (physically) incorporated and has direct effects on everyday practice up to a point where it influences the way we move, sit and chew (Bourdieu 1982: 307–9). In addition, ideas of hygiene and dirt as practices of disposal are connected to incorporated habitual practice. The contributions in Hofmann, Maase and Warneken (1999), especially Silberzahn-Jandt (1999: 165), give an idea of how disposing can be analysed as habitual practice in modern societies. How we feel about our material remains, and what we feel to be correct reactions to them is connected with lifestyle and shaped by habitus. Following disposal practices can provide an insight into habitual processes, as well as helping us to understand a permanent part of medieval life.

The following is a test of the briefly introduced *chaîne éliminatoire* and its relationship to habitus, using data from the medieval village of Diepensee.

Filth and Farming: Animal Bones

The village of Diepensee, southeast of Berlin, was nearly completely excavated between 2004 and 2007 (Figure 3.1). The written sources as well as the material culture (mainly ceramics) date to the thirteenth and fourteenth centuries. The excavation recovered over 170,000 finds from an area of 14

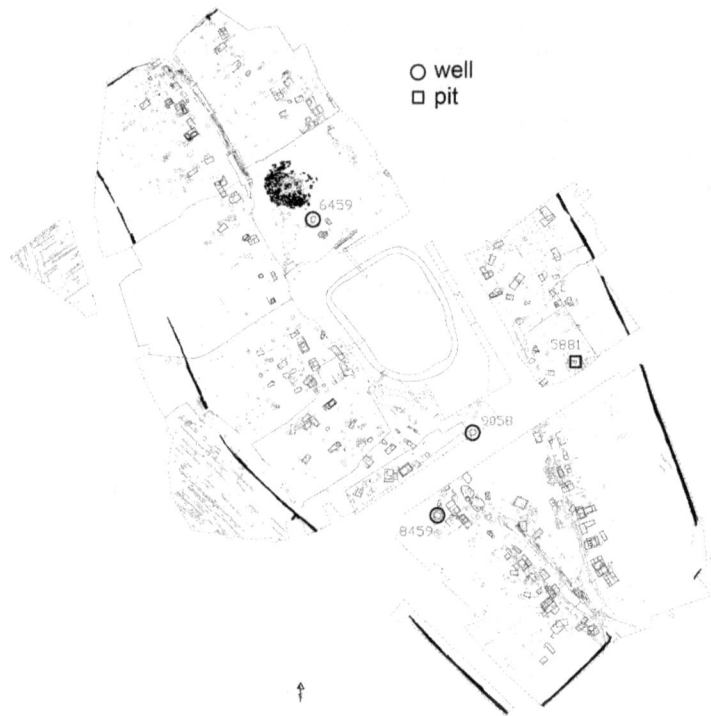

Figure 3.1 Excavation plan of Diepensee. Archaeological features mentioned in the text are marked: circle = well; square = pit; black line = ditch (illustration by Greta Civis/Brandenburg Authorities for Heritage Management and Archaeological State Museum)

hectares. More than 50,000 finds were human bones from the cemetery. Without these, the number of finds from medieval contexts totals more than 75,000 objects. The following analysis mainly concentrates on the animal bones. In Diepensee, 10,882 animal bones were recorded, of which 7,097 can currently be dated to nondisturbed medieval contexts. Franka Höppner (2010) was able to analyse 7,323 of all recorded animal bones (from excavation areas I, II, III, VI, IX and XI) in Diepensee. Of these, 5,400 were from medieval contexts, allowing Höppner to analyse a representative amount of the animal bones from Diepensee for data relating to species, sex, age, diseases/deformation, use- and gnawing-marks.

Sheep/goat (*ovis*) was the most common species in Diepensee, according to both the number of bone fragments (1,168) and the minimum number of individuals (MNI: 36) (Höppner 2010: 9). The amount of horse (*equus*) bones at Diepensee was surprisingly high, with at least twenty-two individuals and 1,167 bone fragments being present. After the disturbed contexts were removed, this becomes even more significant, with horse being the most common species (1,101 fragments), followed by dog (*canis*) (936 fragments) and ovis (701 fragments). The other species mirror the usual medieval spectrum of animals: cattle (*bos*), pig (*sus*), cat (*felis*) and chicken (*gallus*) appear, as well as several wild animals and animals that live close to human settlements, such as rat, fox and wolf.

Abrasion on Animal Bones: Gnawing Marks

It can be assumed that the majority of the bones were disposed of as kitchen refuse. This is likely for single bones from pig, chicken and cattle. Presumably they were disposed of with other remains from food, which are now decayed (see also Jones 2011). Since horse and, especially, dog, which were unlikely to be eaten (Doll 2003: 275), are more often present in cadaver pits, they should not affect the analysis of the record too heavily. The animal bones give hints as to how the Diepensee population dealt with their everyday refuse, especially with the parts that were likely to create bad smells. Gnawing marks on animal bones are an indicator of whether bones have been lying on the surface (see e.g. Morris 2011: 17), accessible for animals like dogs, rats and foxes to chew on, and can be used to determine the approximate proportion of bones that were not immediately buried. Höppner (2010: 78) found gnawing marks on only twelve of the bones studied. After removing the modern disturbed contexts, only five contexts contained bones with gnawing marks. Höppner (2010: 78) interprets this as a careful disposal of kitchen refuse, or at least of the animal bones. I fully agree with this interpretation and would add that the disposal must have happened relatively quickly.

The Spreading of Animal Bones

At the moment, the spreading of the animal bones can only be compared between some of the complexes and excavation areas (henceforth: TF). Since the TFs are of different sizes and contain different quantities of finds, the relative quantities of finds per TF will be compared. The basis for this was the inventory list of the Brandenburg Authorities for Heritage Management and Archaeological State Museum. On average, animal bones account for 11 per cent of the finds from each TF. In relation to animal bones, the finds groups can be divided into three groups (Figure 3.2):

> The first group consists of TFs with a high amount of animal bones (around 20 per cent of finds from these groups) (TFs III, IV and V).

The second group consists of TF with animal bones accounting for between 11 and 17 per cent of finds (TFs VI, VII and IX).

The third group are TFs in which animal bones account for less than 10 per cent of the finds present (TF II, VIII and XI with c. 8 per cent and TF XII with 5.8 per cent).

Across the site, the exclusion of cadaver pits does not change these groupings significantly. Human bones were not included in the calculation.

Blandine Wittkopp (2014) has reconstructed four phases of settlement. The TF with the highest quantities of animal bones present in relation to other finds are all in the core district of Diepensee, in the permanently settled area. The rather meagre TFs II and XII are also situated here, but still I interpret these bones as having accumulated in the permanently inhabited area. TFs VI, VII and IX (in which animal bones comprise between 11 and 17 per cent of finds) are located in the first expansion of the village, during the second phase of occupation. Logically TFs VIII and XI (with low quantities of animal bones) are in the outer area of the village, not inhabited until the third settlement phase.

The sacred character of TF IX (which includes the church and the cemetery) demands a separate debate. Here, as everywhere in Diepensee, animal bones were found. Most of the animal bones from TF IX were recovered from the well (6,459). Without these, animal bones only account for around 8 per cent of the finds from TF IX, which also revealed a rather high amount of nonidentifiable animal bones. This might point to a variety of nondomestic animals that died in the area of the graveyard, but were not actually disposed there. Further investigations will hopefully clarify this issue.

Chronological Development

Blandine Wittkopp has been able to date 582 of the 718 complexes with animal bones according to their horizontal or vertical stratigraphy.[2] I was able to date 636 of the complexes containing animal bones via ceramics, although it should be noted that dating complexes by ceramics is very problematic in a medieval village that existed for only around 150 years. The complexes that could already have been dated to one phase show a nonrandom distribution of finds and phases (on a 1 per cent significance level according to a Chi-square test). Table 3.1 shows some relationship between phase and relative amount of animal bones. Phases 2 and 3 in particular show considerably higher amounts of the animal bones than do later phases. Phase 1 has a much higher proportion of animal bones than

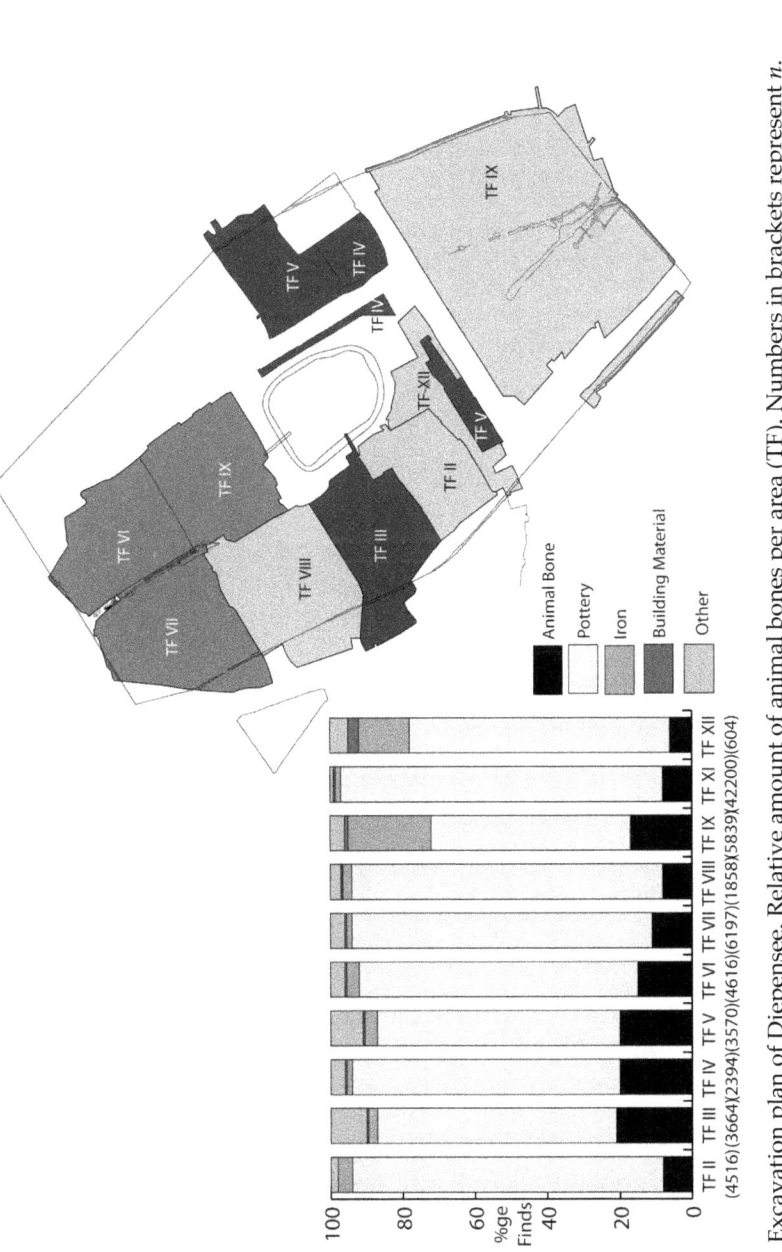

Figure 3.2 Excavation plan of Diepensee. Relative amount of animal bones per area (TF). Numbers in brackets represent *n*. (illustration by Greta Civis/Brandenburg Authorities for Heritage Management and Archaeological State Museum)

Table 3.1 Chronological development of find spectrum in Diepensee.
n: Sum=75,265. Phase 1=713; Phase 2=9,047; Phase 3=19,429; Phase 3–4=6,280; Phase 4=11,991; Phase 2–3=8,456; Unphased=19,349. Cadaver-pits are not included (Inventory List of the Brandenburg Authorities for Heritage Management and Archaeological State Museum; phases kindly provided by Blandine Wittkopp)

Phase	Other finds	Construction material	Iron	Ceramics	Animal bones	Sum
Observed						
Phase 1	26	0	10	169	508	713
Phase 2	112	5	105	7,407	1,418	9,047
Phases 2–3	94	7	120	7,641	594	8,456
Phase 3	472	26	647	16,026	2,258	19,429
Phases 3–4	81	3	185	5,488	523	6,280
Phase 4	190	41	244	10,713	803	11,991
Sum	975	82	1,311	47,444	6,104	55,916
Expected (%) H0						
Phase 1	1.74	0.15	2.34	84.85	10.92	100.00
Phase 2	1.74	0.15	2.34	84.85	10.92	100.00
Phases 2–3	1.74	0.15	2.34	84.85	10.92	100.00
Phase 3	1.74	0.15	2.34	84.85	10.92	100.00
Phases 3–4	1.74	0.15	2.34	84.85	10.92	100.00
Phase 4	1.74	0.15	2.34	84.85	10.92	100.00
%	1.74	0.15	2.34	84.85	10.92	100.00
Difference between observed and expected (%)						
Phase 1	1.90	−0.15	−0.94	−61.15	60.33	0.00
Phase 2	−0.51	−0.09	−1.18	−2.98	4.76	0.00
Phases 2–3	−0.63	−0.06	−0.93	5.51	−3.89	0.00
Phase 3	0.69	−0.01	0.99	−2.36	0.71	0.00
Phases 3–4	−0.45	−0.10	0.60	2.54	−2.59	0.00
Phase 4	−0.16	0.20	−0.31	4.49	−4.22	0.00

expected. Admittedly, phase 1 contains only 713 finds and therefore much less material than other phases, so some distortion might be possible. The 508 bone fragments from phase 1 are from only twelve complexes, of which one complex (no. 5881) contains 364 fragments. On the other hand, it is remarkable that a phase that contains less than 1 per cent of the total amount of finds holds 6 per cent of all animal bones and, even without the 364 fragments from complex no. 5881, holds 2 per cent of the total amount of medieval animal bones.

Therefore, I argue that the disposal of the animal bones happened in the inhabited area – kitchen refuse and dead animal cadavers were not brought far away from the direct living space. Close to the houses, dead animals, animal bones and kitchen refuse seem to have been buried to prevent accessibility for wild animals or to prevent further confrontation with the swill from the last meal. The risk of contamination was presumably too high for these substances to be collected and carried away.

Another interpretation might be that the economic situation or the diet of the Diepensee population changed from the early thirteenth century to the mid fourteenth century. At the moment, the comparison with the dated ceramics does not indicate this: there is no significance in the amount of animal bones combined with early or late ceramic types. On the contrary, phase 1 shows a significant high amount of very small sherds (<2.5 cm). These are not in their primary deposit, but have been moved several times. All of this argues against an economic interpretation; rather, it was the way of disposal that led to the accumulation of large amounts of kitchen refuse in areas inhabited over a long time.

The Functional Context

Of further interest is the function of the complexes that contained bones: animal bones were found in higher percentages than expected in burials, wells, public and private ditches (assuming a random distribution). They were underrepresented in public streets, in pits of technical and unclear function, ovens and hearths, and in several parts of former houses such

Table 3.2 Animal species as represented in selected features: (a) well no. 6459; (b) ditch surrounding the village (data kindly provided by Franka Höppner).

Species	Weight in g (sum)	Fragments (sum)
(a) Well no. 6459		
Bos	225.6	8
Canis Lupus	9.9	2
Equus	1,163.3	29
Gallus	53.5	66
Ovis	1,461.7	382
Sus	392.3	91
Undetermined	144.5	226
Total	3,450.8	804
(b) Ditch around the village		
Bos	378.1	14
Bos/Equus	65.6	35
Equus	484.1	29
Ovis	4.6	1
Undetermined	54.7	59
Total	987.1	138

Table 3.3 General find spectrum in Diepensee (Inventory List of the Brandenburg Authorities for Heritage Management and Archaeological State Museum; interpretations kindly provided by Blandine Wittkopp)

Complex	Other finds	Construction material	Clay	Iron	Ceramics	Animal bones	Total
Observed							
Well	67	0	0	34	426	674	1,201
Village ditch	5	1	0	28	158	132	324
Fireplace	7	0	3	1	365	5	381
Building	47	27	57	79	2,879	269	3,358
Ditch	25	0	0	37	2,154	76	2,292
Pit	252	40	584	379	22,267	1,971	25,493
Cadaverpit	6	4	0	1	630	855	1,496
Cellar	142	6	313	168	13,546	1,224	15,399
Oven	29	0	176	16	1,152	129	1,502
Posthole	10	1	111	29	1,137	166	1,454
Other interpretation	2	0	0	6	207	0	215
Cellar with stone construction	184	35	1,094	966	13,877	1,588	17,744
Street	4	0	0	42	74	8	128
Total	780	114	2,338	1,786	58,872	7,097	70,987
Expected (%) H0							
Well	1.10	0.16	3.29	2.52	82.93	10.00	100.00
Village ditch	1.10	0.16	3.29	2.52	82.93	10.00	100.00
Fireplace	1.10	0.16	3.29	2.52	82.93	10.00	100.00
Building	1.10	0.16	3.29	2.52	82.93	10.00	100.00
Ditch	1.10	0.16	3.29	2.52	82.93	10.00	100.00
Pit	1.10	0.16	3.29	2.52	82.93	10.00	100.00
Cadaverpit	1.10	0.16	3.29	2.52	82.93	10.00	100.00
Cellar	1.10	0.16	3.29	2.52	82.93	10.00	100.00

Oven	1.10	0.16	3.29	2.52	82.93	10.00	100.00
Posthole	1.10	0.16	3.29	2.52	82.93	10.00	100.00
Other interpretation	1.10	0.16	3.29	2.52	82.93	10.00	100.00
Cellar with stone construction	1.10	0.16	3.29	2.52	82.93	10.00	100.00
Street	1.10	0.16	3.29	2.52	82.93	10.00	100.00
Difference between observed and expected (%)							
Well	4.48	-0.16	-3.29	0.32	-47.46	46.12	0.00
Village ditch	0.44	0.15	-3.29	6.13	-34.17	30.74	0.00
Fireplace	0.74	-0.16	-2.51	-2.25	12.87	-8.69	0.00
Building	0.30	0.64	-1.60	-0.16	2.80	-1.99	0.00
Ditch	-0.01	-0.16	-3.29	-0.90	11.05	-6.68	0.00
Pit	-0.11	0.00	-1.00	-1.03	4.41	-2.27	0.00
Cadaverpit	-0.70	0.11	-3.29	-2.45	-40.82	47.15	0.00
Cellar	-0.18	-0.12	-1.26	-1.42	5.03	-2.05	0.00
Oven	0.83	-0.16	8.42	-1.45	-6.24	-1.41	0.00
Posthole	-0.41	-0.09	4.34	-0.52	-4.74	1.42	0.00
Other interpretation	-0.17	-0.16	-3.29	0.27	13.35	-10.00	0.00
Cellar with stone construction	-0.06	0.04	2.87	2.93	-4.73	-1.05	0.00
Street	2.03	-0.16	-3.29	30.30	-25.12	-3.75	0.00

as postholes, cellars and buildings. Some complexes were interpreted as cadaver pits (Hanik and Wittkopp 2012). A Chi-square test indicates a nonarbitrary distribution of finds groups in relation to the types of complexes (below the 1 per cent significance level). The complex with the absolute highest amount of animal bones is well no. 6459 from TF IX. This contained 804 animal bones, mainly *ovis* but also *bos*, *canis*, *equus*, *gallus* and *sus* (Table 3.2a). Wells no. 9058 and no. 8459 contained remarkably high amounts of animal bones. In the following I will contrast the relative amount of animal bones to the amount of other finds groups. With proportions of more than 50 per cent, the wells seemed to have been a place in which animal bones (and kitchen refuse) were regularly disposed of. The quantities present in the ditch enclosing the village are surprisingly high, with 138 bones from a total of 324 finds, making the relative amount of animal bones far beyond the average of 11 per cent, at around 40 per cent. In urban contexts, rules to keep the ditch clean are known (see e.g. the example of the medieval town of Konstanz: Hausmair and Barwitzki 2016: xvi–xvii). For example, Schenk (2009: tables 31 and 32, also personal information) demonstrated there was a low concentration of ceramics in the castle ditch in the town of Freyenstein. The ditch in Diepensee also contains a remarkably low quantity of ceramic sherds. It might be that this caused the seemingly high amount of bones, mainly from domestic animals (Table 3.2b).

The proportion of the total amount of all cellars is compared in relation to the total amount of all postholes to avoid distortions caused by small amounts of finds in small complexes (Table 3.3). The cellars contained a low quantity of bone. Small structures, which could have been filled and closed quickly, seem to have been preferred for the disposal of smelly refuse, especially animal bones. Deposits or features that remained open or exposed for long periods, such as hearths, streets, ovens and private ditches, contained extremely low quantities of animal bones. One feature that was chosen for the deposition of kitchen waste, including animal bone, was the village ditch. The choice of this feature perhaps shows that efforts were made to dump material at the edge of the village in order to avoid confrontation with neighbours.

Summary: Disposal Rules and Practice in Diepensee

The concept of how to ideally dispose of kitchen refuse in Diepensee appears visible in the archaeological record. Refuse that carried a high risk of contamination (that is, rubbish) was quickly buried close to the house. Large, open and rather shallow pits like open cellars were definitely less adequate than wells or smaller pits close to the houses.

Dead animals were also buried. In the village, no separate place appears to have been reserved for this special purpose. Instead, dead animals were buried quite close to houses. It is likely that these were their owner's houses and that the cadaver pits mark the activity area of the animals and/or their owners. This technique shows some confidence in the encapsulating power of the soil. 'In the ground' seemed to be the best place for worrying materials such as animal corpses and bones, and, presumably other smelly and rotting remains. A ditch might have been a good place for swill. This can be interpreted as a semi-private sphere in Diepensee, which was the best place to bury ominous material. Using the vocabulary of the *chaîne éliminatoire*, introduced above, animal bones (and food remains) can be termed as *contaminating* material and can therefore be named rubbish in the sense described above. Effort was taken, and rules of how-to-dispose were followed, to prevent further *confrontation*. Broken ceramics, on the contrary, seemed not to be *contaminating*. The average sherd size across Diepensee is very small, and very few sherds from the same complex fit together, so there must have been a large amount of movement of the sherds and a repeated *confrontation* with broken ceramics. This result correlates with the basic idea of smells being dangerous, which is known from the written record. The basic concept of the human body documented in medieval written sources was humoral theory (e.g. Gilchrist 2012: 32). Smell was central to medieval hygiene. Bad smells promoted miasmas (e.g. Isenmann 2012: 70, 82), toxic emanations of the earth and standing water. Miasmas penetrated the body and disturbed the equilibrium of the humours and the blood in the human body. This, along with foul food, could cause diseases. Infections were possible, too, transmitted by breath and evaporation, but also by eye contact (Isenmann 2012).

Recently, Richard Jones (2011) introduced humoral theory as a central concept shaping medieval disposal practice, especially in English manors. Whether different substances in medieval Diepensee were disposed of differently in order to manipulate the ground according to humoral theory cannot be discussed here and now, but offers a fascinating hypothesis to be tested in the future.

It is not entirely clear if the management of waste was privately organized or if there were also public rules governing how waste might be treated. The animal corpses were all buried close to houses on different private tenements. This shows that dangerous substances were managed privately by individual households. However, the enormously high amount of sherds in TF XI gives the impression of the transport of solid substances to the southeast area of the village. It is likely that this happened after a big fire around 1300, when the southeast area was deserted and the village shrank. The ceramic dating seems to indicate something similar.

Privacy and Body: A Selection of Medieval Written Sources Concerning Rubbish and Hygiene

Written sources often provide quite extreme descriptions about the levels of hygiene in medieval cities (Dirlmeier 1981: 113–14). For example, Hösel (1990: 45–62) describes a disgusting amount of dirt in medieval cities that must have led to hygiene problems. The rural population is described as not even having reservations against their own excrement (Hösel 1990: 40). Isenmann (2012: 66–68) applies this description to the medieval city, but does argue for mental rejections of dirt and describes a certain helplessness on the part of the city councils. This is illustrated by the example from Göttingen, where the city council decided to simply flood the city twice a month (Isenmann 2012: 67) in order to manage the impossible situation. The repeated declarations of laws, threats, appeals, etc. from the Göttingen city council, but also authorities from other medieval towns (e.g. Konstanz – see Hausmair and Signori 2016), towards the medieval population, which largely shape this image, are a clear indicator of conflicts in medieval cities over issues of pureness and rubbish. Höfler and Illi (1992) concentrate on the practices relating to refuse and rubbish. Their argument that the range of medieval professions show extensive repair and reuse is of interest (Höfler and Illi 1992: 363). They also highlight that rather than being indifferent to dirt, according to medieval hygienic conceptions, it was correct to dispose of fluid substances in rivers (see also Dirlmeier 1981: 124). Here Kühnel's (1986: 66) list of features of living quality is also intriguing. Apart from simply fighting pollution, citizens tried to improve the atmosphere and quality of their city with trees, herbs, singing birds and public parks.

Schubert (2002: 96–98) also follows the descriptions shaped by declarations, laws and complaints, but on the other hand assumes that the general quality of water and air must have been better than today (2002: 35, 95). This selection is not exhaustive, but illustrates the range of opinions about the actual situation in medieval cities.

Most likely it is a complex situation, in which concepts of miasmas were present, but so too were conflicts about the resulting practice and serious danger to human health. The conflicts are well documented in medieval written sources. To get a glimpse of the everyday management practice of refuse, archaeological findings are required. Certainly, the city latrines were a permanent risk, for water and botanical analyses from

Bodensee indicate a high level of eutrophication (Küster 1992: 351). On the other hand, we have several archaeologically recorded attempts to control latrines, more and more indicators of extensive private cleaning, and several hints for recycling of refuse, for example, as filling material (for more on this, see Oexle 1992; Kluge-Pinsker 2003: 89–90; Scholkmann 2009: 41; Fay 2011: 175; see also Sczech 2000: 74–79 for a case study).

Comparison and Interpretation: Habitus and Hygiene

Did urban and rural populations share similar ideas about dirt, did they react in similar ways to similar substances and is a form of habitus relating to the treatment of waste visible in the archaeological record? These questions shall now be summed up and discussed within the framework of the *chaîne éliminatoire*.

Compared with the picture drawn by the historical sources, the situation in Diepensee seems surprisingly well-organized. The Diepensee population had a concept of more and less *contaminating* refuse and could, for example, more easily accept a repeated *confrontation* with ceramic sherds while making efforts to avoid *confrontation* with animal remains, be it as cadavers or part of food refuse. Since animal bones are likely to share the dangerous processes of rotting, fouling and stinking, this basically mirrors the hygienic concepts written down by scholars in urban or monastic contexts. The basic danger of rotten animal meat was the smell produced by this. Burying your rubbish was a sufficient prevention against the dangerous influences ascribed to bad smells. The solution of burying dead animal corpses was also practised in the city. Dumping solid refuse in a ditch or river was relatively uncommon in the village and was viewed more harshly in the city.

The image of permanent conflicts in the cities concerning disposal becomes clearer if it is not interpreted in the sense of total indifference of the city population towards dirt and rubbish. More likely is the attempt of the citizens to maintain techniques of disposal that work in the context of a village, but do not work at all in the context of a highly densely populated medieval city. Attempts to dispose of rubbish in a medium private sphere led in a city context to an immediate confrontation with one's neighbour. The medium private sphere did not exist in the city and everything done out of one's immediate personal space affected others. A relevant new feature was the latrine, which also offered a way to dispose in the ground, which was felt to be a correct place for rubbish (Scholkmann (2011: 392) describes a similar picture). The position of latrines close to wells might also indicate a belief in the encapsulating power of soil. The village habitus of disposal was maintained, but did not completely work in the city context, and the council reacted to this with repeated declarations and penalties. These education programmes also show the attempts to establish a new habitus of disposal, which fit the city conditions better. Dirt was changing from a private to a public issue. Norbert Elias (1997) debated the growing awareness (mainly of the elites) of maintaining the borders of one's own body from the late Middle Ages onwards. But while the knights and knaves learned to control their emanations, the city population had to learn to organize disposal as a public task. Sonja Windmüller (2004: 110–12) identified a large education programme for industrialized cities in the early twentieth century to teach the millions of new proletarians how to dispose properly. With an immense urbanization process around 1200, just as occurred around 1900, the historical situation might be comparable in terms of disposal problems. Apart from other aspects, the underlying concepts of hygiene were different. While in the Middle Ages, the antique theories of miasmas and humours were used to explain diseases; by 1900, the ideas of bacteriology were the dominant concept behind the understanding of pollution. Humoral theory (as well as bacteriology) fulfils the role of a naturalized explanation for the chosen practice of hygiene (see above, Douglas 1986: 48). The categories at work (e.g. smell) are part of a complex cosmology. The latter dominates concepts of body and hygiene and influences practices to deal with unwanted parts of the physical world. When the conflicts relating to disposal in the city context are compared with the solutions for rubbish found in the medieval village Diepensee, the change of habitual practice concerning disposing techniques comes into sight. This mirrors the way change takes place according to Bourdieu: as a reaction of a changed structure, which tries to apply old managements to new situations or integrates new situations by developing new solutions (Reichhardt 1997: 87).

Acknowledgements

Franka Höppner wrote her M.A. dissertation on the animal bones of Diepensee. This chapter is largely based on her work, on the work of Susanne Hanik, Blandine Wittkopp and on the finds-inventory from the Brandenburg Authorities for Heritage Management and Archaeological State Museum. I am glad for the opportunity to thank my colleagues for their cooperation and help. I also owe a lot to Lucas Quensel von Kalben, who gave me great assistance in reflecting on my data. All mistakes are of course the results of my work.

Greta Civis is an independent researcher based in Berlin, Germany, who focuses on medieval disposal practices and rubbish management in rural contexts. Before being awarded her Ph.D. in Prehistoric and Historical Archaeology from the University of Vienna, Austria in 2015, she worked for the Brandenburg Authorities for Heritage Management, received a research grant from the Heinrich-Böll-Foundation for her Ph.D. studies concerning ceramics and disposal in the medieval village Diepensee and was associated with the 'Untersuchungen zu Lebensbedingungen, Siedlungsdynamik und menschlicher Ernährungsweise im mittelalterlichen ländlichen Siedlungen in Brandenburg' project supported by the German Research Foundation and the Brandenburg Authorities for Heritage Management.

Notes

1. This chapter was written in 2013, while work was in progress, and many of the presented numbers were provisional. The final analysis (Civis 2015) did not significantly change. This chapter, in the first instance, aims to test theoretical and methodological concepts applicable to the issue 'rubbish' from a regulatory perspective.
2. At the time of writing (August 2013).

References

Appadurai, A. 1986. 'Introduction: Commodities and the Politics of Value', in A. Appadurai (ed.), *The Social Life of Things*. Cambridge: Cambridge University Press, pp. 3–63.
Bar-Yosef, O., and P. van Peer. 2009. 'The Chaîne Opératoire Approach in Middle Palaeolithic Archaeology', *Current Anthropology* 50: 103–31.
Berlin, B., and P. Kay. 1969. *Basic Color Terms: Their Universality and Evolution*. Berkeley, CA: University of California Press.
Blum, S.W.E. 2002. 'Vom Hausfleiß der Trojaner', in R. Aslan (ed.), *Mauerschau*. Remshalden-Grunbach: Greiner, pp. 106–51.
Bourdieu, P. 1982. *Die feinen Unterschiede: Kritik der gesellschaftlichen Urteilskraft*, trans. B. Schwibs and A. Russer. Frankfurt am Main: Suhrkamp.
Butler, J. 1990. *Gender Trouble: Feminism and the Subversion of Identity*. New York: Routledge.
Corbin, A. 1984. *Pesthauch und Blütenduft: Eine Geschichte des Geruchs*. Berlin: Wagenbach, pp. 9–12.
Dirlmeier, U. 1981. 'Die kommunalpolitischen Zuständigkeiten und Leistungen süddeutscher Städte im Spätmittelalter', in J. Sydow (ed.), *Städtische Versorgung und Entsorgung im Wandel der Geschichte*. Sigmaringen: Thorbecke, pp. 113–50.

Doll, M. 2003. *Haustierhaltung und Schlachtsitten des Mittelalters und der Neuzeit: Eine Synthese aus archäozoologischen, bildlichen und schriftlichen Quellen Mitteleuropas*. Rahden/Westfahlen: VML.
Douglas, M. 1986. *How Institutions Think*. London: Routledge.
———. 2002. *Purity and Danger*. London: Routledge.
Elias, N. 1997. *Über den Prozeß der Zivilisation: Soziogenetische und psychogenetische Untersuchungen. Erster Band. Wandlungen des Verhaltens in den weltlichen Oberschichten des Abendlandes*. Frankfurt am Main: Suhrkamp.
Fay, I. 2011. 'Box 4.2: English Hygiene', in M. Carver and J. Klápště (eds), *The Archaeology of Medieval Europe*. Aarhus: Aarhus University Press, pp. 172–75.
Foucault, M. 1969. *Wahnsinn und Gesellschaft: Eine Geschichte des Wahns im Zeitalter der Vernunft*, trans. U. Köppen. Frankfurt am Main: Suhrkamp.
Gilchrist, R. 2012. *Medieval Life: Archaeology and the Life Course*. Woodbridge: Boydell.
Gosden, C., and Y. Marshall. 1999. 'The Cultural Biography of Objects', *World Archaeology* 31(2): 169–78.
Hanik, S., and B. Wittkopp. 2012. 'Tierhaltung und archäologischer Befund: Wirtschaftliche Verhältnisse in Diepensee, Lkr. Dahme-Spreewald', *Archäologie in Berlin und Brandenburg* 2010: 122–26.
Hausmair, B., and L. Barwitzki. 2016. 'Entsorgungs- und Abfallprobleme', in B. Hausmair and G. Signori (eds), *Spruch von den sibnen: Die ältesten Konstanzer Baugerichtsprotokolle (1452–1470)*, Konstanzer Geschichts- und Rechtsquellen XLVI. Ostfildern: Thorbecke, pp. xi–xviii.
Hausmair, B.. and G. Signori (eds). 2016. *Spruch von den sibnen: Die ältesten Konstanzer Baugerichtsprotokolle (1452–1470)*, Konstanzer Geschichts- und Rechtsquellen XLVI. Ostfildern: Thorbecke.
Hill, J.D. 1995. *Ritual and Rubbish in the Iron Age of Wessex: A Study on Formation of a Specific Archaeological Record*, BAR British Series 424. Oxford: Archaeopress.
Höfler, E., and M. Illi. 1992. 'Versorgung und Entsorgung der mittelalterlichen Stadt: Versorgung und Entsorgung im Spiegel der Schriftquellen', in Landesdenkmalamt Baden-Württemberg (ed.), *Stadtluft, Hirsebrei und Bettelmönch*. Stuttgart: Theiss, pp. 351–64.
Hofmann, M., K. Maase and B.J. Warneken. 1999. *Ökostile: Zur kulturellen Vielfalt umweltbezogenen Handelns*. Marburg: Arbeitskreis Volkskunde und Kulturwissenschaft.
Höppner, F. 2010. 'Aussagen zur Ernährung und Soziotopographie des mittelalterlichen Dorfes Diepensee anhand der Tierknochenfunde', M.A. dissertation. Berlin: Freie Universität of Berlin.
Hösel, G. 1990. *Unser Abfall aller Zeiten: Eine Kulturgeschichte der Städtereinigung*. Munich: Kommunalschriften-Verlag.
Isenmann, E. 2012. *Die deutsche Stadt im Mittelalter 1150–1550: Stadtgestalt, Recht, Verfassung, Stadtregiment, Kirche, Gesellschaft, Wirtschaft*. Vienna: Böhlau.
Jenkins, R. 2000. 'Categorization: Identity, Social Process and Epistemology', *Current Sociology* 48(3): 7–25.
Jones, R. 2011. 'Elemental Theory in Everyday Practice: Food Disposal in the Later Medieval English Countryside', in J. Klápště and P. Sommer (eds), *Processing, Storage, Distribution of Food*. Turnhout: Brepols, pp. 145–54.

Kluge-Pinsker, A. 2003. 'Zum Stellenwert von Fäkalien, Schmutz und Müll im mittelalterlichen Alltag', in S. Wolfram and M. Fansa (eds), *Müll*. Mainz: Von Zabern, pp. 87–97.

Kopytoff, I. 1986. 'The Cultural Biography of Things: Commoditization as Process', in A. Appadurai (ed.), *The Social Life of Things*. Cambridge: Cambridge University Press, pp. 64–91.

Kühnel, H. (ed.). 1986. *Alltag im Spätmittelalter*. Vienna: Styria.

Küster, H. 1992. 'Wasser und Luft: Botanische Untersuchungen zur Umweltverschmutzung in der mittelalterlichen Stadt', in Landesdenkmalamt Baden-Württemberg (ed.), *Stadtluft, Hirsebrei und Bettelmönch*. Stuttgart: Theiss, pp. 350–51.

Lakoff, G., and M. Johnson. 2003. *Metaphors We Live by*. Chicago, IL: University of Chicago Press.

Leroi-Gourhan, A. 1980. *Hand und Wort: Die Evolution von Technik, Sprache und Kunst*, trans. M. Bischoff. Frankfurt am Main: Suhrkamp.

Morris, J. 2011. *Investigating Animal Burials: Ritual, Mundane and beyond*, BAR British Series 535. Oxford: Archaeopress.

Morsel, J. 2006. 'Soziale Kategorisierung oder historische Phantasmorgie: Erkundungen zum historischen Gebrauch von mittelalterlichen sozialen Kategorien', in H.-P. Baum, R. Leng and J. Schneider (eds), *Wirtschaft – Gesellschaft – Mentalitäten im Mittelalter*. Stuttgart: Steiner, pp. 212–37.

Mytum, H. 2010. 'Ways of Writing in Post-medieval and Historical Archaeology: Introducing Biography', *Post-medieval Archaeology* 44(2): 237–54.

Oexle, J. 1992. 'Versorgung und Entsorgung der mittlelaterlichen Stadt: Versorgung und Entsorgung nach dem archäologischen Befund', in Landesdenkmalamt Baden-Württemberg (ed.), *Stadtluft, Hirsebrei und Bettelmönch*. Stuttgart: Theiss, pp. 364–74.

Rathje, W., and C. Murphy. 1994. *Müll: Eine archäologische Reise durch die Welt des Abfalls*, trans. A. Böcker. Munich: Goldmann.

Reichhardt, S. 1997. 'Bourdieu für Historiker? Ein kultursoziologisches Angebot an die Sozialgeschichte', in T. Mergel and T. Welskopp (eds), *Geschichte zwischen Kultur und Gesellschaft*. Munich: Beck, pp. 71–93.

Rosch, E. 1978. 'Principles of Categorization', in E. Rosch and B. Lloyd (eds), *Cognition and Categorization*. Hillsdale, NJ: Lawrence Erlbaum, pp. 27–48.

Schenk, T. 2009. *Die Altstadt von Freyenstein, Lkr. Ostprignitz-Ruppin: Rekonstruktion der brandenburgischen Stadtwüstung des 13. Jhs. auf der Grundlage archäologischer Grabungen und Prospektionen und Grundzüge eines denkmalpflegerischen Konzepts*. Rahden/Westfahlen: VML.

Schiffer, M.B. 1987. *Formation Processes of the Archaeological Record*. Albuquerque, NM: University of New Mexico Press.

Scholkmann, B. 2009. *Das Mittelalter im Fokus der Archäologie*, Archäologie in Deutschland Sonderheft PLUS 2009. Stuttgart: Theiss.

———. 2011. 'The Anatomy of Medieval Towns', in M. Carver and J. Klápště (eds), *The Archaeology of Medieval Europe*. Aarhus: Aarhus University Press, pp. 379–403.

Schubert, E. 2002. *Alltag im Mittelalter: Natürliches Lebensumfeld und menschliches Miteinander*. Darmstadt: Wissenschaftliche Buchgesellschaft.

Sczech, K.J. 2000. 'Archäologische Befunde zur Entsorgung im Mittelalter: Dargestellt am Beispiel der Städte Konstanz und Freiburg im Breisgau', Ph.D. dissertation. Freiburg: Albert-Ludwigs-Universität zu Freiburg.

Silberzahn-Jandt, G. 1999. 'Frauen, Müll und Geld: Zum Zusammenhang von haushälterischem Handeln und Müllkultur', in M. Hofmann, K. Maase and B.J. Warneken (eds), *Ökostile*. Marburg: Arbeitskreis Volkskunde und Kulturwissenschaft, pp. 145–69.

Sommer, U. 1991. 'Zur Entstehung archäologischer Fundvergesellschaftungen: Versuch einer archäologischen Taphonomie', in E. Mattheusser and U. Sommer, *Studien zur Siedlungsarchäologie I*, Universitätsforschungen zur prähistorischen Archäologie 6. Bonn: Habelt, pp. 51–197.

Thompson, M. 1979. *Rubbish Theory: The Creation and Destruction of Value*. Oxford: Oxford University Press.

———. 2003. *Mülltheorie: Über die Schaffung und Vernichtung von Werten*, trans. M. Fehr. Essen: Klartext-Verlag.

Thüry, G.E. 2001. *Müll und Marmorsäulen: Siedlungshygiene in der römischen Antike*. Mainz: Von Zabern.

Windmüller, S. 2004. *Die Kehrseite der Dinge: Müll, Abfall, Wegwerfen als kulturwissenschaftliches Problem*. Münster: Lit.

Wittkopp, B. 2014. 'Diepensee: Gründung, Umgestaltung und Wachstum einer ländlichen Siedlung im Mittelalter', in A. Diener, J. Müller and M. Untermann (eds), *Gründung im archäologischen Befund*. Paderborn: Mitteilungen der Deutschen Gesellschaft für Archäologie des Mittelalters und der Neuzeit, pp. 161–70.

Zimring, C.A., and W. Rathje. 2012. *Encyclopedia of Consumption and Waste: The Social Science of Garbage*. Los Angeles: Sage.

Chapter 4

How to Plant a Colony in the New World
Rules and Practices in New Sweden and the Seventeenth-Century Delaware Valley

Magdalena Naum

Introduction

The colony of New Sweden (1638–55), like other colonial settlements in America, was structured by a set of laws and regulations. The comprehensive instructions given to the subsequent governors ordered the particulars of everyday life. They dictated settlers' means of sustenance and rights to trade, detailed rules of engagement with other European colonists and Native Americans, established a system of criminal justice and regulated religious life. Most of these regulations were unquestioned and followed because they constituted a cohesive set of rules that helped to reconstruct settlers' lives in the colony and instilled a sense of continuity. Others, particularly those laws pertaining to moral and orderly conduct and trade with Native Americans, were frequently transgressed by the colonists, despite the risk of severe punishments.

Using historical and archaeological records, this chapter examines obedience and disobedience of the Swedish population of New Sweden and colonial Delaware and Pennsylvania. To better understand the logic behind these actions, the study is set in the context of transatlantic migration as well as the geopolitical realities of the colonial settlements in northeastern America during the seventeenth century.

The Planting of New Sweden

The colony of New Sweden was established in 1638 along the Delaware River in northeastern America (Figure 4.1). It was the earliest Swedish colonial venture outside of Europe, prompted in part by the successful lobbying of the Dutch merchants disappointed with the politics of the Dutch West India Company and searching for new venues for their colonial visions. The decision to establish a settlement in America was mainly grounded in the political ambitions of the Swedish Crown and the prospects of income from the beaver pelt and tobacco trade – New World commodities sought after in Europe. It was also hoped that the Delaware Valley would be rich in other natural resources and a suitable market for Swedish copper (Dahlgren and Norman 1988).

In March 1638 the first Swedish ships reached the Delaware Bay. A piece of land was bought from the Native Americans and the first settlement – Fort Christina – was established. Soon, however, as profits failed to materialize, the initial commitment of the investors vanished. Disappointed with the economic failure of the venture, the foreign shareholders withdrew from this colonial endeavour.

Colonial dreams, however, were not given up. The Company was reorganized and connected with the Swedish Court, which, although not indifferent to the economic profit, perceived the colony as a geopolitical asset, a visualization of the country's aspiration to be Europe's dominant power. The new governor, Lieutenant Johan Printz, equipped with comprehensive instructions, arrived in America in 1642. His long governorship (1642–53) was a period of considerable economic and territorial growth of the colony. However, it was inhibited by an insufficient commitment of the Crown to the project. Swedish colonial ambitions in America were ultimately crushed in 1655 as a result of a Dutch attack and takeover. The last governor of the colony, Johan Risingh, returned to Sweden with thirty-seven soldiers and colonists. The majority, about three hundred people, stayed under the Dutch, and from 1664 the English rule, forming 'the Swedish Nation' – a community united by a common language, Swedish customs and adherence to Lutheranism (Acrelius 1874; Johnson 1911; Lindmark 2005).

Initially, the recruitment of settlers willing to relocate proved to be difficult. The common push factors – religious persecutions, lack of land and capitalist drive – were of minimal impact in the scarcely populated, relatively poor, and mostly rural and Lutheran Sweden. Consequently, the Crown had to use diverse strategies to secure the colonists. One of them was imposing displacement on convicted petty criminals – adulterers and those

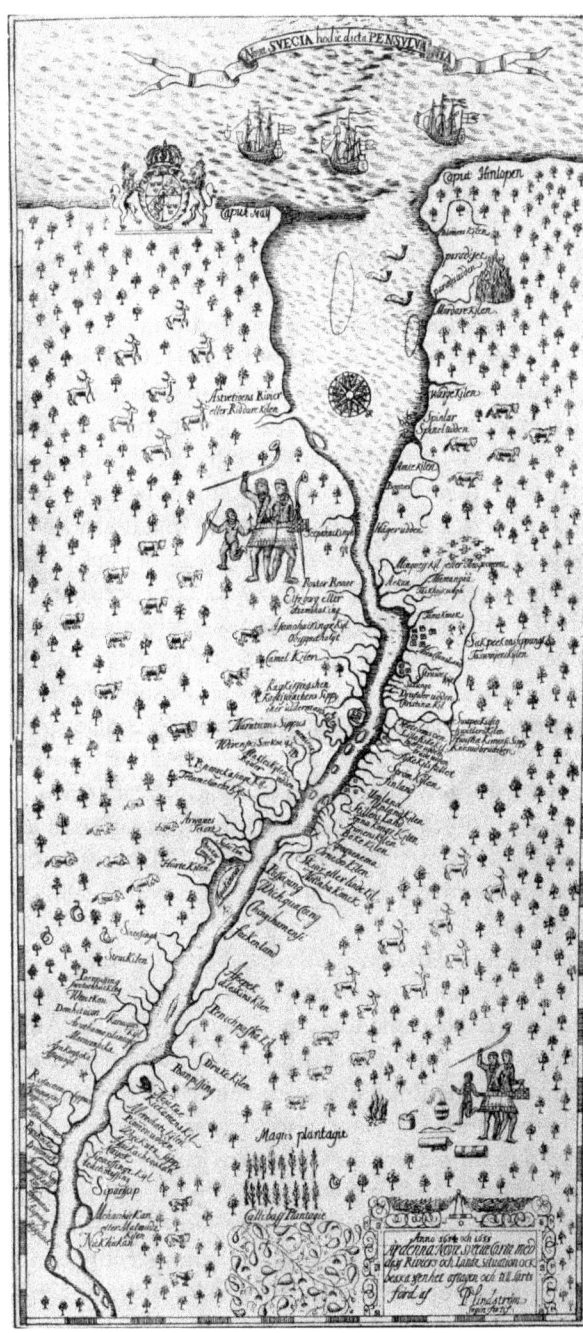

Figure 4.1 Geography of New Sweden. Map drawn by P. Lindström in 1644/55 (Holm 1702: 36)

who encroached on royal prerogatives (*Handlingar* 29: 217–20; Johnson 1911: 239; Carlsson 1995). Deserters and those who evaded army drafting were also forced to serve in New Sweden. The wars that Sweden engaged in since the middle of the sixteenth century took a heavy toll on the population. The continuous conscriptions were commonly dreaded and many took measures to escape drafting. Aware of a popular bad reputation of America, the Swedish government deemed the deportations to the colony as an appropriate form of punishment for stubborn and noncompliant soldiers (*Handlingar* 29: 210–12; Johnson 1911: 268). The exact number of these forced migrants is hard to estimate; they might have constituted about 30 per cent of the colonists who arrived before 1654 (Carlsson 1995: 181).

Between 1640 and 1655, the everyday life in the small colony was regulated by instructions written by the Swedish Royal Council (*Instructions*). They were concerned with the three major aspects of colonial life. They confirmed the status of the colony as an integral part of the Swedish kingdom and expected that the legal and cultural norms that underlined the conduct of everyday life in Sweden would serve as the guidelines in the colony. The Royal Council instructed Governor Printz that 'all occurring controversial matters he shall administer according to Swedish law and justice, custom and usage; likewise in all other matters, so far as [it] is possible, [he shall] adapt and fit the laudable customs, habits and usages of this most praiseworthy kingdom' (*Instructions*: §23). The *Instructions* also specified a range of economic activities to be undertaken by the settlers for their own well-being and for the profit of the Company. Traditional agriculture and husbandry were to support the settlers, while the cultivation of tobacco, sheep keeping for wool, whaling and extraction of natural resources were to be developed for the advantage of the shareholders and the kingdom. The pelt trade, to which the Company had the exclusive rights, was another important source of revenue. Finally, the *Instructions* provided basic guidelines for interactions with the Native Americans and other European colonists. The Swedish Court recommended treating the Native Americans with humanity and respect. The attitude of non-confrontation was to underline the relationship with the English and the Dutch in the neighbouring colonies of New Netherland, Maryland and Virginia.

A short Dutch tenure along the Delaware River (1655–64) did not cause many changes for the Swedish settlers who decided to remain in America, although they had to swear loyalty to the Dutch and adopt the laws of New Netherland. The articles of surrender granted the Swedish community a right to retain a minister of the Swedish Lutheran confession; however, this right was later revoked for the southern portion of Delaware, which became a property administered by the city of Amsterdam. In 1659 the commissioners of the colony stated that: 'The bold undertaking of the

Swedish Parson to preach in the Colonie there without permission does not greatly please us. And as we will assuredly, that, as yet, no other religion but the Reformed can nor may be tolerated there, so you must, by proper means, put an end to or prevent such presumption on the part of other secretaries' (*Pennsylvania Archives* 2.5: 329). The same year, peremptory orders were issued for all Swedes to move from their scattered farms into villages and towns (Ferris 1846: 108–9).

Under the rule of Duke of York (1664–81) and the governorship of William Penn (1681–1718), the inhabitants of Delaware and Pennsylvania enjoyed liberal government and religious tolerance. In the course of the late seventeenth century and in the eighteenth century, Swedish congregations were serviced by pastors regularly sent from Sweden, which undoubtedly helped to preserve a sense of ethnic identity and cultural values.

During the periods of Dutch and English rule, some aspects of the interactions with Native Americans became more regulated. A history of intergroup violence, anti-Dutch sentiments and threats of war led the Dutch to strictly prosecute of any instances violating a ban on powder and weapon sale to the natives. These laws were also acknowledged by New Sweden's governors and other early colonies in northeastern America, but they were notoriously disregarded. The Dutch and later the English administrators were also concerned with the frontier violence and public disorder caused by the drunkenness, and consequently outlawed the sale of strong liquors to the Native Americans.

'I Will Live and Direct Myself Submissively in All Obedience': Rule Following

When members of the Swedish Royal Council designed New Sweden, they envisioned a place that would be a mirror image of Sweden, with its hierarchical social order, adherence to the customs and laws of the country, and devotion to the Royal Court and Lutheran Church. This confessional, linguistic and cultural unity was to ensure a constant link with the homeland and to reinforce the identity and allegiance of the colonists as subjects of the Swedish Crown:

> The Swedish language should be kept, spoken and written, purely without any mixture of other languages. All rivers and streams as well as herbs and woods [should] be called with old Swedish names; abolish all expressions from the Dutch, which now seem to be somewhat ingrained. In fine, both in manners and customs, as far as possibly can be managed, everything should be conformed to old Swedish. (*Brahe to Printz, 9 November 1643*)

Governors Johan Printz and Johan Risingh tirelessly directed a wholesome process of turning a newly acquired foreign landscape into a recognizable and orderly space that would resemble the old country by setting boundaries marked with national emblems, clearing the land and inscribing the landscape with familiar-sounding names. Hopokehocking became Christina, Chamassung was known as Finland, Meckoponacka was christened Upland and Tenakong (Tinicum) Island hosted Fort New Gothenburg (Acrelius 1874: 67–69). Other settlers chose to reside in places named Mölndal, Vasa or Kårsholm (Figure 4.1). The colonial landscape was further transformed by newly erected churches, water mills, forts, docks, farms, orchards and pastures (*Report* 1647).

Of all these undertakings, resuming religious services and furnishing churches were deemed as particularly important:

> The Governor shall endeavor and see to it that ... divine service be zealously performed according to the true Augsburg Confession, the Council of Uppsala, and the ceremonies of the Swedish Church; and [he shall see to it that] all persons, especially the young, be well instructed in the articles of their Christian faith ... all good church discipline be [duly] held and exercised. (*Instructions*: §26)

This urgency is understood considering the close connections between the State and the Church and its role in conforming parishioners into dutiful and obedient subjects. In a 1644 letter to Per Brahe, Printz proudly reported that 'divine service with its ceremony' was held just as in Sweden, 'in the good old Swedish language'. (*Printz to Brahe, 19 July 1644*; see Figure 4.2)

Equally crucial to the process of domestication were more mundane endeavours of clearing the land and establishing farms undertaken by the settlers themselves. Turning foreign and unpredictable surroundings into recognizable and comfortable spaces was achieved through material means of house building, home making and traditional means of sustenance. When choosing suitable places for plantation, freeholders tried to find places that would offer possibilities comparable to those in the old homelands and were drawn to the areas offering a versatile economy, enabling agriculture, husbandry, fishing and hunting. The architecture and layout of the farms resembled the rural settings of central Sweden, where many of the colonists came from. Still-standing houses, historical documents and archaeological surveys document degrees of conservatism in architecture and spatial arrangement of the farm buildings (Ekengren, Naum and Zagal-Mach Wolfe 2013; Naum 2016; see also Figure 4.3).

One of the better-studied properties that can provide insights into the daily life of the settlers belonged to the family of Mårton Mårtonsson (Frens and Frens 1989). The family arrived to the colony in 1654 and in the 1670s acquired a large tract of land in a mostly Swedish neighbourhood

Figure 4.2 Gloria Dei (Old Swedes') Church in Philadelphia, serving a Swedish-speaking Lutheran congregation throughout the late seventeenth and eighteenth centuries (photograph by Magdalena Naum)

Figure 4.3 Lower Swedish Cabin in Drexel Hill, Pennsylvania (photograph by Magdalena Naum)

south of Philadelphia. The property provided fishing and fresh water supplies and quick access to the Delaware River. Marshy areas at the creek's banks were used as winter fodder for the animals, while most of the land was planted with crops (including rye, which was also commonly grown in Sweden) and kept as meadows for grazing sheep, cattle and horses. The excavations and architectural survey conducted at the property indicated that the oldest part of the still-standing dwelling, constructed in c. 1698 (the date carved on the back of the fireplace lintel), was a simple log cabin built with white cedar logs. The cabin was a one-room house (4 x 6 m) with a large corner stove and a sleeping loft (Frens and Frens 1989). Its size and construction details find parallels in the contemporary Swedish vernacular architecture (Erixon 1982). The cabin must be one of the buildings mentioned in the inventory of Morton Mårtonsson Jr. made in 1718, which also described the outhouses and an additional dwelling house (not found during the excavations). The excavated material culture dated to the late seventeenth and early eighteenth centuries and essentially did not differ from other contemporary Pennsylvanian farms. The Mårtonssons, like other families, shopped at the local stores and paddlers, and purchased English tobacco pipes, Staffordshire ceramics and English and German stoneware, along with locally made earthenware. However, their inventories mention objects such as old trunks, chests and spinning wheels, perhaps brought from Sweden, as well as a Swedish Bible and psalm book betraying their ethnic and religious identity.

Foreign and Swedish visitors to the colony noticed the cultural particularities of the area and connected them closely with ethnic identities. Jasper Dankers and Peter Sluyter, two Dutchmen who visited the Delaware region in 1679/80, commented on the rigid traditionalism and simplicity of the Swedish houses. Cabins were made of logs split or shaped from whole tree trunks and attached by incisions at the corners without the use of nails. They were warmed by a fireplace in the corner and although simple in their appearance, they were tight and warm (Dankers and Sluyter 1867: 175). The unmistakable Swedishness of the settlers was also noted by the Lutheran pastors, such as Andreas Rudman, who served the congregations along the Delaware: 'All the houses are timbered in the Swedish manner. The women cook food according to the Swedish custom and brew fine and pleasant tasting drinks ... [they speak] their mother tongue as clear as it was ever spoken in Sweden' (*Rudman to Arhhenius, 29 October 1697*). Late seventeenth- and early eighteenth-century wills and inventories complement this picture of continuous reliance on a set of cultural norms. Houses and their outbuildings (including granaries, storage buildings and saunas) were ordered according to the familiar cultural schemes and partially furnished with chests and other objects brought from Sweden (Naum 2016).

Although many of the regulations issued for New Sweden's governors had a clear political goal and were designed to produce loyal citizens properly belonging to a situated community of Swedish subjects, the insistence on keeping customs had another meaning for the settlers. It helped to re-create a sense of communal belonging, security and familiarity. Displacement subjected the colonists to the loss of confidence and ease with which they would conduct their daily lives and forced them to sever intimate ties with well-known landscapes. Fostering cultural norms and traditions helped to counter these feelings of alienation and fuelled 'homing desires', hopes that what was declared as a home would eventually feel like home (cf. Brah 1996: 193, 197). Following the rules established for the colonial government was perceived less as a means of shaping a compliant and devout subject, and more as a way to ensure continuity of self, despite dramatic disconnection with one's home landscapes.

'Such a Sort of People [that] Must Be Kept under Else They will Rebell': The Disobedience of the Swedish Settlers

New Sweden and later the 'Swedish Nation' were not immune from mutiny, acts of political disobedience and transgressing the norms of moral behaviour. In 1653 about one-third of the colony's male population signed a petition complaining about the abuse of power by Governor Printz. The settlers complained about being forced to work on Printz's and the Company's projects without pay, being in a constant fear for their lives, the brutal treatment of the poor settlers, and the Governor's lack of compassion and promotion of his self-interest (*Settlers' Petition* 1653; *Settlers' Supplemental Complaint* 1654). The Governor treated the complaint as a mutiny and a serious breach of law. The supposed ringleader and two other settlers who signed the letter were executed.

During the Dutch period (1655–64), the Swedish and Finnish settlers were the largest European group living in the colony. The Dutch colonial government treated them with a certain amount of suspicion, fearing possible uprisings and mutinies (*Pennsylvania Archives* 2.5: 304). Although generally liberal in his approach to the Swedish settlers, Peter Stuyvesant, Director-General of the colony, ordered them twice to move from their widely scattered farmsteads to towns and villages (*NYHM XVIII–XIX*: 201). This was to ensure tighter fiscal and social control over the population and provide better protection against any future Native American attacks. However, these orders were ignored and went unpunished (Ferris 1846: 109). The prohibition to preach and practise Lutheranism in the territory overseen by the city of Amsterdam, was met with similar disregard.

More serious cases of disobedience towards the colonial government erupted after the territories along the Delaware River were incorporated into the English possessions. In 1669 forty-two Swedes and Finns (about one-quarter of the adult male Swedish-speaking population) were charged and heavily fined for participation in a conspiracy to overthrow the government. The whole affair became known as 'the Long Finn Rebellion' (*NYHM XX–XXI*: 6–10; Haefeli 2006). By appealing to the Swedish population's sentiments, the instigator, John Binckson, fuelled the rebellion against the English rule. Perceiving this action as a serious threat, the English Governor tried it as an act of treason. Binckson was publicly whipped, branded and sold to slavery in Barbados, while his confederates were fined according to their suspected involvement (Haefeli 2006: 162–65).

Six years later, Swedish and Finnish settlers were involved in another insurgence, this time over their work contribution in the construction and maintenance of the dykes in New Castle (*NYHM XX–XXI*: 92–93), making William Tom, Sheriff of New Castle, utter frustrating remarks that 'the Sweeds and Fynnes being such a sort of people … must be Kept under else they will rebell and of that nation these here are the worse sort' (*NYHM XX–XXI*: 93).

Swedish settlers were from time to time accused of transgression of religious conformity and immoral or violent behaviour. Violence and

Table 4.1 Criminal cases reviewed by the Court of Upland between 1676 and 1681. Approximately 60–66 per cent of the residents under the Court's jurisdiction were Swedes; Englishmen were the second-largest group

Accused	Slander, assault and battery	Theft or unlawful appropriation of property	Adultery	Mistreatment or killing of somebody else's livestock
Swedes	14	1	1	2
Englishmen	2	5	1	2
Dutchmen	2	–	–	–

misbehaviour were problems in all the colonies and the Swedes were no more or less prone to breaking the laws (Bailyn 2012). The cases reviewed by the Court of Upland between 1676 and 1681 illustrate this point (*Record of the Court of Upland* 1860). Of eighteen tried cases of slander, assault and battery, Swedes were involved in fourteen of them. In half of these incidents the accused was one Måns Petersson Stacke, a known drunkard who frequently stirred feuds with his neighbours. The accusations of theft and unlawful appropriation of property were more common among the English, while cases of adultery and mistreatment of livestock involved members of both groups (Table 4.1). The type of tried cases in the colony finds correlation with the most common crimes investigated by the contemporary Swedish courts, where physical violence and libel were the most common misdemeanours (Österberg 1996).

Extramarital relationships, drunkenness and abuse were the most common complaints, but courts also handled graver accusations of witchcraft. In the seventeenth century, Europe and colonial America were swept by the witch craze. Delaware and Pennsylvania stayed at the margins of the religious persecution. There are only four known indicted cases of witchcraft and all of them involved Finnish and Swedish individuals. In around 1653, Karin the Finn and her husband Lasse the Finn were convicted of witchcraft by Governor Printz. The details of the accusation and trial are unclear, but both received harsh punishments in accordance with Swedish law (see Ankarloo 1990; Heikkinen and Kervinen 1990). Lasse was outlawed and Karin was tortured, starved and kept chained for over a year. Upon her release, she allegedly went mad and disappeared into the woods (*Settlers' Supplemental Complaint* 1654). The fate of Margaret Mattson and Yeshro (Gertrud) Hendrickson was less tragic (*Minutes of the Provincial Council of Pennsylvania* 1: 93–96). Margaret was accused by several witnesses of conjuring and bewitching the neighbours' cows, allegations she scorned as untrue and based on hearsay. The court found her guilty of 'having the Comon fame of a witch, but not guilty in manner and fame as Shee stands Indicted' (*Minutes of the Provincial Council of Pennsylvania* 1: 96). Margaret and Gertrud were released after their families posted a bail as a warranty for their good behaviour. The women were saved by the fact that in 1684, when the trial took place, there was no law against witchcraft in Pennsylvania, and that William Penn had abolished the death penalty in his colony for all but 'willfull murder'. Laws against witchcraft were not imposed until 1718, when they were forced upon the colony by England's Privy Council.

Beliefs in supernatural forces as well as the possibility to protect oneself against evil forces were deeply rooted in early modern European culture. In Sweden and Finland the practice of sorcery and healing, beliefs in harmful and protective magic were neither erased by the Reformation nor by the violent witchcraft trials in 1668–76 (Ankarloo 1990). The Lutheran Catechism from 1689 still contained the strictures against the worship of the sun, the moon and mythical creatures. These beliefs and ideas migrated across the Atlantic (Godbeer 2013). Archaeological evidence from colonial Pennsylvania and Delaware suggests that many European settlers took measures to protect their households against malevolent acts and misfortune (Becker 1978; Donmoyer 2014; Manning 2014). A copper coin of Charles II dated to 1672 recently found in the foundations of the Mouns Jones' house in Douglassville, Pennsylvania (Gene Delaplane, personal information) and the so-called witch bottle found in the base of a chimney of an eighteenth-century house in Essington, Pennsylvania might be examples of the use of sympathetic magic (Becker 1978).

'Some Bad, Straggling People Brought Too Much Rum amongst Them & Debauched Their Young men': Illegal Trade with Native Americans

The colonial governments that subsequently staked their claims to the areas along the Delaware imposed diverse regulations on trade and interactions between European settlers and Native American groups. The most radical, and the most contested, were the laws regarding the sale of weapons and strong alcohol.

Among the early colonial governments, there seemed to exist an agreement prohibiting the officers and settlers from exchanging guns and powder with indigenous groups. Its existence is hinted by the correspondence between the Governor of New Netherland Peter Stuyvesant and Governor Printz and mentioned by officer and engineer Per Lindeström, who visited New Sweden in 1655 (Lindeström 1925: 227; *NYHM XVIII–XIX*: 26–28).

Preserved documents from New Sweden do not include regulations concerning gun trade; however, the governors and company officials in New Netherland repeatedly issued laws forbidding the sale of muskets, powder and lead, under severe penalties, including the death sentence (*Pennsylvania Archives* 2.5: 88, 95, 101–2). These laws were also adopted along the Delaware River after the Dutch takeover in 1655 (*NYHM XVIII–XIX*: 89).

Obeying the laws in the American context posed a difficult conundrum for the colonial administrators and led to double standards when dealing with the transgression of gun regulations. The ban on the weapons trade was introduced to avoid or minimize the risk of bloodshed at the hands of the indigenous groups. Colonial administrators were well aware of the potentially lethal consequences of arming the Native Americans and instructing them in the use of the guns. Yet in the geopolitically complex landscape of colonial America, guns became key objects exchanged for alliances, peace and land. European weapons quickly became an object of desire and an indispensable tool for the Native Americans. Recognizing this want of guns, colonial governors used weapons to bribe native groups to take their side in disputes concerning land claims and other conflicts. Aware of the European want of land and competition between different colonies, Native Americans requested guns in exchange for their collaboration, e.g. in the 1640s, when Governors Printz and Stuyvesant contested each other's right to trade and settle along the Delaware. Both sent gifts including muskets and ammunition to diverse clans of Susquehannocks to gain support (*NYHM XVIII–XIX*: 28, 34; *Settlers' Supplemental Complaint* 1654: 24). Guns were used as standard gifts in confirming peace and friendship. These ceremonies were particularly important to the thinly populated and resource-poor New Sweden, whose fragile existence hinged on good relationships with the natives.

Although the Governors saw their own illegal actions as an unavoidable step in preventing the greater evil, they dealt harshly with individual settlers, soldiers and merchants accused of dealing in contraband. Per Cock, who supposedly lost his gun to an Indian but succeeded in retrieving it, was sentenced by Printz to three months of unpaid labour for the Company (*Settlers' Supplemental Complaint* 1654: 23–24). Govert Lookermans, a Dutch merchant who smuggled guns and ammunition and conducted shady dealings along the Delaware, was sentenced to three years of banishment from New Netherland (*NYHM XVIII–XIX*: 26–28).

The flow of European weapons to the native groups could also be inferred from archaeological material. Gunflints made of European flint and local lithic material dated to the mid seventeenth century were found in the Native American settlements and burial sites in Delaware (archaeological site 7NC-E-60) and southeastern Pennsylvania on Roberts, Strickler and Frey Haverstick sites (Kent 1983; 2001; Custer et al. 1998; Beisaw 2008). All of these sites were located within the trading zone of New Sweden. While Roberts Site and Frey Haverstick, both Susquehannock settlements used in the 1630s and 1640s, contained a limited number of gunflints and metal parts of guns, at the large village at Strickler Site, dated between 1645 and 1665, over one hundred gunflints and several metal gun parts were uncovered (Kent 1983: 30; Kent 2001: 292, 348–67, table 19).

Liquor was another contested commodity. Despite colonial regulations, brandy and rum were routinely traded with the Native Americans and consumed during negotiations, the signing of treaties and land sale. This novelty consumed in excess had addictive and devastating effects on the indigenous communities. It led to violence within indigenous groups and against the colonists, community disruptions, poverty and, on occasion, death (Mancall 1997). The first known prohibitions from the Delaware region were issued in 1655 by the Dutch administrators. They instituted corporeal and monetary punishment for breaching the ban (*NYHM XVIII–XIX*: 50) and were later confirmed several times by the English governors (*NYHM XX–XXI*; *Pennsylvania Archives* I: 154). Under the rule of the Duke of York (1664–81), distilling strong alcohol, being the cause of 'debauchery and idleness of the inhabitants', was also prohibited. In many cases these regulations were introduced upon the requests of the villagers living in the frontier exposed to the violent effects of excessive drunkenness and Native American communities growing aware of the damaging effect of addiction.

Despite the obvious harms, colonial settlers kept selling brandy, rum and beer to the Native groups. On several occasions, the Swedish community was singled out as breakers of the liquor laws. Individual Swedes were accused of illegal trade (*NYHM XVIII–XIX*: 60; *Pennsylvania Archives* I: 435) and they were pinpointed as the root of the problem by the Native community (*NYHM XVIII–XIX*: 266–67). Late seventeenth- and early eighteenth-century inventories from Pennsylvania and New Castle counties indicate that the distilling of alcohol and brewing was a common household activity among the Swedish-speaking settlers. Stills and brewing equipment are listed in more than half of inventories. Although most of this liquor was produced for house consumption, Swedes, many of whom acted as Indian traders and interpreters, treated alcohol as a commodity and a necessary element in rituals of hospitality.

The Anatomy of Colonial Obedience and Disobedience

The lives of the Swedish population along the Delaware River under shifting governments were regulated by sets of changing rules. In reviewing the cases of following and breaking the laws, it is possible to discern certain patterns, especially in the settlers' attitudes towards the rules that touched the core of their community and daily lives. Those regulations that allowed for the continuity of traditions and those that introduced obligations that did not depart too far from the expected duties were generally followed. Those that threatened the fabric of newly reconstituted life, such as Dutch orders to abandon Lutheranism, were commonly disobeyed. This consistency is in many ways not surprising. Reproducing familiar norms guided by the habitual knowledge was a necessary step to counter the unsettling break caused by transatlantic relocation. For the colonists, whose lives were disrupted by migration, engagement in well-known material practices and the ability to reconstruct patterns of everyday routines contributed to the act of emplacement (Malkki 1992; Brah 1996), while at the same time this place-making meant keeping at bay an endemic sense of anxiety and instability caused by displacement (Casey 2001; Turton 2005).

Many of the settlers and residents were unwilling immigrants, forced to move to the colony as a consequence of their petty crimes and army desertion (*Handlingar* 29: 210–12, 217–20; Johnson 1911: 239, 268; Naum 2013). They regarded transatlantic displacement as a frightening and irreversible step in their lives. Even for voluntary settlers, the initial impression of America upon arrival stood in strong contrast to the places they left behind. They moved from intimate places of rich textures constructed through memories, daily routines, interactions with family, neighbours and friends to a site that was foreign and devoid of the characteristics of home. A sense of place and community had to be created anew and bodily memory, cultural dispositions, values and norms were the necessary guiding forces in this project of domestication (Malkki 1992; Casey 2001; Turton 2005: 277). The same dispositions underlined New Sweden's laws, and although their primary goal was to create obedient and controllable subjects, they were followed by the settlers because these rules were coherent and well-known to them and instilled a sense of familiarity and constancy.

The disregard for Dutch orders prohibiting Swedish pastoral activities and forcing the 'Swedish Nation' to resettle was undoubtedly motivated by the need to preserve traditions, re-establish homes and a sense of community – i.e. the same factors that motivated following the laws during the New Sweden period. Dutch orders came at a time when many of the Swedish settlers successfully pieced together their daily existence shattered by relocation, established their own farms and created a cohesive community with its network of social relations marked by mutuality and emotional bonds. Interaction caused by daily, weekly, seasonal and annual congregational and social events and responsibilities brought the community together and 'territorialized' it (Leach 2005). The new legislation was thus objected to and disobeyed because it was perceived as potentially threatening to the Swedish community as a whole.

On occasion, the grip of the homeland associated with the past prior to migration, identification with it through spoken language and Lutheran practice turned into deeper sentiments that prompted political mobilization, as in the case of 'the Long Finn Rebellion'. The mutiny, ignited by false rumours of Swedish plans to retake the colony, is a good illustration of the 'engagement of even the most obscure colonists with a transatlantic world of connections both real and imagined' (Haefeli 2006: 139). Clearly illegal and punished, this common action of the 'Swedish Nation' was grounded in an overt identification with a European homeland and perhaps it was spurred on by a nostalgic longing. As the society and culture of seventeenth-century American colonies were continuously shaped by their European roots, the actions of those accused of conspiracy can be seen as an expression of how deep the Old World lingered in the hearts and minds of those in America (Haefeli 2006: 139; Fur, Naum and Nordin 2016: 4–6).

Breaching the laws that regulated trade between the European colonists and the Native Americans had different roots. The illicit trade of guns, ammunition and strong alcohol was partly motivated by the particularities of the American market and early colonial geopolitics. In the seventeenth century the success of the trading enterprises and the growth of the colonies depended on collaboration with the Native Americans. Land purchases often required specific baskets of goods. Alcohol and guns were staples in these transactions (*Pennsylvania Archives* 1.1: 32, 34, 47, 95). Upon Native American requests, they were also to be included as gifts exchanged during friendship ceremonies and treaties. Consequently, the individuals accused of breaching the laws sometimes argued that Native Americans would not trade or deal with them, or worse they would harass them and threaten their lives, if alcohol and guns were not offered. However, breaking the law to accommodate the new conventions was only part of the story. Illicit trade involving guns and alcohol was motivated by the promise of profit. Guns quickly became highly prized items and the ban on their sale in the 1630s–1660s elevated their exchange value and promised sizeable profits. Trading involving liquor was equally profitable. Unlike other goods offered by the colonial merchants, alcohol was quickly consumed and there always seemed to be a market for it. In shady and dishonest dealings, traders would offer excessive amounts of alcohol to the Native Americans and would encourage them to drink in order to cheat them on the prices of the offered commodities (Mancall 1997). Illicit trade was thus closely connected to personal gains and economic opportunities.

In their pattern of obeying and disobeying the laws, the Swedish population did not show striking differences from other European colonists (e.g. Bailyn 2012). In all seventeenth-century settlements the customary laws and regulations were usually followed as they constituted an important link with the past and offered common-sense guidelines for establishing communities in America (e.g. Goodfriend 1999). Ethnic and religious minority groups occasionally brushed with the law due to their ignorance of specific regulations or conscious protest against unjust treatment. Strict religious policies favouring state churches or particular denominations were in place in other colonies, and un-Christian, immoral behaviour and heresy were severely punished (Godbeer 2013). The temptation of profit enticed settlers in New Netherland, Maryland and New England to engage in forbidden trade involving guns, powder and alcohol. Breaching these laws and suspicious behaviour were often attributed to the colonists venturing to the outskirts of colonial possessions. Even there, however, disobedience and disregard for the laws could have had serious consequences.

Magdalena Naum is an associate professor at the Department of Archaeology and Heritage Studies, Aarhus University, Denmark. Her research focuses on migration in the late medieval and early modern period, early modern Scandinavian colonialism and border landscapes. She is co-editor of *Scandinavian Colonialism and the Rise of Modernity* (Springer, 2013) and author of numerous articles on the subject of her research.

References

Primary Sources

Brahe to Printz, 9 November 1643, ed. A. Johnson. 1930. *The Instruction for Johan Printz, Governor of New Sweden: The First Constitution or Supreme Law of the States of Pennsylvania and Delaware*. Philadelphia, PA: Swedish Colonial Society, pp. 155–58.

Handlingar rörande Skandinaviens Historia 29. 1848. Stockholm: Kungliga Samfundet för utgivande av handskrifter rörande Skandinaviens historia.

Instructions for the Governor of New Sweden Johan Printz, ed. A. Johnson 1930. *The Instruction for Johan Printz, Governor of New Sweden: The First Constitution or Supreme Law of the States of Pennsylvania and Delaware*. Philadelphia, PA: Swedish Colonial Society pp. 62–99.

Minutes of the Provincial Council of Pennsylvania from the Organization to the Termination of the Proprietary Government, Vol. 1. 1852. Philadelphia, PA: J. Severns.

Narratives of Early Pennsylvania, West New Jersey and Delaware, 1630–1707. 1953. New York: Barnes & Noble, pp. 156–65.

NYHM Dutch, Vol. XVIII–XIX. Delaware Papers (Dutch Period) 1655–1644, ed. C. Gehring. 1981. Baltimore, MD: Genealogical Publishing Co.

NYHM Dutch, Vol. XX–XXI. Delaware Papers (English Period) 1664–1682, ed. C. Gehring. 1977. Baltimore, MD: Genealogical Publishing Co.

Pennsylvania Archives Vol. I. Minutes of the Provincial Council of Pennsylvania 1683–1700. 1852. Philadelphia, PA: J. Severns & Co.

Pennsylvania Archives Series 1 Vol. 1. Commencing 1644. 1852. Philadelphia, PA: J. Severns & Co.

Pennsylvania Archives Series 2 Vol. 5. Papers Relating to the Colonies on the Delaware, 1644–1682. 1896. Harrisburg, PA: Clarence M. Busch.

Printz to Brahe, 19 July 1644, ed. A. Johnson. 1930. *The Instruction for Johan Printz, Governor of New Sweden: The First Constitution or Supreme Law of the States of Pennsylvania and Delaware.* Philadelphia, PA: Swedish Colonial Society, pp. 162–68.

Record of the Court at Upland, in Pennsylvania, 1676 to 1681. And a Military Journal Kept by Major E. Denny 1781 to 1795, ed. J. Harmar and E. Armstrong. 1860. Philadelphia, PA: Historical Society of Pennsylvania.

Report of Governor Johan Risingh, 1655, ed. A. Cook Myers. 1959. New York: Charles Scribner's Sons.

Report to the Right Honorable West India Company in Old Sweden, Sent from New Sweden, February 20, 1647, ed. A. Johnson. 1930. *The Instruction for Johan Printz, Governor of New Sweden: The First Constitution or Supreme Law of the States of Pennsylvania and Delaware.* Philadelphia, PA: Swedish Colonial Society, pp. 127–43.

Rudman to Arhhenius, 29 October 1697, ed. P. Stebbins Craig and K.-E. Williams. 2006. *Colonial Records of the Swedish Churches in Pennsylvania. Vol. 2 The Rudman Years 1697–1702.* Philadelphia: Swedish Colonial Society, pp. 65–71.

Settlers' Petition to Governor Printz, 1653, ed. P. Stebbins Craig and K.-E. Williams. 2006. *Colonial Records of the Swedish Churches in Pennsylvania. Vol. 1.* Philadelphia, PA: Swedish Colonial Society, pp. 11–13.

Settlers' Supplemental Complaint against Printz, 1654, ed. P. Stebbins Craig and K.-E. Williams. 2006. *Colonial Records of the Swedish Churches in Pennsylvania. Vol. 1.* Philadelphia, PA: Swedish Colonial Society, pp. 19–24.

Secondary Literature

Acrelius, I. 1874. *A History of New Sweden: or, The Settlement on the Delaware River.* Philadelphia, PA: Historical Society of Pennsylvania.

Ankarloo, B. 1990. 'Sweden: The Mass Burnings (1668–1676)', in B. Ankarloo and G. Henningsen (eds), *Early Modern Witchcraft.* Oxford: Clarendon Press, pp. 285–317.

Bailyn, B. 2012. *The Barbarous Years: The Peopling of British North America: The Conflict of Civilizations, 1600–1675.* New York: Alfred A. Knopf.

Becker, M. 1978, 'An Eighteenth Century Witch Bottle in Delaware County, Pennsylvania', *Pennsylvania Archaeologist* 48(1–2): 1–11.

Beisaw, A.M. 2008. 'Untangling Susquehannock Multiple Burials', unpublished report. Harrisburg, PA: Pennsylvania Historical and Museum Commission.

Brah, A. 1996. *Cartographies of Diaspora, Contesting Identities*. London: Routledge.

Carlsson, S. 1995. 'The New Sweden Colonists, 1638–1655: Their Geographical and Social Background', in C.E. Hoffecker, R. Waldron, L.E. Williams and B.E. Benson (eds), *New Sweden in America*. Newark, DE: University of Delaware Press, pp. 171–87.

Casey, E. 2001. 'Between Geography and Philosophy: What Does it Mean to Be in the Place-World?', *Annals of the Association of American Geographers* 91(4): 683–93.

Custer, J.F., K.R. Doms, A. Allegretti and K. Walker. 1998. 'Preliminary Report on Excavations at 7NC-E-60 in New Castle County, Delaware', *Bulletin of the Archaeological Society of Delaware* 35: 3–27.

Dahlgren, S., and H. Norman. 1988. *The Rise and Fall of New Sweden*. Uppsala: Almqvist & Wiksell.

Dankers, J., and P. Sluyter. 1867. *Journal of a Voyage to New York and a Tour in Several of American Colonies, 1679–80*. New York: Long Island Historical Society.

Donmoyer, P. J. 2014. 'The Concealment of Written Blessings in Pennsylvania Barns', *Historical Archaeology* 48(3): 179–95.

Ekengren, F., M. Naum and U. Zagal-Mach Wolfe. 2013. 'Sweden in the Delaware Valley: Everyday Life and Material Culture in New Sweden', in M. Naum and J. Nordin (eds), *Scandinavian Colonialism and the Rise of Modernity*. New York: Springer, pp. 169–87.

Erixon, S. 1982. *Svensk Byggnadskultur: Studier och Skildringar Belysande den Svenska Byggnadskulturens Historia*. Malmö: Walter Ekstrand Bokförlag.

Ferris, B. 1846. *A History of the Original Settlements on the Delaware*. Wilmington, DE: Wilson & Heald.

Frens, D., and S. Frens 1989. 'The Morton Homestead. A Historic Structure Report', unpublished report. Harrisburg, PA: Pennsylvania Historical and Museum Commission.

Fur, G., M. Naum, and J.M. Nordin 2016. 'Intersecting Worlds: New Sweden's Transatlantic Entanglements', *Journal of Transnational American Studies* 7(1): 1–22.

Godbeer, R. 2013. 'Witchcraft in British America', in B.P. Levack (ed.), *The Oxford Handbook of Witchcraft in Early Modern Europe and Colonial America*. Oxford: Oxford University Press, pp. 393–411.

Goodfriend, J.D. 1999. *Before the Melting Pot: Society and Culture in Colonial New York City, 1664–1730*. Princeton, NJ: Princeton University Press.

Haefeli, E. 2006. 'The Revolt of the Long Swede: Transatlantic Hopes and Fears on the Delaware, 1669', *Pennsylvania Magazine of History and Biography* 80(2): 137–80.

Heikkinen, A., and T. Kervinen. 1990. 'Finland: The Male Domination', in B. Ankarloo and G. Henningsen (eds), *Early Modern Witchcraft*. Oxford: Clarendon Press, pp. 319–38.

Holm, T.C. 1702. *Kort beskrifning om provincien Nya Swerige uti America: som nu förtjden af the Engelske kallas Pensylvania*. Stockholm: Wankifjs Änkia.

Johnson, A. 1911. *The Swedish Settlements on the Delaware, 1638–1664. Vol. 1–2.* Philadelphia, PA: Swedish Colonial Society.

Kent, B.C. 1983. 'More on Gunflints', *Historical Archaeology* 7(2): 27–40.

———. 2001. *Susquehanna's Indians.* Harrisburg, PA: Pennsylvania Historical and Museum Commission.

Leach, N. 2005. 'Belonging: Towards a Theory of Identification with Space', in J. Hillier and E. Rooksby (eds), *Habitus.* Farnham: Ashgate, pp. 297–311.

Lindeström, P. 1925. *Geographia Americae with an Account of the Delaware Indians.* Philadelphia, PA: Swedish Colonial Society.

Lindmark, D. 2005. *Ecclesia Plantanda: Swedishness in Colonial America.* Umeå: Umeå universitet.

Malkki, L. 1992. 'National Geographic: The Rooting of Peoples and the Territorialization of National Identity among Scholars and Refugees', *Cultural Anthropology* 7(1): 24–44.

Mancall, P.C. 1997. *Deadly Medicine: Indians and Alcohol in Early America.* Ithaca, NY: Cornell University Press.

Manning, C.M. 2014. 'The Material Culture of Ritual Concealments in the Eastern United States', *Historical Archaeology* 48(3): 52–83.

Naum, M. 2013. 'The Malady of Emigrants: Homesickness and Longing in the Colony of New Sweden (1638–1655)', in M. Beaudry and T. Parno (eds), *Archaeologies of Mobility and Movement.* New York: Springer, pp. 165–77.

———. 2016. 'Displacement and Emplacement in New Sweden and Colonial Middle Atlantic (1638–1750)', in I. Gustin, M. Hansson, M. Roslund and J. Wienberg (eds), *Mellan slott och slagg: Vänbok till Anders Ödman.* Lund: Lund University, pp. 177–82.

Österberg, E. 1996. 'Criminality, Social Control and the Early Modern State: Evidence and Interpretation in Scandinavian Historiography', in E.A. Johnson and E.H. Monkkonen (eds), *The Civilization of Crime.* Champaign, IL: University of Illinois Press, pp. 35–62.

Turton, D. 2005. 'The Meaning of Place in a World of Movement: Lessons from Long-Term Field Research in Southern Ethiopia', *Journal of Refugee Studies* 18(3): 258–80.

Part II

Space and Power

Introduction
Rules and the Built Environment

Harold Mytum

Part II focuses on case studies associated with buildings, varying in function from the purely domestic, through administrative and leisure sites, to institutions such as asylums and prisons, where explicit control through rules and regulations is at its most extreme. In some cases the wider landscape within which the built structures operate is also considered. These chapters consider not only normative behaviour and the rules that can be identified in cultural practices, but also, in some cases, the ways in which these rules were challenged and subverted in various forms of resistance. Working within documented periods, there are also expectations created by our readings of these texts, and what we expect to find materially: the chapters in this section consider how structures, sites and landscapes conform to, or challenge, our reading of documents, forcing us to consider whether explicit written rules or ones we infer from historical sources were followed in the ways we expected, or whether there is variation in their past application.

That buildings and landscapes have followed rules in their design and use has long been recognized, and is the underlying principle of many classic studies in architectural and art history, cultural geography and archaeology. These rules underlie the order in typology and style. Theoretical developments considering underlying structural principles in building construction and design (Glassie 1975; Deetz 1977) are not overtly considered in these chapters, but the more recent considerations of medieval communality versus increasing early modern emphasis on enclosure and privacy (Johnson 1996) is apparent. Marianne Hem Eriksen sees the open hall of the Middle Ages in its early manifestation in the

Viking Age longhouse, where internal divisions of domestic space were primarily by activity, linked to status, primarily using the hall for human habitation and the byre for animals. However, in later medieval houses a fixed item of furniture possibly indicates where the lord sat, carrying out his social obligations of hospitality, with lesser areas within the space identified through hearths with food preparation. Although some low-status individuals might, at times, be consigned to living within the byre or a compartment of it, generally all were housed together, albeit separated spatially and in terms of role within that space. The medieval structures at Frodsham discussed by Rachel Swallow, whether castle or manor house, would have followed a similar communal format, as both forms of settlement were products of the same cultural mindset.

The medieval landscapes discussed by both Eriksen and Swallow were more physically open than those that were to be created later, but this is not to imply that there were not extensive rules as to ownership, access and symbolic association. The Frodsham hunting landscapes, with the *haiae* enclosures for roe deer, denoted an elite land use with symbolic associations (Swallow), as did the Viking Age farm boundaries linked to cosmological forces and materially represented by burial mounds and wetlands where votive deposits could be made (Eriksen): it may be that such deposits were also made elsewhere, but have not survived.

By the early modern period, cultural, social and ideological forces were encouraging a greater emphasis on individual identity, whilst still retaining significance for family, religious groups and, increasingly, nationality. This tension between communality and shared experience on the one hand, and individual concerns with differentiation and personal space on the other, is explored by Ruth Nugent through examination of the use of space in Shakespearian playhouses. Yet underlying these necessary aspects of form lie layers of rules about behaviour and sociability linked to status: conscious and unconscious rules about gender, class-based behaviour, and privacy and private space. The tension between communality and privacy was also exemplified in other structures and in elite domestic dwellings, but also in churches where post-Reformation changes opened up the intervisibility of interior space, facilitated the new wall memorial, and saw a rise in the ownership of pews, internal family burial areas and an increased concern with rules of spatial identity (Mytum 2004).

The chapters on later periods by Justin E. Eichelberger, Katherine Fennelly and Laura McAtackney all consider institutional contexts, where powerful rules of spatial segregation and order are seen as natural and necessary, with the studies focusing on their exact formation and implementation. In these places rules were explicitly set out in written form and were known by those managing the spaces, but with varying degrees of awareness, understanding and acceptance by those on whom they were enforced. Even the resistance to the rules in these case studies does not demonstrate opposition to the presence of spatial ordering, but only its form of implementation, and the power structures and authority thus implied.

The ways in which regulations were enforced and challenged is not a simple binary opposition, as McAtackney acknowledges. At Long Kesh/Maze, the nature of regulation and conflict varied between comparatively relaxed controls within the compounds of Nissen huts, and the heightened tensions and controls in the H Blocks. Here the levels of noncompliance meant that the normal patterns of control and authority were significantly undermined and subverted, to the point where aspects of the power structure were reversed as the authorities wished to control the interior whilst maintaining a level of integrity in the wider external political and media contexts. These tensions were experienced – and remembered – differently, and are revealed in a range of material culture, oral history and written testimony. The US Army camp examined by Eichelberger is beyond the reach of oral history, but the rich archaeological record, combined with key documentary sources, reveals the ways in which the officially sanctioned tobacco smoking was performed in full public view, while the illicit consumption of alcohol took place inside, away from authority's gaze. Rules were there to be complied with, but even more importantly they had to be seen to be apparently supported. At Fort Yamhill, resistance was hidden and, indeed, may even have been tolerated, as long as it was not overtly challenging the official position on alcohol consumption, unlike Long Kesh/Maze, where resistance was in and of itself the point – a political statement. In asylums, Fennelly concentrates on resistance caused by mental illness and the degree to which patient agency was controlled by physical restraint by the authorities – here, issues of intentionality come to the fore in terms of the extent to which deliberate breaking of rules could be discerned within those whose rationality was uncertain. Prohibited conduct is certainly identified by McAtackney and Eichelberger where coherent planned and repeated rule-breaking was part of established behaviour patterns, though with very different motives.

Through these chapters, we see a tension between physical marginality and social liminality on the one hand and centrality of both on the other – people move apart or between spaces for shorter or longer periods of time, through symbolically significant thresholds into specially formed spaces, only to re-emerge, at least sometimes, into broader society. The investment in physical structures and cultural institutions reveals their centrality to society in terms of managing diversity, separating off the imagined (Nugent), the sick (Fennelly), the protesting (McAtackney), the elite (Eriksen, Swallow) and the military (Eichelberger) from the everyday, either temporarily or permanently. Some were created by a state apparatus, others were private initiatives, but all were products of the normative cultural mindsets that saw these physical forms and their rules of space and behaviour as natural.

Only with our comparative eye can we see the rules regarding the design and use of buildings and landscapes as deeply culturally constituted, both reflecting but also reinforcing and re-creating those cultural attitudes and behaviours that, despite the elements of resistance, largely remained, even if details of their implementation were altered by these alternate practices. The studies in Part II all carry the thread of the role of the person being present and active within the institutions – the physicality of the body and that body's actions are central to the conscious decision-making and underlying normative attitudes and assumptions that are visible in the material conditions that then form the archaeological record. From the domestic life of the longhouse through army drinking, asylum praying or prison furniture breaking, agency within and against the structure of rules can be discerned. The built environment of buildings and landscapes provides an effective arena in which to explore past rule systems and the extent to which they were fixed, challenged and altered.

Harold Mytum is Professor of Archaeology at the University of Liverpool, United Kingdom and currently President of the Society for Post-Medieval Archaeology. His research focuses on issues of identity and memory through mortuary studies, rural settlement and internment camps in Britain, Ireland, North America and Australia. He is currently exploring biography, different forms of narrative and network approaches to expand the ways in which archaeology can be done and reported. His publications include *Recording and Analysing Graveyards* (CBA, 2000), *Mortuary Monuments and Burial Grounds of the Historic Period* (Springer, 2004) and *Prisoners of War: Archaeology, Memory and Heritage of 19th- and 20th-Century Mass Internment* (with Gilly Carr; Springer, 2013).

References

Deetz, J.F. 1977. *In Small Things Forgotten: The Archaeology of Early American Life*. Garden City, NY: Anchor Books.
Glassie H. 1975. *Folk Housing in Middle Virginia: A Structural Analysis of Historic Artifacts*. Knoxville, TN: University of Tennessee Press.
Johnson, M. 1996. *An Archaeology of Capitalism*. Oxford: Blackwell.
Mytum, H. 2004. *Mortuary Monuments and Burial Grounds of the Historic Period*. New York: Kluwer Academic/Plenum.

Chapter 5

Embodied Regulations
Searching for Boundaries in the Viking Age

Marianne Hem Eriksen

Introduction

This chapter is first and foremost intended as a theoretical exploration of how landscapes and domestic space in Viking Age Scandinavia (c. 800–1050) were regulated by the use of sensory experienced boundaries. A dwelling constitutes patterned human behaviour and movement within a structured space (e.g. Rapoport 1969; Bourdieu 1977; Wilson 1988). The materiality of the typical Viking Age longhouse, with its diverse physical and mental spaces, will have constituted a reciprocally influencing arena for the behaviour of its inhabitants. The built environment, and its surroundings, prompts associations with acceptable rules of conduct within the social space. Using eclectic and qualitative material from archaeology and the earliest texts from Scandinavia – and focusing specifically on boundaries and thresholds – this chapter asks: what kinds of physical and cognitive boundaries ordered the Viking settlements? Moreover, what was the nature of spatial transgression and how was it dealt with?

Regulating Spaces and People in the Viking Age

The Viking Age longhouse sprang from a nearly three thousand-year-old tradition of spatial ideals. Even though the Viking Age is a period of innovation in architectural designs, the basic layout of the longhouse with internal roof support – still the most common house type in the

Viking Age (e.g. Skov 1994; Eriksen 2015a) – alludes to ancient, shared north European ideals introduced in the Neolithic. The architecture of the Vikings constituted a meaningful part of their social memory and social production.

I argue that the longhouse was a focal point of society throughout the Iron Age. This applies particularly to central and northern Scandinavia, which had few urban sites and central places. The house was the major social and ritual arena in a pre-state society, where people were born, grew up, worked, held rituals and feasts, and in the end, died and were buried. It has been pointed out that the Norse re-created their architecture when they settled new areas, even if they needed to amend their traditions due to a lack of building material (Stoklund 1984; Stumman Hansen 2000). There are clearly shared architectural ideals over vast spaces, ideals that were deeply rooted in the populations' own past and ancestry.

It is difficult to assess the role of legal rule in the Viking Age. We know that there were legal assembly sites, *things*, mentioned on rune stones and in Scandinavian toponyms (Brink 2008). Several medieval landscape laws also survive that were closely connected to certain geographical areas, although these later law texts were strongly influenced by King and Church (Skre 2007). However, medieval provincial laws may preserve strata of older, orally transmitted rule (Hoff 2002; Brink 2008: 27). A phrase from the Forsa rune ring (discussed below) may indicate the existence of a landscape law in Hälsingland, Sweden as early as the ninth century (Brink 2008: 29). At any rate, the laws of the Vikings were probably more connected to custom and tradition than strict legal rules (Skre 2007: 389). These customs nonetheless regulated practices, behaviour and spaces in the period.

Boundaries and Thresholds

> '[A] border is not so much an object or a material artefact as a belief, an imagination that creates and shapes a world, a social reality'
> —H. van Houtum, O. Kramsch and W. Zierhofer, *B/Ordering Space*.

Viking Age landscapes and settlements were intersected with visible and invisible boundaries: between farmsteads; between infield and outfield; between humans and animals; between agents of different status; between differentiated social spaces; and between the living and the dead (Hållans and Andersson 1997). Boundaries constitute functional, psychological and social partitioning of space, and order empty volumes of space into meaningful entities. They delimit land and territories; they create both borders and passages to cross them; paths and patterns of movement that allow you to transcend the boundaries and move between activity zones (van Houtum, Kramsch and Zierhofer 2005).

Simultaneously, boundaries can be used to separate agents, control movement and people. Defining borders means imposing your own ideals on your surroundings. The power of defining boundaries is the power to define relationships (cf. Lefebvre 1991). Roland Barthes (2012: 116–17) discussed how the words for rule and regulation are related to words for space and boundary. Studying boundaries can generate insights into land ownership, socioeconomic questions, access control, hierarchy and ritual behaviour. This chapter focuses specifically on everyday borders, their social and phenomenological aspects, and their connection to cognitive and cosmological boundaries.

Settlement Boundaries

Settlement boundaries can be readily identified in the archaeological record as enclosures and boundary markers. However, borders could also be constituted by rivers, marshlands and shorelines. The etymology of the Old Norse word *garðr* – 'house, farm, world', modern Scandinavian *gård*, 'farm' – means 'fence, enclosure' (Bjorvand and Lindeman 2007: 343). Borders could also be purely cognitive; invisible but known to everyone in the vicinity. Even empty spaces can constitute boundaries in Iron Age landscapes (Hållans and Andersson 1997). This constitutes a paradox for archaeologists studying material remains of the past. Still, as Nico Roymans (1995: 32) states: 'The culture-bound, ideological-mental dimension of space is also a prominent topic of research for archaeologists studying the cultural landscape.'

For much of Scandinavia, territorial rights are interpreted as being reorganized during the beginning of the late Iron Age, around the middle of the first millennium. From this period onwards, settlements were generally more stable in terms of placement, and the importance of land ownership and appropriation increases (Skre 1998; Widgren 1998). Appropriating land and creating new settlement boundaries are events with political, economic and ritual overtones (Strang and Busse 2011). The *Landnámabók* reveals how land could be appropriated in various rituals by Iceland's earliest settlers. Lit torches were carried around a territory's edges, thereby drawing the boundaries of the land with fire (Kvideland 1993: 13; Zachrisson 1998: 197–99). An arrow could be shot over the territory (perhaps alluding to an Odinnic ritual) or wooden posts erected to claim ownership (Strömbäck 1928). Although the oldest surviving copies of the *Landnámabók* date from the thirteenth century, the rituals described have several allusions to pre-Christian religion. These rituals may well be memories of the Icelanders' not-so-distant past – it is pointed out in some of the texts that this was done 'after ancient custom' (Strömbäck 1928).

According to Aaron Gurevich (1969: 43), transferral of territorial rights in medieval Scandinavia constituted a 'concrete sensual attitude to possession'. One ritual encompassed the former owner giving the new owner a handful of earth from the plot, or placing the earth in the new owner's lap. This ritual was executed in the assembly place – the *thing* – with many witnesses to the transaction of rights. The emphasis on earth and soil in the territorial rituals may be echoed in other cultures. Nicole Boivin (2008: 138–39) suggests that the practice of cultivating the earth creates a strong link between people and the land, and therefore the soil itself becomes a metaphor for land ownership rights – a material expression of a sense of *belonging*.

Regulating boundaries between single farmsteads could also be an area of conflict, at least in later folkloric sources. The legendary *deildegasten* was the ghost of a man who had appropriated land illegally by moving boundary stones. According to these legends, when the perpetrator died, he was forced to haunt the area relentlessly, carrying the boundary stones for eternity. The same could happen if a participant in boundary disputes placed earth from his own land in his shoes and swore falsely that he was 'standing on his own soil' (Kvideland 1993). As late as the 1751 treaty regulating the national border between Norway and Sweden, the punishment for moving or destroying boundary cairns was death by hanging on the spot, as a warning to others (*Grensetraktaten av 1751*: art.VII).

The placement of burial mounds and the erection of rune stones may be seen as strategies for enforcing territorial claims in the Viking period, as well as being boundary markers (Zachrisson 1998). The right to be free and the right to own lands in this period may be two sides of the same coin (Skre 1998). One term for a free man was *óðalsmaðr*. Odal is the inherited territorial right of a family. Whether odal was a ubiquitous organization of inheritance and land ownership in this period or related to all Scandinavian areas is unclear. Written sources suggest that odal was inherited from familial ancestors, and both Aaron Gurevich (1985) and Torun Zachrisson (1994) interpret odal as a *mentality*, not just as a legal regulation. The legitimacy of territorial claims was dependent on social memory, and possibly the material manifestation of the ancestral burial mounds. The *haugbúi*, ancestors thought to live in burial mounds, were connected to odal. Even into the Christian period, *Magnus Lagabøte's Law* (1270s) cites the *haugodalsmann*, the man who has odal rights from the burial mound. Skre (1998: 199–203) argues that burial mounds were, to some extent, legal documents; landscape manifestations of odal and inheritance. Thus, the ancestors may have guarded these important boundary zones and the outfields of the farm (Zachrisson 1998: 200).

Cosmological Boundaries

Farm boundaries may be linked to cognitive and cosmological boundaries. Based on later textual sources, the cognitive landscape of the Vikings has been suggested to resemble three concentric circles: an inner circle representing *Ásgarðr*, the home of the gods; a middle circle representing *Miðgarðr*, the home of humankind; and the outer circle *Útgarðr*, a wild domain where giants and the powers of chaos ruled (Gurevich 1985). This model has rightly been critiqued as structuralist, simplified and static (e.g. Hedeager 2003: 159). The fluidity of Scandinavian pre-Christian religion suggests that many worldviews and cosmologies potentially coexisted. Yet, mythology and later folklore, where supernatural, powerful and dangerous beings were associated with natural places such as mountains, marshlands and forests, may support the concentric-circle model.

Cognitive boundaries, however they were envisaged, did not only exist on a metaphysical, distant plain, but sprang from, and were constituted by, materiality and practice (*contra* Hastrup 1985: 137). Archaeological and anthropological studies reveal how cosmological ideals are frequently expressed, influenced and mediated by architecture, funerary monuments and cognitive landscapes (Wilson 1988; Parker Pearson and Richards 1994; Carsten and Hugh-Jones 1995; Roymans 1995), and practice (Bourdieu 1977). In Iron and Viking Age Scandinavia, cosmological ideals may have been particularly potent in the aristocratic, ritualized halls. Lotte Hedeager (2002) proposed the late Roman 'central place' of Gudme on the island of Funen, Denmark as an 'Ásgarðr reconstructed'. The surrounding landscape and monumental halls were formed in a cosmological image, creating a transcendental space, which connected the supernatural spheres (Odin's *Valhall*) with the earthly (the hall at Gudme).

There was probably a reciprocal relationship between the material and mythological world, with the ideas of a mythological hall, supplying gold, meat and drink for continuous, eternal feasting, based on the new elites' architectural ideals and practices. If the material world was used as a model for mythological ideas, the chieftain/king became an earthly representative of Odin in his Valhalla. This also constitutes a potent strategy for power legitimation.

Cosmological boundaries were not only expressed in the built environment. Through their studies of depositional sites, Torun Zachrisson (1998), Lotte Hedeager (2003) and Julie Lund (2005) have all suggested that rivers and wetlands may have constituted important cognitive boundaries in Viking landscapes. Depositional places should be seen as 'borders of topography' where landscape characteristics change, e.g. from dry land to wetland or from fields to mountains (Lund 2005: 120). Zachrisson (1998), studying metal depositions in central Sweden, sees a connection between silver deposits in wetlands and historical farm boundaries. In the *Svarfdöla Saga*, which claims to take place under the rule of Harald Fairhair (c. 850–932), the protagonist, Thorsten, appropriates new land by depositing his broken comb and pieces of silver in three places in a valley (*Svarfdöla Saga*: Chapter 11; Zachrisson 1998: 198–99). He then calls witnesses and claims the entire valley in his name. Since precious metal was recognized as extremely personal, the deposition of personal metal items created and reinforced the boundaries of his newly appropriated land. Although potentially fictional, this episode attests to a recognizable practice, contemporary with the saga, of landscape deposition connected with land appropriation. The tradition of depositing silver at boundary places may simultaneously be linked with the liminal character of rivers, borders and wetlands (cf. Lund 2010).

Longhouse Boundaries

From landscape boundaries and cosmological boundaries, we now turn to boundaries close to and within the house itself. The settlement constitutes a delimited territory. One of the most famous poems of the Edda, *Hávamál* (stanzas 36–37), states that within the house, every man is master. Within the settlement, it is conceivable that there were visible and invisible boundaries that were known by the inhabitants.

A key social code of the Vikings was hospitality, one of the central themes in *Hávamál*. There was a social obligation to accept guests and travellers arriving at the door, the major access point and boundary of the dwelling (Figure 5.1). Since being hospitable was a social requirement, there was the concept of *heimfriðr* – 'peace/sanctity of the home'. This was a sociolegal concept of the right to sanctity in your own home, possibly connected to pagan cult and the exclusive high seat of the ruler/master and his spouse (Carlsson 1935; Palme 1959). According to the medieval law *Kristofferslagen*, the right to *heimfriðr* extended to the enclosure around the farm – the drawn boundary. The right to peace was also extended to the house guests.

Current research suggests that the typical Viking Age longhouse in Norway would have had one or two entrances (Eriksen 2015a). The number of entrances, however, increases with the size of the house and the interpreted social status of the inhabitants. The elite hall buildings had the highest number of entrances. Frands Herschend (1998: 171–72)

Figure 5.1 The doorway of the reconstructed Iron Age longhouse of Ullandhaug, Stavanger, Norway. The door is the boundary into the domestic space of the house, and the border where guests would be welcomed into the home (photograph by Marianne Hem Eriksen).

suggests royal hall buildings had one door used exclusively by the King and the most prominent guests. Therefore, entering a particular space, whether domestic, an enclosure, or perhaps particularly sacral space, could constitute ritualized and regulated behaviour.

Although at times difficult to determine archaeologically, there were internal boundaries within domestic space. In longhouses, with a byre at one end and dwelling quarters at the other, a key boundary must have been between humans and animals. This type of spatial ordering was dominant in the Roman and Migration periods, but by the late Iron Age, animals were increasingly moved to auxiliary buildings. Nevertheless, a substantial number of late Iron Age and Viking Age longhouses were still divided into a byre and dwelling quarters. In southern Scandinavia (Denmark and parts of Sweden), this spatial order was often aligned with cardinal directions, i.e. humans in the west and animals in the east (e.g. Hvass 1988). This spatial order must have been important in both everyday physical movement and perceptions of world order – animals belonged in one part of the world and humans in the other.

Elite hall buildings often generate more knowledge of internal boundaries than regular settlements, as they generally produce more artefacts and constructional evidence. A well-documented example of such a building is Borg in Lofoten, northern Norway (Munch, Johansen and Roesdahl 2003). At 82 metres in length, it is the largest longhouse ever excavated in Northern Europe (Figure 5.2). The hall was used for ritual, feasting and representation by a chieftain/petty king, his family and his retainers – the

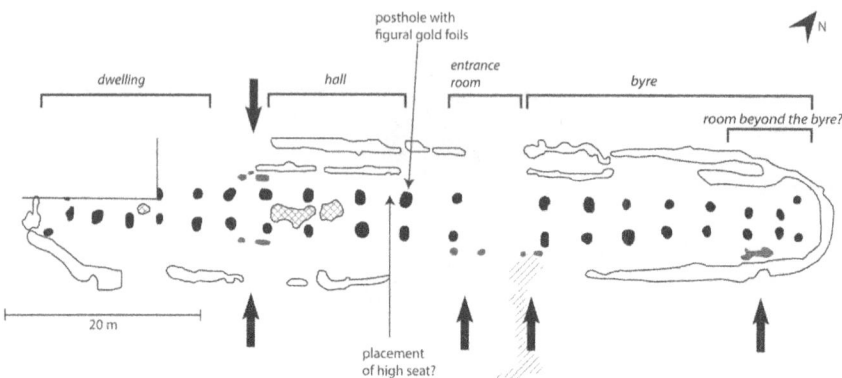

Figure 5.2 The hall building at Borg in Lofoten, northern Norway (illustration by Marianne Hem Eriksen after Herschend and Mikkelsen 2003: 52)

Figure 5.3 The Forsa ring from Hälsingland, Sweden, with its runic inscription. It is a striking object, probably intended to be ornamental rather than purely functional, hanging on a door – the archetypical boundary to regulated space (photograph by Marianne Hem Eriksen).

commitatus (Herschend 1997). The Borg hall, in the southwest-central part of the building, is c. 120 m² with two central hearths and a fixed piece of furniture in the north, possibly a high-seat (Munch 2003: 261). The hall was frequently delimited by depositing ritual artefacts in the postholes, possibly done to sacralize or initiate the hall space and draw boundaries between different spaces within the building.

An artefact intimately connected with the hall is the *gullgubber*; small gold foils stamped with human figures, often an embracing couple. These figures have been interpreted as the mythological couple Frøy and Gerd, the alleged ancestors of one of the most powerful royal lines in Viking Age Scandinavia (Steinsland 1991). *Gullgubber* are usually deposited in one or more postholes in the hall; at Borg, five gold foils were deposited in the northern posthole of the hall room (Munch 2003). I interpret this as both a way to sacralize the hall space and to connect the hall owners with the archetypal royal couple.

Some longhouses and hall buildings show clear differentiation between areas used for cooking and domestic activities, and spaces used for social purposes, representation and drinking. This is usually evidenced by several contemporary hearth rooms within the domestic space. The hearths for cooking may have been primarily associated with thralls or dependants, as thrall names known from rune stones, Eddic poetry and saga material are often associated with cooking and food preparation (Brink 2012: 121–24).

Another case that may reveal social and spatial boundaries within the internal house-space is the so-called 'room beyond the byre' (Norr 1996). Towards the end of the early Iron Age in areas of modern-day Sweden, an extra room emerges in the gable, identified by a hearth and sometimes an extra entrance. The hypothesis is that when power was consolidated in fewer hands, the extra room was for an emerging social group, of dependents or thralls who lived with animals. One of the thrall names listed in the Edda is *Fjósnir*, 'he who belongs in the byre'. A handful of Norwegian late Iron Age houses may display a similar, if not identical, spatial order (Eriksen 2015a). One of them is Borg, which has two entrances to the byre, one cattle track and one presumably used by humans, the latter possibly leading to a small dwelling space within the byre. However, there is no extra hearth found in the byre at Borg, which may undermine this interpretation. Herschend (2009: 219) discusses an earlier case, Nørre Tranders, Denmark (first century), where a longhouse caught fire. Three adults and one child burned inside with the animals in the byre, which indicates that these were 'byre-living people'. The room beyond the byre gives insight into a mentality that expected some people to live away from the household and enter separately from other humans to dwell with the animals.

Trespassing

What happens when someone, or something, trespasses the boundaries of the settlement? We have already seen the later, folkloristic idea of what happened to those who cheated with farm boundaries. Legal sources may shed further light on this question. The aforementioned idea of concentric boundaries regulating the intimacy of space may be found in medieval legal sources of transgression. The *Hälsingland Law* from Sweden (the oldest copy dates from the fourteenth century) has a section entitled 'On Wilful Killing and Guests'. It opens by defining the sanctity of the home, which 'extends as far as cattle and sheep graze'. It states the penalties for trespassing the farm and assaulting or killing the inhabitants, with fines increasing with the number of boundaries crossed to the place of assault. The boundaries are described from the outside moving inwards and include: the outer boundary of the farm (i.e. the edge of the grazing lands); the middle pasture; in the byre; in the farmyard; on the extended entrance; between the threshold and the hearth; by the hearth; between the hearth and gable bench; on the gable bench; between the gable bench and the women's bench; on the women's bench; and finally 'if a man is struck in his bed, forty-eight marks to each of the three parties [the plaintiff, the king, the community]' (*Hälsingeland Law*: VI, §2).

The innermost, most protected space of the settlement was thus the sleeping area, the space where one is least guarded. But on the perpetrator's way to the bed, we catch a glimpse of other meaningful boundaries in the settlement: concentric circles encompassing the increasingly private and intimate spheres of the house. It is noteworthy that the largest increase in the size of the fine happens between the extended entrance/porch (twelve *merker*) and after the threshold has been crossed. When the crime happens between the threshold, the boundary of the house and the hearth, which was the focal point of the dwelling, the fine triples to thirty-six *merker* (*Hälsingeland Law*: VI, §2).

Whether the zones of intimacy described in this law from a specific region in Sweden applied to other Scandinavian areas is unknown. Furthermore, a medieval law text may not be wholly relevant to a late Iron Age mindset. Yet this text presents an inkling of how domestic space and the settlements may have been perceived and experienced in terms of boundaries.

The oldest known Scandinavian law, the runic inscription on the large iron Forsa ring from Hälsingland, Sweden (Figure 5.3), may underline the importance of spatial boundaries and regulation. Originally thought to be medieval, it has recently been redated to the ninth century on runological and linguistic grounds (see the debates in Brink 2010; Källström 2010; Löfving 2010). The ring once hung on a door in the medieval church of Forsa, but I have suggested that the ring may have originally belonged to the door of a pre-Christian cult building, before being transferred to the Christian cult building – the church – after the conversion (Eriksen 2015b). The inscription's meaning is heavily debated, but it has recently been interpreted as listing fines a transgressor has to pay the first, second and third time he destroys the cult place, thus regulating the punishment for desecration (Brink 2008). Therefore, instead of fines increasing according to boundaries crossed, as in the later *Hälsingland Law*, fines increased according to frequency of a transgressive act.

I have argued elsewhere (Eriksen 2015b) that it is not a coincidence that a door ring was used as a medium for regulating accepted social behaviour in the cult building. The doorway is the border between spaces, between the inside and the outside, and the door to the sacral space may therefore be experienced as a particularly powerful boundary. Rings, on the other hand, in the Iron Age were perceived as magical objects with connotations of legality and swearing oaths. The door ring with a legal text, hanging on the door to the cult building, may therefore have constituted a forceful reminder of accepted social behaviour. Perhaps the ring even had sensory, mnemonic qualities in reminding a person crossing the boundary to the sacral space of the rules of conduct that applied (Eriksen 2015b).

The two legal texts described – the medieval *Hälsingland Law* and the Viking Age inscription on the Forsa ring – mention fines in terms of money and livestock that should be paid when someone transgresses social rules and boundaries. But in the Viking Age, one of the most severe forms of punishment was exile. Contrary to modern-day ideas of punishment, where transgressors are kept behind locked gates and high fences, perpetrators of severe crimes in the Viking Age were 'locked out'. They were exiled from the community and had to live outside in the wilderness, the *útangarðs* ('outside the farm'). These people were called *skogarmaðr* ('forest-men'), *útlagi* ('out-law') or *vargr* ('wolf'). They could be killed on sight by anyone (Hastrup 1985: 137–40).

The mentality of this punishment underpins the perception that the settled areas were under social control and regulation, whilst those banished were moving outside of society, outside of the law. This constitutes a different way of thinking about punishment, where the harshest punishment, except death, was to be denied access to the social and cosmological centre of the settlement. The transgressor was confined outside the boundaries of society, i.e. outside the house.

Controlling Thresholds

Placing deposits in buildings was a tradition over the longue durée in Scandinavia, from the Neolithic into the Medieval period (Carlie 2004). Deposited artefacts range from flint axes, knives, ceramics, and coins, to whole animals deposited in constructional elements of the house (Carlie 2004; Kristensen 2010). Deposition can, amongst others, be approached as a strategy for enforcing the boundaries of the house. The phenomenon of intentional deposition has in recent years been critiqued on the grounds of creating a dichotomy between everyday and ritual practices (Morris and Jervis 2011; Garrow 2012). I argue that in prehistoric Scandinavia, the spheres of economy, ritual and social production were interwoven (cf. Bradley 2005). Deposition was an exceptionally long-lived and multi-faceted phenomenon defying strict categorization. This should not exclude us from studying deposition or render deposits in boundary/liminal spheres meaningless.

According to Tove Paulsson-Holmberg, who has studied deposition in the Swedish Iron Age and medieval material, artefacts 'were placed at critical positions in the building: under the threshold, above the front door, inside or under the oven, or under the floor in the middle of the house' (Paulsson-Holmberg 1998: 163). In late Iron Age Norway, artefacts were generally deposited in postholes, wall lines and doorways of the longhouses.

Not only things but also people could be placed on the boundaries of settlements (Eriksen 2013; cf. Hamerow 2006). A grave containing burnt bone and a fragmented whetstone was cut into the extended entryway of a small longhouse from the site of Storrsheia, southwest Norway. Burying or depositing human remains in the entrance of the house is a particular practice that must be embedded with a particular social meaning. The intention could be to keep the dead person on the threshold between spheres, in a between-space where the connection with the household continues. Burying someone on the boundary, in a liminal place, could also imply deviance in some way (Eriksen 2013; cf. Reynolds 2009). But it is also possible that the ancestor buried by the entrance was placed there to protect the descendants by guarding the threshold – the boundary to the home.

After the conversion to Christianity, medieval folklore reveals continuing depositional traditions, such as striking nails into the wooden thresholds so that the dangerous dead would hurt their feet if they tried to force their way in. However, the cultic focal point was now the church, and church portals became ritualized boundary spaces. Portal ornamentation was accessorized with apotropaic motives to keep dangerous powers away, probably associated with the devil (Karlsson 1988: 252–54). These portal motifs derived almost exclusively from pre-Christian mythology, are somewhat oxymoronic on the portals to a Christian building. Particularly popular were Sigurd motifs, visualizing the narrative of Sigurd the Dragonslayer from *Völsunga saga* (Gjærder 1952: 58–65). Even profane doors could, in the Middle Ages, be engraved with crosses adorned with protective runic inscriptions or other ornamentation to guard the domestic space within and keep dangerous powers out (Gjærder 1952). Per Gjærder suggests that apotropaic symbols may have been carved and recarved at particular times of the yearly cycle, when the threat from the Otherworld was strongest. In the Middle Ages, this may have been during *jól* (Christmas), when *Åsgårdsreia* – a flying flock of dark forces and dead corpses – came to haunt the living. Åsgårdsreia was perceived as a great threat to people and animals, and the best precaution was to make the sign of the cross and paint crosses on all doors (Bø 2013) to defend the boundaries of the building

Conclusions: Embodied Regulations

Using a qualitative, eclectic dataset, I have suggested that important Viking Age boundaries and focal points of landscapes and settlements included farm boundaries, rivers, enclosures, infields, the threshold and door, and the hearth. Subsequently, I have proposed some strategies used to control these thresholds, such as depositional practices, and have outlined possible consequences when borders were transgressed.

Boundaries are bodily experienced elements of physical and cognitive surroundings. Drawing boundaries can be a strategy for making oneself at home; of creating a sense of belonging to the earth and to a place. The boundaries of the farm may also have been understood as a material analogy of the household or the small community that belonged within (Wilson 1988: 60). Attempts to control thresholds by depositing artefacts at the threshold-space, in the wall lines of the house, or in rivers and wetlands, was possibly a powerful strategy for enforcing the border and protecting the intimate space within. The ancestors buried in the grave mound, placed by the border of the farm, may have guarded the settlement, making sure that no one, whether earthly or supernatural, could trespass and approach the intimate zones of the house. There were personal items deposited along the wetland boundaries, or on dry land, delimiting this space from the surrounding world, linking the territory with the founder and his family. Upon entering the house and crossing the threshold, there could be powerful items placed under the doorsill or ornamentation on the door itself, guarding the intimate space of the house. On a very rare occasion, there could even be human remains under the doorway to protect the household and bring good years.

The experience of entering another person's land, opening the gate to their fields and crossing the threshold to their house would be a practice filled with its own embodied experience and its own set of social rules. Visible and invisible boundaries in the landscape could constitute mnemonic, bodily experienced reminders of social regulation. As Kevin D. Fisher (2009: 455) argues: '[Elements of the built environment] ... helps ensure that social actors recognize the signs that remind them of "proper" or expected behavior.' We can imagine Viking Age boundaries to express social regulations of hospitality, of *heimfriðr*, of the spatial and cosmological order between people and animals, of feasting practices and required behaviour in the hall, of the differences between free and enslaved people.

We cannot from the archaeological material and the textual sources grasp all perceptions of space, regulation of zones, and accepted and inappropriate behaviour in the past. But we must assume that Viking Age people also brought with them a cultural and social conceptualization of space and borders. Unwritten rules of privacy, of rank, of social roles within the household, of gender and of belonging were expressed in a practical, material way inside and around the longhouse. Boundaries affect the embodiment of social rules and regulations. The embodied experience of crossing the boundary, perhaps several social and cosmological boundaries at once, may have had a profound influence on both practice and mentality in the Viking Age.

Acknowledgements

I am grateful to Lotte Hedeager, Lars Erik Gjerpe, Vibeke Viestad, and Astrid Nyland for commenting on an early draft of this chapter. Many thanks to the anonymous reviewer for insightful suggestions, and the editors for comments, as well as for inviting me to contribute to this volume.

Marianne Hem Eriksen is an Associate Professor of Archaeology at the University of Oslo. She is currently on a Research Council of Norway/ Marie Curie Mobility Fellowship at the University of Cambridge. Her research interests include houses and households, ritual, archaeology of death, archaeological theory and social archaeology. Her Ph.D. dissertation was awarded H.M. The King's Gold Medal in 2016.

References

Primary Sources

Grensetraktaten av 1751, ed. Kongelige Norske Utenriksdepartement. 1967. *Norges traktater 1661–1966, Vol. 1, 1661–1944*. Oslo: Grøndahl.
Hälsingland Law, ed. Å. Holmbäck and E. Wessén. 1940. *Svenska landskapslagar, Vol. 3*. Stockholm: Geber.
Hávamál, ed./trans. L. Holm-Olsen. 1985. *Edda-dikt*. Oslo: Cappelen.
Kristofferslagen, ed. D.C.J. Schlychter. 1869. *Corpus Iuris Sueo-Gotorum Antiqui: Samling af Sweriges gamla Lagar, Vol. 12*. Lund: Berlingska Boktryckeriet.
Landnámabók, trans. J.R. Hagland. 2002. Hafrsfjord: Erling Skjalgssonsekskapet.
Magnus Lagabøte's Law, ed. R. Keyser and P.A. Munch. 1848. *Norges gamle Love indtil 1387, Vol. 2*. Christiania: Grøndahl.
Svarfdöla Saga, trans. N.M. Petersen. 1844. *Historiske Fortællinger om Islændernes Færd hjemme og ude*. Copenhagen: Det Kongelige Nordiske Oldskriftselskab.

Secondary Literature

Barthes, R. 2012. *How to Live Together*. New York: Columbia University Press.
Bjorvand, H., and F.O. Lindeman. 2007. *Våre Arveord*, Instituttet for Sammenlignende Kulturforskning, Serie B, Skrifter 105. Oslo: Novus.
Bø, O. 2013. 'Oskoreia', *Store Norske Leksikon*. Retrieved 17 May 2017 from http://snl.no/oskoreia.
Boivin, N. 2008. *Material Cultures, Material Minds: The Impact of Things on Human Thought*. Cambridge: Cambridge University Press.
Bourdieu, P. 1977. *Outline of a Theory of Practice*, trans. R. Nice. Cambridge: Cambridge University Press.
Bradley, R. 2005. *Ritual and Domestic Life in Prehistoric Europe*. London: Routledge.
Brink, S. 2008. 'Law and Society', in S. Brink and N.S. Price (eds), *The Viking World*. London: Routledge, pp. 23–31.
——. 2010. 'Är Forsaringen Medeltida?', *Hälsingerunor* 2010: 109–17.
——. 2012. *Vikingarnas Slavar*. Stockholm: Atlantis.
Carlie, A. 2004. *Forntida Byggnadskult*, Riksantikvarieämbetet Arkeologiska Undersökningar 57. Stockholm: Riksantikvarieämbetet.
Carlsson, L. 1935. 'Högsätet och Hemfriden', *Rig* 18: 65–92.
Carsten, J., and S. Hugh-Jones. 1995. *About the House: Lévi-Strauss and Beyond*. Cambridge: Cambridge University Press.
Eriksen, M.H. 2013. 'Doors to the Dead: The Power of Doorways and Thresholds in Viking-Age Scandinavia', *Archaeological Dialogues* 20(2): 187–214.
——. 2015a. 'Portals to the Past: An Archaeology of Doorways, Dwellings, and Ritual Practice in Late Iron Age Scandinavia', Ph.D. dissertation. Oslo: University of Oslo.
——. 2015b. 'The Power of the Ring: Door Rings, Oath Rings, and the Sacral Place', in M.H. Eriksen, U. Pedersen, B. Rundberget, I. Axelsen and H. Berg (eds), *Viking Worlds*. Oxford: Oxbow, pp. 73–89.

Fisher, K.D. 2009. 'Placing Social Interaction: an Integrative Approach to Analyzing Past Built Environments', *Journal of Anthropological Archaeology* 28(4): 439–57.
Garrow, D. 2012. 'Odd Deposits and Average Practice: A Critical History of the Concept of Structured Deposition', *Archaeological Dialogues* 19(2): 85–115.
Gjærder, P. 1952. *Norske Pryd-Dører fra Middelalderen*, Universitetet i Bergen Skrifter 24. Bergen: University of Bergen.
Gurevich, A. 1969. 'Space and Time in the *Weltmodel* of Medieval Scandinavia', *Medieval Scandinavia* 2: 42–53.
———. 1985. *Categories of Medieval Culture*, trans. G.L. Campbell. London: Routledge & Kegan Paul.
Hållans, A.-M., and C. Andersson. 1997. 'No Trespassing: Physical and Mental Boundaries in Agrarian Settlements', in H. Andersson, P. Carelli and L. Ersgård (eds), *Visions of the Past*. Stockholm: Central Board of National Antiquities, pp. 583–602.
Hamerow, H. 2006. '"Special Deposits" in Anglo-Saxon Settlements', *Medieval Archaeology* 50: 1–30.
Hastrup, K. 1985. *Culture and History in Medieval Iceland: An Anthropological Analysis of Structure and Change*. Oxford: Clarendon Press.
Hedeager, L. 2002. 'Scandinavian "Central Places" in a Cosmological Setting', in L. Larsson and B. Hårdh (eds), *Central Places in the Migration and Merovingian Periods*, Acta Archaeologica Lundensia Series in 8° nr. 39. Stockholm: Almqvist & Wiksell, pp. 3–18.
———. 2003. 'Kognitiv Topografi: Ædelmetaldepoter i Landskapet', in P. Rolfsen and F.-A. Stylegar (eds), *Snartemofunnene i Nytt Lys*, University Museum of Cultural Heritage Occasional Papers 2. Oslo: University of Oslo, pp. 147–66.
Herschend, F. 1997. *Livet i Hallen*, Occasional Papers in Archaeology 14. Uppsala: Uppsala University.
———. 1998. *The Idea of the Good in Late Iron Age Society*, Occasional Papers in Archaeology 15. Uppsala: Societas.
———. 2009. *The Early Iron Age in South Scandinavia*, Occasional Papers in Archaeology 46. Uppsala: Societas.
Herschend, F. and D. Kaldal Mikkelsen. 2003. 'The Main Building at Borg (I:1)', in G.S. Munch, O.S. Johansen, and E. Roesdahl (eds), *Borg in Lofoten*. Trondheim: Tapir, pp. 41–76.
Hoff, A. 2002. 'The Farm Buildings on Basis of the Northwest-European Lawbooks: ca. 900–1200', in J. Klapste (ed.), *The Rural House from the Migration Period to the Oldest still Standing Buildings*, Ruralia 4. Nieders: Institut für historische Küstenforschung, pp. 45–48.
Hvass, S. 1988. 'Jernalderens Bebyggelse', in P. Mortensen and B.M. Rasmussen (eds), *Fra Stamme Til Stat I Danmark 1: Jernalderens Stammesamfund*. Aarhus: Jysk Arkæologisk Selskabs Skrifter, pp. 53–92.
Karlsson, L. 1988. *Medieval Ironwork in Sweden Vol. 1*. Stockholm: Almqvist & Wiksell.
Kristensen, T.S. 2010. 'Husgeråd Som Husoffer', *Primitive Tider* 12: 61–70.

Kvideland, R. 1993. 'Establishing Borders: The Narrative Potential of a Motif', in H.R. Ellis Davidson (ed.), *Boundaries and Thresholds*. Stroud: Thimble Press, pp. 13–20.
Källström, M. 2010. 'Forsaringen er Vikingtida', *Fornvännen* 105: 228–32.
Lefebvre, H. 1991. *The Production of Space*, trans. D. Nicholson-Smith. Oxford: Blackwell.
Lund, J. 2005. 'Thresholds and Passages: The Meanings of Bridges and Crossings in the Viking Age and Early Middle Ages', *Viking and Medieval Scandinavia* 1: 109–35.
———. 2010. 'At the Water's Edge', in M.A. Carver, A. Sanmark and S. Semple (eds), *Signals of Belief in Early England*. Oxford: Oxbow, pp. 49–66.
Löfving, C. 2010. 'Forsaringen Är Medeltida', *Fornvännen* 105: 48–53.
Morris, J., and B. Jervis. 2011. 'What's so Special? A Reinterpretation of Anglo-Saxon "Special Deposits"', *Medieval Archaeology* 55: 66–81.
Munch, G.S. 2003. 'Borg as a Pagan Centre', in G.S. Munch, O.S. Johansen and E. Roesdahl (eds), *Borg in Lofoten*. Trondheim: Tapir, pp. 253–63.
Munch, G.S., O.S. Johansen and F. Roesdahl (eds). 2003. *Borg in Lofoten*. Trondheim: Tapir.
Norr, S. 1996. 'A Place for Proletarians? A Contextual Hypothesis on Social Space in Roman and Migration Period Long-Houses', *Current Swedish Archaeology* 4: 157–64.
Palme, S.U. 1959. 'Fridlagstiftning', in *Kulturhistorisk Leksikon for Nordisk Middelalder Vol. 4*. Copenhagen: Kulturhistorisk Leksikon for Nordisk Middelalder, pp. 622–26.
Parker Pearson, M., and C. Richards. 1994. *Architecture and Order: Approaches to Social Space*. London: Routledge.
Paulsson-Holmberg, T. 1998, 'Iron Age Building Offerings', *Fornvännen* 92: 163–75.
Rapoport, A. 1969. *House Form and Culture*. Englewood Cliffs, NJ: Prentice Hall.
Reynolds, A. 2009. *Anglo-Saxon Deviant Burial Customs*. Oxford: Oxford University Press.
Roymans, N. 1995. 'Archaeology, Folklore, and the Ideational Dimension of Space', *Archaeological Dialogues* 2(1): 32–38.
Skov, H. 1994. 'Hustyper i Vikingetid og Tidlig Middelalder: Udviklingen af Hustyperne i det Gammeldanske Område fra ca. 800–1200 e. Kr.', *Hikuin* 21: 139–62.
Skre, D. 1998. 'Herredømmet: Bosetning og Besittelse på Romerike 200–1350 e. Kr.', Ph.D. dissertation. Oslo: University of Oslo.
———. 2007. 'The Skiringssal Thing site Thódalyng', in D. Skre (ed.), *Kaupang in Skiringssal Vol. 1*, Norske Oldfunn 22. Aarhus: Aarhus University Press, pp. 385–406.
Steinsland, G. 1991. *Det Hellige Bryllup og Norrøn Kongeideologi*. Oslo: Solum.
Stoklund, B. 1984. 'Building Traditions in the Northern World', in A. Fenton and H. Pálsson (eds), *The Northern and Western Isles in the Viking World*. Edinburgh: John Donald, pp. 96–115.
Strang, V. and M. Busse. 2011. *Ownership and Appropriation*. London: Academic Press.

Strömbäck, D. 1928. 'Att helga land: Studier i Landnáma och det äldste rituella besittningstagandet', in E. Liljeqvist (ed.), *Festskrift tillägnad Axel Hägerström den 6 September 1928 av filosofiska föreningarna i Uppsala*. Uppsala and Stockholm: Almqvist & Wiksell, pp. 198–220.

Stumman Hansen, S. 2000. 'Viking Settlement in Shetland', *Acta Archaeologica* 71: 87–103.

Van Houtum, H., O. Kramsch and W. Zierhofer 2005. 'Prologue', in H. van Houtum, O. Kramsch and W. Zierhofer (eds), *B/Ordering Space*. Aldershot: Ashgate, pp. 1–16.

Widgren, M. 1998. 'Kulturgeografernas Bönder och Arkeologernas Guld: Finns det Någon väg till en Syntes?', in L. Larsson and B. Hårdh (eds), *Centrala Platser, Centrala Frågor*, Acta Archaeologica Lundensia Series in 8° nr. 28. Lund: Almqvist & Wiksell, pp. 281–96.

Wilson, P.J. 1988. *The Domestication of the Human Species*. New Haven, CT: Yale University Press.

Zachrisson, T. 1994. 'The Odal and its Manifestation in the Landscape', *Current Swedish Archaeology* 2: 219–38.

———. 1998. 'Gård, Gräns, Gravfält: Sammanhang Kring Ädelmetalldepåer och Runstenar från Vikingatid och tidig Medeltid i Uppland och Gästrikland', Ph.D. dissertation. Stockholm: Stockholm University.

Chapter 6

What Law Says That There Has to Be a Castle?
The Castle Landscape of Frodsham, Cheshire

Rachel Swallow

Introduction

Power of place and the dynamics of landscape manipulation are the focus of current research into the number, location and distribution of castles raised in Cheshire (United Kingdom) in the period of the Earldom of Chester (c. 1066–1237). Previous studies have focused on individual castles within the county only, underlining the need for a multidisciplinary approach to landscape, using archaeological and textual evidence to further our understanding of the Norman Conquest and the development of Norman lordship.

This chapter explores the nature of rules and regulations regarding the definition of a castle and their relationship with the archaeological record. Within this context, the chapter considers Frodsham Castle, Cheshire. Believed to have been constructed by the first Earl of Chester within an administrative centre of a pre-existing and substantial Anglo-Saxon estate, the location of Frodsham's vanished castle has proved elusive with reference to available historical sources alone.

Drawing on a reinterpretation of the available archaeological, documentary and antiquarian evidence, this chapter explores the relationship between comital law and regulation and the power of place in considering the functions and role of Frodsham Castle.

Broken Rules? The Interchangeable Use of *Castellum* and *Castrum*

The generally accepted and fairly fluid definition of a castle is that it was a fortified residence of a lord (Brown 1969: 13–14, 136 and references therein; Brown, Preswich and Coulson 1980: 13–14). There are variations on this theme, reflecting more recent debate regarding a castle's military deterministic versus, or as well as, symbolic function (Coulson 1979: 74–77; Platt 2007; Creighton and Liddiard 2008). Such debate has resulted in the development of an interdisciplinary research environment contributing a fresh approach to castle studies, which in turn has led to the categorization of the term 'castle' revolving around the two elements of military strategy or social movement in isolation (Coulson 2003: 29–63; Cowan 2014 and pers. comm.). The question posed by Brian Davison back in 1967 therefore remains: 'In archaeological terms, in what way did [the Anglo-Saxon *burh*] differ from the private defended residence of a Norman Lord of equivalent status? This really is the crux of the whole problem: just what do we in fact mean by the term "castle"?' (Davison 1967: 204, quoted in Wheatley 2004: 10).

Ironically, while we continue to problematize this issue of definition in modern scholarship, we have so far failed to uncover any rules and regulations as regards the contemporary understanding of the castle. Indeed, historical and archaeological research points to the fluidity of each of the contemporary terms, all of which we understand to be castles, and this has been discussed at length (Chibnall 1989: 43–56; 2003: 129; Coulson 2003: 29–63; Creighton and Barry 2012: 65; White 2012: 184). This fluidity is evidenced in Domesday Book (*E 31*) of 1086, a period when we might expect castles to have been built for predominantly military purposes. Of the forty-nine castles mentioned in Domesday Book, eight of these were listed as a *castrum* (castle), two as a *domus defensibilis* (fortified house) and the significant remainder (thirty-nine) as a *castellum* (castle). The apparent lack of distinction between the three terms has been noted (Harfield 1991: 377). It is to be wondered whether the Domesday Book scribes had been given any rules as regards the terms they used to cite a castle, when in Lincolnshire, for example, the term *castellum* is employed for Lincoln and *castrum* for Stamford (Harfield 1991: 377) in respect of the two castles listed within the county.

One example related to a site investigated through archaeological excavation, cited by Thomas A. Heslop (2003) to highlight the danger of interpretations of contemporary use and subsequent translations of the same term, is at Castle Acre in Norfolk. This residence was held by the Warenne

Earls. The development of the country house and keep on its mound seems to have spanned almost a century and involved a series of major adaptations over that period (Heslop 2003: 52). Heslop concludes that permutations of interpretations are endless, not only with the term 'castle', as discussed here, but in analysing typological development, where, as with his case study of Weeting Castle in Norfolk, it is impossible to assess the place of a 'castle' design within a larger picture (Heslop 2003: 55). Contemporary rules and regulations of the terms used for a castle thus evade us, and to quote Charles L.H. Coulson (2003: 34): 'To fuss and refine upon language too inexact to be treated as "technical terminology" would lack sense of proportion: but the drift of that original language ... is consistent.'

While heeding such warnings, it is to be wondered to what extent recent archaeological research at Frodsham Castle, Cheshire can add any clarity as to the 'drift' of what was meant by the various terms used by medieval contemporaries and subsequently translated as 'castle'.

Frodsham Castle, Cheshire

Frodsham's vanished castle (Figure 6.1) is believed, without evidence, to have been constructed by the first Earl of Chester (*CHER*: 984/1/0) within an administrative centre of a pre-existing and substantial Anglo-Saxon estate in Cheshire (Higham 1993: 152). The estate was originally held by King Edward the Confessor (1042–1066) (Morgan 1978: 263d; Harris and Thacker 1987: 346). Frodsham is in mid Cheshire and is 14.5 km east of Chester. Chester Castle was the main seat of the quasi-independent Earls of Chester within their separate feudal domain of Cheshire. Law and regulation was clearly significant in late eleventh-century Frodsham: the Earl took a Third Penny of the fines in its Hundred Court, the remaining two-thirds of the fines being payable to the King (Harris and Thacker 1987: 346). This was an unusual arrangement for quasi-independent Cheshire in the latter half of the eleventh century, where the only other example of the Earl taking the Third Penny was at Macclesfield in east Cheshire, within Macclesfield Forest. In addition, the Earls at Frodsham were privileged enough to own a salt house that served their hall (Morgan 1978: 263d). Yet, despite this pre-existing administrative importance of Frodsham, the only castle referred to in Domesday Book (*E 31*) for Cheshire was that of Rhuddlan, where the term *castellum* was applied (Morgan 1978: 269a, 269b; Harfield 1991: 377). Clearly, the absence of evidence of an Anglo-Norman castle at Frodsham is not necessarily the evidence of absence. That said, there is no known contemporary law that states that there had

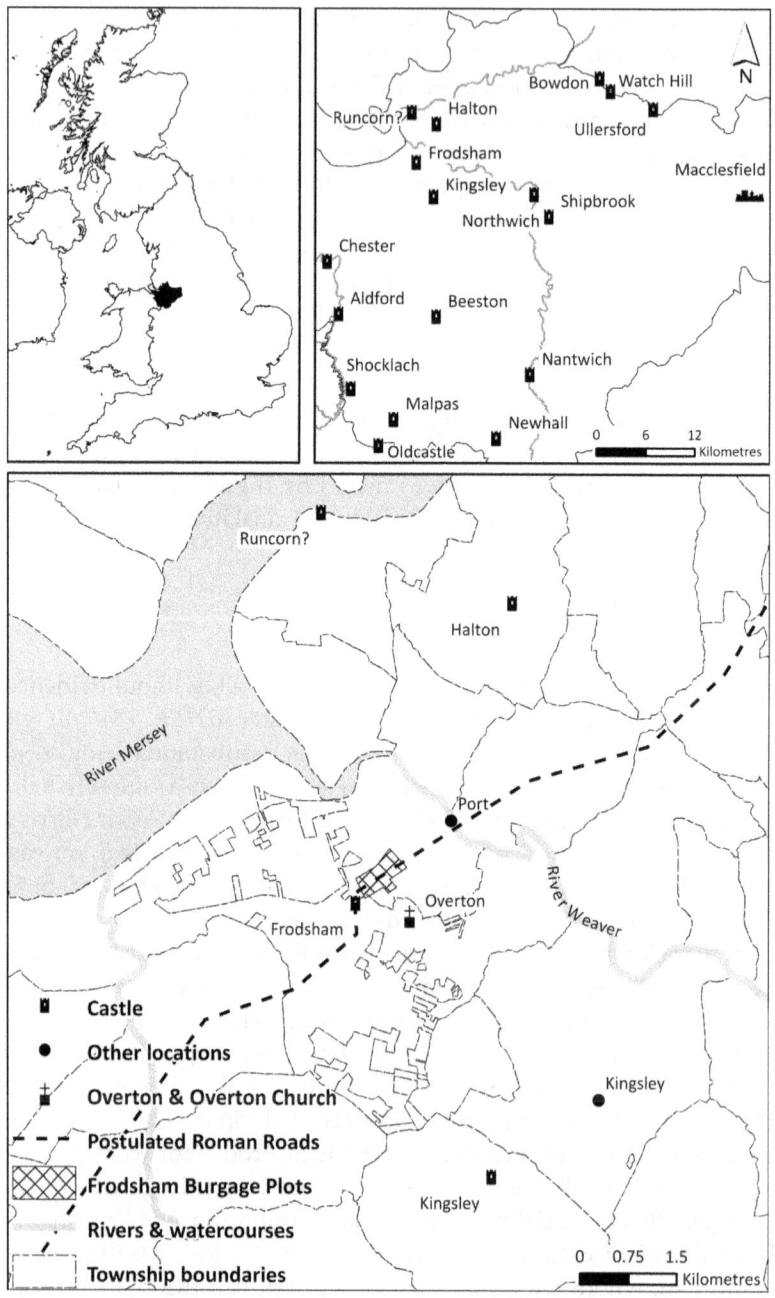

Figure 6.1 Location of Frodsham Castle within (a) England, (b) Cheshire (section) and (c) its immediate landscape (illustration created by Rachel Swallow and drawn by Rob Edwards)

to have been an early medieval castle built at such a settlement of continuing Anglo-Norman significance.

In fact, it is only from the fourteenth century that we first have documentary evidence of a *castellum* at Frodsham (see Chamberlain's accounts references below). In terms of law and legislation at this time, Frodsham clearly continued to enjoy its earlier and unusually privileged jurisdiction within Cheshire, experienced by three courts: the borough court (portmote), the manor court (halmote) and the Forest Eyre of the Justiciar of Chester, which was a special session held just for Frodsham manor (Booth pers. comm.; Stewart-Brown 1910: 190; *SC6 801/12*). Late thirteenth- and fourteenth-century documentary evidence indicates that the sixth Earl of Chester, Ranulf de Blundeville (1170–1232), created a borough at Frodsham, politically separate from its manor, between 1208 and 1215 (Barraclough 1988: 365–66). Some of the 110 burgage plots (Dodd 1987: 14) are still visible in the street plan today. There was also a highly successful medieval port on the River Weaver (*SC6 801/12*; Booth 1981). Significance continued into the thirteenth century, when in 1237, Cheshire passed to the Crown, and Frodsham was valued at 126 pounds, exceeded only in value within the county by the county's chief town at Chester (Hewitt 1929: 112).

The fourteenth-century use of *castellum* at Frodsham is translated as 'castle', although it has been described from the nineteenth century as a 'fortified manor house' (Beamont 1881; 1280 extent: *C145 38(4)*, trans. by P.H.W. Booth in 1978 (unpublished)). The *castellum* may have been categorized in this way because post-1237 documents give us some clues as to elite, seemingly weakly defended, architectural and landscape features at Frodsham. Chamberlain's accounts tell us about the herbage of the park (Stewart-Brown 1910: 81; Hewitt 1929: 106n; Booth and Dodd 1979: 34; *SC6 786/1; SC6 801/12; SC6 801/15*), along with mentions of gardens, barns, stables, a dovecote and garderobes (Beamont 1881: 62; *SC6 801/15; SC12 22/96*). In 1315, the water mill next to the *castellum* had been repaired (*SC6 801/12*; Stewart-Brown 1910: 82, 124) and needed repairing again in 1361/62 (*Account of Master John de Burnham*: 95). Importantly, in 1312/13, the accounts tell us that the great chamber was being amended and repaired (Stewart-Brown 1910: 81). King Alfred's (849–99) paraphrase of *St Augustine's Soliloquies* regarding the descending order of accommodation at any royal palace indicates the early significance of the great chamber in residential buildings of high status, which continued throughout the medieval period: 'some men are in the chamber, some in the hall, some on the threshing-floor, some in prison' (*St Augustine's Soliloquies*: 77 [44.25–46.10]; Blair 2003: 309). In 1347, a not overly defensive Oriel window (a projecting room on an upper floor) was made for the manor of Frodsham, a water mill was (again) being repaired and the kitchens were rebuilt (Stewart-Brown 1910: 271; Hewitt 1929: 92; *SC6 801/12; SC6 801/13; SC12 22/96*). Between 1351 and 1360, a new hall was built (Booth and Dodd 1979: 48) and in 1358, the wooden kitchen buildings were again being repaired, as was the stone tower of the manor (Stewart-Brown 1910: 252; Hewitt 1929: 96, 99–100). A later entry for the same year tells us that two doors were made for the tower and 'divers windows and other defects' of the tower were mended (Stewart-Brown 1910: 271). Was this Ranulf de Blundeville's castle built alongside the borough he had established about 150 years beforehand, now in need of repair? The tower was presumably to some extent fortified. Perhaps the subsequent translation of *castellum* to manor house is correct, but only as far as we understand the contemporary term upon the application of our problematized rules and regulations. Indeed, it could well have been the thirteenth-century lords of wealth and rank – in this case, Earl Ranulf de Blundeville and his royal successors – as well as the prestige and antiquity of Frodsham itself that determined the contemporary castle (*castellum*) status, and not necessarily the quality of the castellated residence itself (Coulson 2003: 40, 61).

This considerable wealth, rank and prestige at Frodsham is evident in the fourteenth century, when it is notable that only 'Frodsham Manor', not a castle of any description, is listed in Edward The Black Prince's (1330–76) register in 1337 (*SC12 22/96*). Earlier, in 1278, Prince Dafydd ap Gruffudd (1238–83) was staying at Frodsham at the invitation of Edward I (1239–1307) (Pryce and Insley 2005: 646–47). Dafydd wrote to the King, describing his stay as hard and tedious. Notably, rather than highlight the difficulties of staying in the Frodsham residence, which was clearly in need of considerable repair at the time (see above), Dafydd bemoaned the fact that he was without the solace – and therefore the privilege – of hunting at Frodsham. Dafydd thus prayed that King Edward would grant him a licence to hunt in the common of the vill. This was granted (Pryce and Insley 2005: 648). It is possible, then, that Frodsham's manor tower with the later insertion of an oriel window (1347) served as the solar or private living and sleeping quarters of the lord, with a view across the fourteenth-century park landscape. Indeed, about three hundred years earlier, the Domesday Book records two enclosures (*haiae*) at Frodsham (Morgan 1978: 263d), presumably for keeping deer (Liddiard 2003: 4), although there is no specific qualification in the Domesday entry. In Cheshire, the concentrations of *haiae*, or hays, lay predominantly in the well-wooded and sparsely populated east and southeast of the county on the upland areas of the Forests of Mara and Mondrem, which became known as Delamere Forest. In addition, the privileged Forest Eyre of the Justiciar at Frodsham (see above), situated to the immediate west of Delamere, indicates a significant power of place for both the Mercian and Norman earls' hunting.

Kingsley, situated about 3 km to the southeast of Frodsham, was also within Eddisbury Hundred. At Domesday it was listed as having four *haiae*, specifically for catching roe deer, and a hawk's eyrie (Morgan 1978: 267d). The small motte at Kingsley, known as Castle Cob Motte (Hogg and King 1963; King 1983: 68; *CHER*: 898) (Figure 6.1), could have been part of Frodsham's wider hunting landscape. Kingsley is first mentioned in Domesday Book (Ormerod 1819a, 87–97; 1819b: 896; Morgan 1978: 267d), and its place name significantly means 'the King's wood or clearing' (Dodgson 1981: 239; Higham 1993: 152). We know that by 1086, the Norman Earl Hugh had created a considerable tract of his Forest (one league square) lying within the Forests of Mara and Mondrem. Because Dunning held Kingsley as a free man prior to holding it from Earl Hugh at 1086, the implication is that there was continuity across the Anglo-Norman period as regards the management of the Forest for hunting, as well as with the Earls' steward for their court at Frodsham (Ormerod 1819a: 46; Higham 1993: 153). In Bourne's (2012) discussion of 'Kingston' place names in Anglo-Saxon England, it is notable that there is a dearth of the 'King' prefixes in northwest English place names. The presence of 'Kingsley' so close to the previous royal vill of Frodsham, and within the township of Delamere Forest called Kingswood, therefore reinforces the suggestion that some aspect of royal activity took place, or royal power was enforced (Bourne 2012: 280), connected with the *caput* at Frodsham and its mother church at Overton on Overton Hill to the immediate south (Morgan 1978: 263d; Higham 1993: 152–53). It is possible that 'Kingsley' represented the last 'toe-hold of land' that the King held on to when the rest of the Anglo-Saxon estate had been granted away (Bassett 2007; Bourne 2012: 280). Retaining elite and valuable forest for hunting from Frodsham would be a reasonable conclusion to make here. Frodsham, then, was a significant settlement within an elite hunting landscape, where the Mercian hall mentioned in the Domesday Book could well have been part of an Anglo-Saxon royal palace complex held first by King Edward. These early lordly architectural and landscape components could have remained unaltered until the early thirteenth century, when Frodsham developed as a borough under Earl Ranulf the Blundeville.

We do have tantalizing clues as to Frodsham Castle's existence following its first mention in the mid fourteenth century, when it was at that stage in ruins, as we have seen. By 1654, it had been burnt down (*CHER*: 984/1/0; MacKenzie 1896: 172; Shaw and Clark 2003: 5). The Buck Brothers' engraving of Frodsham Castle in 1727 (Buck and Buck 1774: 3) shows the castle ruins upon a seemingly elevated site. The ruins, of a long hall with rounded windows, are set against two water mills within the castle landscape, which were possibly those pulled down at the north of Castle Park when the railway was constructed (*CHER*: 984/1/4; *CRO EDT 162/1* and *2*; Burdett 1777; Ormerod 1819a: 46; 1819b: 203), as well as Halton Castle in the hinterland, 2 km to the northwest. The settlement of Frodsham is shown on the wrong side of the River Mersey, and it would be impossible to view the brothers' entire landscape context for the castle from any one position within Frodsham. Indeed, evidence from excavation, and comparison with other illustrations of Halton Castle (e.g. Buck (Buck and Buck 1774: 10)), suggest that the Buck Brothers used similar artistic licence with regard to the position of Halton Castle ruins, the anomalies of which are detailed in the 1987 archaeological excavation report (McNeil 1987: 59). It is thus impossible to state with confidence today where the elevated site of the Frodsham Castle ruins might have been. Frodsham's present-day Castle Park is yet another clue as to the previous existence and location of Frodsham Castle. However, these later, and obviously post-medieval, clues have not been enough to locate the medieval castle site with any confidence and precision.

The Case for Frodsham Castle

While we do not have any evidence that Frodsham was once the site of an Anglo-Norman castle, cartographic research of the immediate landscape context of Frodsham Castle points to what were once elite landscape features in Frodsham Castle Park. For instance, the Buck Brothers' 1727 engraving of Frodsham Castle (Buck and Buck 1774: 19), pictorial evidence on Burdett's map of 1777, documentary sources (*SC6 801/4*; *SC6 801/12*) and field names on the Tithe Map and Award of about 1846 (*CRO EDT 162/1* and *2*) all confirm the existence of water mills and a complex leat and damming system around and within the current boundaries of Frodsham Castle Park (Figure 6.2). Further, a previously unrecorded, curved bank and ditch feature to the west of the park, which appears to be an extension of Dig Lane to its north, is clearly visible on the 1836 Tithe Map. The evidence of cartographic research, LiDAR – optical remote sensing technology (*DTM Frodsham*) – and ground survey in 2013 all point to what might well have been the early castle site: a motte and bailey. This evidence could indicate the ditches of the castle's bailey to the west, running north of Dig Lane, and seeming to curve around to the earthwork remains of the former mill site and fishpond (Figure 6.3). The evidence could also point to the existence of the castle's motte, much later worn down and employed as a viewing mound within Edward Kemp's

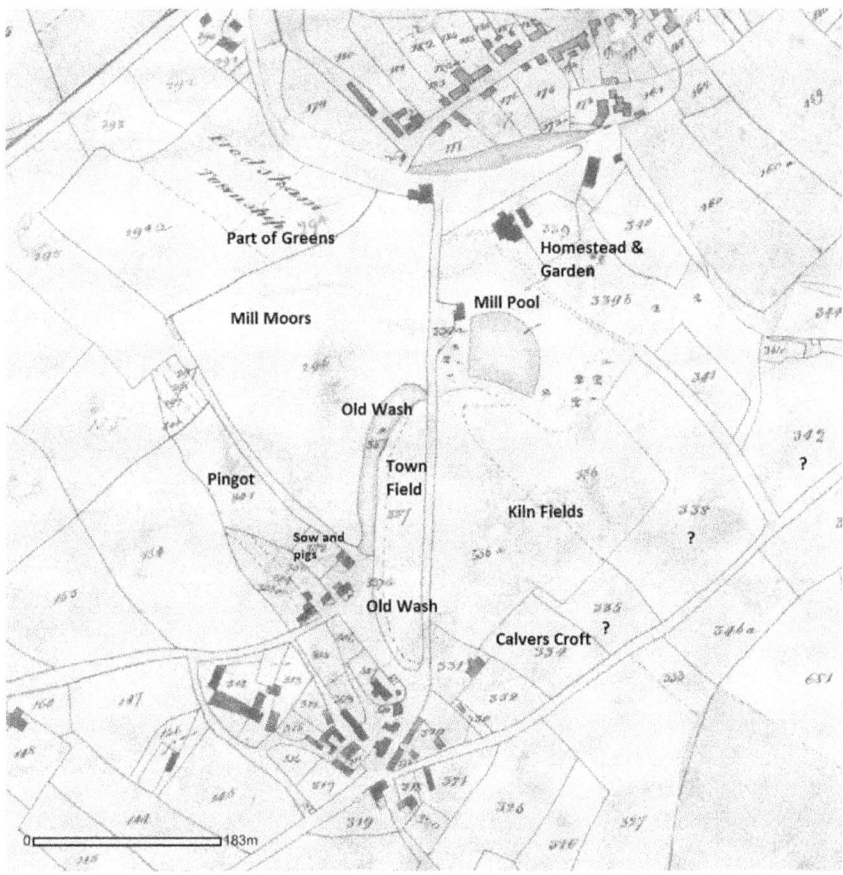

Figure 6.2 Tithe Map with field name annotations (after *CRO EDT 162/1* and *2*)

garden landscape design for Castle Park in the mid nineteenth century (Kemp 1858: Figure 185) (Figure 6.4). Of all the sites in Frodsham, this mound takes the most defensible position, overlooking with clear views Wales and the Dee estuary to the west, and both the town and the port of Frodsham on the River Weaver to the north and east. Indeed, this could be the elevated site upon which the Buck Brothers depicted the remains of Frodsham Castle in 1727.

However, magnetometry geophysics surveys undertaken in Castle Park in March 2013 have not supported this theory (Figure 6.5). Rather than evidence for a castle bailey, the banks, ditches and palisades to the west and north of Castle Park, and referred to in primary source documents from about 1312 (*SC6 784/8*; *SC6 787/5*; *SC6 801/12*; *SC6 801/15*), could have been moated enclosure ditches for the elite medieval landscape of Frodsham's

Figure 6.3 Earthwork remains running north of Dig Lane, to the west of Castle Park, Frodsham (photograph by Rachel Swallow)

Figure 6.4 Mound in Castle Park, view to south (photograph by Rachel Swallow)

What Law Says That There Has to Be a Castle?

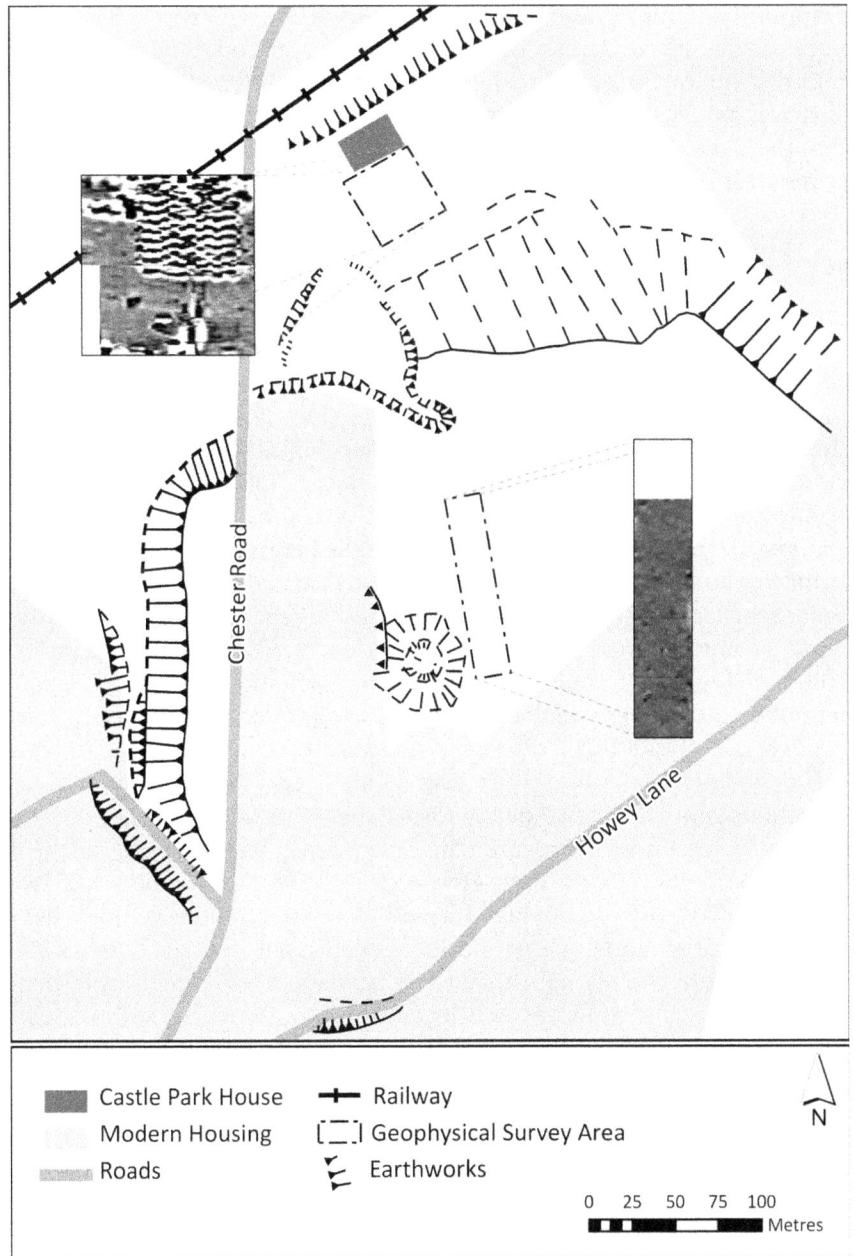

Figure 6.5 Ground and magnetometry geophysics surveys at Castle Park, Frodsham (illustration created by Rachel Swallow, drawn by Robert Edwards)

manorial complex adjacent to its borough town. Indeed, there is late Saxon period evidence at Goltho, Lincolnshire for a hall and at least one other building sited within a ditched enclosure. Just as at Frodsham, this enclosure was associated with a water mill (Hamerow 2012: 117). This suggests that the moated enclosure ditches at Frodsham could have pre-dated the borough and that they can neither confirm nor deny the presence of a later Anglo-Norman castle. It is also important to note that the defining line for a 'castle' for the Dukes of Normandy was the nature of the enclosing barrier and its accompanying ditch (White 2012: 185), thus suggesting that the ditched enclosure could date from the second half of the eleventh century. Whatever their original date of construction, the ditches at Frodsham were probably constructed, in whole or in part, to prevent the frequently cited inundations of the River Mersey at this time (Hewitt 1929: 32). As regards the mound in Castle Park, there are archaeological considerations to be taken into account: while a stone build upon such an insubstantial mound would not have been structurally sound, and thus highly unlikely, we cannot rule out the existence of a timber castle here; however, any existing scant traces cannot be found, unless explored via intensive and extensive open-area archaeological excavation. Mottes were frequently adapted into garden features, when the locus of the castle shifted away from the motte. Alternatively, the mound could be a later garden mound only; a flagpole mount or hill, as per twentieth-century cartographic indication (*National Heritage List*: no.1001622); the site of a former windmill, possibly the one mentioned in fourteenth-century documents (Dodd 1969: 332), or, indeed, something much older, but in any case, not a motte after all.

Despite secondary source references suggesting that the old castle must have been below Castle Park House (*CHER*: 984/1/0; Ormerod 1819a: 46; 1819b: 203), this low-lying site with a relatively poor outlook over its surrounding landscape would have been much weaker defensively. Antiquarian historians tell us that coffins, cannon balls and an ancient lamp were located at foundation level during some works at the house, but provide no further details to assist in locating the castle here (Beamont 1881: 206; Castlering Archaeology 2005/*CHER* R2564). Frodsham Castle Park landscape has undergone a series of manipulations over the centuries, which must be taken into consideration with any interpretation. For the same reason, the assertion that masonry blocks used in the construction of the current house's basement were those belonging to the castle, and that their use for the present construction must indicate that the original castle must have been located here, cannot be either proved or disproved (Stewart Ainsworth pers. comm.). In addition, the magnetometry geophysics survey to the immediate fore of Castle Park House produced no evidence of any pre-eighteenth-century below-ground archaeology; the foundations of the building appear to be those of its previous projection to the south, as evidenced on the Tithe Map (*CRO EDT 162/2*). Nor are there any indications in the current landscape at Overton to indicate the siting of an early castle there. However, it is recognized that it is unlikely that geophysics surveys would pick up any prior existence of wooden buildings, and evidence of early medieval architecture and material culture in Cheshire is extremely rare in any case (Higham 1986: 242–43; Newman 2006: 91).

Thus, when considering the position of Frodsham's Anglo-Saxon hall and its immediate landscape, it could be significant that the earthen bank and ditch at Goltho, Lincolnshire has been dated to the mid ninth century, and that at Sulgrave in Northamptonshire, a stone hall with earthen ramparts might also pre-date the Conquest (Davison 1977; Beresford 1987; White 2012: 187–88). As noted above, Dig Lane in Frodsham runs to the immediate west of the newly identified bank and ditch bounding Castle Park. Possibly significant in terms of its dating, 'dig' derives from *dīc*, being Old English for 'a ditch' (Dodgson 1981: 159). Indeed, excavations at a number of castle sites indicate that where there is evidence of continuity of power of place straddling the Anglo-Norman period, the building of a motte-and-bailey castle may not have taken place until up to a century after the Conquest. Recent re-interpretation of excavations undertaken at Goltho, for instance, suggests that in the late Saxon period, there was a timber hall within a defensive earthwork enclosure, which only culminated in a castle site during the 'Anarchy' period of c. 1140–50, rather than at the end of the eleventh century, as had been thought previously (Everson 1988; Everson 1990; Creighton 2002: 21). In addition, the physical site chosen for the castle at Goltho had no observable strategic significance of any description, but did occupy the most visible topographical position in the immediate vicinity, adjacent to the medieval village (Bassett 1985; Beresford 1987; Hodges 1988; Stocker 1989). Parallels could be drawn with Frodsham in this respect, as well as the consideration that at Goltho, the castle represented the final stage within a longer sequence of aristocratic occupation. Further, and as Creighton points out, 'rather than reflecting any military considerations, the location of this particular rural castle [Goltho] was determined by a practical need for continuity in the estate centre' (Creighton 2002: 23). Therefore, in the absence of historical and recently carried-out archaeological evidence for an early castle at Frodsham, it is suggested that the pre-Conquest buildings at Frodsham continued in use during the Anglo-Norman period and that the *castellum* – whatever that term meant to its contemporaries – came later. This was possibly during the early thirteenth century, when the borough was established by Earl Ranulf de Blundeville. A similar case has been made for lordly dwellings on the Anglo-Scottish border, where there is increasing evidence of halls, not castles, being founded at surviving baronial or manorial *capita* during the thirteenth century, these possibly directly succeeding the late Saxon timber halls (*aulae*) in some lordships (Dixon 1992: 85–87).

As regards the documentary mention of a stone tower at Frodsham (see above), extant medieval towers in Cheshire are generally believed to date to the later thirteenth and fourteenth centuries, such as at Delves Hall, or Doddington Castle, Newhall Tower and Brimstage Hall (*CHER*: 235/1/2; *CHER*: 2077; Ormerod 1819a: 180, 240–2; 1819b: 265–9, 303; MacKenzie 1896: 166–67; Emery 2000: 477; and, contra, Fradley 2009); tower construction did not necessarily correspond to the tower of an early motte-and-bailey castle. The dilapidated stone tower mentioned in mid fourteenth-century documents at Frodsham could well have been built by Ranulf de Blundeville in the early thirteenth century (see above). Contextual evidence to support this theory is the fact that a freestanding rectangular tower was built, probably by Ranulf, at Whittington Castle, Shropshire in the 1220s (White 2012: 198), at about the time (or shortly after) he created the borough of Frodsham. Ranulf then started a huge building programme across a considerable part of England. This included the building of three castles, one of which was Beeston Castle in Cheshire. The programme, however, also included Cheylesmore manor house and park within Coventry, the south end of which comprised a large stone hall and tower (*MCT 2194*; Coss 1986: 30, 34; Rylatt, Soden and Dickinson 1992: 10; Soden 2009: 53), as well as houses in Sutton Bonnington, Nottinghamshire (Hardy 1844: 561; Soden 2009: 94). Whichever period, or periods, during which the tower at Frodsham was in existence, and to whatever type of defensive or symbolic (or both) complex it belonged throughout its duration, it would have had an 'unmistakable presence – an elevated and iconic architectural features that forcefully stamped the seigneurial mark on the locality' (Creighton 2012: 61).

Discussion

Multidisciplinary, including archaeological, research of both the immediate and wider landscape context of Frodsham in little-examined Cheshire is essential in order to locate the foundations of what has been labelled a castle. Such an approach not only points to the possible date and location of the Anglo-Norman Earls' residence at Frodsham, but also widens the debate concerning the pre-existing symbolic significance of the landscape within which it was sited. With its domestic outbuildings, stables, park and gardens, should we be looking for more of a palatial, manorial residence of the Norman Earl rather than for a castle *per se*? And if so, can we carry this assumption back to the Domesday period of 1086, if not before? For instance, did the incoming Norman Earl of Chester retain the holding as a settlement controlled by a manorial palace or hall within its moated, ditched and fenced enclosure, and adjacent to its mill, sitting beneath its mother church in a defined, elite landscape? Or, as William the Conqueror is reputed to have done at Chester in about 1070 (Cullen and Hordern 1986: 12; Grimsditch, Nevell and Nevell 2012: 100), did the Norman Earl construct a castle at Frodsham immediately post-Conquest, as his significant new seat of power there? Interestingly, the first documentary reference we have to Chester Castle in Cheshire (for which both *castrum* and *castellum* are used) is for 1141 (Dodgson 1981: 42), during the 'Anarchy' period. Having here considered Frodsham's landscape context for the first time, it is suggested that the incoming Norman Earl did not build a formal castle at Frodsham in Cheshire, but retained the use of the Anglo-Saxon hall as the focus of its hundredal domain.

However, we are not party to any contemporary ruling as regards the perceived meaning of the term *castellum* in either a national or a local context. Nor do we know whether or not the appearance and defensibility of the *castellum* were relevant at all in relation to the contemporary use of this term. It could well be that we mistakenly interpret the legal status of the *castellum* in a very narrow sense today by amalgamating complex variations in the status and use of sites over time. This has a direct impact on how we integrate legal documents that define fixed status and identities, with the fluidity of buildings that were closely tied to the varied fortunes of elite families. For instance, building programmes arose as the result of family fortunes, but also from anxieties over inheritance and competition. Conversely, a decline in a family's fortunes or transferred interests to other geographical areas resulted in site decline. Therefore, a fixed status does not apply to inhabited, elite residences and their many components, where a complex interleaving of political, socioeconomic fortunes, aspirations and the biographies of buildings existed. If this is the case, our restricted viewpoint of a fixed status cannot provide us with any clue as to what we might expect to discover archaeologically when looking for a *castellum*. Indeed, was Frodsham *Castle* created purely in the air of later interpretation rather than physically on the ground during the early medieval period?

Conclusion

Despite inconclusive results, the endeavour of trying to match a complex site biography of changing locations and uses to a specific legal status has wider implications. Archaeological and historical context, both at

Frodsham and within and without the county of Cheshire, demonstrates that there were unlikely to have been any fixed rules regarding the building and tight definition of either what we now call 'castles' in the Norman period or regal and comital halls throughout the Anglo-Norman period. This case study at Frodsham appears to represent a national conundrum, and lack of any further clarity, regarding any rules and regulations surrounding contemporary and subsequent nomenclature of the 'castle'. It highlights the fact that the legal terminology of medieval documents might not relate to the archaeology and architecture that survives, and that we should not let the former govern our interpretations and expectations of the latter. A multidisciplinary, critical approach remains essential, as argued by O'Keefe (2013: 261), who has recently expressed frustration at archaeologists who metaphorically 'black-box' seemingly 'new' castles without the 'requisite scrutiny'. Likewise, as Creighton and Barry point out, 'a key challenge for the future is, of course, to address the fact that our understanding of the medieval rural scene has been compartmentalized into these different categories, effectively retarding any ambition we might have towards the appreciation of the countryside *in toto*' (Creighton and Barry 2012: 65). Clearly, then, some sort of an understanding of the medieval landscape, and what *was* meant by those writing our medieval primary sources, would be beneficial for us to understand our medieval archaeology – and vice versa – whether that archaeology is above or below ground, or, perhaps, confined forever to the historical record.

Acknowledgements

As regards assistance with the field and geophysical surveys carried out at Frodsham in 2013, my gratitude is extended to my doctoral research advisor, Visiting Professor Stewart Ainsworth; postgraduate Jo Kirton; graduate Dean Paton and undergraduates Dave Laverty, Tom Sigsworth and Nathaniel Welsby – all of the University of Chester. I am grateful to the Frodsham and District History Society, and in particular to Kath Gee and Kath Hewitt, for their kind assistance and time taken in allowing me access to the society's archive. I am indebted to the generosity of Dr Paul Booth for sharing primary sources transcribed by him, as well as his expert knowledge of Frodsham. I wish to thank Professor Howard Williams of the University of Chester, for his supervisory support throughout my doctoral research (2015 (unpublished): 'Cheshire Castles in Context'), and for commenting on drafts of this chapter. Finally, I am grateful for the valuable comments and guidelines provided by my two anonymous reviewers. Any errors and omissions are entirely my own.

Rachel Swallow, a visiting lecturer and Visiting Research Fellow in the Department of History and Archaeology at the University of Chester, United Kingdom, was recently awarded a Ph.D. for her thesis entitled 'Cheshire Castles in Context' (2015). While researching historical landscapes associated with Cheshire's Anglo-Norman castles, she has published a number of articles, including a landscape study of Aldford Castle in *Cheshire History Journal* (2012), for which she was awarded a runners-up prize by the British Association for Local History, and two case studies published in *The Archaeological Journal* (2014, 2016). Her interests continue in the multidisciplinary and multiperiod research of the historical landscape.

References

Primary Sources

Account of Master John de Burnham, John de Burnham, ed. P.H.W. Booth and A.D. Carr. 1991. *Account of Master John de Burnham the Younger, Chamberlain of Chester of the Revenues of the Counties of Chester and Flint, Michaelmas 1361 to Michaelmas 1362*, Record Society of Lancashire and Cheshire Vol. 125. Stroud, Gloucestershire: Sutton Publishing.

C145 38(4). The National Archives, Kew, UK (hereafter NatArch) (*Chancery, Misc. Inquisitions*: Extent of the manor of Frodsham, with appurtenances, 1280).

CHER. Cheshire West and Chester Council, Chester, UK (*Cheshire Historical Environment Record*; Numbers 984/1/0 and 984/1/4: Frodsham Castle; 898: Kingsley; 235/1/2: Delves Hall/Doddington Tower; 2077: Newhall Tower).

CRO EDT 162/1. Cheshire Record Office, Chester, UK (*Tithe Award*, Frodsham Township, 1844).

CRO EDT 162/2 (apportionment CRO EDT 162/1). Cheshire Record Office, Chester, UK (*Tithe Award*, Frodsham Township, 1844).

DTM Frodsham. Cheshire West and Chester City Council, Chester, UK (Digital Terrain Model (DTM) of Castle Park, Frodsham, 2012).

E 31. NatArch (*Domesday Book*; manuscript record of the 'Great Survey' of most parts of England and parts of Wales, compiled by order of King William the Conqueror, 1086).

MCT 2194. Coventry City Council, Coventry, UK (*Coventry Heritage Environment Record*; medieval Manor House of Cheylesmore Manor).

National Heritage List for England, English Heritage, Swindon, UK (no. 1001622: list entry for Castle Park, Frodsham). Retrieved 10 November 2013, from English Heritage: http://list.english-heritage.org.uk/resultsingle.aspx?uid=1001622

SC12 22/96. NatArch (Survey Demesnes of Cheshire, 1337).

SC6 784/8. NatArch (Cheshire Minsters, 1352–53).

SC6 786/1. NatArch (Cheshire Minsters, 1362–63).

SC6 787/5. NatArch (Cheshire Minsters, 1372–73).

SC6 801/. NatArch (account of the Manor of Frodsham, 10 June to 30 September 1315).

St. Augustine's Soliloquies, King Alfred, ed. T.A. Carnicelli. 1969. *King Alfred's Version of St. Augustine's Soliloquies*. Cambridge, MA: Harvard University Press.

Secondary Literature

Barraclough, G. 1988. *The Charters of the Anglo-Norman Earls of Chester, c. 1071–1237*. Gloucester: Alan Sutton Publishing.

Bassett, S.R. 1985. *Saffron Walden: Excavations and Research 1972–80*, Council for British Archaeology Research Report 45. London: Council for British Archaeology.

Bassett, S. 2007. 'Boundaries of Knowledge: Mapping the Land Units of Late Anglo-Saxon and Norman England', in W. Davies, G. Hassall and A. Reynolds (eds), *People and Space in the Middle Ages, 300–1300*. Turhout: Brepols, pp. 115–40.

Beamont, W. 1881. *An Account of the Ancient Town of Frodsham*. Warrington: Pearse.

Beresford, G. 1987. *Goltho: The Development of an Early Medieval Manor c. 850–1150*. London: HMSO.

Blair, J. 2003. 'Hall and Chamber: English Domestic Planning 1000–1250', in R. Liddiard (ed.), *Anglo-Norman Castles*. Woodbridge: Boydell, pp. 307–28.

Booth, P.H.W. 1981. *The Financial Administration of the Lordship and County of Chester 1272–1377*. Manchester: Chetham Society.

Booth, P.H.W., and J.P. Dodd. 1979. 'The Manor and Fields of Frodsham, 1315-74', *Medieval Cheshire: Transactions of the History Society of Lancashire and Cheshire* 128: 27–57.

Bourne, J. 2012. 'Kingston – The Place-Name and its Context', in R. Jones and S. Semple (eds), *Sense of Place in Anglo-Saxon England*. Donington: Shaun Tyas, pp. 260–83.

Brown, R.A. 1969. 'An Historian's Approach to the Origins of the Castle in England', *Archaeological Journal* 126: 131–48.

Brown, R.A., M. Prestwich and C. Coulson. 1980. *Castles: A History and Guide*. Poole: Blandford Press.

Buck, S., and N. Buck. 1774. *Buck's Antiquities*, London: Robert Sayer.

Burdett, P.P. 1777. *A Survey of the County Palatine of Chester*, the Historic Society of Lancashire and Cheshire Occasional Series Vol. 1. London: Lund Humphries.

Castlering Archaeology. 2005. *Castle Park House, Castle Park, Frodsham, Cheshire. SJ5140 7750*. Archaeological Watching Brief. Pontesbury: Castlering Archaeology (*CHER* R2564).

Chibnall, M. 1989. 'Orderic Vitalis on Castles', in C. Harper-Bill, C. Holdsworth and J. Nelson (eds), *Studies in Medieval History Presented to R. Allen Brown*. Woodbridge: Boydell, pp. 43–56.

———. 2003, 'Orderic Vitalis on Castles', in R. Liddiard (ed.), *Anglo-Norman Castles*. Woodbridge: Boydell, pp. 119–32.

Coss, P.R. 1986. *The Early Records of Medieval Coventry*. London: British Academy.
Coulson, C.L.H. 1979. 'Structural Symbolism in Medieval Castle Architecture', *Journal of the British Archaeological Association* 132: 73–90.
———. 2003. *Castles in Medieval Society: Fortresses in England, France, and Ireland in the Central Middle Ages*. Sheffield: Equinox.
Cowan, K. 2014. 'Defining the Castle through Twelfth-Century Chronicle Perceptions in the Anglo-Norman Regnum'. Unpublished DPhil thesis, University of Oxford.
Creighton, O. 2002. *Castles and Landscapes: Power, Community and Fortification in Medieval England*. Sheffield: Equinox.
———. 2012. *Early European Castles: Aristocracy and Authority. AD 800–1200*. London: Bloomsbury.
Creighton, O., and T. Barry 2012, 'Seigneurial and Elite Sites in the Medieval Landscape', in N. Christie and P. Stamper (eds), *Medieval Rural Settlement Britain and Ireland, AD 800–1600*. Oxford: Windgather Press, pp. 26–30.
Creighton, O., and R. Liddiard. 2008. 'Fighting Yesterday's Battle: Beyond War or Status in Castle Studies', *Medieval Archaeology* 48: 161–69.
Cullen, P.W., and R. Hordern. 1986. *The Castles of Cheshire*. Chorley: Nelson Brothers.
Davison, B.K. 1967. 'The Origins of the Castle in England: The Institute's Research Project', *Archaeological Journal* 124: 202–11.
———. 1977. 'Excavations at Sulgrave, Northants 1960 – 76: An Interim Report', *Archaeological Journal* 134: 105–14.
Dixon, P. 1992. 'From Hall to Tower: The Change in Seigneurial Houses on the Anglo-Scottish Border after c.1250', *Thirteenth Century England* 4: 85–107.
Dodd, J.P. 1969. 'A Survey of Frodsham', *Cheshire Round* 10: 329–36.
———. 1987. *A History of Frodsham and Helsby*. Frodsham: self-published.
Dodgson, J.M. 1981. *The Place-Names of Cheshire: English Place-Name Society, Vol. XLVIII, Part Five I:i, The Place-Names of the City of Chester. The Elements of Cheshire Place-Names*. Cambridge: Cambridge University Press.
Emery, A. 2000. *Greater Medieval Houses of England and Wales, 1300–1500: Volume 2, East Anglia, Central England and Wales*. Cambridge: Cambridge University Press.
Everson, P. 1988. 'What's in a Name? "Goltho", Goltho and Bullington', *Archaeological Journal* 14: 627–29.
———. 1990. 'The Problem of Goltho', *Medieval Settlement Research Group Report* 5: 9–14.
Fradley, M. 2009. 'Field Investigation at Newhall Tower, Newhall, Cheshire', *Medieval Settlement Research* 24: 59–67.
Grimsditch, B., M. Nevell and R. Nevell 2012. *Buckton Castle and the Castles of North West England*. Manchester: University of Salford.
Hamerow, H. 2012. *Rural Settlements and Society in Anglo-Saxon England*. Oxford: Oxford University Press.
Hardy, T.D. 1844. *Rotuli Litterarum Clausarum in Turri Londiniensi: Vol II, 1227–30*. London: Records Commission.
Harfield, C.G. 1991. 'A Hand-List of Castles Recorded in the Domesday Book', *English Historical Review* 106: 371–92.

Harris, B.E., and A.T. Thacker. 1987. *A History of the County of Chester*. Oxford: Oxford University Press.

Heslop, T.A. 2003. 'Weeting "Castle", a Twelfth-Century Hall House in Norfolk', *Architectural History Journal of the Society of Architectural Historians of Great Britain* 46: 42–57.

Hewitt, H.J. 1929. *Medieval Cheshire: An Economic and Social History of Cheshire in the Reigns of the Three Edwards*. Manchester: Chetham Society.

Higham, N.J. 1986. *The Northern Counties to AD 1000*. London: Longman.

——. 1993. *The Origins of Cheshire*. Manchester: Manchester University Press.

Hodges, R. 1988. 'Origins of the English Castle', *Nature* 333: 112–13.

Hogg, A.H.A., and D.J.C. King. 1963. 'Early Castles in Wales and the Marches: a Preliminary List', *Archaelogia Cambrensis* 112: 77–124.

Kemp, E. 1858. *How to Lay out a Garden: A General Guide in Choosing, Forming, or Improving an Estate*. London: Bradbury and Evans.

King, D.J.C. 1983. *Castellarium Anglicanum: An Index and Bibliography of the Castles in England, Wales, and the Islands*, I. Millwood, NY: Kraus International.

Liddiard, R. 2003. 'The Deer Parks of Domesday Book', *Landscapes* 4: 4–23.

MacKenzie, J.D. 1896. *Castles of England; Their Story and Structure*. Vol. 2. New York: Macmillan.

McNeil, R. 1987. *Halton Castle. A Visual Treasure*, North West Archaeology Trust Report 1. Liverpool: North West Archaeological Trust.

Morgan, P. 1978. *Domesday Book, Cheshire*, Chichester: Phillimore.

Newman, R. 2006. 'The Early Medieval Period Resource Assessment', in M. Brennand (ed.), *The Archaeology of North West England: An Archaeological Research Framework for the North West Region, Vol. I. Resource Assessment*. Liverpool: CBA North West, pp. 115–44.

O'Keefe, T. 2013. 'Hall, "Hall-Houses" and Tower-Houses in Medieval Ireland: Disentangling the Needlessly Entangled', *Castles Studies Group Journal* 27: 252–62.

Ormerod, G. 1819a. *The History of the County Palatine and City of Chester, Vol. II*. London: Lackington, Hughes, Harding Mayor and Jones.

——. 1819b. *The History of the County Palatine and City of Chester, Vol. III*. London: Lackington, Hughes, Harding Mayor and Jones.

Platt, C. 2007. 'Revisionism in Castle Studies: A Caution', *Medieval Archaeology* 51: 83–102.

Pryce, H., and C. Insley. 2005. *The Acts of the Welsh Rulers, 1120–1283*. Cardiff: University of Wales Press.

Rylatt, M., Soden, I., and J. Dickinson. 1992. *Cheylesmore Manor Excavations 1992*. Coventry: Coventry Museums Archaeology Unit.

Shaw, M., and J. Clark. 2003. *Cheshire Historic Towns Survey: Frodsham Archaeological Assessment*. Chester: English Heritage and Cheshire County Council.

Soden, I. 2009. *Ranulf de Blundeville: The First English Hero*. Stroud: Amberley.

Stewart-Brown, R. 1910. *Accounts of the Chamberlains and Other Officers of the County of Cheste*, Record Society of Lancashire and Cheshire 59. Liverpool: Record Society of Lancashire and Cheshire.

Stocker, D. 1989. 'Review of G. Beresford, "Goltho": The Development of an Early Medieval Manor c. 850–1150', *Archaeological Journal* 14: 627–29.

Swallow, R.E. 2015. 'Cheshire Castles in Context'. Unpublished Ph.D. thesis: University of Chester.

Wheatley, A. 2004. *The Idea of the Castle in Medieval England*. York: York Medieval Press.

White, G.W. 2012. *The Medieval English Landscape 1000–1540*. London: Bloomsbury.

Chapter 7

Shakespearian Space-Men
Spatial Rules in London's Early Playhouses

Ruth Nugent

Introduction

With their distinctive circular-polygonal shape, London's early playhouses were a short-lived architectural phenomenon. The two earliest short-lived playhouses were probably rectangular (Bowsher 2011: 456–57) and likely developed out of pre-existing buildings; the Red Lion (1567) was in a Middlesex farmhouse courtyard, and the Newington Butts (c. 1575) playhouse was of unknown form converted from a 'messauge' of tenements or domestic dwellings (Wickham, Berry and Ingram 2000: 290, 320). The major circular/polygonal purpose-built playhouses were constructed between 1576 and 1614, excepting the Fortune which was originally rectangular. These were: the Theatre (1576), the Curtain (1577), the Swan (c. 1596), the Rose (1587), the Globe (1599), the Fortune (1600) (rectangular) and the Hope (1613–14) (Wickham, Berry and Ingram 2000; Mackinder et al. 2013). Those not already defunct were closed by Parliament in 1642, meaning the first 'playhouse period' only spanned around seventy-five years. As vernacular buildings designed by the theatrical community, playhouses were unique, purpose-built venues for theatre's new era of commercialism. Yet despite their unusual design, playhouses also present a concise architectural expression of evolving spatial rules in the late sixteenth and early seventeenth centuries.

Late Elizabethan and early Jacobean architectural culture, of which playhouses were a product, were designed to underpin a complex network of state-enforced social identity linked to spatial zones. As will be shown, where a body appeared within a defined spatial plane, particularly vertical planes, was a vital demarcation of social identity. It was within an architectural setting that body-identities were most fully expressed and received. This system of spatial identity was based on an individual's inherited social rank and the office they held. In its simplest, most derivative form, it was the feudalistic hierarchy of royalty, nobility and workers played out in a top-down ordering of space (Hazard 2000). Superficially, playhouses repeated these long-standing rules in what has been termed their 'vertical sociology' (Gurr and Ichikawa 2000: 8).

This chapter, however, approaches playhouse spatiality beyond 'vertical sociology'. It situates playhouses within a broader reordering of space of the late sixteenth and early seventeenth centuries (Girouard 2009). Playhouses are compared to contemporary churches and elite residences, all of which had to accommodate highly stratified social groups of audiences, congregations, and the family-servant spectrum in large houses. Many of the spatial changes discussed were initiated by the *nouveau riche* of a burgeoning Elizabethan middle class (Howard 1994) who were undermining the privilege of inherited status with their purchasing power. This 'middle class' was not homogeneous, but comprised a range of (newer) classes: the artisans, merchant citizens, and the literati in education and clergy (Gurr 2004: 58). In the developing capitalist society of Elizabethan and Jacobean England, exclusive spaces, previously allocated by bloodline, were now available for a price (Howard 1994: 75). Thus, it is suggested that playhouses not only contributed to a reordering of spatial rules, but were also a microcosm of destabilized social categories.

Past Approaches

From an archaeological perspective, playhouses are ripe for exploration. Despite the award-winning monograph on the Rose (1989) and Globe (1988–91) excavations (Bowsher and Miller 2009), the British Museum exhibition 'Shakespeare Staging the World' in 2012 (Bate and Thornton 2012), and recent partial excavations of the Hope (1999–2001) (Mackinder et al. 2013), the Theatre (2008–11) and the Curtain (Bowsher 2012), early playhouses have rarely been incorporated into wider theoretical discussions in archaeology (although see Bowsher 2007). Playhouse studies are predominantly undertaken by theatre historians, with discussions centred on their reconstruction, appraising their audiences, synthesizing plays with staging practices, and debating the extent of the theatrical community's political power and social capital (e.g. Mullaney 1988; Orrell 1988;

Howard 1994; Montrose 1996; Gurr and Ichikawa 2000; Gurr 2004; Karim-Cooper and Stern 2013).

While such studies commonly employ excavated evidence, archaeology has largely served as an empirical benchmark against which various document-derived theories are measured for viability. However, an explicitly archaeological perspective of playhouses is equally capable of going beyond reconstruction. Traditionally, archaeological approaches to space have explored binary structures: front/back, private/public, clean/dirty, male/female, etc., and degrees of access to the innermost zones of a building (e.g. Schofield 1994). Colin Counsell (1996) employed a Foucaldian framework of power and sight to explore how intervisibility was facilitated by spatial codes across pre- and post-Renaissance theatre in buildings both real and metaphorical. Jean Wilson (1995) produced a rare and welcome synthesis of other contemporary built structures and material culture to stimulate fresh approaches to reconstructing the playhouse interiors. Although reconstruction is not the goal here, this study builds on Wilson's contribution by examining more recent contextual evidence to illuminate broader changes to Elizabethan-Jacobean spatial rules.

This approach explores spatial rules prevalent in the architectural culture of the period, contextualizing playhouse design. It synthesizes a variety of micro and macro-boundaries that demarcated, segregated or incorporated body-identities within the built environment of Elizabethan-Jacobean England. This broad-brushstroke approach deliberately moves away from the detailed appraisals of playhouse individuality, concentrating instead on their shared characteristics as a building type. Discussion first centres on the documentary evidence for playhouses as inherently transgressive spaces, which dislocated bodies from the familiar spatial rules of society. Comparisons are then made between the spatial ordering in playhouses and other architectural structures of the period from excavated and standing remains. Specific emphasis on elevation, compartmentalization and mobility illuminates new ways in which body-identity and body-practice were being structured, and existing spatial rules challenged.

Playhouses as Transgressive Spaces

Stephen Mullaney (1988) highlighted the spatial and cultural liminality of playhouses, noting how suburban playhouses were built beyond the jurisdiction of London's city authorities. Indeed, the City's concerted opposition to the suburban playhouses dissolved into 'anything resembling a partnership in regulation' (Whitney 2001: 178) and in his appraisal of City-playhouse relations, Ian Archer (2009: 412) concludes: 'The City authorities had indeed driven the players into the suburbs.' The earliest known purpose-built playhouses (therefore excluding the Red Lion to the east and Newington Butts to the south) appeared north of the city limits (the Theatre, the Curtain), later joined by the Fortune in 1600 (Wickham, Berry and Ingram 2000: 330, 404, 531). The Rose, the Globe, the Swan, and the Hope were in the suburbs of Bankside, south of the River Thames (Wickham, Berry and Ingram 2000: 211, 419, 437, 493, 595). This helped the theatrical community avoid prosecution under the Vagabond Act (1576), which listed unlicensed players on a legal par with thieves, beggars, prostitutes and vagrants (Montrose 1996: 54). Bankside was in a liminal zone known as the 'Liberty of the Clink', which stretched south of the Thames (Mullaney 1988: 1–58). This area held many buildings dedicated to illegal and immoral activities, such as brothels, which, although suppressed in 1546, reappeared in the expensive 'Holland's Leaguer' brothel, contributing to Bankside's reputation (Bowsher 2012: 20). Animal-baiting arenas, 'the Clink' prison (Mullaney 1988: 1–58) and malodorous trades, such as tanning (Johnson 1969: 304) and soap-making (cf. Orrell 1988) also made up Bankside's liminal environment (Carlin 1996).

Despite their popularity across social classes (Gurr 2004: 58–94), playhouses were contested spaces. London's Lord Mayor, Aldermen, and Puritan preachers and concerned citizens repeatedly petitioned the Privy Council for their abolition, citing the moral degeneracy of their plays and the immoral behaviour playhouses facilitated (Yachnin 1997: 21). Antitheatrical tracts of the period brought numerous moral charges against players and their playhouses as a dislocating agent. The transvestism of males playing females, the occult content of certain plays, allusions to Catholic spectacle, and the inclusion of politically and morally volatile themes were all openly and unsympathetically questioned by many outside the profession (see Howard 1994; Montrose 1996).

In her survey of antitheatrical sources, Jean Howard (1994: 24–27) identified a strong denouncement of playhouses for displacing bodies. For example, nonconformist preacher John Northbrook's *A Treatise wherein Dicing, Dauncing, Vaine Playes or Enterludes ... are reproved* (1577) warned females against attending playhouses, because it displaced them from their defining normative locale (the home). Playhouses set their bodies on display to the gaze of male playgoers and, more dangerously, could incite female lust as they returned the male gaze (Howard 1994: 24–25). Northbrook equally condemned playhouses for dislocating the faithful body from church (especially Sunday performances), the idle body from employment and the active body from the workplace (Howard 1994: 27).

Social rules of propriety, bodily proximity and location were considered to be compromised by entering playhouse space.

Moreover, playhouses presented a violation of state-enforced dress codes. Sumptuary Laws, established by Henry VIII, prescribed which social classes could wear certain fabrics, accessories and colours (Gurr and Ichikawa 2000: 4). This meant that playhouse audiences could 'read' the intended identity of the player or playgoer based on composite elements of a single outfit. According to playgoers and antitheatricalists, audience zones played a pivotal role in reiterating rank to fellow playgoers (Gurr 2004). As a Continental tourist, Thomas Platter, noted following a visit to the Globe in 1599:

> There are different galleries and places, however, where the seating is better and more comfortable and therefore more expensive. For whoever cares to stand below [in the yard] pays only one English penny, but if he wishes to sit in the most comfortable seats which are cushioned, where he not only sees everything well, but can also be seen, then he pays yet another English penny at another door. (Wickham, Berry and Ingram 2000: 413)

A similar description was made by Lambarde in 1596 (Wickham, Berry and Ingram 2000: 297). A 'Lord's Room' is mentioned in the Rose accounts of 1592; the Fortune contract mentions 'Gentlemen's rooms' and 'two-penny Rooms', while the 1604 Globe had 'private rooms' and the 1614 Hope contract mentions 'two boxes in the lowermost storey', each available to spectators at an additional cost (Bowsher and Miller 2009: 115–16). The exact location of these rooms is unclear (see below). Presumably the 'rule' was that wealthier patrons were expected to sit or stand in these more exclusive, expensive areas. Yet the rule of 'vertical sociology' was by no means watertight. There are references to playgoers entering the 'wrong' social zone. For example, a Venetian ambassador decided to watch in the Curtain's yard to the horror of his companions (Wickham, Berry and Ingram 2000: 415). Cut-purses, some described as remarkably well dressed, were well known for entering the middle galleries for more fruitful opportunities (Gurr 2004: 78). Alternative activities amongst playgoers in galleries and rooms took place, including sleeping, smoking, gaming, talking and flirting (Gurr 2004: 226; Bowsher and Miller 2009: 158). Gurr and Ichikawa (2000: 68, 141) argue that players performed in upper galleries above the stage, acting out death scenes in amongst the wealthier playgoers. If so, even players broke the spatial 'rules' of playhouse stratigraphy.

Attending playhouses was as much about the playgoer's performance amongst his or her peers as the players onstage. Identity was meant to be 'read' from an interweaving of clothing colours and materials; hairstyle, accessories, gesture and degree of bodily elevation within the crowd (see Hazard 2000). Yet this complex system was hugely undermined by low-born male players dressing as females and impersonating a range of high-born characters (Gurr and Ichikawa 2000: 3). Platter commented:

> The actors are most expensively and elaborately costumed; for it is the English usage of eminent lords or knights at their decease to bequeath and leave almost the best of their clothes to their serving men, which it is unseemly for the latter to wear, so that they offer them for sale for a small sum to the actors. (Wilson 1995: 63)

Players wore costumes in colours and materials well beyond their social rank, thus hiding their true status as servants and encouraging audiences to play along with the deceit (Gurr and Ichikawa 2000: 6, 53). As Howard (1994: 27) surmised, playhouses were 'connected with the loss and confusion of identity... [and] usurpation, seizing a social position which one does not, by one's birth, deserve, aspiring to an identity which can therefore be discredited as illusory, counterfeit, deceptive'. Although licensed companies were exempt from Sumptuary Laws (which were abolished in 1604), antitheatricalists denounced players for their deliberate deception. Elizabeth I's mandatory national sermon 'Against Excess of Apparel' was often cited, which warned against wearing socially inappropriate clothing as it was offensive to both God and the monarch (Howard 1994: 32–33). For antitheatricalists, simply attending playhouses made all playgoers complicit in this deceit, and in Protestant theology any false illusion was the work of the Devil (Howard 1994: 16). Thus, 'Sathan's Synagogues' (Northbrook) became arenas known for social and religious defiance where familiar social rules were undermined and normative locales abandoned.

Physical Space

Having briefly appraised key textual evidence for playhouses as marginal spaces, we turn to the buildings themselves. Unlike churches, elite residences and indoor theatres, playhouses were not inherited spaces. Although each playhouse was unique in its details, they shared general characteristics with some copying and competition between designers. The Globe was built from the dismantled timbers of the Theatre, both owned by different generations of the Burbage family (Wilson 1995: 69–81). The building contract for Henslowe and Alleyn's Fortune playhouse uses and improves upon the Globe (see below). The Rose excavations and the Fortune building contract therefore provide substantial evidence of their overall design and derivatives of their design, and thus form the basis of the following contextualization.

The Rose (1587–c.1606)

The Rose was one of the smaller playhouses, its yard estimated to have originally accommodated between 400 and 530 people, and between 550 and 740 after remodelling in 1592 (Bowsher and Miller 2009: 157). A footbridge over the southern sewer-ditch led to a narrow main entrance, creating a deliberate bottleneck of traffic to ensure that playgoers did not escape paying (Bowsher and Miller 2009: 111). A ceramic money box recovered from the Rose's *ingressus* suggests additional payment was collected at gallery thresholds, mirrored in contemporary references to the Theatre (Bowsher and Miller 2009: 46, 133) (Figure 7.1).

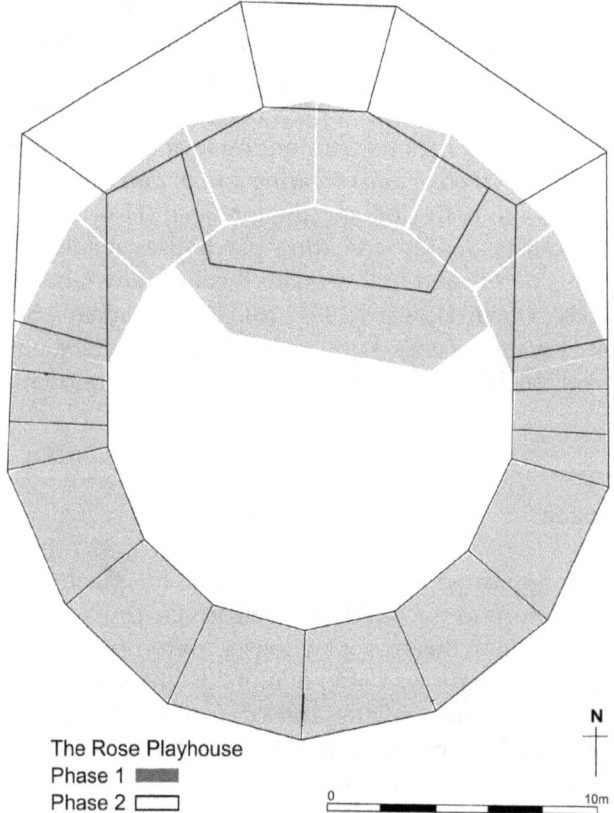

The Rose Playhouse
Phase 1 ■
Phase 2 ☐

Figure 7.1 The Rose Playhouse: phases 1 and 2 (after Bowsher and Miller 2009; redrawn, simplified, coloured and phases overlain by Ruth Nugent)

The Swan, the Globe, the Fortune and the Hope all definitely had three galleries, and though two galleries at the Rose have been conjectured (Greenfield 2007: 31–34), it likely had three, which was the standard. A dripline created by rainwater running off the gallery's eaves into the Rose's yard does not indicate whether one or all of them were jettied. Excavated floors and a timber balustrade suggest that its first gallery was separated from the yard by a 10 ft (3.05 m) timber 'wall' (Bowsher and Miller 2009: 17–18, 113), in an era where the average adult male was only 5'6" (1.67 m) tall (Greenfield and Gurr 2004: 336). Greenfield and Gurr (2004) argue that this height was a safety measure for additional animal-baiting. However, the depth and raking of the floor, which sloped down northwards, and the fact that the Rose had no animal licence, make this an unlikely theory (Bowsher 2007; Bowsher and Miller 2009: 131–32).

The Rose was later remodelled, probably in 1592 according to Henslowe's diary (Bowsher and Miller 2009: 54). The second Rose focused on enhancing the stage by rebuilding it with a new tiring-house/stage wall 2 m north of the first, and two timber columns were installed to support a stage canopy (Bowsher and Miller 2009: 58–59, 64). Although the new stage was almost identical in size (47.6 m^2), it was redesigned to thrust into the yard so that players could perform on several frontages (Bowsher and Miller 2009: 58–59, 136). A plaster surface inside the stage perimeter indicated a below-stage area for trapdoor exits and storage (Bowsher 2007: 64).

The northern galleries were pushed back to increase their sightlines of the newly canopied and thrust stage. Conversely, the yard floor, which was originally raked to enable those standing at the back to see the stage, was levelled before 1592 (Bowsher and Miller 2009: 49, 54, 59). Henslowe's 1592 'penthowsse shed' built against the 'tyeringe howsse doore' was probably placed to the west of the tiring house (Bowsher and Miller 2009: 111–12). Backstage at the first Rose were three 12 ft (3.66 m)-deep 'rooms' built into the gallery, probably for storage, administration and potentially rehearsals (Bowsher and Miller 2009: 137). No physical evidence of the stage *frons scenae* (back wall) survive. DeWitt's sketch of the Swan's interior (Figure 7.2) provides a general idea of construction, although neither definitive nor perfectly rendered (Foakes 1985: 52–55). However, it may represent how the Rose stage was moved forward from the gallery façade (Bowsher pers. comm.). Wilson (1995: 81, 135) argued they were based on existing hall screens from great houses used by patronized troupes for performances.

Stairs from the yard into the galleries (ingresses) were original features (Bowsher and Miller 2009: 45, 111–12). If the Rose had external entrances to the gallery, they were probably later additions, although the small

Figure 7.2 Buchelius' copy of DeWitt's sketch of the Swan c. 1596 (Utrecht, University Library, Ms. 842, f.132r. Reproduced with permission of the University of Utrecht Library).

Figure 7.3 'The Wits, or Sport upon Sport' frontispiece, 1662 (Folger Library, W3218. Reproduced with permission of the Folger Library)

plot of land may not have facilitated this (Bowsher and Miller 2009: 115). The Globe excavations revealed what may be the foundations of a stair-tower to the galleries from the 1614 rebuild, which marries with contemporary depictions of two either side of the main entrance. There are also suggestions of multiple staircases within the Fortune contract (Bowsher and Miller 2009: 115).

The Fortune (1600)

All amphitheatre-style playhouses were timber-framed circular-polygonal structures, except the first Fortune, which was originally rectangular, but seems to have been rebuilt circular in brick (see Bowsher 2012: 101–3). Citing the Globe's layout, Henslowe's building contract for the Fortune required:

> Juttey forwardes in eyther side of the saide Two upper Stories of Tenne ynches of lawfull assize, with ffower [four] convenient divisions for gentlemens roomes,

and other sufficient and convenient divisions for Twoe pennie roomes, with necessarie Seates to be placed and sett, Aswell in those roomes as througheoute all the rest of the galleries ... and with such like steares [stairs], Conveyances and divisions withoute and within, as are made and Contryved in and to the late erected Plaiehowse On the Banck in the saide parishe of Ste Saviours Called the Globe. (Foakes 2002: 307)

Henslowe specifies jettied galleries, potentially suggesting that this new trend was not at the Globe by the time the Fortune contract was written. Although there is a danger of arguing from silence here, jettied galleries at the Fortune may have been a way of outshining a competing playhouse.

The Fortune's gallery heights were to be 12 ft (3.67 m) for the lowest gallery, 11 ft (3.52 m) high for the second and 9 ft (2.74 m) for the third gallery (Foakes 2002: 306–15). The lowest gallery was also to be 'laide over and fenced with strong yron pykes', presumably to prevent 'groundlings' from climbing into the gallery without paying (Foakes 2002: 308). The tiring house was to have 'convenient windows and lightes glazed' and the stage had a canopy copying the Globe's. The main roof, and stage and staircase roofs were tiled and the stage floor was also tiled (Foakes 2002: 308–9).

Summarizing Playhouse Space

Social segregation was enforced using high boundaries between yard and galleries, separate entrances, private rooms and later external staircases to the galleries. This ensured payment and allowed faster access to higher floors without taking up lucrative seating space inside the galleries (Bowsher and Miller 2009: 114–15). The players themselves had arguably the most exclusive, defining spaces. The stage, understage, tiring house and backstage entrance were largely off-limits to playgoers. Unlike the expensive indoor hall-theatres, gallants could not sit on stools on stage at playhouses (Gurr 2004: 36).

A 'Lord's Room' is mentioned in contemporary accounts and plays as an expensive, exclusive space within the public playhouses (Egan 1997). In the Fortune and Hope contracts, the Lord's Room is distinct from 'twopenny galleries' and 'gentleman's rooms' (Gurr 1994: 38). Its location, however, is unclear and two schools of thought have emerged. Some argue that it was situated above or behind the stage (e.g. Hosley 1957; Berry 1987: 50–66; Gurr and Ichikawa 2000: 68, 141; Gurr 2004: 22, 25). Others disagree, emphasizing them as flanking the stage (e.g. Egan 1997; Bowsher and Miller 2009: 115–16; Bowsher 2011: 462). Lords' and gentlemans' rooms may have been paired together on both sides of the stage, or one to the left and the other to the right (Egan 1997: 309).

Whatever their arrangement, the wealthier guests who hired them may have been permitted to share the backstage entrance with players to enter the 'Lords' Rooms' and, as conjectured by Gurr and Ichikawa (2000: 68, 141), players may have acted amongst them in these rooms. If so, players may have subtly communicated a degree of legitimacy for their liminal profession by harnessing spatial rules of restricted space and elite identity. Mingling exclusively with the wealthiest attendees would enhance such a statement.

Introducing thrust stages also recentred the players as the focal point, competing with the bodily display of playgoers. The stage canopy not only protected expensive costumes from bad weather but also accommodated lifting machinery for players and props to rise and descend (Foakes 2002: 7). Its supporting columns meant that the galleries either side were moved outwards to improve their sightlines, with groundlings at the front now able to engage with players on three sides of the stage (Bowsher 2011: 462). However, the yard's slope towards the stage was less pronounced in the remodel (Bowsher 2011: 462), meaning that those at the back would have had a reduced view of the stage. Gaining the attention of the more influential gallery audiences may have been a new priority.

Although the stage was still beneath the higher galleries, by commanding great intervisibility, players situated themselves within the rules of vertical sociology not by spatial plane, but by commanding visual space.

Contextualizing Playhouses: Churches

Communality

In churches, communality was the new spatial rule. Protestant remodelling had decentralized the altar and removed divisions such as rood screens and associated lofts, to form a more open-plan rectangular space (Howard 2007: 60). The axis of medieval churches used for Catholic processions was deactivated and central space made squarer to facilitate communal worship prescribed by the *Common Book of Prayer* (1559) (Howard 2007: 61–62). Thus, creating exclusive areas became the signature of wealth and power in this period. Nowhere was this more overt than inside churches.

In response, those who could afford it were actively purchasing and investing in private spaces, challenging the intention of communal worship. Space was subdivided into private box-pews and the regular pew backs heightened to screen and segregate the body (Llewellyn 2000: 239, 242). Surviving box-pews at Worthenbury church, Wrexham and at Rycote Chapel, Oxfordshire provide early seventeenth-century prototypes for great covered family pews as well as the new canopied box pulpits to

Figure 7.4 Surviving box-pews in Worthenbury church (reproduced with the permission of Howard Williams)

isolate and elevate the preacher (Girouard 2009: 282–83) (Figure 7.4). The early seventeenth century witnessed a surge of new, exclusively owned pews, so being seated for sermons became a luxury. These new pews dominated viewscapes within the church because of their massive height (Llewellyn 2000: 238–39). They were simultaneously attention-seeking yet private spaces, akin to the exclusive but highly visible private rooms at playhouses.

Elevation of the body was also transforming. Although recumbent effigies continued to be installed in churches, a new fashion for the deceased to be depicted kneeling, often surrounded by standing mourners, indicates a movement of the represented body from a static, horizontal position to an active, vertical position (Llewellyn 2000: 368–70). Space will not permit further detailing of the theological shift accompanying this, but suffice to say the monumental body was also being elevated. Similarly, the introduction of wall memorials in the mid sixteenth century meant that new upper-body bust styles were starting to climb the vertical plane of the church walls, looking down on the congregation below (Llewellyn 2000: 239–42, 369).

Funerary monuments had to be appropriate in size, decoration and location to the status of the deceased, and even their raw materials were situated within a hierarchy (Llewellyn 2000: 237–39). New styles of funerary monumentality at the turn of the seventeenth century included four, six and eight-poster tombs and arched-wall tombs to increase the vertical height of the dead (Llewellyn 2000: 242). These created a sense of space and intervisibility between the posters rather than the heavily canopied late medieval tombs. Although this allowed intervisibility between family pews, monuments and sacred space, the sheer size of such tombs was on an unprecedented scale (Llewellyn 2000: 242; Howard 2007: 60). However, Nigel Llewellyn (2000: 239) documents the mockery and resentment aimed at social climbers who commissioned inappropriately oversized tombs, flaunting regulations of space and materiality. Rules of spatial identity were highly contentious, even for the dead.

Commemoration within the chancel rail was considered a prime space since it 'was also a theatrical setting, for the chancel held the congregation's attention throughout much of the service' (Llewellyn 2000: 237). Space here was also limited, putting it at a premium, and inscriptions mention regret that the monument is in a poor location, not as false modesty, but as genuine regret for displacing a worthy person from a worthy space (Llewellyn 2000: 237). In both churches and playhouses, two venues where socially mixed groups met in a defined setting, personal space was not simply enough. Premium space was spatially connected to the most active areas of the building. Now the church faithful, marginal player, and self-aggrandising playgoer in their box were relying not just on proximity to privileged space, but to be remembered within *active* space.

Contextualizing Playhouses: Elite Residences

Elevation and Third Height

Apart from the introduction of galleries, most large Elizabethan residences simply remodelled earlier buildings (Girouard 2009: 76). In the early to mid sixteenth century, residences were usually only two storeys high above ground, although corner towers and attic rooms could give the impression of height and status. But by the 1570s, internal rooms were higher and external towers and gables were being built even taller as a way of demonstrating impressive social standing (Girouard 2009: 272–73). Architectural height within the landscape was a major component of spatial status.

A third floor was commonly added by installing a floor in high-ceilinged halls (Howard 2007: 2) and exterior entrance porches were being built in three tiers to match (Girouard 2009: 118–19). As a result, rooms were reordered. The upper storey had previously been for minor rooms, but three-storey houses were shifting their principal rooms into the third floor, fronted by great windows (Girouard 2009: 273). The power of 'third height' had currency in the playhouse period to communicate prestige, where three tiers of galleries seem to have been standard (see Figure 7.1). For example, the Bear Garden of 1583 was specifically rebuilt as a playhouse with three tiers instead of one or two, which was deliberately copied at the Hope and Davies Bear Garden (Mackinder et al. 2013: 20). Although a third gallery was not necessarily built purely as an expression of social status by the theatrical community – after all, it allowed for more paying customers – it likely resonated with both players and playgoers as a type of new, elite space bolstering 'vertical sociology'. Internal porches developed in the late sixteenth and early seventeenth centuries, with surviving examples at Sizergh Castle, Westmoreland; Bradfield, Devon, and Broughton Castle, Oxfordshire (Girouard 2009: 352–53). These acted as small entrance chambers between two rooms, often only big enough for two or three individuals at most. They were richly decorated portals or holding places between important rooms. The compartmentalization of a (guest) body in this manner suggests a deepening interest in the rules of space as a method of power, controlling rhythms and levels of access.

Similarly, hall screens divided guests from the household, allowing a stranger's social rank to be gauged before entering (Hazard 2000: 155). Although these were traditional elements of Tudor residences, they were either retained or being built into the mid seventeenth century (Girouard 2009: 90). The theatrical community recreated hall-screen designs for their frontispieces depicting the profession, and in their coronation arches which actors performed around as the monarch passed through these symbolic thresholds (Wilson 1995: 81, 135; Ronayne 1997: 125–27; Hazard 2000: 146, 155). Thus, it is very plausible hall screens influenced stage facades. For Tudor performances in elite residences, the gallery above the hall screen was a marginal area used by the musicians (Hazard 2000: 149, 152). However, the gallery above the hall-screen-style playhouse stage generated prestige in terms of price, elevation, visibility and physical segregation. While this resonates strongly with indoor theatres and private residences, DeWitt's Swan sketch depicts screens and balconies in playhouses with similar potential. Berry (1987: 178–79) has argued that boxes for elites to sit in were located behind the stage at the indoor Blackfriars theatre, although this is merely conjecture. Nonetheless, private rooms seem to have been in prominent places, adjoining or above the stage, providing the worst view of the stage but the most self-aggrandizing position in the playhouse, as depicted in the later 'The Wits, or Sport upon Sport' frontispiece of 1662 (Figure 7.3). A minor space in grand houses was now equated with the luxuries of privacy and restricted access, emphasizing an inversion of spatial rules in playhouses. The appropriation of hall screens by the theatrical profession would indicate awareness of spatial segregation as a characteristically elite privilege. Increased compartmentalization such as this, combined with new elevations, redefined spatial orders in grand residences. These new rules are analogous to the elevated rooms compartmentalizing elite bodies in playhouses, where people were prepared to pay extra for this privilege.

Galleries

The new Elizabethan architectural innovation for larger residences was the gallery (later termed a 'long gallery') (Girouard 2009: 69). Galleries were glazed corridors on upper stories, some running the length of the building, to promenade, enjoy the view, and display family and royal portraits (Girouard 2009: 71). They were particularly popular at royal residences, such as Hampton Court (e.g. the Queen's Gallery, built 1533–37), with more modest versions appearing in mid to late sixteenth-century non-royal houses as well (Girouard 2009: 69–70). Owners competed to have the most impressive gallery and 'from the 1570s till the 1620s every new house of any importance had to have a gallery no less than 100 ft in length' (Girouard 2009: 70–71). Flat, lead-floored roofs also became popular installations for elevated promenading and impressive vistas (Girouard 2009: 91). A new desire for movement and vistas influenced architectural codes of status.

Tiffany Stern (2000) demonstrates from a variety of textual sources that promenading through playhouse galleries during performances was commonplace. Not all performances were sell-out affairs, leaving playgoers room to manoeuvre to better viewpoints in both the yard and the galleries. This also suggests that gallery seats did not always provide an ideal view of the stage. It raises the issue as to whether seating was fixed or moveable. Views of a static stage would have been easier to orchestrate, unlike the Bear Gardens where action moved around the arena, forcing spectators in upper galleries to leave their seats in order to see (Bowsher pers. comm.). Moving about also occurred in private rooms. At the Fortune in 1617, Orazio Busoni, chaplain to the Venetian embassy, had an 'elegant dame' move around with her entourage to sit with him during the performance, apparently a common occurrence (Stern 2000: 215; Gurr 2004: 236, 276). Stern (2000: 212–13) has pointed out that DeWitt labelled the third gallery at the Swan a 'porticus', which was defined in *Riders Dictionarie* (1606) as 'a porch, gallerie, or walking place'. DeWitt was using classical Vitruvian architectural grammar to describe what he was seeing, relating it to an open walkway atop a building (Bowsher pers. comm.). The third gallery in the Fortune contract was much lower in height than the preceding two galleries, which may have prevented as many bleacher-style tiered seats being installed because of reduced head height. Fewer seats but the same room depth would have provided room to promenade. Although playhouse galleries were designed for sitting, the new fashion for promenading at home was transferred to these zones. In churches, seating was a new privilege and the cost of seats at playhouses suggests that the same rule applied. Those who promenaded in galleries and rooms, however, may have been citing this new, elite trend in architectural culture. They were potentially distinguishing themselves not only through elevation and compartmentalization, but also through mobility, suggesting a complex layering of spatial cues. Again, the fresh emphasis on *active* zones added a new dimension to spatial identity.

Great Chambers

Kent Rawlinson (2012) highlights the importance of great halls at royal residences under Henry VIII for the performance of 'triumphs'. In Elizabethan great houses, the great chamber was the focal point of the building and lavishly furnished (Girouard 2009: 68). Here guests were formally received, command performances were held, and the owner would eventually be laid in state in this room (Girouard 2009: 68). When not in formal use, it acted as a common room for servants not on duty, where they could play cards and board games; Lord Berkeley was known to have joined in during the 1570s, whereas the Earl of Huntington banned yeomen from gaming in his great chamber in 1609 (Girouard 2009: 68). These multifunctional great chambers were simultaneously formal and informal spaces, defined not so much by their decoration as by the activities performed by different social groups. Likewise, alternative activities taking place in the six-penny and two-penny rooms (hereinafter penny-rooms; Bowsher and Miller 2009: 115–16) of playhouses may have been a reflection of this multilayered understanding of space. Although playhouse rooms were meant to be privileged spaces, akin to the larger great chambers, they could be treated in an informal manner, paying only a fraction of attention to their primary function. Wealthier playgoers could adapt penny-rooms to their own purposes of playgoing and gaming or reading, just as servants could adapt great chambers for their own informal entertainment. From this perspective, the rules of space did not so much dictate how a room must be used, but rather provided a template of idealized activity. Less formal behaviour relaxed the rules of intended room use. This reflects the dialectical relationship between architectural intention and the subversion or dilution of those intentions through group behaviour.

Discussion

Spatial rules were evolving along similar lines in playhouses, churches and elite residences. Similarities were not necessarily intentional since each building had specific goals: playhouses were businesses, churches defined and expressed religious practice, and residences were statements of familial prestige. Yet each building type was part of a broader architectural culture that was manipulating rules of space and identity in new ways.

Potentially, the efficacy of the 'feudalistic' 'top-down' vertical sociology was diluted by the rise of the *nouveau riche* (e.g. Howard 1994: 75). Thus, rules of spatial identity were subtly redefined across a range of buildings. Elevation was still a status symbol, but was now emphasized through a 'third height'. Expensive effigial bodies were also moving into elevated, vertical positions on church walls and tombs. The luxury of being seated in church contrasts with the luxury of promenading in new residential galleries, but playhouses offered the best of both in their galleries and rooms. Although playhouse promenading was not necessarily a design feature, the transferral of this activity from residence to playhouse reveals the agency of playgoers in renegotiating the intended rules of certain spaces. This is mirrored in residential great chambers, where behaviour could challenge intentions of space. Its most extreme form is the subversion of the marginal hall-screen gallery into a prestigious playhouse zone. Old and new rules of space were synthesized rather than usurped.

Elevation was accompanied by compartmentalization to signify elite status, especially under imposed communality in churches. Pews, box-pews and pulpits, hall screens, internal porches, playhouse galleries and rooms all segregated bodies on multiple sides, dividing up visual space as well. Prime locales for living and dead bodies were next to active spaces, such as chancels or stages, where high visibility and proximity to the kinetic could endorse status claims. In playhouses, a dialectical relationship developed between those in expensive rooms and the players onstage, each relying on proximity to the other as a statement of social validity.

Conclusion

Playhouses destabilized rules dictating where a body should be, displacing a range of people at macro (house, workplace, church) and micro (yard, auditorium, and stage) scales. Yet these liminal buildings were employing new spatial rules found in the wider, nonmarginal world. Thus, space was simultaneously reordered and commodified. Playgoers purchased a vista – some to see the stage, some to see and be seen – but all were buying admission to socially appropriate space. Indeed, space was arguably the most tangible attribute of an otherwise 'intangible' business.

Citations of broader spatial privileges inside playhouses may have been a useful tool in legitimizing an otherwise marginal profession in a liminal landscape.

Acknowledgements

My sincerest thanks go to Julian Bowsher for his insights and suggestions on an earlier version of this chapter, to Howard Williams for his image permission, and to the editors and peer reviewers for their immensely beneficial comments.

Ruth Nugent completed her doctoral thesis on mortuary culture in English cathedrals in the Department of History and Archaeology at the University of Chester, United Kingdom, where she is a visiting lecturer in History and Archaeology, and a post-doctoral researcher in Digital Humanities. She has previously published on mortuary practices and perceptions of bodies, material culture and their spatial arrangements. Her research interests include interactions between bodies (living or dead) and physical/conceptual spaces, and the role of touch in navigating this intersection.

References

Archer, I.W. 2009. 'The City of London and the Theatre', in R. Dutton (ed.), *The Oxford Handbook of Early Modern Theatre*. Oxford: Oxford University Press, pp. 396–413.
Bate, J., and D. Thornton. 2012. *Shakespeare: Staging the World*. London: British Museum Press.
Berry, H. 1987. *Shakespeare's Playhouses*. New York: AMS Press.
Bowsher, J. 2007. 'The Rose and its Stages', in P. Holland (ed.), *Shakespeare Survey 60*. Cambridge: Cambridge University Press, pp. 36–48.
———. 2011, 'Twenty Years on: The Archaeology of 'Shakespeare's' London Playhouses', *Shakespeare* 7(4): 452–66.
———. 2012. *Shakespeare's London Theatreland: Archaeology, History and Drama*. London: MOLA.
Bowsher, J., and P. Miller. 2009. *The Rose and the Globe-Playhouses of Shakespeare's Bankside, Southwark*, MOLA Monograph 48. London: MOLA.
Carlin, M. 1996. *Medieval Southwark*. London: Hambledon Press.
Counsell, C. 1996. 'Traversing the Known: Spatiality and the Gaze in Pre- and Post-Renaissance Theatre', *Journal of Dramatic Theory and Criticism* 9(1): 19–33.

Egan, G. 1997. 'The Situation of the "Lords Room": A Revaluation', *Review of English Studies* 48(191): 297–309.
Foakes, R.A. 1985. *Illustrations of the English Stage, 1580–1642*. London: Scolar Press.
———. 2002. *Henslowe's Diary*. Cambridge: Cambridge University Press.
Girouard, M. 2009. *Elizabethan Architecture: Its Rise and Fall, 1540–1640*. New Haven, CT: Yale University Press.
Greenfield, J. 2007. 'Reconstructing the Rose: Development of the Playhouse Building between 1587 and 1592' in P. Holland (ed.), *Shakespeare Survey 60*. Cambridge: Cambridge University Press, pp. 23–35.
Greenfield, J., and A. Gurr. 2004. 'The Rose Theatre, London: The State of Knowledge and What We Still Need to Know', *Antiquity* 78(300): 330–40.
Gurr, A. 1994. 'The Bare Island', *Shakespeare Survey* 47: 29–43.
———. 2004. *Playgoing in Shakespeare's London*. Cambridge: Cambridge University Press.
Gurr, A., and M. Ichikawa. 2000. *Staging in Shakespeare's Theatres*. Oxford: Oxford University Press.
Hazard, M.E. 2000. *Elizabethan Silent Language*. Lincoln, NE: University of Nebraska Press.
Hosley, R. 1957. 'The Gallery over the Stage in the Public Playhouse of Shakespeare's Time', *Shakespeare Quarterly* 8: 15–31.
Howard, J.E. 1994. *The Stage and Social Struggle in Early Modern England*. London: Routledge.
Howard, M. 2007. *The Building of Elizabethan and Jacobean England*. New Haven, CT: Yale University Press.
Johnson, D.J. 1969. *Southwark and the City*. Oxford: City of London Corporation and Oxford University Press.
Karim-Cooper, F. and T. Stern. 2013. *Shakespeare's Theatres and the Effects of Performance*. London: Bloomsbury.
Llewellyn, N. 2000. *Funeral Monuments in Post-Reformation England*. Cambridge: Cambridge University Press.
Mackinder, A., L. Blackmore, J. Bowsher and C. Phillpotts. 2013. *The Hope Playhouse, Animal Baiting and Later Industrial Activity at Bear Gardens on Bankside: Excavations at Riverside House and New Globe Walk, Southwark, 1999–2000*, MOLA Archaeology Studies Series 25. London: MOLA.
Montrose, L. 1996. *The Purpose of Playing: Shakespeare and the Cultural Politics of the Elizabethan Theatre*. Chicago, IL: University of Chicago Press.
Mullaney, S. 1988. *The Place of the Stage: License, Play and Power in Renaissance England*. Chicago, IL: University of Chicago Press.
Orrell, J. 1988. *The Human Stage: English Theatre Design, 1567–1640*. Cambridge: Cambridge University Press.
Rawlinson, K. 2012. 'Hall's Chronicle and the Greenwich Triumphs of 1527', in T. Betteridge and G. Walker (eds), *The Oxford Handbook of Tudor Drama*. Oxford: Oxford University Press, pp. 402–28.
Ronayne, J. 1997. 'Totus Mundus Agit Histrionem: The Interior Decoration Scheme of the Bankside Globe', in J. Mulryne and M. Shrewing (eds), *Shakespeare's Globe Rebuilt*. Cambridge: Cambridge University Press, pp. 121–46.

Schofield, J. 1994. 'Social Perceptions in Medieval and Tudor London Houses', in M. Locock (ed.), *Meaningful Architecture*. Aldershot: Avebury, pp. 188–206.

Stern, T. 2000. '"You That Walk i'th Galleries": Standing and Walking in the Galleries of the Globe Theatre', *Shakespeare Quarterly* 51(2): 211–16.

Whitney, C. 2001. 'The Devil His Due: Mayor John Spence, Elizabethan Anti-theatricalism, and the Shoemaker's Holiday', *Medieval and Renaissance Drama in England* 14: 168–85.

Wickham, G., H. Berry and W. Ingram. 2000. *English Professional Theatre, 1530–1660*. Cambridge: Cambridge University Press.

Wilson, J. 1995. *The Shakespeare Legacy: The Material Legacy of Shakespeare's Theatre*. Stroud: Sutton Publishing.

Yachnin, P. 1997. *Stage-Wrights: Shakespeare, Jonson, Middleton, and the Making of Theatre Value*. Philadelphia, PA: University of Pennsylvania Press.

Chapter 8

US Army Regulations and Spatial Tactics
The Archaeology of Indulgence Consumption at Fort Yamhill, Oregon, United States, 1856–66

Justin E. Eichelberger

Introduction

Fort Yamhill (35PO75), a mid nineteenth-century US Army post in Western Oregon, existed during a critical period in the Army's ever-evolving policy concerning the consumption of indulgence items such as alcohol and tobacco. Established in 1856 and occupied until 1866, the post experienced several periods of the institutional acceptance and prohibition concerning the consumption of alcohol and tobacco. Since the occupation of the post, substantial archaeological deposits representing the consumption of indulgence items within the company kitchen and associated with the enlisted men of the post have since been recovered. This chapter examines this collection of alcohol bottles, drinking vessels and tobacco pipes in order to explore the drinking and smoking behaviour of the enlisted men and their negotiation of military regulations concerning the acceptable and/or unacceptable consumption of these items.

Over the last decade, there has been a growing interest in the archaeology of institutions. Institutions have been largely defined as established, significant and recognized practices, relationships or organizations within a society or culture (Wilson 2008). According to Wilson (2008: 16), institutions are a specific type of organization that exhibits three characteristics: (1) they are defined through their members; (2) they are identified by their buildings or some other specific location and require the use of symbols to distinguish members from nonmembers and to serve as a focal point of identity; and (3) institutions are characterized by the interaction amongst members, between members and nonmembers, and collectively as institutions with other institutions. These institutions can take many forms, such as schools, prisons, orphanages, communes, prisons, asylums, workhouses and hospitals (Beisaw and Gibb 2009). Peter Davies (2011) describes these organizations as 'total institutions', where those with authority control the routines and activities of the members through a process of rules and punishment. Members are withdrawn from society and isolated within the institution, where their former identities are broken down, before receiving instruction in the rules and expectations of the institution via a system of rewards and punishments (Davies 2011: 83). The nineteenth-century US Army was one such 'total institution' where recruits were removed from their respective communities and stationed at remote and isolated frontier posts; their individual identities were broken down, and their day-to-day activities were tightly controlled by superior officers through the use of regulations, orders and punishment in order to indoctrinate them with the culture of the US Army.

Military culture can be defined as the values, norms and assumptions that guide a soldier's actions, whether individually or in formation, in battle or in garrison (Wilson 2008: 14). This culture is largely based on military discipline or the behaviour of military personnel in conformity with previously prescribed rules (Burke 1999: 447). The rules usually come in the form of US regulations or military orders from specific officers. In general, these rules are meant to maintain order through the process of social control. During the years in which the post was occupied, the US Army codified 1,909 rules in the US Army Regulations (USWD 1857, 1861a, 1861b, 1863) designed to dictate nearly every form of behaviour of the soldier, from what he wore and what he ate to where he slept and what times of the day these activities were to take place. In addition, commanders issued hundreds of 'orders' each year, further adding to the number of rules each soldier was required to observe. Some of these rules were explicit in that they dictated every aspect of behaviour and left no room for officer or soldier interpretation. Other regulations were rather broad and were treated more as general guidelines that individual officers were to refer to when making specific decisions in the field or in garrison. Adding to the complexity of these rules was a bewildering array of measures aimed at eliminating or regulating indulgence consumption on post. For example, while the Army Regulations (USWD) might permit the sale of alcohol to enlisted men, individual company commanders might ban all alcohol sales to their men, while the post commander might allow on-post alcohol sales at certain times of the day (Adams 2009: 94).

US Army Use of Space

The officers within the US Army used the layout of their post as another form of social control. By controlling the spatial layout of the post, officers were able to control the level of surveillance they had over their men. Although most mid nineteenth-century US Army posts in the western United States followed a similar layout, no standardized plans were ever adopted by the Army (Hoagland 2004: 41). The buildings in the post were arranged hierarchically around a hollow quadrangle, with each building grouped by function and military rank and social position. For most posts, the officers' quarters were positioned on one side of the quadrangle, with the enlisted men's quarters opposite or sometimes adjacent, but usually at a considerable physical and social distance away from the officers. The third side of the quadrangle contained the administrative buildings such as guardhouses and adjutants' offices, while the fourth side was either left open or sometimes contained the primary storehouses or defensive structures such as a blockhouse. The ancillary structures such as kitchens, bakeries, carpenter and blacksmith shops, stables and occasionally hospitals were located outside the quadrangle and away from the parade ground. In a study of 214 nineteenth-century military posts located in the western United States, Douglas Scott (2009: 304) found that 90.7 per cent of these posts were constructed using this plan.

The parade ground, positioned in the physical centre of the post, was the social, ideological and ceremonial hub of the post. As the ceremonial centre, the parade ground was where all of the ritual activities of military life were performed, such as dress parade, drills, reading of official orders and punishments. This area was also the ideological and symbolic centre of the post where the post flag was located and served as the official meeting place for officers and enlisted men (Adams 2009: 133). This expanse of open ground between the primary buildings of the post not only played host to official functions, but also allowed an unobscured view and surveillance of the enlisted personnel by their commanding officers.

US Army and Indulgence Consumption

The pattern associated with the consumption of indulgence items varied greatly depending on the level of acceptance by the Army of the item consumed. Whereas the consumption of tobacco-related indulgence items was accepted and often encouraged, the consumption of other indulgence items, such as alcohol, was often forbidden. Noticing a general trend towards temperance in civilian society, Army officers generally took an oppositional position to alcohol consumption not only because it was viewed as a moral evil, but also, more importantly, because of a fear of alcohol-fuelled unruliness among enlisted men in relation to discipline and social order (Adams 2009: 116). Alcoholism was in turn linked to desertion, the Army's most consistent problem during the nineteenth century. Between 1820 and 1860, the desertion rates averaged nearly 15 per cent per year, with as many as 37 per cent deserting as the result of alcoholism (Schablitsky 1996: 87; Wooster 2009: 68). Following on the heels of a temperance movement, begun by the American Temperance Society in 1826, the US Army removed alcohol from the ration in 1838, replacing it with an allowance of coffee and sugar (Breck 1875: 2; Tate 1999: 165). Over the course of the nineteenth century, the public perception of alcohol grew increasingly negative, culminating in the prohibition of alcoholic beverages in fifteen states and territories, including the Oregon Territory, by 1855 (Burns 2004: 82). The Army followed suit by amending the *Regulations for the Army of the United States* in 1857 and the *Articles of War* in 1861, banning all sutlers from keeping or selling liquor, victuals, ardent sprits or other intoxicating drinks under penalty of losing their stations (USWD 1857: 28). Facing strong opposition from sutlers, soldiers and lobbyists, this ban on the sale of intoxicating substances was soon modified by allowing post sutlers to sell intoxicating beverages, but only the weaker varieties, from a specified location within the sutler's store and during specific times during the day and certain days of the week (USWD 1863: 37; Adams 2009: 95). Although the US Army attempted to regulate the use of alcohol, there is no evidence that soldiers cut back on the consumption of alcoholic beverages and in many cases they seemed to have drunk more (Burns 2004: 91). Instead of abandoning the consumption of alcohol as it was now 'against regulation', soldiers invested their time in elaborate schemes to acquire and hide their consumption (Adams 2009: 93).

However, the US Army did sanction alcohol for specific purposes, such as medicine and as a reward. Most nineteenth-century medicines contained alcohol for its anaesthetic properties (Fike 1987) and alcohol-related artefacts are commonly retrieved from US Army hospitals and other medical contexts (Hardesty 1981; Trussel 1996). Alcohol was also an official reward for soldiers serving extra or fatigue duties, including harvesting timber or constructing the quarters. Moderate consumption of alcohol either before or after 'ordinary' fatigue or exposure was believed to be beneficial by either providing transient strength or helping soldiers recover strength afterwards (Butterfield 1862: 104; Kautz 1864: 40–41). Alcohol was also a reward during holiday celebrations (Davis

2003) and in farewell rituals for soldiers permanently leaving military service. Corporal Royal A. Bensell, Company D., Fourth California Infantry (stationed at Fort Yamhill 1862–64), frequently commented on alcohol accompanying holiday celebrations, including Christmas and the Fourth of July (Barth 1959). Alcohol consumption also had ritualized importance in toasting (Barth 1959: 181).

Recognizing the role that alcohol played in breaking the lonely, boring and exhausting conditions of Army service and its role in social ritual, but condemning its inebriating effects, the Army sought to replace the consumption of alcohol with that of tobacco. By the mid 1800s, smoking tobacco was an American tradition favoured by all social classes of society, and many soldiers, both enlisted and commissioned, were already tobacco smokers when they began their service (Burns 2007: 125). Where 'scientific' studies of alcohol by the US Army found that 'ardent spirits are not necessary to health in the healthy' (Ordronaux 1863: 97), other studies advocated adding tobacco to the army ration. Dr Horsford in his study of the US Army ration concluded that:

> The experience of camp life has shown conclusively that there is an article contributing greatly to the comfort of the solder, of which no note is taken in the Government ration. This article is tobacco. It is the universal testimony of officers, chaplains, and especially of the rank and file, that the cheerfulness, good spirits and even general health of the men are greatly promoted by the temperate indulgence of the taste of tobacco. (Horsford 1864: 28)

Following his recommendations, the Army added tobacco to the ration by Section 6 of the Army Appropriation Act of 3 March 1865 (Barringer 1877: 104). Not only was smoking tobacco the preferred indulgence choice for the enlisted ranks amongst the officer corps, it also became very popular amongst the soldiers themselves. In order to foster this new habit, Senate Bill no. 136, passed into law by Congress on 21 March 1862, required post sutlers to provide for sale to officers and enlisted men tobacco, cigars, pipes and matches, and explicitly forbade them to sell liquor under penalty of losing their licence (USWD 1902: 938).

The examination of the consumption of indulgences at military sites has traditionally been tangential to primary research interests and usually reflected little more than commenting on the presence, absence or relative abundance of indulgences found at military sites (South 1977; Crass and Wallsmith 1992: 8–10; Balicki 2000: 143). A few published studies have gone beyond these basic studies to examine the spatial distribution of alcohol-related artefacts and to interpret the behavioural meaning of these distributions (Clouse 1999: 103–4; Bush 2000: 74). In his seminal work on the archaeology of alcohol and drinking, Frederick Smith (2008:

97–99) places the consumption of alcohol within military sites under a broader functional interpretation of drinking as a method of reducing soldier anxiety. He states that evidence for excessive alcohol use is especially strong at military sites and may reflect the anxieties caused by the unpredictable nature of warfare and beliefs in the courage-promoting effects of drinking (Smith 2008: 98). Others have argued that the high consumption of alcohol at military posts represents the soldiers' attempt to break the boredom and monotony of frontier garrison duty (Utley 1967: 40; Ball 2001: 58).

In this chapter, alcohol bottles, drinking vessels and clay tobacco pipes are used as a basis for exploring the deviant and conformist consumption of indulgence items of the enlisted soldiers at Fort Yamhill. Beginning with a brief overview of the history of the fort, the chapter describes the alcohol and tobacco artefact assemblage, especially in terms of its spatial distribution within the company kitchen. Discussion then focuses on the nature of alcohol and tobacco consumption within the nineteenth-century US Army and specifically how this was negotiated within Fort Yamhill's company kitchen. This behaviour is contextualized within other institutions of control, arguing that soldiers could assert their agency in resistance to military regulations through alcohol consumption. Yet consuming tobacco allowed them to display their conformity to such regulations, ultimately giving soldiers a sense of personal power within the nineteenth-century Army's institution of control.

Background: The History of Fort Yamhill

Fort Yamhill was established in March 1856 as a resolution to the cross-cultural conflict between American settlers and the Native American tribes of Western Oregon (Figure 8.1). The post was charged with monitoring traffic in and out of the reservation; guarding the reservation's boundaries from Euro-American incursion; and protecting and assisting the Grand Ronde Indian Agency (Adams 1991:16).

After the American Civil War (1861–65), Fort Yamhill lost its military usefulness and was closed by General Order No. 19 of 3 August 1866, and the post buildings, livestock and surplus supplies were sold at public auction (Barth 1959: 197).

Fort Yamhill covered c. 50 acres, contained twenty-four buildings and was designed to garrison up to three hundred men (Figure 8.2). The buildings were arranged around a quadrangle, creating a rectangular area in the centre known as the parade ground. The eastern side had six officer's houses; the western and opposite side of the parade ground contained

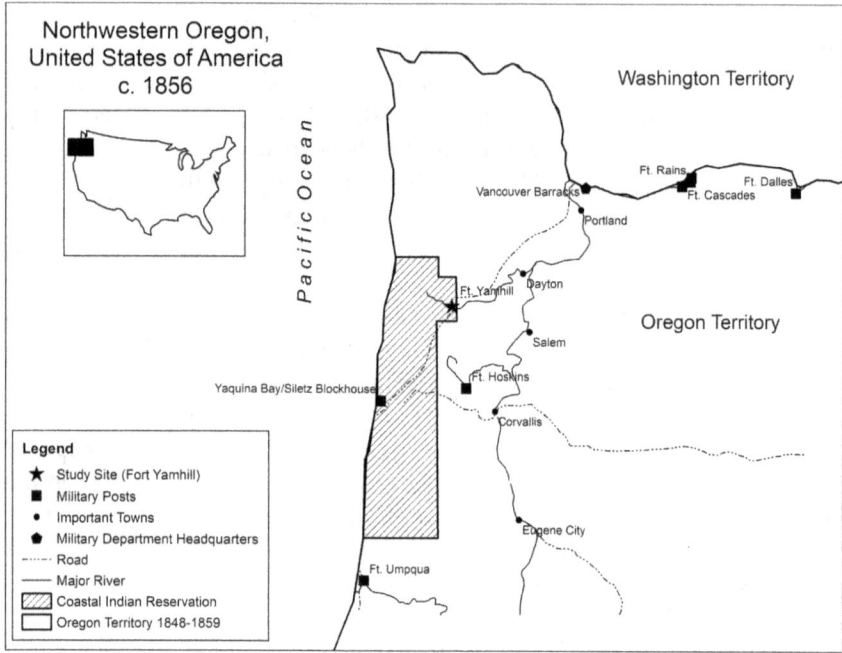

Figure 8.1 Northwest Oregon Territory c. 1856, showing the location of Forts Yamhill, Hoskins, and Umpqua, and the Coastal Indian Reservation (illustration by Justin E. Eichelberger)

the blockhouse. The north side contained the adjutant's office, the guardhouse and the quartermaster and commissary storehouse. The southern side had the enlisted men's barracks, mess room and company kitchen. Outside this quadrangle were auxiliary and civilian structures such as the hospital, laundress houses, bake house, stables, blacksmith shop, carpenter shop and sutler's store.

Figure 8.2 shows the location of the company kitchen on the south side of the parade ground, centred and behind the company barracks and mess hall. According to the 1864 Davison map (reprinted in Adams 1991: 51), it was 16 x 20 ft (4.87 x 6.09 m), with a large chimney on the east end. The map depicts four doors/windows: two on the north side, one on the west and one on the south.

Archaeological Investigations at the Company Kitchen

Between June 2005 and August 2007, the company kitchen of Fort Yamhill (35PO75) was excavated for the Oregon State Parks Recreation Department

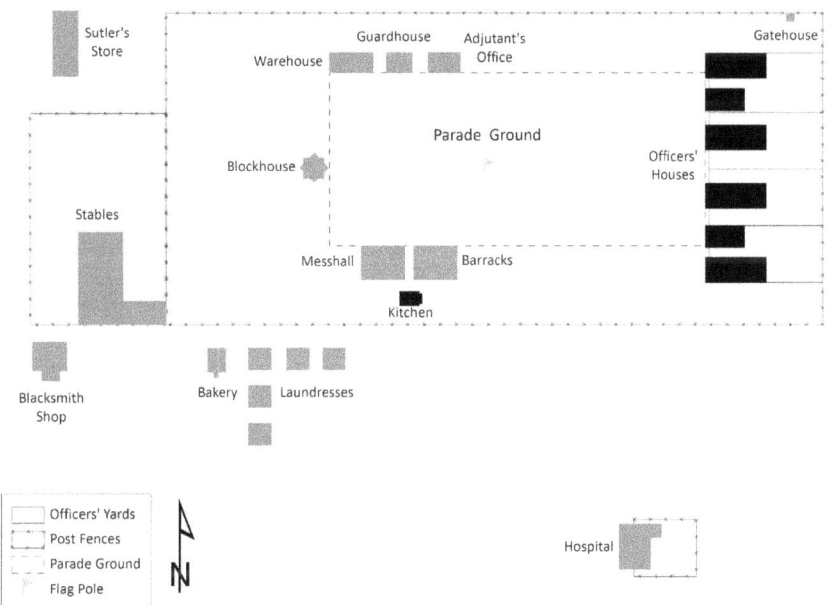

Figure 8.2 Map of Fort Yamhill c. 1864, showing the fort layout and the location of company kitchen in relation to the parade ground and the officers' quarters (illustration by Justin E. Eichelberger)

during several field seasons by archaeologists at Oregon State University, concluding with the full exposure of the building's foundations and interior, and exploration of areas to the west and north of the kitchen (Figure 8.3; Eichelberger 2010). The kitchen's hearth and foundations, a paved exterior working area, a front porch and a back porch were identified (Figure 8.3).

All excavated sediment was screened through a quarter-inch mesh and all artefacts were mapped in situ to the nearest centimetre or collected by excavation unit and level. Archaeological deposits at the company kitchen were relatively shallow, ranging from approximately 10 to 30 cm below the surface, and showed little vertical stratigraphy in artefacts or sediments. The archaeological deposits appear to have accumulated during use through either loss or discard and represent discrete activities areas associated with the primary functions of the company kitchen (Eichelberger 2010: 261–64). The site showed little post-depositional disturbance except for the demolition and/or salvage of the brick and sandstone material from the kitchen firebox and chimney, and the intrusion of tree roots in the northwest and southeast corners of the structure (Figure 8.3).

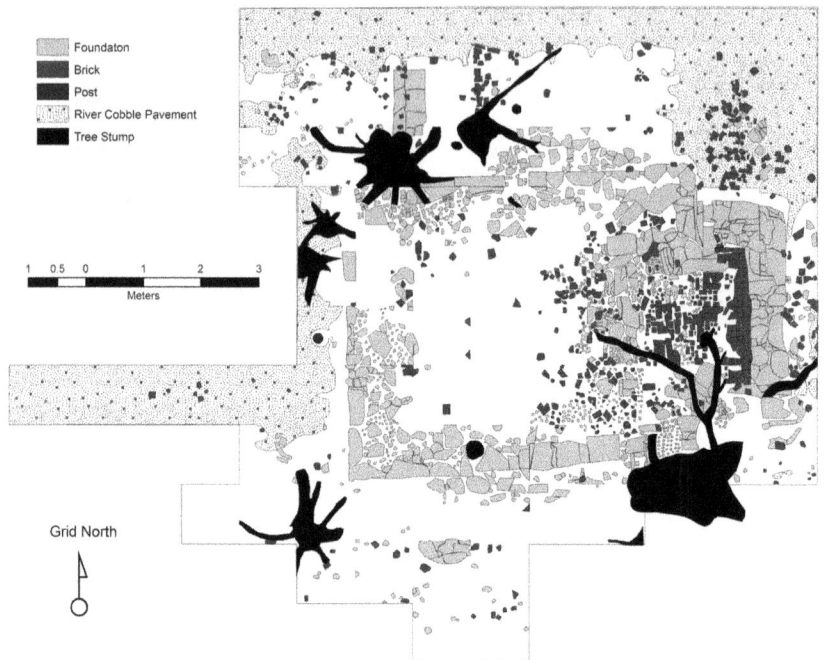

Figure 8.3 Feature map and schematic drawing of the company kitchen (illustration by Justin E. Eichelberger)

Artefact Assemblage

The company kitchen feature produced 1,072 indulgence-related artefacts (Table 8.1), representing 22.4 per cent (1,072 out of 4,776 artefacts) of the total company kitchen artefact assemblage – a far greater percentage than any other excavated feature at Fort Yamhill (Eichelberger 2010: 168). Indulgence-related artefacts only represent 16 per cent of the artefact assemblage at the post bakery; 9 per cent at the company barracks, and 4 to 5 per cent of the assemblages at each of the officers' quarters (Brauner and Eichelberger 2009; Brauner, Eichelberger and Boulware 2009; Eichelberger 2010, 2014; Eichelberger and Brauner 2011). It is this significantly higher concentration of indulgence-related artefacts at the company kitchen and their spatial distribution that forms the basis of the following analysis and discussion.

The majority of alcohol bottles were identified by their dark olive and 'black glass' colour since the majority of these bottles were made for alcoholic beverages, including hard liquor, wine, champagne and ale (McKearin and Wilson 1978; Fike 1987: 13; Van den Bossche 2001). The

Table 8.1 Alcohol and tobacco artefacts recovered from the company kitchen

Indulgence type	Description	Count
Alcohol artefacts	Ale/whiskey bottle	5
	Wine bottle	3
	Udolpho Wolfe's Schiedam Aromatic Schnapps bottle	2
	Dr. J. Hostetter's Stomach Bitters bottle	1
	Champagne bottle	1
	Pressed glass tumbler	2
	MNV (bottle = 12, tumbler = 2)	14
	Total fragments (bottle = 1,014, tumbler = 20)	1,034
	Total weight (g, both bottles and tumblers)	3,770.71
Tobacco pipes	Presidential Campaign pipe bowl	3
	Soldier Effigy pipe bowl	2
	'T.D.' Stars and Laurel pipe bowl	2
	Knobby pipe bowl	2
	Geometric pipe bowl	2
	Plain pipe bowl	2
	MNV	13
	Total fragments	38
	Total weight (g)	93.16

consumption of alcohol is also represented by the recovery of glass tumblers. Nineteenth-century alcohol consumption could be ritualized, such as toasting, facilitated by specialized glass tableware, for example, tumblers. The minimum number of alcohol vessels (MNV) was primarily based on the total number of distinct bottle finishes and bottle glass colour for the alcohol bottles and minimum number of distinct bases for the pressed glass tumblers.

Tobacco consumption at the kitchen is represented by clay tobacco pipes. In comparison to alcohol-related items, tobacco-related items represent a much smaller percentage (4 per cent) of the indulgence artefact assemblage (fragments = 38, weight = 93.16 g, MNV = 13) (Table 8.1). The entire tobacco indulgence collection comprised at least thirteen tobacco pipes, including Millard Fillmore, Lewis Cass and Henry Clay presidential campaign pipes (n=3), soldier effigy pipes (n = 2), 'T.D.' star and wreath pipes (n=2), knobby pipes (n=2), pipe bowls with geometric designs (n=2) and plain bowl pipes (n=2) (Figure 8.4). One brass spark cap and one white clay pipe stem with a raised 'MCDOUGALL / GLASGOW' mark were also recovered, but did not contribute to the MNV calculations. The minimum number of tobacco pipes was based on the number of

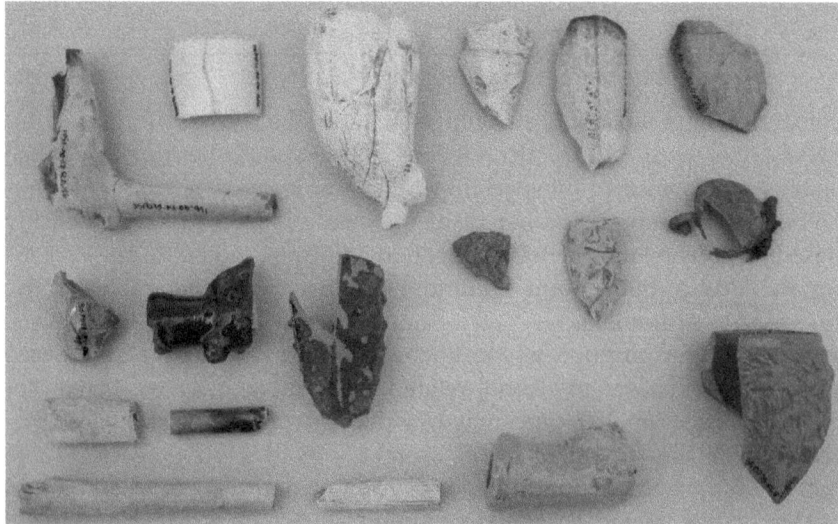

Figures 8.4 and 8.5 Sample of alcohol bottles and tobacco pipes recovered from the company kitchen (photographs by Justin E. Eichelberger)

distinct shank/bowl junctures, fabric colour and the presence or absence of a glaze or slip.

Spatial Contexts

In order to explore indulgence consumption at the company kitchen, each artefact type was analysed based on its spatial location as defined by proximity to the parade ground (the professional and military centre of the post) and to the officers' quarters (the authoritative and hierarchical apex of the post) (Figure 8.2). Three sets of binary pairs of spatial context were defined and used in this study: front/back, inside/outside and open/closed (Figure 8.6). Each point-provenanced artefact was classified based on its excavated position to the nearest centimetre. Artefacts not recovered in situ but collected from 1 x 1 m excavation units were classified according to the unit's spatial location in reference to the officers' quarters, the parade ground and the company kitchen foundations.

Excavation units in front of the kitchen within a clear view of the parade ground and the officers' quarters were classified as 'front' (n=32),

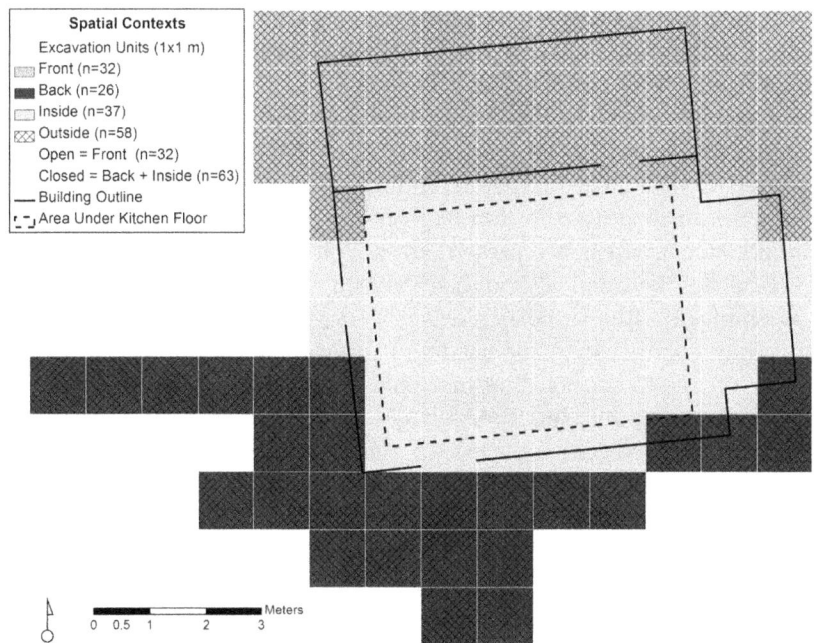

Figure 8.6 Spatial contexts at the company kitchen (illustration by Justin E. Eichelberger)

and those behind the kitchen hidden from the parade ground and the officers' quarters were classified as 'back' (n=26). The front/back spatial analysis did not include artefacts or excavation units located inside the original company kitchen, since they were neither 'front' nor 'back'. The same method was used to classify artefacts according to inside/outside spatial contexts. Excavation units located inside the kitchen foundations were classified as 'inside' (n=37) and those outside the building foundations were 'outside' (n=58). Lastly, these two binary pairs were combined to represent the overall exposed or hidden location of indulgence artefacts. Excavation units located in front and outside the company kitchen, within clear view of the parade ground and the officers' quarters, were classified as 'open' (n=32), and those located behind and inside the company kitchen, and thus hidden from the parade ground and the officers' quarters, were classified as 'closed' (n=63). All 1,072 indulgence-related artefacts were classified within one of these three binary spatial contexts (Tables 8.2, 8.3 and 8.4 and Figure 8.6).

Spatial Distribution of Indulgence Artefacts

Both alcohol-related and tobacco-related artefacts were unevenly distributed across the company kitchen, representing differing consumption and disposal patterns. The majority of alcohol-related artefacts were recovered from the front, inside, and closed spatial contexts of the kitchen and, conversely, the majority of tobacco-related artefacts were recovered from the back, outside, and open spatial contexts (Tables 8.2, 8.3 and 8.4 and Figure 8.7). Although fragment counts and total weight of indulgence artefacts are presented, they are omitted from the following discussion because, although important in understanding the overall assemblage within a particular site (Voss and Allen 2010), fragment and weight counts cannot be used as substitutes for object or minimum number of vessel counts (Sussman 2000). It is important to note that both fragment counts and total weight of indulgence artefacts within their spatial context reflect the overall patterns seen in the distribution of indulgence-related artefacts by minimum number of vessels (Tables 8.2, 8.3 and 8.4 and Figure 8.7).

The greatest number of alcohol-related artefacts by fragment, weight and MNV were recovered from the back, inside and closed spatial contexts (Tables 8.2 and 8.4 and Figure 8.7). Three of the four alcohol items in the front/back context were recovered from behind the company kitchen, and only a single pressed-glass tumbler was recovered from in front of the company kitchen. A similar distributional pattern is observable in the

Table 8.2 Artefact, weight and MNV counts for alcohol-related artefacts recovered from the company kitchen by spatial context

Spatial context	No. of artefacts	Weight (g)	MNV	Artefacts per unit	Weight (g) per unit	MNV per unit
Front	198	407.84	1	6.19	12.75	0.03
Back	389	710.72	3	14.96	27.34	0.11
Inside	447	2,652.15	10	12.08	71.68	0.07
Outside	587	1,118.56	4	10.12	19.28	0.07
Open	198	407.84	1	6.18	12.75	0.03
Closed	836	3,362.87	13	13.27	53.38	0.21

Table 8.3 Artefact, weight and MNV counts for tobacco-related artefacts recovered from the company kitchen by spatial context

Spatial context	No. of artefacts	Weight (g)	MNV	Artefacts per unit	Weight (g) per unit	MNV per unit
Front	18	45.12	7	0.56	1.41	0.22
Back	7	14.59	1	0.27	0.56	0.04
Inside	13	33.45	5	0.35	0.90	0.13
Outside	25	59.71	8	0.43	1.03	0.14
Open	18	45.12	7	0.56	1.41	0.22
Closed	20	48.04	6	0.32	0.76	0.09

Table 8.4 Percentages of indulgence-related artefacts by spatial context

Spatial context	Fragments		Weight (g)		MNV	
	Alcohol	Tobacco	Alcohol	Tobacco	Alcohol	Tobacco
Front	33.7	72	36.5	75.6	25	87.5
Back	66.3	18	63.5	24.4	75	12.5
Inside	43.2	34.2	69.3	35.9	71.4	38.5
Outside	56.8	65.8	30.7	64.1	28.6	61.5
Open	19.1	47.4	10.8	48.4	7.1	53.8
Closed	80.9	52.6	89.2	51.6	92.9	46.2

inside/outside and open/closed contexts. Out of fourteen alcohol-related items, ten were recovered from within the company kitchen, including a small cache of four complete and near-complete alcohol bottles. The remaining four alcohol items recovered from outside the kitchen were a glass tumbler recovered from in front of the kitchen, and a glass and two alcohol bottles recovered from behind the kitchen. Within the open/closed context, over 92 per cent (n=13) of the alcohol-related artefacts were

182   Justin E. Eichelberger

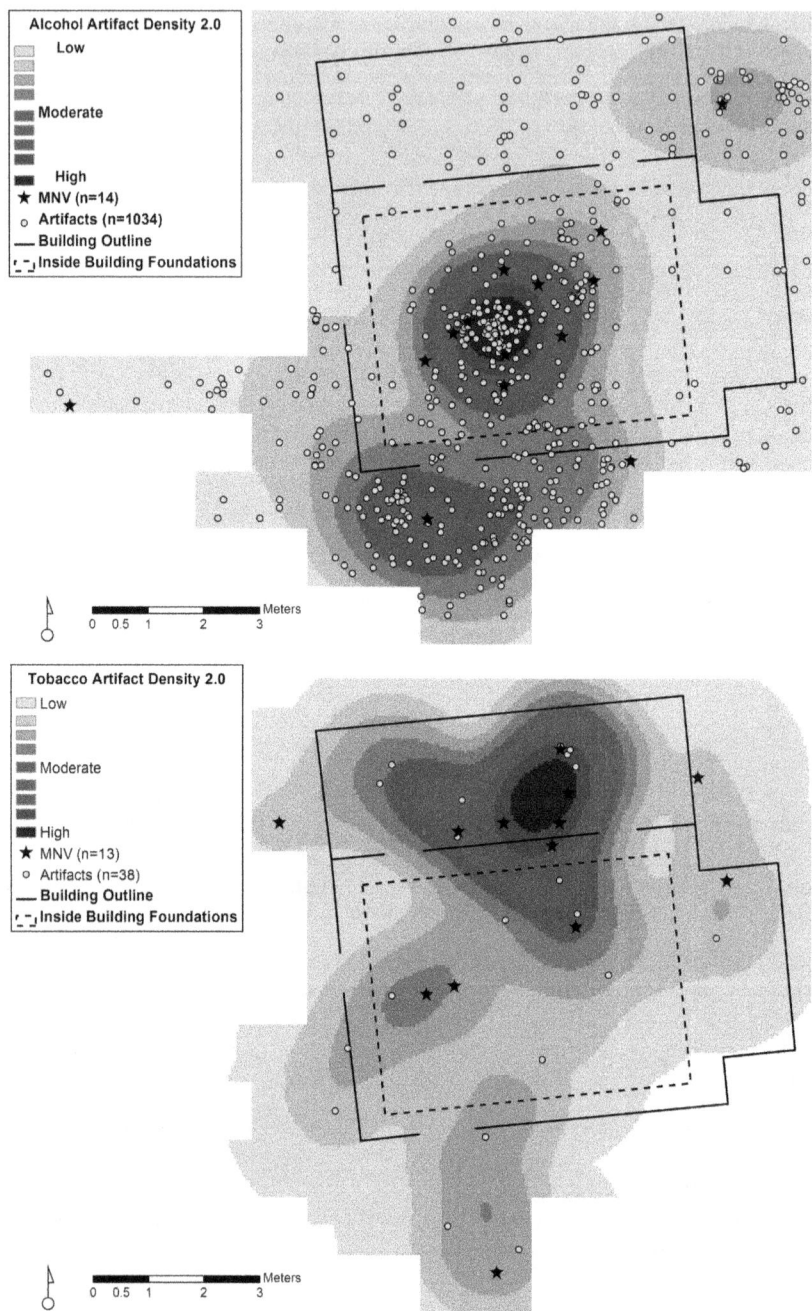

Figure 8.7 Kernel density distributions of alcohol and tobacco related artefacts by Justin E. Eichelberger

recovered from a context that would have been hidden from public view. These items represent the ten bottles recovered from within the building foundations and the two bottles and one glass tumbler recovered from behind the company kitchen. The remaining 8 per cent are represented by the single pressed-glass tumbler recovered from in front of the kitchen. When the unequal sample sizes within each spatial context is accounted for by dividing the total number of items by the total number of archaeological units within each spatial context, the patterns observed in the spatial distribution of alcohol-related items remain the same (Table 8.2).

In direct contrast to the distribution of alcohol-related artefacts, the greatest number of tobacco-related artefacts by fragment, weight and MNV were recovered from the front, outside, and open spatial contexts (Tables 8.3 and 8.4 and Figure 8.7). Over 87 per cent (n=7) of the tobacco items were recovered from in front of the company kitchen, primarily in the area of the front porch. The remaining 13 per cent are represented by a single tobacco pipe recovered from behind the kitchen. Eight (61.5 per cent) of the tobacco-related items were recovered outside the kitchen, as opposed to only five (38.5 per cent) recovered from inside the kitchen. Less dramatic but still reflecting a similar pattern with the front/back and inside/outside contexts, over 53 per cent (n=7) of the tobacco items were recovered from open contexts, while only 47 per cent (n=6) of the tobacco items were recovered from the closed contexts. When the unequal sample sizes within each spatial context is accounted for by dividing the total number of items by the total number of archaeological units within each spatial context, the patterns observed in the spatial distribution of tobacco-related items remain the same (Table 8.3).

When mapped using kernel density distributions, alcohol fragments and alcohol-related items tended to cluster inside and behind the company kitchen as well as in the closed spatial contexts, and tobacco-related items tended to cluster outside and in front of the company kitchen as well as in the open spatial contexts (Figure 8.7).

Statistical Analysis

The level of significant difference in the spatial distribution of indulgence-related artefacts within the binary spatial contexts was tested using a Pearson's chi-squared goodness of fit test to compare the observed frequency distribution of indulgence-related artefacts to a hypothetical frequency of equal distribution within each spatial context. Expected frequency distributions were determined by assuming that the distributions of each artefact type would be equal across all spatial contexts. Samples

Table 8.5 Results of Pearson's chi-square statistical analysis for alcohol-related artefacts

Measure	Spatial context	Expected	Observed	X²	df	p
Weight (g)	Front	626.39	407.84			
	Back	492.17	710.72	173.301	1	<0.001
	Inside	1,470.58	2,652.15			
	Outside	2,300.13	1,118.56	1,556.330	1	<0.001
	Open	1,282.04	407.84			
	Closed	2,488.67	3,362.87	903.138	1	<0.001
No. of fragments	Front	382.72	198			
	Back	258.28	389	118.140	1	<0.001
	Inside	403.26	447			
	Outside	630.74	587	7.770	1	0.005
	Open	351.56	198			
	Closed	682.44	836	101.630	1	<0.001
Minimum no. of vessels (MNV)	Front*	1.65	1			
	Back*	1.34	3	–	–	–
	Inside	5.46	10			
	Outside	8.54	4	6.189	1	0.012
	Open	4.76	1			
	Closed	9.24	13	4.500	1	0.033

sizes for each spatial context were unequal, so each expected frequency was calculated by normalizing the values based on the percentage of units within each spatial context. By comparing the observed frequency distributions to the expected frequency distributions, it is possible to determine the level of significant difference in the distribution of artefacts between the two classifications within each spatial context (Preacher 2001).

The results of these tests suggest that the differences in the distributions of alcohol-related material were statistically significant at the $p<0.03$ or greater significance level for all measures (object, weight and MNV) and within all spatial contexts (front/back, inside/outside and open/closed) (Table 8.5). The one exception is the MNV measure for the front/back context, which had an inadequate sample size. The results for the spatial distributions of the tobacco-related material were more mixed. In six of the nine Pearson's chi-square tests, there was no significant difference found in the distributions of tobacco-related items. But a significant difference in distributions was found within the front/back and open/closed contexts by the weight measure and in the open/closed contexts of the fragment measure (Table 8.6).

Table 8.6 Results of Pearson's chi-square statistical analysis for tobacco-related artefacts

Measure	Spatial context	Expected	Observed	X^2	df	p
Weight (g)	Front	33.43	45.12			
	Back	26.27	14.59	9.281	1	0.002
	Inside	36.33	33.45			
	Outside	56.83	59.71	0.374	1	0.541
	Open	31.67	45.12			
	Closed	61.49	48.04	8.654	1	0.003
No. of fragments	Front	14	18			
	Back	11	7	2.597	1	0.107
	Inside	14.82	13			
	Outside	23.18	25	0.366	1	0.545
	Open	12.92	18			
	Closed	25.08	20	3.026	1	0.081
Minimum no. of vessels (MNV)	Front	5.6	7			
	Back	4.4	1	2.977	1	0.084
	Inside	5.07	5			
	Outside	7.93	8	0.002	1	0.968
	Open	4.42	7			
	Closed	8.58	6	2.282	1	0.13

Discussion

Dietler (2006) argues that the consumption of indulgences is usually accompanied with a set of cultural rules that dictate when, where, why, how and by whom these indulgences can be consumed. Because of these cultural rules, the consumption of indulgences, as embodied material culture, constitutes a prime arena for the negotiation, projection and contestation of power (Dietler 2006: 232). Within this arena, enlisted soldiers contested the Army's prohibition of alcohol through a process of social performance and the renegotiation of space through the use of spatial tactics. Spatial tactics are the use of space as a strategy or technique of power and social control (Low and Lawrence-Zúñiga 2003: 30). Army officers used spatial tactics, evidenced in the spatial layout of the post, to physically separate themselves from the rest of the post and as a tool to monitor their enlisted men. Located at the top of the hill, Officers' Row not only had a superior vantage point for monitoring the daily activities of the post, but also created a physical barrier in terms of distance (150 m) and elevation (15 m) between officers and enlisted soldiers. The commissioned officers also erected physical barriers in terms of post fences designed to exclude civilians from military personnel (the post fence) and soldiers of different social and military rank from each other (officers' fenced yards) (Figure 8.2). Although they did not have the authority of the commissioned officers to erect physical barriers, the enlisted personnel also employed spatial tactics for their own means. Instead of employing spatial tactics as a form of social control, enlisted men used spatial tactics to reappropriate space for the clandestine consumption of alcohol. In the case of the soldiers at Fort Yamhill, they reappropriated the company kitchen for use as a locale of social gathering and indulgence consumption using the building's semi-hidden location to conceal their consumption of alcohol.

The overwhelming concentration of alcohol-related artefacts in the hidden contexts suggests that the enlisted soldiers were actively consuming and disposing of the alcohol-related artefacts in a clandestine manner. As the consumption of alcohol on post was generally forbidden (*Fort Yamhill Post Orders* 1856–66; Barth 1959), enlisted soldiers were participating in acts of subversive resistance to authoritative control by the commissioned officers. The enlisted soldiers' affinity for drinking was not unusual and they resorted to all sorts of schemes to get alcohol, such as purchasing 'medicinal' alcohols (Adams 2009) or smuggling alcohol onto the post in nonalcohol bottles or concealed in other items such as cakes or turkeys (Davis 2003). Caches of alcohol bottles under the floorboards of the company kitchen (Figure 8.7), hidden in the abandoned bakery oven at Fort Yamhill (Eichelberger 2010: 229) and discreetly deposited in the company privies at Fort Hoskins (Bowyer 1992) demonstrates that enlisted soldiers were finding ways to thwart the 'dry fort' orders of their commanding officers. Known to have hosted 'cat fights' and other gambling activities, the company kitchen was the ideal venue for concealing the consumption of alcohol that most certainly accompanied these activities (Barth 1959: 78). After these items were consumed, it would have been easy enough to erase all evidence of their indulgence by discreetly depositing the used and empty bottles under loose kitchen floorboards. Not only were the enlisted personnel actively, although discreetly, resisting their superior officers, they also participated in the public display and consumption of the accepted indulgence item, smoking tobacco through a social performance. The higher concentration of tobacco-related artefacts in the front, outside, and open contexts than in the back, inside, and clandestine contexts demonstrates that the soldiers were actively participating, or at least making an attempt to appear so to their superior officers, in the consumption of Army-sanctioned indulgences as a form of social performance, demonstrating their willingness to conform to the Army regulations concerning indulgence consumption.

Interpreting this behaviour through a dramaturgical perspective (Goffman 1959), it becomes apparent that the soldiers were enacting a social performance, for the benefit of their superior officers, when engaging in the consumption of indulgences. Many soldiers viewed their service in the US Army as akin to being actors in a performance, balancing their personal desires with military discipline. One soldier wrote: 'All the Army, like the world's, a stage.' He continued, 'and the soldiers are "supes." Each in his time plays many parts' (Adams 2009: 145). Using this theatrical metaphor, we can begin to understand the attitudes and motives of the soldiers concerning the consumption of indulgences. They were consuming the acceptable indulgence (tobacco) in what Goffman (1959) called the 'front stage', or in open contexts, exposed to the view, and judgement, of their commanding officers. But when consuming the forbidden victuals (alcohol), they did so in the 'back stage', or closed contexts, where they could not be viewed by their superiors and thus were able to participate in banned behaviour of alcohol consumption without the censure of the officers. By consuming the different indulgences in different contexts, soldiers were 'putting on a show' or performance for their superior officers in an attempt to demonstrate their adherence to Army regulations concerning the consumption of tobacco and alcohol.

As in wider American society, the prevalence of alcohol in the Army incited reactions traceable to class differences (Reckner and Brighton 1999; Smith 2008). The patterns of indulgence consumption seen at the Fort Yamhill company kitchen reflect similar patterns seen at other nineteenth-century 'total institutions', such as at Boot Cotton Mills (Mrozowski, Ziesing and Beaudry 1996; Beaudry and Mrozowski 2001), Hyde Park Barracks (Davies 2011) and the Lakehurst Shops (Veit and Schopp 1999), where lower and working-class members of these communities expressed class solidarity and individual agency through their clandestine consumption of forbidden indulgences. US Army officers believed in their own superiority and the inferiority of the men who served under them, and went to extravagant lengths to keep alcohol from their men, while openly participating in the consumption of alcohol themselves (Adams 2009). This double-standard had its roots in the very structure of social difference within nineteenth-century American culture. In the Army, the officers were seen as gentleman with the self-control to limit their own alcohol consumption, but the enlisted soldiers needed firm guidance and restraint from their propensity for drunkenness. Strict discipline and harsh penalties were seen as the best corrective measures, so rather than publically disobeying their officers, the soldiers continued to indulge their vices through the consumption of alcohol in more clandestine contexts.

Justin E. Eichelberger is a Ph.D. candidate in Historical Archaeology at Oregon State University, United States. He earned his M.A. in Historical Archaeology at Oregon State University in 2011, where he studied the rules and regulations of the foodways system of the US Army as it operated at Fort Yamhill, Oregon. As part of a larger Oregon State University project exploring nineteenth-century US Army posts in the Pacific Northwest, he is currently involved with excavations at several forts in the region examining the relationship between military rules and cultural practice. His doctoral dissertation continues this work by examining the role of architecture, space and material culture in the creation of social boundaries between members of different military ranks.

References

Primary Sources

Fort Yamhill Post Orders. Oregon Historical Society, Portland, United States (microfilm collection of post orders, 1856–66).
USWD. 1857. New York: Harper & Bros. (United States War Department (hereinafter USWD): *Regulations for the Army of the United States*).
——. 1861a. Washington, DC: George W. Bowman (USWD: *Regulations Concerning Barracks and Quarters for the Army of the United States*).
——. 1861b. Washington, DC: Government Printing Office (USWD: *United States Army Regulations*).
——. 1863. Washington, DC: Government Printing Office (USWD: *Revised United States Army Regulations. 1861*).
——. 1902. Washington, DC: Government Printing Office (USWD: *The War of the Rebellion*).

Secondary Literature

Adams, K. 2009. *Class and Race in the Frontier Army: Military Life in the West, 1870–1890*. Norman, OK: University of Oklahoma Press.
Adams, W.H. (ed.). 1991. *Fort Yamhill: Preliminary Historical Archaeological Research Concerning the 1856–1866 Military Post*. Corvallis, OR: Department of Anthropology, Oregon State University.
Balicki, J. 2000. 'Defending the Capital: The Civil War Garrison at Fort C. F. Smith', in C. Geier and S. Potter (eds), *Archaeological Perspectives on the American Civil War*. Gainesville, FL: University Press of Florida, pp. 125–47.
Ball, D. 2001. *Army Regulars on the Western Frontier*. Norman, OK: University of Oklahoma Press.
Barth, G. 1959. *All Quiet on the Yamhill: The Civil War in Oregon*. Eugene, OR: University of Oregon Books.
Barringer, J.W. 1877. *Legislative History of the Subsistence Department of the United States Army from June 16. 1775 to August 15. 1876*. Washington DC: Government Printing Office.

Beaudry, M.C., and M.S. Mrozowski. 2001. 'Cultural Space and Worker Identity in the Company City: Nineteenth-Century Lowell. Massachusetts', in A. Mayne and T. Murray (eds), *The Archaeology of Urban Landscapes*. Cambridge: Cambridge University Press, pp. 118–31.

Beisaw, A.M., and J.G. Gibb (eds). 2009. *The Archaeology of Institutional Life*. Tuscaloosa, AL: University of Alabama Press.

Bowyer, G.C. 1992. 'Archaeological Symbols of Status and Authority: Fort Hoskins. Oregon. 1856–1865', M.A. dissertation. Oregon: Oregon State University.

Brauner, D., and J.E. Eichelberger. 2009. *Archaeological Investigations at the Fort Yamhill Site: Field Season 2008*. Corvallis, OR: Department of Anthropology, Oregon State University.

Brauner. D., J. E. Eichelberger and B. Boulware. 2009. *Archaeological Investigations at the Fort Yamhill Site: Field Season 2007*. Corvallis, OR: Department of Anthropology, Oregon State University.

Breck, Major S.A.A.G. 1875. *Remarks on the Food of the U.S. Army*. Washington DC: United States War Department.

Burke, J. 1999. 'Military Culture', in L. Kurtz (ed.), *Encyclopaedia of Violence Vol. II*. New York: Academic Press, pp. 447–62.

Burns, E. 2004. *The Spirits of America: A Social History of Alcohol*. Philadelphia, PA: Temple University Press.

———. 2007. *The Smoke of the Gods: A Social History of Tobacco*. Philadelphia, PA: Temple University Press.

Bush, D. 2000. 'Interpreting the Latrines of the Johnson's Island Civil War Military Prison', *Historical Archaeology* 21(1): 67–80.

Butterfield, D. 1862. *Camp and Outpost Duty for Infantry*. New York: Harper & Brothers.

Crass, D.C., and D.L. Wallsmith. 1992. '"Where's the Beef?": Food Supply at an Antebellum Frontier Post', *Historical Archaeology* 26(2): 3–23.

Clouse, R.A. 1999. 'Interpreting Archaeological Data through Correspondence Analysis', *Historical Archaeology* 33(2): 90–107.

Davies, P. 2011. 'Destitute Women and Smoking at the Hyde Park Barracks. Sydney. Australia', *International Journal of Historical Archaeology* 15: 82–101.

Davis, W.C. 2003. *A Taste for War: The Culinary History of the Blue and the Gray*. Mechanicsburg, PA: Stackpole Books.

Dietler, M. 2006. 'Alcohol: Anthropological/Archaeological Perspectives', *Annual Review of Anthropology* 35: 229–49.

Eichelberger, J.E. 2010. 'Foodways at Fort Yamhill. 1856–1866: An Archaeological and Archival Perspective', M.A. dissertation. Oregon: Oregon State University.

Eichelberger, J.E., and D.R. Brauner. 2011. *Archaeological Investigations at the Fort Yamhill Site: Field Season 2011*. Corvallis, OR: Department of Anthropology, Oregon State University.

Fike, R.E. 1987. *The Bottle Book: A Comprehensive Guide to Historic, Embossed Medicine Bottles*. Salt Lake City, UT: Peregrine Smith Press.

Goffman, E. 1959. *The Presentation of Self in Everyday Life*. New York: Doubleday.

Hardesty, D. 1981. 'Historical Archaeology at Fort Churchill', *Nevada Historical Society Quarterly* 24(4): 283–97.
Hoagland, A.K. 2004. *Army Architecture in the West*. Norman, OK: University of Oklahoma Press.
Horsford, E.N. 1864. *The Army Ration*. New York: D. Van Nostrand.
Kautz, A.V. 1864. *Customs of Service for Non-commissioned Officers and Soldiers*. Philadelphia, PA: J.B. Lippincott & Co.
Low, S.M., and D. Lawrence- Zúñiga. 2003. 'Locating Culture', in S.M. Low and D. Lawrence- Zúñiga (eds), *The Anthropology of Space and Place*. Malden, MA: Blackwell, pp. 1–48.
McKearin, H., and K.M. Wilson. 1978. *American Bottles & Flasks and their Ancestry*. New York: Crown.
Mrozowski, S.A., G.H. Ziesing and M.C. Beaudry. 1996. *Living on the Boott: Historical Archaeology at the Boott Mills Boardinghouses, Lowell, Massachusetts*. Amherst, MA: University of Massachusetts Press.
Ordronaux, J. 1863. *Hints on Health in Armies, for the Use of Volunteer Officers*. New York: D. Van Nostrands.
Preacher, K.J. 2001. 'Calculation for the Chi-Square Test: An Interactive Calculation Tool for Chi-Square Tests of Goodness of Fit and Independence'. Retrieved 21 May 2017 from http://www.quantpsy.org/chisq/chisq.htm.
Reckner, P.E. and S.A. Brighton. 1999. '"Free from All Vicious Habits": Archaeological Perspectives on Class Conflict and the Rhetoric of Temperance', *Historical Archaeology*, 33(1): 63–86.
Schablitsky, J.M. 1996. 'Duty and Vice: The Daily Life of a Fort Hoskins Soldier', M.A. dissertation. Oregon: Oregon State University.
Scott, D. 2009. 'Studying the Archaeology of War: A Model Based on the Investigation of Frontier Military Sites in the American Trans-Mississippi West', in D. Gaimster and T. Majewski (eds), *International Handbook of Historical Archaeology*. New York: Springer, pp. 299–317.
Smith, F.H. 2008. *The Archaeology of Alcohol and Drinking*. Gainesville, FL: University Press of Florida.
South, S. 1977. *Method and Theory in Historical Archaeology*. New York: Academic Press.
Sussman, L. 2000. 'Object vs. Sherd: A Statistical Evaluation', in K. Karklins (ed.), *Studies in Material Culture Research*. Tucson, AZ: Society for Historical Archaeology, pp. 96–103.
Tate, M.L. 1999. *The Frontier Army in the Settlement of the West*. Norman, OK: University of Oklahoma Press.
Trussel, T. 1996. 'Frontier Military Medicine at Fort Hoskins. 1857–1865'. M.A. dissertation. Oregon: Oregon State University.
Utley, R. 1967. *Frontiersman in Blue: The United States Army and the Indian, 1848–1865*. New York: MacMillan Company.
Van den Bossche, W. 2001. *Antique Glass Bottles*. Woodbridge: Antique Collectors Club.
Veit, R., and P.W. Schopp. 1999. 'Who's Been Drinking on the Railroad? Archaeological Excavations at the Central Railroad of New Jersey's Lakehurst shops', *Northeast Historical Archaeology* 28: 21–40.

Voss, B., and R. Allen. 2010. 'Guide to Ceramic MNV Calculation Qualitative and Quantitative Analysis', *Technical Briefs in Historical Archaeology* 5: 1–9.

Wilson, P.H. 2008. 'Defining Military Culture', *Journal of Military History* 72: 11–41.

Wooster, R. 2009. *The American Military Frontiers*. Albuquerque, NM: University of New Mexico Press.

Chapter 9

Religion in the Asylum
Lunatic Asylum Chapels and Religious Provision in Nineteenth-Century Ireland

Katherine Fennelly

Introduction

In the summer of 2012, a fire at a church in Wakefield, West Yorkshire drew the attention of the local media (Figure 9.1). A number of pre-fire photographs of the site taken by urban explorers offered a sharp juxtaposition to the burned-out shell. The church, on the grounds of a former nineteenth-century asylum, had become dilapidated, and the urban explorers' photographs of the intact church showed the extent of neglect after years of abandonment. Photographs also recorded the stained-glass windows, which stood intact until the fire, depicting asylum-related imagery such as a nurse and a motif of the asylum's name. The stained glass linked the institution to the church, even after the closure and redevelopment of the hospital buildings into apartments.

Church buildings are a common feature of many former asylum sites. Despite this, the historiography on lunatic asylums presents religious practice and provision as a contested issue, due to the perceived risk that religious fervour posed to an unstable mind (Pinel 1806: 78; Conolly 1847: 122; Foucault 2006: 242). Much of the literature on the history of asylums, their architecture and material culture, has drawn a correlation between asylums and contemporaneous institutions like prisons and workhouses; not least the work of sociologist Erving Goffman (1961), who associated asylums with prisons and other institutions of incarceration. Goffman considered asylums to be 'total institutions, that is an institution catering for the three spheres of life – work, sleep and play – in one central facility' (1961: 17). The foundation of pauper asylums can be linked to the popular ideology of the 'undeserving poor', a popular concept in England and Ireland that drew a distinction between those who were genuinely in need and those who claimed charitable support but were able-bodied or otherwise could potentially support themselves (Crossman 2006: 5). This ideology was supported by scholars like Thomas Malthus, who argued that poverty was a result of the improvidence and immorality of the poor themselves (Emsley 1996: 37). The social and spatial marginalization of asylums, reinforced by the provision of all asylum facilities within the walls of the total institution, including religious services, supports this link. Where religion was increasingly seen as a common ground between the community and the patients in the asylum, the construction of asylum

Figure 9.1 Stanley Royd Hospital Church, Wakefield, nine months after its destruction by fire (photograph by Katherine Fennelly)

Figure 9.2 The grounds of the former Maryborough District Lunatic Asylum chapel site, with the Roman Catholic church in centre middle-ground and the Anglican church in left middle-ground (photograph by Katherine Fennelly)

Figure 9.3 The interior of Maryborough Asylum Roman Catholic Church (now St Fintan's Church; photograph by Katherine Fennelly)

chapels and designated spaces for religious service within the asylum meant that the patients were further separated from society. Through examination of the historical documents, contemporaneous reform literature and the physical built environment, this chapter will outline the extent to which communication between the asylums and the wider population can be identified. Taking asylum churches as an example of the many features of asylum architecture, it will argue that the consolidation of patient space within the asylum was driven by political, social and economic factors.

Total institutions included onsite features such as laundries, leisure facilities, farms and chapels; unlike many contemporaneous features, chapels survive largely intact. This chapter will focus on a distinctive Irish case study, the Maryborough District Lunatic Asylum, with reference to other contemporaneous Irish asylums. The nineteenth-century asylum system in Ireland comprised just twenty-seven institutions, nine of which were designed between 1825 and 1835 by public works architects Francis Johnston and William Murray. Asylum construction was overseen by the Board of General Control from 1817 until 1835, and by the Inspectors for Lunacy and the Board of Works from 1845 (Reuber 1996: 1183). The Irish system was thus more architecturally and administratively homogeneous than the English and Welsh system, where asylums were constructed and run at county level, or the Scottish system, where many asylums were constructed under royal charter rather than state bodies. As such, the Irish system offers more scope for comparative analysis.

As a result of downsizing and closure of psychiatric hospitals in the late twentieth century, former lunatic asylum buildings that had, up to that point, been used as hospitals, now face dilapidation, development or even demolition. In a few cases, the buildings are still used for mental health services; however, access to those buildings is restricted. For this research, permission was sought and granted for access to St Fintan's Hospital (formerly Maryborough District Lunatic Asylum), an Irish hospital still operating as a psychiatric facility. The continuous use of the building as a hospital from 1833 to the present has meant that it is in a good state of preservation, with many of its original features still intact. This chapter builds on archaeological approaches to lunatic asylum buildings and the material culture of mental illness, conducted largely in Australia and the United States (Coleborne 2001; Piddock 2007; Psota 2011).

Historical Background

The buildings considered within this chapter were constructed within the broader context of asylum building in the nineteenth century. Therefore, a brief overview of the history and development of the asylum systems in the British Isles is necessary to understand why the development of Irish sites is significant.

Growing urban populations and developments in healthcare contributed to interest in provision for lunatics towards the end of the eighteenth century (Scull 1993: 26). Migration to increasingly industrial urban centres for work meant that the traditional family-centred care for lunatics was destabilized. On the back of the success of asylums like St Luke's in London, provincial asylums were founded in cities such as Manchester and Newcastle (Porter 2004: 138). A series of acts – the 1808 County Asylums Act (48.Geo.3.c.96), the 1817 Irish Lunatic Asylums for the Poor Act (57.Geo.3.c.106) and the 1845 Lunacy Acts (8 & 9.Vict.c.100.s.3) – revolutionized the care of lunatics by providing for the establishment of dedicated lunatic asylums.

The new asylums were to be run according to a 'moral' approach to the management of lunatics, advocated and popularized by French physician Philippe Pinel, and English reformer and private asylum owner Samuel Tuke (Pinel 1806: 51–54; Tuke 1813; Thompson and Goldin 1975: 58). This approach became known contemporaneously as 'moral management'. 'Moral' referred to the mental and interpersonal nature of the treatment, and 'management' related to the hands-on, caretaking approach that promoted patient self-regulation under paternalistic supervision (Porter 2004: 213–14; Yanni 2007: 24). The Retreat in York opened in 1796 and was run as a 'moral' institution. The Retreat was purpose built and became a model for the architecture and management of asylums (Yanni 2007: 27–28). The building was organized into two separate wings, joined at the centre by an administration block and common room facilities. It gained particular notoriety under the stewardship of founder William Tuke's grandson, Samuel, who published a treatise on the management of the Retreat and the architecture that supported it (Tuke 1813; Porter 2002: 104).

Religion in the Asylum

Religion was central to the establishment of the Retreat. The death of a Quaker patient at the nearby York Asylum in 1790 inspired William Tuke, also a Quaker, to establish a private institution for Quaker patients, though it remained so exclusive for less than a generation (Digby 1986: 10; Porter 2004: 136). After the 1808 County Asylums Act (48.Geo.3.c.96), many of the features of the Retreat were applied in public asylums; however, religious provision was not a priority amongst architects and reformers who oversaw construction. Despite the lack of material provision for practice, religion was nonetheless an ever-present feature in the daily lives of the patients. For example, asylum reform commentator and physician John Conolly (1847: 72) noted that the diet at his asylum, Hanwell in Middlesex, offered an alternative to meat for Roman Catholic patients during Lent. In the early public asylums, exposure to religion was identified as a cause and aggravator of mania and depression (Foucault 2006: 242–46). Attitudes towards religion and mental illness are evidenced in the lack of religious provision in early asylum buildings; the abovementioned West Riding Asylum, which opened in 1818, did not make provision in the estate for a separate chapel until the middle of the century (C85/1/1/2). The Irish asylums constructed between 1815 and 1835 likewise did not originally build any chapels on their grounds, despite the fact that the patient populations in Irish asylums reflected the religious demographic in their surrounding areas (Reynolds 1992: 63). In the mid nineteenth century, about 80 per cent of inmates in Irish asylums were Roman Catholic, with the remaining 20 per cent made up of Church of Ireland Protestants, Presbyterians, Quakers and other religious denominations (Prior and Griffiths 1997: 137). Considering the political associations of different religious groups and the prominence of religion in Irish politics, the absence of churches from original asylum plans is conspicuous.

From 1845, the Commissioners for Lunacy in England made the provision of a chapel compulsory in all asylums (Taylor 1991: 166). This was due to a shift in attitudes towards the role of religion in the management of the insane. Notably, in his treatise on the construction of asylums, Conolly (1847: 123–24) underpinned his concerns over the dangers of religious fervour in asylums with the point that many patients he observed gained comfort from religious service. He described a religious service at an asylum, noting that patients participated in responses and singing during services, suggesting that the routine of religious services offered a degree of normalcy to institutionalization. The Commissioners' actions may also have been informed by the unauthorized use of asylum spaces for religious service. In the Northampton General Lunatic Asylum, for example, a chapel was requested by the asylum's management committee for the 'cheering and solacing' as well as the sanitary wellbeing of the patients who had, until this time, been crowded into one of the male wards to hear services (Foss and Trick 1989: 108). This created a different hazard: the potential mixing of male and female patients.

The provision for religious service in asylums coincided with the 1845 County Asylums Act (8 & 9.Vict.c.100.s.3) in England and Wales, which stipulated that all counties must construct a lunatic asylum for the pauper insane. The outlying effects of this Act were felt in Ireland; new asylums were built in provincial towns such as Kilkenny and Sligo, and were overseen by the newly established Inspectors of Lunacy. However, unlike their English and Welsh counterparts, the new Irish asylums did not incorporate chapels into their plans. Services in early asylums continued to be carried out by a chaplain inside the building, in day rooms and dining rooms (*Inspector's Reports* 1891; Scully 1983: 29; Saris 1996: 548). The provision of a chaplain but not a designated space for worship was part of the government's efforts to maintain impartiality in religious matters in charitable public institutions, while also facilitating inmates in religious practice (Robins 1986: 117). A dispute between the government and the Belfast District Lunatic Asylum regarding the provision of chaplains highlights the level of contention over this issue. In the 1850s, the governors of the Belfast Asylum so opposed the government (in the person of the Lord Lieutenant) on the issue of appointing three asylum chaplains that they successfully brought legal action to prevent their appointment (Robins 1986: 118–19; Prior and Griffiths 1997: 148–50).

However, the conflict in Belfast was exceptional, and religious services continued to be commonly held in Irish asylums. By the end of the nineteenth century, religious services were interfering with the running of the asylums, as communal rooms in the buildings were being used for religious worship (*Inspector's Reports* 1891: 150). Finally, bowing to the individual demands of different asylums, chapels began appearing on the grounds of asylums; these chapels were distinctive in style from their host institutions. Many new chapels were neo-Gothic in style. This style was typified by architects like Augustus Pugin and the Ecclesiologist Movement, who espoused the connection between religious truth, moral authority and architectural design. Pugin advocated for a return to medieval-style architecture to recapture the spirit of the high Middle Ages, which was seen in the nineteenth century as a lost age of morality (Watkin 2001: 21–22; Hill 2009: 118). The style was popular amongst Anglican church-builders (Brück 2013: 205); its use in the new asylum churches is therefore unsurprising. The moral character of chapel architecture was juxtaposed to an increasing regulation of mental illness by professionals trained in psychiatry and superseding moral management (Scull 1981: 6). Arguably, the construction of neo-Gothic churches in asylums may have been an attempt to re-establish the caretaking and humanitarian approach to management that characterized the establishment of early asylums in the face of increasing clinicization, echoing the attempts of the ecclesiologists to recapture a golden age of religious fervour. Regardless, positioning chapels within the asylum walls affirmed the authority of the asylums, both spatially and literally, over the lives of patients, and reinforced the 'total institution'. Considering the Maryborough Asylum, the following will outline the efforts of asylum managers and commissioners towards consolidating the insularity of the asylums through the provision of religious services, though with a view primarily to addressing, and catering for, patient needs.

Case Study: Maryborough District Lunatic Asylum, Queen's County, Ireland

The Maryborough Asylum was constructed in 1833 to serve Queen's County (now Laois), King's County (now Offaly) and the counties of Westmeath and Longford. The institution was constructed 1 km to the east of the market town of Maryborough (now Portlaoise) in the Irish midlands. Maryborough's geographical position at the confluence of several arterial routes made it an ideal locale to host a provincial asylum. Minimal local industry may have further influenced the decision to situate the asylum in the town (*CP/2/440/9*). Religious provision at Maryborough reflects a changing attitude towards religious practice in public institutions during the nineteenth century, and a response to advances or reforms in mental healthcare and the evolution of the total institution.

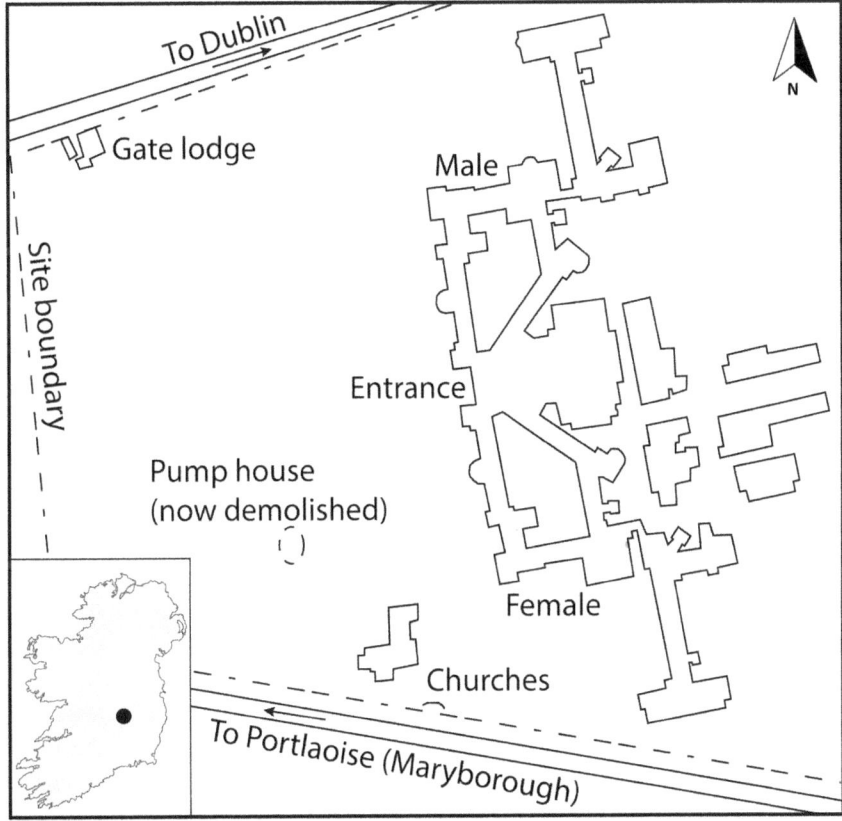

Figure 9.4 Plan of the Maryborough Asylum site as it stood in 2014, with significant features labelled (illustration by Katherine Fennelly)

Johnston and Murray designed Maryborough Asylum in a K-shape, with an administration block in the centre flanked by two lateral corridors and two diagonal wings to the rear with patient rooms (Figure 9.4). Vaulted interior corridors bounded the north and south ranges, creating two interior courtyards. The building was divided symmetrically, with male patients to the north and female patients to the south.

The grounds were designed with patient recreation in mind, negating the need for extended use of the enclosed airing yards. By the end of the nineteenth century, the building had expanded beyond the original K-shape. Previous features such as store rooms to the north and south had been converted to patient accommodation to cater for increasing demand. However, despite major development works throughout the century, no provision was made for religious services until the 1890s.

In 1833, the asylum's physician, John Jacob (1833: 57), noted that a chaplain was required for the asylum, albeit under the direction and at the behest of the physician. His directions were clearly ignored as no chaplain (of any denomination) appeared on the asylum books until 1844, when a Protestant and a Catholic chaplain are both listed for the first time in the account books. The delay in offering regular religious provision is conspicuous; Conolly (1847: 127) observed that Irish Catholic patients in England were notable for their regular requests for religious provision, deriving consolation from it. Therefore, it is surprising that there was not a demand for the appointment of any chaplains before 1844. It must be assumed that the asylum was visited by clergymen or that patients attended services outside the institution.

The manager of the asylum, William Abbot, noted that two chaplains – Roman Catholic (RC) and Church of Ireland (COI) – were both appointed in 1843/44 and that henceforth divine service was performed on Sundays and festival days (*AO/19/48/14*). Up to twenty patients attended Protestant services, while up to seventy regularly attended Catholic services that year. This accounts for roughly half the patient population, so it is reasonable to assume that those who attended services were exceptional. Either they had requested religious service (as Conolly noted) or they were the convalescent (recovering) and quiet patients. Abbot (*AO/19/48/14*) also noted that 'such of the household as [could] be spared' also attended services with the patients. Interestingly, Abbot followed his note on divine service attendance with one on the asylum's recent introduction of the 'non-restraint system'. Non-restraint was one of the central principles of moral management and refers more specifically to the cessation of the use of mechanical restraints such as manacles, chains and cuffs (orders of purchase for which had previously appeared on the asylum's books). The close association between religious service and moral management in Abbot's account suggests that the asylum was, ten years after opening, slowly beginning to take on the principles of lunacy reform and patient management, which had been behind the development of the asylum system since the 1817 Act (57.Geo.3.c.106). However, Maryborough was still lacking in providing and regulating patient access to formal religious services. This was largely due to the gross underestimation of demand for services that resulted in massive overcrowding and the use of dedicated spaces for multiple purposes (such as the conversion of work rooms for patient dormitories in the 1840s).

From the late 1830s, new asylums constructed in England, such as the Derby Asylum, responded to massive overcrowding in the Georgian asylums by expanding patient capacity and modifying asylum design accordingly. The Derby Asylum, much lauded by Conolly, allowed for dedicated rooms for leisure activities like music, maximum patient classification according to severity of illness and, notably, a chapel (Piddock 2007: 63). Asylums constructed before the 1845 Lunacy Acts (8 & 9.Vict.c.100.s.3) in England and Ireland were rather slower to respond to the architectural and management trends that asylums like Derby were taking on board. The patient population in Maryborough swelled from its original capacity of one hundred on construction to 349 in 1891. The building programme brought the asylum into line with other lately constructed institutions like Enniscorthy and Portrane, which were built along the lines of the British models like Derby. Due to the massive expansion of the asylum, provision was made for specific activities. Like the asylums in England and the new asylums in Ireland, Maryborough began to consolidate and regulate all aspects of patient life and routine within the walls of the institution.

Hygiene was the primary concern underlying the construction of specialist facilities for religious provision. In 1891, the Inspectors of Lunatics in Ireland noted that the dining room at the Maryborough had been converted into a chapel for the use of divine service. This development left the patients bereft of a separate space for meals, which were by necessity taken in day rooms (*Inspector's Reports* 1891: 12, 150). The practice of using the dining room for the purpose of a chapel was not uncommon; anthropologist Jamie Saris (1996: 548) pointed out that a room in the Sligo Asylum was occasionally referred to amongst staff in the twentieth century as the 'Chapel', presumably due to its use as such in the past. The commissioning of chapels for their use by patients demonstrates the concern of the Inspectors and the asylum authorities over the misappropriation of designated spaces, and the need to spatially regulate the asylum interiors. If day rooms were taken up with dining patients, the patients' negotiable space would be confined to their own rooms or to the new open-plan wards that began to appear in public asylums from the 1840s. In the increasingly clinical atmosphere of the later nineteenth-century lunatic hospitals, the need to maintain a level of cleanliness in sleeping areas was paramount. Therefore, the dining room could not continue to be used as a chapel. To do so would be to increase the likelihood of a hygiene risk in the appropriated day rooms, which the patients were eating in, or the wards, where patients were spending increasingly more time.

The Inspectors recommended that a separate chapel be constructed for the use of the patients. The logic behind their decision was economic: a new dining room, in a central space, would be more expensive to build than a separate chapel on the asylum's extensive grounds. Church buildings were constructed at Maryborough and completed in 1896, at a cost of £5,559 (*Inspector's Reports* 1896) (Figure 9.2). One building was constructed, though both major denominations were catered for. The churches were situated beside a gate in the south perimeter wall, facing the female wing.

The buildings were designed by Sir Thomas Drew, notable for his various chapel buildings such as the Kilkenny District Lunatic Asylum church. Drew's Maryborough chapels were constructed of undressed stone arranged in overlapping style. The church buildings stand at the southeastern entrance to the asylum, backing onto gardens at the rear, which were landscaped for the purpose of constructing the chapels. This is evidenced by the sharp break of slope directly behind the buildings marked later by a low kerb and an abrupt change from grass to gravel; pathways from the main building were also redirected (Figure 9.5). The deliberate positioning of the chapels at this location on the grounds shows that there was no hesitation in allowing the public full view of the presence of religious service within the asylum. It must therefore be assumed

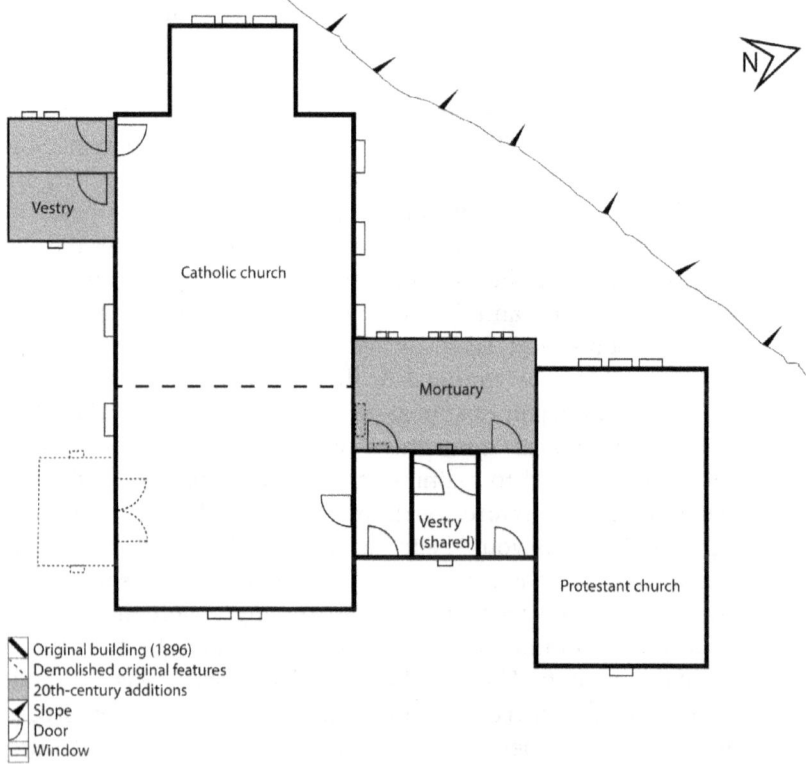

Figure 9.5 Plan of the Maryborough Asylum churches (illustration by Katherine Fennelly)

that the opinions of the authorities and locals on the construction of chapels at Maryborough differed greatly to those of the governors at Belfast (as discussed above).

The shape of the buildings separate them from other asylum chapels built at this time. Maryborough was originally supposed to build just one RC chapel; COI patients could be provided for in the asylum board room. One external building was common: the Johnston/ Murray Asylums at Armagh and Clonmel both constructed large detached RC chapels. Drew's chapels at Kilkenny were similar in style and proportion to their Maryborough counterparts; however, they were not attached despite their close proximity on the site. The Maryborough churches were constructed next to each other, connected at the centre by a shared vestry, making them a single building (Figure 9.6). The Maryborough churches were an innovative approach to chapel construction and are distinctive in their plan. The continued use of both chapels at Maryborough for their respective purposes is also unusual. A similar plan was executed at Carlow thirty years previously; a single building with separate chapels and separate entrances was constructed, but by the end of the nineteenth century, this building was exclusively used for RC services (Irish Architectural

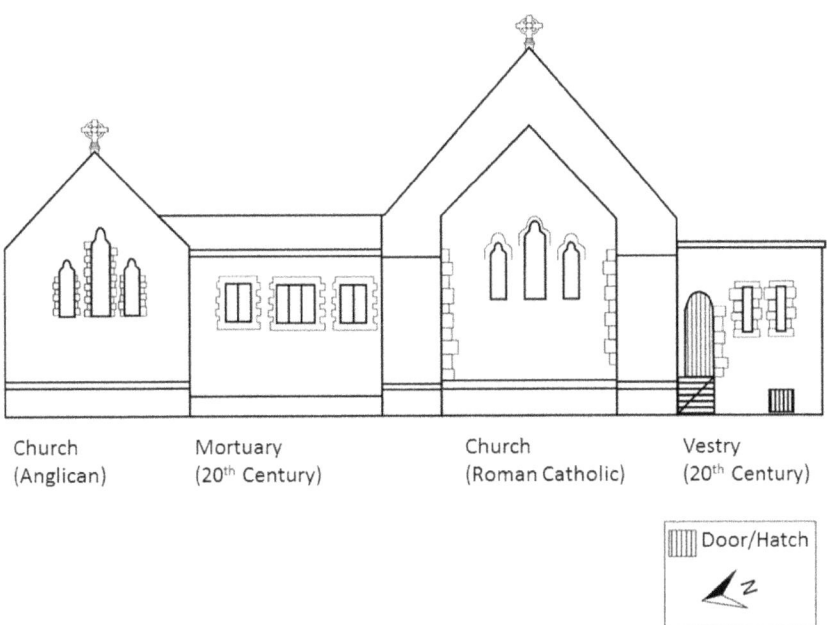

Figure 9.6 Rear elevation of the Maryborough Asylum churches (illustration by Katherine Fennelly)

Archive 2014). COI services were catered for in a smaller chapel attached to the asylum building's eastern interior courtyard.

The two-chapel solution was common in Irish asylums, though British lunatic asylums commonly only had one church to cater to the institution. Examples include the churches at Prestwich and Wakefield Asylums in Lancashire and Yorkshire respectively (*Ordnance Survey* 1855, 1891). The joint chapels at Maryborough suggest a degree of cooperation and tolerance with regard to religion in the area.

The importance placed on the consecration of RC churches in Ireland may also have contributed to the construction of two separate churches. When the Maryborough churches were built, Ireland had recently undergone a sustained period of church building following the 1829 Catholic Emancipation Act, which removed a series of laws and tithes imposed on Irish Catholics since the seventeenth century (Brooks 1995: 16). The consecration of a dedicated RC church at the Maryborough Asylum rather than the construction of one nondenominational church correlated with the ongoing affirmation of Irish Catholic identity, expressed through church building. The two churches at Maryborough are not significantly materially different in terms of layout or design, aside from a size difference. The churches shared a vestry until the middle of the twentieth century. Both are rectangular in plan, with a shallow chancel to the west of the RC church. Two separate entrances at the front of the building, flanking either side of the shared vestry's lancet window, offered access to the churches without mixing the congregations of either faith. The original main entrance to the RC church was through a porch facing the south perimeter wall. The porch and entranceway do not survive, possibly due to a fire in the church in the mid twentieth century; the wall where the entranceway stood has been filled in. A mortuary and RC vestry were added in the 1970s. Maryborough's RC chapel is significantly larger (almost double in length) than the COI chapel (Figure 9.3). The difference in size between the two reflected the demographics of the asylum.

The material arrangement of the buildings played a pivotal role in the regulation and control of patient movement and interaction. As mentioned above, patients were separated in the asylum according to gender, with male patients to the north and female patients to the south. Considering this attention to patient gender classification, it must be assumed that patients were separated inside the church too. Patient separation may be the reason behind the two separate entrances to the RC church. The small number of COI patients in the asylum meant that patients could be easily filtered into the building; however, the large number of RC patients may have necessitated careful spatial separation. A 1968 plan of the asylum churches indicates that there was a gallery in the church, which no longer exists. The gallery was accessed by a staircase to the left of the rear-left doorway to the RC church. It is reasonable to assume that patients who entered through the rear were directed to the gallery, while patients who entered through the south entrance porch were seated in the main body of the church.

It is not possible to ascertain which gender group would have entered through which door, if indeed patients were separated at all. However, given the strong emphasis on classification in much of the contemporaneous literature (including an essay on modern asylum building penned by George Hine in 1901) and the fundamentality of patient classification and separation to the regulation of the asylum architecture, it is reasonable to assume that the large body of patients entering the RC church were separated by gender. Minimizing fraternization between the patients may have been a moral issue: historian Maria Luddy (2007: 19) has pointed out in her work on Irish prostitution that many women engaged in this activity ended up in asylums. Therefore, the separation of a certain class of female patient may have been deemed necessary to preserve the moral character of the institution, just as patients with venereal disease were either relegated to separate institutions or housed in separate wards in contemporaneous public infirmaries (Taylor 1991: 102). In order to access the chapel, male patients would have been required to cross the asylum grounds in front of the female side. If male patients entered through the south porch, they may have crossed paths with female patients entering the rear-east door. Therefore, it must be surmised that male patients either entered through the rear-east door (the back door) or their journey to the church was staggered with that of the female patients, so as to minimize any fraternization.

The asylum churches were constructed in an unexpected location, further adding to the probability that their spatial arrangement in the asylum was chosen to reflect asylum protocol and the regulation of the asylum space. The asylum had extensive land to the front and an expanse of farmland to the rear, on which was built a mortuary and a graveyard for patients. The construction of the church to the rear of the asylum near to these two features makes more sense as a spatial arrangement than the construction of the churches in their present position beside the south gate. The placement is not consistent with Drew's other churches at Kilkenny, which were built to the rear of the building. Conversely, the spatial placement of the Kilkenny churches may inform us of the reasons behind the placement of the Maryborough churches. Both the Maryborough and Kilkenny churches were built beside main roads and close to gates. Placing the churches near a gate meant that chaplains did not need to enter the grounds proper to carry out their tasks, sparing the asylum outside interference and maintaining distance between the patients and any established religious body. The placement of stone crosses on the apex of each church's gable end also indicates the importance of constructing the chapel within view of the public. Public opinion and concern over the workings of asylums had been an issue of asylum management since the exposure of abuses at the York Asylum in 1790. Therefore, construction of the asylum church within view of the road meant that one feature of patient treatment – religious service – was consistent with the routine of onlookers outside the asylum, normalizing the routine and behaviour of patients in the asylum.

Discussion: Religion, Asylums and the Local Area

Maryborough was not alone in separating religious provision between denominations. At the Sligo Asylum, pressure from a Catholic-controlled Sligo County Council to fund an RC chapel over a COI chapel at the asylum led to a compromise solution: two chapels were built, but the RC chapel was six times larger than that of the COI (Saris 1996: 548). The ornately decorated RC chapel was designed in a neo-Gothic style, with a lead-capped cupola, a polygonal feature atop of the church building, with shaped gables and ashlar (horizontally laid) tracery. The COI chapel was rather understated in comparison with pointed arch openings for the windows and door (*Co.Sligo.Reg.no:32323002*). The two chapels stand facing each other in stylistic contrast, 140 m apart at the front of the asylum building, which has now been converted into a hotel. Their oppositional stance reflects the conflict surrounding their construction.

The chapels of the Richmond Asylum in Dublin also face each other. The Richmond chapels had an extra distinctive feature: a tunnel, linking the asylum annexe where the chapels stood to the original asylum building, across a public thoroughfare. The tunnel enabled the passage of patients to the chapels (and a nearby infirmary) without requiring them to exit the asylum grounds (Bedford 2008: 12). This tunnel, which ensured the maintenance of security and the minimization of outside influence on the patients, was still in operation by the 1930s. Like the chapels, the tunnel reinforced the totality of the institution by keeping patients within the walls.

As Goffman (1961: 17) stated, lunatic asylums catered for work, rest and play, controlling the patient's routine. The addition of chapels on the sites removed the asylum from the local community further by providing a facility that the staff, as well as the patients, could use. The importance placed on constructing dedicated spaces for worship in asylums is curious considering the proximity of asylums to their host towns. Though religion may be said to be a means of keeping patients integrated in wider society (Prior 1997: 506), the separate nature of inmates from that society was stressed by keeping them from public religious services. This separation may have inadvertently contributed to the increasing marginalization of some asylums by their local communities. In the community of 'Kilronan' in the twentieth century, Saris (1999: 694) noted that the social faux pas of hospitalization in the nearby Sligo Asylum meant that patients were neither mentioned nor alluded to. It is reasonable to assume that people in the towns without connection (employment or otherwise) to the asylum were able to ignore its presence, due to the patients' lack of visibility at even the most public of local events: religious service. The exclusion of patients from public religious service in Maryborough is marked considering the proximity of the asylum from the town: the asylum was 1.09 km from the RC church and 1.38 km from both the COI and Methodist churches. In the town of Carlow, which also hosted an asylum, this exclusion is even more conspicuous considering the sheer number of churches in the local area. Here, there were seven public churches and two private abbeys, including an RC diocesan cathedral and a church across the street, immediately to the west of the asylum. The construction of dedicated asylum chapels reinforced the totality and domination of the asylum in the routine of patients' lives and their ability to relate or communicate with wider society. However, it is not reasonable to interpret the provision of chapels solely as an active means of marginalizing the patients from their local community; it is more likely that the marginalization occurred through the increasing self-regulation of the asylum.

Furthermore, the expansion of the farm and the construction of the asylum chapels overlapped with other building works in the asylum. Maryborough Asylum updated the lighting system inside the buildings, replacing the gas lamps with electric lights; this coincided with wider attempts to make the asylum more 'home-like' through the addition of domestic material culture. Pictures, ornaments and filled bookcases for patient recreation were recommended for each room (*Inspector's Reports* 1899: 186). The Commissioners praised the economy of the electric light, but also expressed relief at the cessation of building works due to the distress of having 'strange workmen' in the asylum (*Inspector's Reports* 1900: 170). The Commissioners were concerned with the impact of building works on the ambience of the asylum, which was central to the treatment of the patients, through careful control of the asylum space.

The movement to consolidate all aspects of patient life within the walls of the asylum may also have had an economic motivation. The District Asylums appropriated approximately 150 acres of extra land in the 1890s. Extra land meant that asylum farms could be expanded, providing more occupation for the male patients who worked in the farms as part of their therapy (ninety-three patients in Maryborough in 1899) (*Inspector's Reports* 1899: 13, 188). The expansion of the farms furthered the asylum's ability to self-regulate without recourse to the local area. In Ireland, institutional self-regulation of foodstuffs was likely a particular concern after the mid nineteenth-century famine, during which asylums like Maryborough were forced to overspend on provisions provided by external suppliers due to the failure of the institution's food staple, the potato (*AO 19/48/14*). Therefore, the regulation of asylum space and the consolidation of asylum resources in one place made economic sense as a failsafe against another crisis.

Conclusion

The motivations behind the construction of dedicated facilities for the patients were driven by a concern for patient welfare and health, and in response to political and economic trends. The sentiments of the asylum Commissioners with regard to patient welfare stand in stark contrast to the ideology of the 'undeserving poor'. By adopting minimal restraint and domestic interiors, and supporting the patients' religious beliefs through hiring chaplains, and ultimately building chapels, the asylums attempted to cater for patient needs and normalize their routine and regulation in the eyes of public onlookers. However, the consolidation of patient services within the asylum grounds may have contributed to their marginalization from the local community. This chapter has argued that religious provision is a lens through which the amalgamation of many aspects of patient life and the regulation of routine within lunatic asylums may be glimpsed. Through the construction of chapels and the strict regulation of patient services, contemporaneous political and economic movements were addressed and a clear concern can be evidenced with normalizing patient experience within the secure environment of the lunatic asylum.

Katherine Fennelly is Lecturer in Heritage at the University of Lincoln, having gained her Ph.D. from the University of Manchester. Her research focuses on the material and documentary histories of public institutions, their built heritage and social legacy. Prior to joining the College of Arts, Lincoln, she was Teaching Associate in Landscape Archaeology at the University of Sheffield, United Kingdom, having previously worked for a commercial archaeology unit in Lincolnshire as a Heritage Research Archaeologist. She is Assistant Editor of *Post-Medieval Archaeology* and has published on the built heritage and historical management practice of institutions for mental health treatment in Ireland and England.

References

Primary Sources

48.Geo.3.c.96. Parliament of the United Kingdom. 1808. County Asylums Act.

57.Geo.3.c.106. Parliament of the United Kingdom. 1817. Irish Lunatic Asylums for the Poor Act.

8 & 9.Vict.c.100.s.3. Parliament of the United Kingdom. 1845. Lunacy Act – Provision for the Commissioners of Lunacy and County Asylums Act.

AO/19/48/14. The National Archives of the United Kingdom, Kew, United Kingdom (audits of Maryborough District Lunatic Asylum, 1842–66).

C85/1/1/2. West Yorkshire Archive Service, Morley, United Kingdom (*Minutes of the Visiting Magistrates of the West Riding District Lunatic Asylum*, 1814–89).

Co.Sligo.Reg.no:32323002. National Inventory of Architectural Heritage, Dublin, Ireland (buildings survey: Saint Columba's, St Columba's Road, Sligo, 2006). Retrieved 3 April 2016 from http://buildingsofireland.ie/niah/search.jsp?type=record&county=SL&regno=32323002.

CP/2/440/9. National Archives of Ireland, Dublin, IE (*Cholera Papers*, 15 November 1832).

Inspector's Reports. *The Fortieth Report of the Inspectors of Lunatics on the District, Criminal and Private Lunatic Asylums in Ireland*. 1891. Dublin: Her Majesty's Stationery Office.

Inspector's Reports. *The Forty-Fifth Report of the Inspectors of Lunatics on the District, Criminal and Private Lunatic Asylums in Ireland*. 1896. Dublin: Her Majesty's Stationery Office, 1896.

Inspector's Reports. *The Forty-Eighth Report of the Inspectors of Lunatics (Ireland)*. 1899. Dublin: Her Majesty's Stationery Office.

Inspector's Reports. *The Forty-Ninth Report of the Inspectors of Lunatics (Ireland)*. 1900. Dublin: Her Majesty's Stationery Office.

Ordnance Survey County Series 1st Edition, Scale 1:10560, Yorkshire. 1855. Southampton: Ordnances Survey Office.

Ordnance Survey County Series 1st Edition, Scale 1:2500, Lancashire. 1891. Southampton: Ordnances Survey Office.

Secondary Literature

Bedford, W. 2008. 'Archaeological Appraisal: Grangegorman Masterplan Dublin 7'. Unpublished Archaeological Report. Grangegorman Development Agency and Margaret Gowan and Co. Ltd.

Brooks, C., 1995. 'Introduction', in C. Brooks and A. Saint (eds), *The Victorican Church: Architecture and Society*. Manchester: Manchester University Press, pp.1–29.

Brück, J. 2013. 'Landscapes of Desire: Parks, Colonialism, and Identity in Victorian and Edwardian Ireland', *International Journal of Historical Archaeology* 17(1): 196–223.

Coleborne, C. 2001. 'Exhibiting Madness: Material Culture and the Asylum', *Health and History* 3(2): 104–17.

Conolly, J. 1847. *The Construction and Government of Lunatic Asylums and Hospitals for the Insane*. London: John Churchill.

Crossman, V. 2006. *The Poor Law in Ireland 1838–1948*. Dundalk: Irish Economic and Social History Society.

Emsley, C. 1996. *Crime and Society in England 1750–1900*. Harlow: Longman.

Foss, A., and K.Trick. 1989. *St. Andrew's Hospital, Northampton: The First 150 Years (1838–1988)*. Cambridge: Granta.

Foucault, M. 2006. *Madness and Civilization: A History of Insanity in the Age of Reason*. London: Routledge.

Goffman, E. 1961. *Asylums: Essays on the Social Situation of Mental Patients and Other Inmates*. Harmondsworth: Penguin.

Hill, R. 2009. *God's Architect: Pugin and the Building of Romantic Britain*, New Haven, CT: Yale University Press.

Hine, G.T. 1901. 'Asylums and Asylum Planning', *Journal of the Royal Institute of British Architects* 8: 161–84.

Irish Architectural Archive (ed.). 2014. 'George Wilkinson', in *Dictionary of Irish Architects 1550–1900*. Retrieved 18 March 2014 from http://www.dia.ie/architects/view/4918/Wilkinson,+George.

Jacob, J. 1833. *Observations and Suggestions on the Management of Maryborough District Lunatic Asylum*. Dublin: P. Dixon Hardy.

Luddy, M. 2007. *Prostitution and Irish Society, 1800–1940*. Cambridge: Cambridge University Press.

Piddock, S. 2007. *A Space of their Own: The Archaeology of Nineteenth Century Lunatic Asylums in Britain, South Australia and Tasmania*. New York: Springer.

Pinel, P. 1806. *A Treatise on Insanity*. London: Cadell and Davis.

Porter, R. 2002. *Madness: A Brief History*. Oxford: Oxford University Press.

———. 2004. *Madmen: A Social History of Madhouses, Mad-Doctors and Lunatics*. Stroud: Tempus.

Prior, P. 1997. 'Mad, Not Bad: Crime, Mental Disorder and Gender in Nineteenth-Century Ireland', *History of Psychiatry* 8(32): 501–16.

Prior, P., and D. Griffiths. 1997. 'The Chaplaincy Question: The Lord Lieutenant of Ireland versus the Belfast Lunatic Asylum', *Eire/Ireland* 32(2–3): 137–53.

Psota, S. 2011. 'The Archaeology of Mental Illness from the Afflicted and Caretaker Perspective: A Northern California Family's Odyssey', *Historical Archaeology* 45(4): 20–38.

Reuber, M. 1996. 'The Architecture of Psychological Management: The Irish Asylums (1801–1922)', *Psychological Medicine* 26(6): 1179–89.

Reynolds, J. 1992. *Grangegorman: Psychiatric Care in Dublin since 1815*. Dublin: Institute of Public Administration.

Robins, J. 1986. *Fools and Mad: A History of the Insane in Ireland*. Dublin: Institute of Public Administration.

Saris, A.J. 1996. 'Mad Kings, Proper Houses and an Asylum in Rural Ireland', *American Anthropologist* 98(3): 539–54.

———. 1999. 'Producing Persons and Developing Institutions in Rural Ireland', *American Ethnologist* 26(3): 690–710.

Scull, A.T. 1981. 'The Social History of Psychiatry in the Victorian Era', in A.T. Scull (ed.), *Madhouses, Mad-Doctors and Madmen*. London: Athlone Press, pp. 5–32.

———. 1993. *The Most Solitary of Afflictions: Madness and Society in Britain, 1700–1900*. New Haven: Yale University Press.

Scully, S. 1983. 'From Minute to Minute 1886–1905', in D.A. Murphy (ed.), *Tumbling Walls*. Portlaoise: Imperial Print, pp. 28–37.

Taylor, J. 1991. *Hospital and Asylum Architecture in England, 1840–1914: Building for Health Care*. London: Mansell.

Thompson, J.D., and G. Goldin. 1975. *The Hospital: A Social and Architectural History*. New Haven, CT: Yale University Press.

Tuke, S. 1813. *Description of the Retreat, an Institution near York for Insane Persons of the Society of Friends*. York: W. Alexander.

Watkin, D. 2001. *Morality and Architecture Revisited*. London: John Murray.

Yanni, C. 2007. *The Architecture of Madness: Insane Asylums in the United States*. Minneapolis, MN: University of Minnesota Press.

Chapter 10

Prison-Issue Artefacts, Documentary Insights and the Negotiated Realities of Political Imprisonment
The Case of Long Kesh/Maze, Northern Ireland

Laura McAtackney

Introduction

Historically, studies of prisons have had a tendency to replicate narratives that dichotomize domination and resistance with an emphasis on control by prison authorities and varying degrees of noncompliance by the inmates. Often these narratives are based on singular sources, with prison records being particularly utilized by historians (e.g. Morris and Rothman 1998) and standing prison buildings by archaeologists and architectural historians (e.g. Johnston 2000). This chapter argues for a move beyond the usual sources of prison regulations, i.e. transcripts of imprisonment, to reveal the underlying realities of negotiated power relations. Using the case study of Long Kesh/Maze prison in Northern Ireland, it is suggested here that both historians and archaeologists need to move beyond extracting superficial details from traditional sources in order to uncover the nuances of institutional relationships.

Approaches to Studying Imprisonment

Michel Foucault's volume *Discipline and Punish* (1991) is probably the most influential work on the development of penal institutions, their connection with modernity and the increasing institutionalization of citizens by their governments. Its ubiquity in examinations of prisons or institutions ensures that there is an interpretative emphasis on the perceptions and effectiveness of the prison authorities to control. However, it does have notable problems when used to understand a place of political imprisonment where prisoners actively contested the form and right to imprisonment. Long Kesh/Maze is an extreme example of the negotiated realities of imprisonment that are, in reality, much more reliant on mutual negotiation than we would assume from government files or public pronouncements of defiance by political prisoners. The most glaring deficiency in Foucault's work is that it does not sufficiently address the agency of the incarcerated and their ability to defy their conditions of imprisonment. Fundamentally, the free will of the individual or communal prisoner body is downplayed. This emphasis is replicated in many examinations of prisons that concentrate on architecture and aesthetics, which present prison buildings as shells, with little engagement with how these places adapted over their lives or functioned in practice (including Johnston 2000; see also Brodie, Croom and Davies 2002).

The historians' preference for written sources ensures that there is an overreliance on the records that governments create to administer institutions. Government files naturally emphasize the administration of such places, but this does not necessarily mean that evidence of prisoner noncompliance is absent. However, noncompliance is often an aside, marginalia or not overtly discussed, and can be missed if a reader is extracting facts rather than questioning the source. Following Ann Laura Stoler (2002), it is clear that the researcher should note the context and interplay of the archives, since continual updating of protocol or the collation of out-of-place papers may reveal the unforeseen nature of, or responses to, these incidences. One must treat government archives as reflecting both imaginary and situated realities that 'fashioned histories as they concealed, revealed, and reproduced the power of the state' (Stoler 2002: 97). Often these subtleties are not the focus of the historian's gaze and it is more difficult, certainly as one descends back in time, to be able to locate documentary trails from the imprisoned. Prior to the twentieth century, we are often dealing with largely illiterate prison populations who did not leave many retrievable written traces. Even in more recent times, when illiteracy is not such a widespread issue, prisoners do not routinely leave written accounts of imprisonment. Celebrated cases can provide insights, with writers as contrasting as Oscar Wilde (1898) and Brendan Behan (1965) emotively detailing their experiences of imprisonment as Irishmen in England, but these survivals are rare. The mainstream prisoner does not often leave a documentary trail and so we must work with government sources with caution and care.

Increasingly, documents have become a central form of evidence in historical archaeology, but their exact relationship with other forms of material culture remains unresolved. Martin Hall's work on the historic Atlantic is important in proposing a less-than-straightforward link between documentary and other material forms of evidence, as 'a multi-stranded rope that links together a complex network of sources and connects the present with the past' (2000: 9). He asserts that whereas documentary and other forms of material culture are often used as mutually exclusive sources, usually with one deemed of primary importance and the other used to supplement, one should instead exploit the discrepancies between them. Historical archaeologists' increasing attempts to juxtapose and combine multiple sources in this way has reduced the gap between how governments present their regimes and the actual experiences of prisoners.

In recent years there has been a concerted effort to move away from the reliance on extant institutional buildings as the primary form of evidence in order to combine a number of sources to reveal the negotiated realities of prison life. Eleanor Casella (2000, 2001a, 2001b) has used her research at Ross Female Factory, Tasmania to emphasize the experiences of the female prisoners and their ongoing relationships both within, and external to, the prison. Using judicial records, relating to cases brought against existing prisoners, as well as prisoners' illicit material culture, she explores facets of identity and agency of prisoners in order to reveal the tensions inherent in the prisoner–prison regime relationship. Likewise, Lu Ann DeCunzo's (2006) dual emphasis on both the impact of institutional choices relating to material culture, and the inmates' ability and desire to negotiate it, has been influential. Her research emphasizes institutions as 'places that embody and challenge the boundaries of socially, philosophically, scientifically, or legally acceptable actions, minds and bodies' and as such allows us to conceive of institutions as places to challenge and subvert authority (DeCunzo 2006: 167). She highlights the need to examine institutions in an open-minded way in order to 'negotiate an emotion-laden terrain with compassion, outrage and openness' (DeCunzo 2006: 185). Such a contention is important when considering the reaction that prisons, and particularly political prisons of recent vintage such as Long Kesh/Maze, have on the wider public, as well as those who study them.

Lateral Approaches to Understanding Experiences of Imprisonment

In this investigation of Long Kesh/Maze, I add to the established use of government documents and/or structural remains of the carceral environment by including oral testimonies and material culture as retrieved through documentary sources. Due to Long Kesh/Maze's recent operational status, one can include the living memories of those who were associated with the prison. Oral testimonies conducted at the prison have revealed that there is not one overarching experience of place. Long Kesh/Maze was not only a complicated place, due to its entanglement with the ebbs and flows of the conflict that produced the majority of its population, but the experience of place was impacted by time, place and circumstances of imprisonment. Whether a prisoner was held in the relative freedom of the Nissen huts of Compounds (1971–88) or was involved in the heightened protests of Republican prisoners in the H Blocks (c. 1976–81) would have hugely impacted prisoner experiences and memories of place. However, even during periods of protest, prisoners had different experiences due to their decision to be actively involved (known as 'non-complying' in government files) or, as the majority did, to stay within prison rules and regulations as 'complying' prisoners. However, one also needs to consider the role of memory. Cillian McGrattan (2013: 10) asserts that in transitional societies such as contemporary Northern Ireland, the past, and how it is collectively remembered, remains a difficult and disruptive influence on the present because it is innately connected to ideas about contemporary identity (McGrattan 2013: 7). Therefore, we need to exercise caution while using oral testimonies, treating them as guides of opinion and perspectives rather than factual records.

Contemporary archaeologists have the ability to locate, assess, interrogate and incorporate an overwhelming range of material culture. As highlighted by Harrison and Schofield (2010: 5): 'Archaeological sites of the contemporary past are places that in some ways we know all about, but in others can seem almost as mysterious and "distant" as sites of prehistory or the medieval period.' The closeness of a site to the present does not necessarily mean we know about it more than distant, historical examples. The potential for contradictory information to be revealed by different sources means there are no simple readings. Indeed, the contemporary archaeologist is often confronted with so many potential sources that they are forced to be highly selective, which almost inevitably leads to the accidental or deliberate exclusion of potential sources of information.

In such circumstances, rather than trying to superficially include a wide range of sources, we should engage with them in multifaceted and lateral ways. This includes considering and locating their life biographies (regardless of how short), moving beyond aesthetics to illuminate use values, questioning later accepted mythologies, reveal multiple narratives and locate lost material culture that may inadvertently be revealed through other sources. While large quantities of moveable material culture emanate from a site such as Long Kesh/Maze, there is a need to question how different forms may have changed in terms of use and significance over time. For example, prison-issue artefacts include a wide range of forms, such as furniture, bedding, lighting, cookware, crockery and cutlery and prisoner's personal artefacts, including prison art, tools, stationery, books, letters, games, musical cassettes, toiletries and clothing. One should examine their survival and how they are integrated into other sources, which often unintentionally provides vital information on their mutable roles and meanings. This chapter argues that the emphasis that is currently placed on 'prison art', as exemplifying prisoner creativity and expression, is in danger of misinterpreting its role in prison life and inadvertently conceals the importance of mundane, prison-issue artefacts in contesting the rights and forms of imprisonment.

Retrieving Specific Experiences of Imprisonment at Long Kesh/Maze

Long Kesh/Maze is widely considered to be one of the iconic sites of the Northern Irish Troubles (c. 1968–c. 1998). Its biography as a place of paramilitary imprisonment mirrors – and is implicated in – the course and longevity of this low-level war, which resulted in the deaths of c. 3,600 people during its thirty-year duration (McKittrick et al. 1999). It was first utilized as an internment camp in 1971 and was eventually closed, almost bereft of prisoners released as a condition of the 1998 Good Friday Agreement, in 2000. Many of the turning points of the conflict originated in, and centred on, Long Kesh/Maze – including debates about the legalities of internment, disputes regarding the 'political' status and nature of prisoners and their crimes, the legality of Diplock Court convictions, the hunger strikes of 1980/81, the mass prison escape of 1983 and the brokering of peace agreements in the 1990s. Long Kesh/Maze not only facilitated the continuation of the conflict, it also enabled the faltering, protracted moves towards the eventual cessation of violence. It contained an overwhelmingly paramilitary prisoner population who were communalized in their actions, and who often strategically moved – individually and en masse – between 'complying' and 'noncomplying' status. This was a means of performing their self-proclaimed political status and disrupting the prison regime. Indeed, an ex-governor, contradicting official government narratives of control, admitted: 'anyone who said they governed the Maze was a liar, they could only say they tried to govern the Maze ... The story of the Maze really was that the prisoners were in control' (XX 2007).

Due to the prison population at Long Kesh/Maze being essentially unique to the temporal and spatial dimensions of the Northern Irish Troubles, it provides an interesting, if unusual, case study as to the effectiveness of a prison – as a material structure, ideology and regime – in controlling an essentially noncomplying prison population. It also has wider significance in judging whether material conditions, the nature of the regime or the steadfastness of prisoner resolve are ultimately most effective in determining the control and experiences of institutional space. In this study, artefacts connected to the prison that are no longer in existence but are retrieved from oral and documentary sources are used as a means of gaining a partial insight into specific, temporal experiences of imprisonment. Artefacts have been selected as previous investigations have shown that they represent the widest and most varied range of evidence for individual interactions and negotiations of the prison environment in comparison to other material scales of analysis (McAtackney 2014). Therefore, while other sources could be used, artefacts shall remain the focal point as the most heterogeneous, numerous and telling survival of the prison environment.

Artefacts relating to Long Kesh/Maze are vast in quantity and range of forms. They came from a wide number of sources (both in situ and moved around and beyond the prison site) and include prison-issue artefacts that were provided for the prisoners by the prison authorities; artefacts that the prisoners owned and held legitimately; illicit artefacts that the prisoners held without the authorities' permission and that may have been created in the prison or smuggled from outside; and prison art that was created in the prison but was later passed to contacts and relatives outside the prison. A significant number of artefacts moved between these categories during their life biographies, as some artefacts were initially held legitimately and were later reassigned by the authorities as contraband or were held legitimately, but were later physically altered to have an illicit use, or contraband elements were hidden within them.

On examining a narrative history of the prison, it is apparent that particular periods of the prison's existence witnessed escalations of protests, prisoner noncompliance and contestation of imprisonment status. Orchestrated prisoner noncompliance against the regime was particularly notable during the escalation of Republican protests on the introduction of newly sentenced prisoners to the new prison form – the H Blocks (Figure 10.1) – and its association with criminalization, from 1976 until the end of the hunger strikes in 1981. While these prisoner protests involved substantial numbers, they were always in a minority, despite greatly impacting on the material environment for the prisoners involved. One ex-prisoner described the difference in moving from a noncomplying to a complying wing: '[H5 was] like Butlins [holiday camp] compared to the last place' (McMullan 1994: 19). Accessing the materiality of noncompliance at this time presents a problem for the archaeologist. There is difficulty in

Figure 10.1 Front entrance of an H Block (copy by Laura McAtackney)

accessing any artefacts associated with this period of imprisonment due to the time that has elapsed since the protests, the prison's continued functioning during and after the protests, and the sparse nature of the material world of noncomplying prisoners at this time. However, partial insights into their roles, usages and meanings can be located in a small number of government files from this period.

Experiences of the H Blocks, c. 1976–81

One of the difficulties in exploring recent archaeological remnants, such as the abandoned prison site of Long Kesh/Maze, is that they can swiftly become politically loaded sites of memory. Mythologizing about experiences of such a site not only impacts on memories of what happened and where, but even determines what material culture was considered important. An ex-prisoner Felim O'Hagan (1994: 71) states: 'There are tales of certain events of almost mythical status which appear to have taken place in all the Blanket Blocks. It could be a collective mind at work but, me, I reckon the men who were on H3 and H5 are just liars.' If we want to avoid what Alan Mayne and Tim Murray (2001: 1) call 'the homogenising, universalising and changeless qualities of myth', we need to critically assess these sources and consider why they were created, if they had a propagandist intention and what narratives they wished to present.

When one asks ex-prisoners about material culture that was important during their imprisonment at Long Kesh/Maze, there is often an emphasis placed on prison art. The term 'prison art' covers an almost indefinable range of artistic and creative objects made by prisoners either for their own use or circulation beyond the prison walls. They varied in form, style and material across the life of the prison, but included decorated banners, flags, handkerchiefs, leather goods and wooden trophies covered in nationalist or unionist symbols and emblems such as flags, shamrocks, Celtic crosses, red poppies, Orange Order motifs and football team names. Prisoners created them as personal mementoes, or for loved ones, or to be sold to supporters in order to provide funds for the movement or support for families. These cultural artefacts were made in great quantities at specific times in prison life and are particularly associated with the culture, and availability of tools and materials, in the Nissen huts of the Compounds (Figure 10.2). As such, their creation and existence is often considered a symbol of political status, especially by later noncomplying prisoners in the H Blocks.

Figure 10.2 A Nissen hut contained within a wired compound (copy by Laura McAtackney)

Prison art can legitimately be interpreted as a materialization of identity; however, the perception of it as being a product of creativity and artistic licence is a misrepresentation. Mike Moloney, an ex-instructor from Long Kesh/Maze, has asserted that prison art is unusual in that 'your artistic skill is judged on your craft, not on your artistic interpretation' (2009: 4). This judgement is confirmed by the degree of uniformity of artefact form and type found in various private and public collections. Prison art often displayed individualized aspects, but they were essentially specialized forms that followed templates and were created communally for external markets 'as being symbols of the continuation of the struggle within the cages' (Moloney 2009: 6). Prison art materialized very specific identities within the prison that were used to maintain group cohesion, underline sectarian divisions (see Figure 10.3) and (just as importantly) pass time, but they were not made by all prisoners or throughout the life of the prison, especially in the escalating tensions of the H Blocks, c. 1976–81.

The constraints on prisoner freedom and control of their environments during the protests in the H Blocks meant that the material culture from this time was very different from the preceding period associated with prisoner freedom of the Compounds. Indeed, as the protests escalated, the mundane, everyday and functional material culture that was available to prisoners took on a heightened role in negotiations between the regime, prisoners, and the contestation/assertion of prisoner status. Prison art is largely absent from the environment at this time and is therefore not central to understanding the material environment of noncomplying H Block wings. The imposed material culture of imprisonment takes on new and context-specific meanings at this time that are difficult to retrieve in material form, but can be partially located through alternative sources of government files and oral testimonies.

Oral testimonies and artefactual assemblages throughout prison life reveal that subversive or unforeseen usages of prison-issue artefacts often left an ambiguous or no trace on the material object. There are innumerable examples from both manifestations of prison revealing how prison-issue artefacts were used in ingenious ways to facilitate a range of actions from light-hearted subversions – such as metal bins being used as alcohol stills (Figure 10.4) – to sinister activities, such as metal parts of windows being used as weapons. In a number of government files relating to imprisonment in the early years of the Compounds, it is clear that there was growing concern amongst government officials at the prisoners' abilities to use prison-issue artefacts to plan and execute escapes. These fears were confirmed by the interception of a prisoner 'comm.' (prison terminology, meaning 'communication') imparting a detailed escape plan that is located in one file:

Figure 10.3 Loyalist banner used for marching in the Compounds. Confiscated and held in the Northern Ireland Prison Service Museum, Millisle (copy by Laura McAtackney)

Figure 10.4 Metal household bin being used to distilled alcohol in the Compounds. Confiscated and held in the storage room of the Northern Ireland Prison Service Museum, Millisle (copy by Laura McAtackney)

> No 4 Squad would carry 10 lockers to be placed against fence in a series of steps, 4 lockers placed on edge against fence, then three, two and one. When lockers are in position, mattresses would then be placed on barbed wire coils to prevent barbs catching on clothing thus slowing up movement. Mattresses to be weighted down with bricks on road side of fence and tied to lockers on inside to prevent them from falling when men are going over. (CJ4/456)

When these fears became a reality – with the rioting and burning of the camp by Republican prisoners in October 1974 – the acceptance that the current environment could not control prisoners was central in the decision to build a more standardized, cellular structure in the form of the H Blocks. However, it is equally clear that the government did not consider that a communalized and noncomplying prison population could continue to disrupt and negate the intentions of the prison structures and regime with the use of prison-issue artefacts in this new, purpose-built facility.

The move to a cellular carceral environment meant that the previous communal nature of the Compounds was altered and the regime could now isolate and control prisoners on an individual basis in their cellular structures. On introduction, and throughout imprisonment, the prisoners had to make decisions as to whether they would comply or not with the new prison regime. The form of this compliance or noncompliance was shaped by the material culture provided for prisoners. The prisoners were assisted in their ability to coordinate noncompliance by inherent deficiencies in the prison buildings, which became apparent on their introductions to the H Blocks. This includes their ability to establish oral communications 'along the [heating] pipes' down wings, through sliding weighted written messages on strings across corridors and shouting messages from wing to wing through windows' (see McAtackney 2014: 137–82). This ability to communicate in various ways provided the non-complying prisoners with a means of planning and coordinating communal protests, even if they took a different and more laboured form than in the Compounds.

The prison regime focused their attempts to control prisoners on their ability to separate and isolate individual prisoners using the cellular structures and limiting the material environment through the number and form of prison-issue artefacts provided. Therefore, to assess the ability of the prisoners to bypass or subvert this control, one must explore the (mis)use of these seemingly innocuous artefacts. Prison-issue artefacts from the H Blocks of the late 1970s through to the early 1980s are no longer in existence; they have long since been destroyed, replaced or reused through the actions of protesting prisoners or normal cycles of use at a functional prison. However, information gleaned from various documentary and oral sources detail their central role in power struggles, degrees of material comfort and identification amongst fellow prisoners. Retrieving the now-absent prison-issue artefacts through documentary sources reveals the heightened role of mundane material culture at this specific period, which was central not only to prisoner experiences but also in negotiating power relations with prison staff.

Numbers of conforming and nonconforming prisoners in the H Blocks fluctuated on a daily basis. Prisoners continually went 'on' and 'off' protest due to personal decisions or prisoner hierarchies wishing 'to keep track of what is happening on the hunger strike front' (*NIO/12/160A*). There were often disputes regarding exact figures and the location of noncomplying and complying wings due to these frequent changes. By the time the protests on the H Blocks were established – originating with the first Republican prisoners to enter the wings in the autumn of 1976 – noncomplying prisoners were moved to specifically noncomplying wings where their sparse material conditions acted as an indicator of their antagonistic relationship with the prison authorities. In a materially controlled environment, unremarkable artefacts were ascribed heightened, and often overtly political, meanings. These artefacts, for short times in their biographies, were no longer unseen and unconsidered, but became important. They were actively constructed to negotiate status and power relations between the prisoner (individually and communally) and the regime. Their form was at times significant – in allowing particular usages to take place – but often their imposition or demand was their most important attribute. These artefacts provide insights into how prison-issue material culture was used to perform claims of political status. They reveal the nature of reciprocal relationships within the prison and demonstrate hierarchies of control within the prisoner body that defied official proclamations of power and control located overtly in government files, and symbiotically in the standing structures of the prison.

Contemporary government files inadvertently reveal the negotiated realities of prison life at this time. They claim that the austere and extremely restrictive conditions in which many prisoners found themselves were largely of their own doing. Internal communications argued that there was a degree of self-selection in the extent of material deprivation and that prisoner choices as to whether they acquiesced or rejected the fundamental conditions of the prison regime created these conditions. If prisoners 'undertook to keep their cells clean and to slop out and accordingly their accommodation was re-furnished within 24 hours' (NIO/10/14/1A). To noncomplying prisoners, such arguments were disingenuous. Particularly at times of heightened protest, it is clear that both the regime and prisoners understood that access to and treatment of prison-issue artefacts was an indicator of compliance and noncompliance, and was symbolically associated with prisoner status. At specific times and locations within Long Kesh/Maze, the presence, use and misuse of limited prison-issue artefacts became the focus of power struggles between the prisoner and the regime. Beds, furniture and even clothing became representative of conditions and levels of acceptance. Protesting prisoners would not compromise their right to protest – or risk categorization as 'criminal' – by making promises to maintain or comply with prison authority demands they intended to break. Indeed, there was official recognition of this state of affairs. When prisoners did comply, received prison-issue artefacts and then later destroyed them, it was often noted in government files that this happened because the prisoners felt they had legitimate grievances. As one official noted: 'They took this action after being told that they would not be issued with their own clothing until they were conforming completely to the prison rules' (NIO/10/14/1A).

Clothing was one of the most important battlegrounds in the negotiation of prisoner and prison relationships. While efforts were belatedly made by prison authorities to make their imposed prison uniforms look like civilian clothing – including examples created in denim and tailored in contemporary styles – the fact of their imposition, not reflecting the free choice of the individual prisoners, ensured that this became a major material obstacle in the negotiation of prisoner status. Daniel Miller (2010) has argued that clothing is a primary identifier of personal individuality and freedom of choice. In his study of Trinidadian culture, Miller links clothing choices and style to conceptions of individuality and freedom, which he suggests may be a reaction to the previous status of control associated with historical slavery (Miller 2010: 16). This argument has resonance with a materially controlled environment of political imprisonment, where clothing was not merely a superficial concern but a material identifier of political, rather than criminal, status. Miller states that clothing can be viewed as unimportant in a normative UK context, but its links to exercising freedom of choice are paramount: 'Clothes are among our most personal possessions. They are the main medium between our sense of our bodies and our sense of the external world' (Miller 2010: 23). This view is supported by ex-prisoner Laurence McKeown, detailing the discomfort he felt at wearing any form of prison clothing when he entered a complying wing after the end of the 1981 hunger strike: 'I was horrified at the thought of wearing prison gear ... The argument made a lot of sense but for us at that period it still seemed wrong to adopt such a pragmatic outlook in relation to the prison issue clothing' (McKeown 2001: 100). The choice, style or quality of the clothes were not important; their significance lay in the role they played in communicating internal worlds and states of being to external audiences. In a materially controlled environment, such as Long Kesh/Maze, clothing choices were viewed as a major identifier of personal freedom – a symbol of political status – rather than the superficial afterthought as presented to a normative society by the government.

Noncomplying prisoners were placed into the gloomy surroundings of a cubed shape cell with Perspex windows, where every prison-issue blanket, chair and table became part of the arsenal of protest or symbols of compliance. A prison official writing in August 1979 noted that: 'Yesterday prisoners who were returned to a clean and newly painted wing in H5 were given clean mattresses, pillows, pillowcases and blankets. However within a short time the pillows were thrown out of the cells' (NIO/10/14/1A). In early February 1980, another prison official wrote: 'On Tuesday at dinner time the NCP's [Non-Complying Prisoners] in C3 refused to leave their knives, forks, plates etc at their doors for collection. Instead they scattered them in different parts of their cells' (NIO/10/14/1A). However, not all misuses/abuses of prison-issue artefacts by noncomplying prisoners were benign. A letter in February 1981 noted that the prisoners had 'proceeded to break up their furniture and used it to attack the windows of their cells' (NIO/10/14/1A), reinforcing why, at an

Figure 10.5 Photograph taken by prison officers of debris after prisoners had broken all the windows of their non-complying H Block wing. Northern Ireland Prison Service Museum, Millisle (copy by Laura McAtackney)

early stage, Perspex windows were considered a necessary addition to all noncomplying wings (Figure 10.5).

The accounts of noncomplying prisoners describe situations where furniture was often destroyed not only as a symbol of prisoner noncompliance but also out of frustration and annoyance at the tensions inherent in the situation. The prisoners often channelled the breaking of artefacts as an orchestrated, collective act of defiance and communality: 'it wasn't just the satisfaction of breaking furniture but the message that it would be sending to the Brits' (McCann 1994: 137). The responding prison officers, utilizing the now piecemeal and broken shards and chunks of furniture as de facto obstacle courses, could in turn subvert these prisoner acts of defiance to facilitate and compound injuries as prisoners were dragged from their cells. Following Alfred Gell's (1998) interpretation of the agency of objects, the furniture retained the potential to act as an 'index' of multiple human actions. Furniture broken by prisoners could be used to attack their surroundings and contest their imprisonment, but it could then 'act back' in performing the agency of the prison officers in legitimating the injuring of the prisoner as they were trailed 'over broken furniture and beds that lay all over the wing' (Campbell et al. 1994: 33).

The Roman Catholic Cardinal of Ireland, Tomás Ó'Fiaich, remarked in a letter to the government: 'Many violent scenes took place *between prisoners and warders* [underlining and marginalia of "!!" added by hand] in which the furniture in the cells was broke [*sic*] and used in these battles' (*NIO/12/160A*). The Cardinal's assertions that these 'battles' were orchestrated and enacted by both sides may be contradicted officially by the '!!', but his statement indicates his belief of the negotiated relationship between noncomplying prisoner and prison guard, and inadvertently confirms the heightened role of prison-issue material culture at this time.

Conclusions

Traditional examinations of prisons from historical and archaeological perspectives can overly rely on extracting facts from government files and examining standing buildings. Such approaches can bypass the more nuanced and evolving narratives of imprisonment that can emerge from a careful examination of less obvious sources. Following Ann Laura Stoler, there is a need to 'move from archive-as-source to archive-as-subject' (2002: 93), to explore documents within official archives with the perspective of revealing the mechanisms and assumptions of governance. This allows us to interpret and understand 'archives not as sites of knowledge retrieval but of knowledge production, as monuments of states as well as sites of state ethnography' (Stoler 2002: 90). Equally, the archaeologist needs to think laterally in their retrieval of material culture. Archaeologists can move beyond reifying extant material culture from the end points of site biographies to retrieving material culture that inadvertently appears in other sources, such as documents and oral testimonies.

In this case study, prisoner interactions with the structures at Long Kesh/Maze during periods of heightened tensions left few lasting traces. However, there is evidence in both documentary and oral sources of prison-issue artefacts being used to articulate protesting status and noncompliance by prisoners that is revealed through their inclusion in government files. It is clear from documentary and oral sources from both prison administrators and prisoners that the material environment of the prison provided both the weapons and battleground that allowed otherwise mundane and unexceptional prison-issue artefacts to become signifiers of compliance and protest. In the context of contemporary archaeological studies, where our material sources are rich and varied, this case study highlights the need to continually question the quantity and availability of the material world we study and to delve beyond the obvious. We must dissect accepted narratives and attempt to retrieve materially absent sources from elsewhere in order to reveal the most nuanced and telling narratives of the tensions between rules, regulations, contestation and noncompliance.

Laura McAtackney is Associate Professor in Sustainable Heritage Management at Aarhus University, Denmark. An archaeologist by training, her current research spans areas as diverse as post-conflict memory and memorialization in Northern Ireland, female experiences of political imprisonment during the Irish Civil War and race/social relations on early modern Montserrat in the Caribbean (the latter as a member of the SLAM project). She is the author of *An Archaeology of the Troubles: The Dark Heritage of Long Kesh/Maze* (Oxford University Press, 2014) and created http://kilmainhamgaolgraffiti.com in 2015. She is secretary of CHAT (Contemporary and Historical Archaeology in Theory Group) and co-assistant editor of *Post-Medieval Archaeology*.

References

Primary Sources

CJ4/456. National Archives, Kew, United Kingdom (proposed and existing security arrangements in Maze prison, 31 July 1973 to 29 November 1973).

NIO/10/14/1A. Public Record Office of Northern Ireland, Belfast, United Kingdom (*Maze Cellular – Dirty Protest – Cleaning Reports*, 1979 –81).

NIO/12/160A. Public Record Office of Northern Ireland, Belfast, United Kingdom (prison protest action: protest action arising from claim to special category status – hunger strike; 22 October 1979 to 2 January 1981).

XX 2007. Ex-Governor of Maze Compounds and Maze Cellular, interview conducted in his home in 2007 (names randomized and abbreviated to protect identities).

Secondary Literature

Behan, B. 1965. *Confessions of an Irish Rebel*. London: Hutchinson.
Brodie, A., J. Croom and J. Davies. 2002. *English Prisons: An Architectural History*. Swindon: English Heritage.

Campbell, B., L. McKeown and F. O'Hagan (eds). 1994. *Nor Meekly Serve My Time: H-Block Struggle, 1976–81*. Belfast: Beyond the Pale.

Casella, E.C. 2000. '"Doing Trade": A Sexual Economy of Nineteenth-Century Australian Female Convict Prisons', *World Archaeology* 32(2): 209–21.

———. 2001a. 'To Watch or Restrain: Female Convict Prisons in 19th Century Tasmania', *International Journal of Historical Archaeology* 5(1): 45–72.

———. 2001b. 'Every Procurable Object: A Functional Analysis of the Ross Female Factory Archaeological Collection', *Australasian Historical Archaeology* 19: 25–38.

DeCunzo, L.A. 2006. 'Exploring the Institution: Reform, Confinement, Social Change, Boundaries and Crossings', in M. Hall and S. Silliman (eds), *Historical Archaeology*. Oxford: Blackwell, pp. 167–90.

Foucault, M. 1991. *Discipline and Punish: The Birth of the Prison*, trans. A. Sheridan. London: Penguin.

Gell, A. 1998. *Art and Agency: An Anthropological Theory*. Oxford: Clarendon Press.

Hall, M. 2000. *Archaeology and the Modern World: Colonial Transcripts in South Africa and Chesapeake*. London: Routledge.

Harrison, R., and Schofield, J. 2010. *After Modernity: Archaeological Approaches to the Contemporary Past*. Oxford: Oxford University Press.

Johnston, N. 2000. *Forms of Constraint: A History of Prisoner Architecture*. Urbana, IL: University of Illinois Press.

Mayne, A., and Murray, T. 2001. 'The Archaeology of Urban Landscapes: Exploration in Slumland', in A. Mayne and T. Murray (eds), *The Archaeology of Urban Landscapes*. Cambridge: Cambridge University Press, pp. 1–11.

McAtackney, L. 2014. *An Archaeology of the Troubles: The Dark Heritage of Long Kesh/Maze Prison*. Oxford: Oxford University Press.

McCann, J. 1994. In B. Campbell, L. McKeown and F. O'Hagan (eds), *Nor Meekly Serve My Time*. Belfast: Beyond the Pale.

McGrattan, C. 2013. *Memory, Politics and Identity: Haunted by History*. Basingstoke: Palgrave Macmillan.

McKittrick, D., S. Kelters, B. Feeney and C. Thornton.1999. *Lost Lives: The Stories of the Men, Women and Children Who Died as a Result of the Northern Ireland Troubles*. Edinburgh: Mainstream.

McMullan, J. 1994. In B. Campbell, L. McKeown and F. O'Hagan (eds), *Nor Meekly Serve My Time*. Belfast: Beyond the Pale.

Miller, D. 2010. *Stuff*. London: Wiley.

Moloney, M. 2009. *Prison Art and the Conflict in Northern Ireland: A Troubles Archive Essay*. Belfast: Arts Council of Northern Ireland.

Morris, N., and Rothman, D. 1998. *The Oxford History of the Prison*. Oxford: Oxford University Press.

O'Hagan, F. 1994. In B. Campbell, L. McKeown and F. O'Hagan (eds), *Nor Meekly Serve My Time*. Belfast: Beyond the Pale.

Stoler, A.L. 2002. 'Colonial Archives and the Arts of Governance', *Archival Science* 2: 87–109.

Tarlow, S., and S. West. 1999. *The Familiar Past? Archaeologies of Later Historical Britain 1150–1950*. London: Routledge.

Wilde, O. 2012 [1898]. *The Ballad of Reading Gaol*. London: CreateSpace.

Part III

Corporeality

Introduction
Maleficium and Mortuary Archaeology
Rules and Regulations in the Negotiation of Identities

Duncan Sayer

In a letter to Jean-Baptiste Leroy, dated to 13 November 1798, Benjamin Franklin wrote: 'Nothing can be said to be certain, except death and taxes.' This phrase popularly describes the inevitability of death and taxes, but the presence and scale of taxation varies between circumstances and civilizations. Perhaps if Franklin had the long contextual view of an archaeologist, he would have rephrased his letter to describe the reliability of both rules and death, as it is rules that require us to pay taxes. It is in this context that the chapters presented in Part III describe social, religious or legal rules as we can see them in the burial record. But there are universal themes connecting these five pieces of research: who makes the rules, what are the societal mechanics that define or change regulations and what happens if they break down?

Like other socially constructed objects, rules and regulations are rarely straightforward. A useful illuminative example of this complexity can be found in a series of early seventeenth-century witch trials in Lancashire, England, often referred to as the 'Pendle witches' and the 'Samlesbury witches'. These witch trials offer a useful way of thinking about rules and the situations in which they might emerge or be enforced, particularly in terms of the relationship between individuals and wider society. Of the two men and nine women tried as Pendle witches, ten were executed by hanging. On the surface, the trials were the consequence of mistrust within tight-knit rural communities and focused on the apparent breach of specific social, religious or legal regulations. This was articulated with accusations of murder using magic, and child murder or cannibalism via *maleficium* – causing harm using witchcraft. These trials have been interpreted as the persecution of pre-Christian traditions, but this is unlikely as few of the women accused were healers or midwives (Hutton 2000: 379). In this vein, the Samlesbury witch trials are particularly interesting in the way they highlight individual guilt and responsibility within wider rules and regulation. For example, the accused were acquitted after it was demonstrated that the complainant had been an instrument of a Catholic priest (Pumfrey 2002). Consequently, another interpretation describes how these witch trials were the result of a struggle between Catholic and Protestant spirituality in a period of heightened religious conflict; early modern Lancashire remained a haunt for Catholics who were prohibited from practice in post-Reformation England (Hasted 1993; King and Sayer 2011). It has also been argued that these cases were show-trials designed to demonstrate that Lancashire was not a wild or lawless region (Pumfrey 2002). And yet, a few years later, witch trials took place in East Anglia: these rural counties were the home of puritanism and Parliament, not the lawless periphery.

This concern with the relationship between private and public religious observances, individual identity and culpability, social practice and the use of practice to present or mask a particular image is a central theme of the chapters in this part. It is particularly addressed in the contributions by Sarah Inskip and Eleanor Williams. Inskip describes burial evidence for the observance of Islamic tradition used to publicly demonstrate distinction from Christian or Jewish practice, which allowed surviving relatives to avoid heresy charges in medieval Iberia. The political elite actively used mortuary rules to legitimize their role as a religious and political power reinforcing the authority of the Umayyad Caliphate. As she notes, we must be careful of using mortuary rules to reflect social identities because they are the result of historically contingent decisions and may not identify ethnic or internal religious alignment, something that may be explored in private spaces (Lenton 2015). Williams also explores a religious context; in her example, shared burial practice can be used to express group affiliation, and the doctrinal proximity of Cluny Abbey's dependent houses to their motherhouse. Even with Benedictine practicality inbuilt into the rulebooks, which describe burial customs, Williams is able to explore senior monastics' choices to adhere to, or reinvent, Cluniac custom as part of localized contexts.

But what of instances where rules were broken and what were the contributing factors to such a breakdown? Here the witch trials again illuminate the relationship between social instability and the renegotiation of rules by groups and individuals, authority figures and the general populace. The Lancashire witch trials may have resulted from the dissolution of societal rules, which left a vacuum of economy and authority, perpetuated by the dissolution of the powerful Catholic monastery at Whalley (Hasted 1993). Although the witch trials in East Anglia were conducted with the support of some local authorities, who paid the expenses of the witch finder, the trials took place during the insecurity of the English Civil War (Geis and Bunn 1997; Sharpe 2004). Thus, when governing social structures appear precarious, rules and regulation may also appear more flexible and open to interpretation. Rejection of regulation may therefore follow amongst certain groups. This particular outcome is explored in two chapters concerning the archaeology of medieval and post-medieval practice. In Barbara Hausmair's study of unbaptized infant burials, she explores social order, implicitly the rejection of medieval church doctrine by the laity and some local clergy. She highlights the importance of church space for infant and child burial (see also Sayer 2013). Significantly, she describes how finding the youngest infant graves within consecrated burial grounds across Europe highlights a conflict between the established Church's position, the assignment of unbaptized babies to a realm adjunct to Hell, and to unconsecrated burial space, and the desperation of the recently bereaved to secure salvation for their deceased child.

Louise Fowler and Natasha Powers explore a different rejection of rules in describing the results of excavation work at the Royal London Hospital, which was founded in the eighteenth century. Their chapter focuses on the supply of corpses to the medical fraternity for dissection. In theory, the use of resurrection men to acquire corpses for medical teaching was illegal. However, a new scientific establishment was able to create hegemony through 'secrecy and delicacy' so that the government turned a blind eye to such activities until the passing of the Anatomy Act in 1832, which made fresh corpses legally available.

In both cases, the breaking of rules comes about through a tension between societal norms and the necessities of practice, be that the emotional needs of bereaved parents or the academic requirements of the scientific community. Just as rules are broken for reasons intimately linked to their context, there was probably no single social cause for the witch trials. Moreover, multiple and multiscale circumstances created locally determined frustrations, suspicion, disenfranchisement, misogyny, empowerment or the exploitation of powerlessness and personality. The Civil War and spiritual uncertainty left localized civil regulation impotent and contributed to the failure of individual social negotiations; the rules that people used to define and reproduce their place within society failed.

Rules therefore become increasingly important in such times of change, an issue addressed by Kristopher Poole's analysis of dog burial in the early Anglo-Saxon period, in which the decline of this phenomenon in the later Saxon period is seen as evidence of the growing influence of the

Church. Whether we are focusing on the political use of burial, as discussed by Inskip, the societal regulation of human–animal relationships, as discussed by Poole, or the growth of phenomena such as the witch trials, it is evident from the contributions in this part that rules surrounding the body are both shaped by and shape the societal contexts to which they relate.

What all of these chapters show is that, just like the witch trials example, agents act as individuals within social structures and use or reject regulations as a way to define their identity. Agents may be empowered by association with an institution (Inskip); they may follow or develop rules to express belonging to a bigger group or to align themselves to a wider community (Williams; Poole). They may reject rules as a way to create new hegemonies (Fowler and Powers) or define specific relationships within local environments such as monasteries or local parish dynamics (Williams; Hausmair). Rules are a significant part of society and whether someone finds themselves a rule maker or rule breaker is part of how they negotiate their place within society. The disenfranchised women who accused witches took an opportunity to align themselves with authority figures – witch finders, churchmen or magistrates – and in so doing they redefined their relationship with an authority during a state of instability. Through this, they separated themselves from those they marginalized by their accusation. For some accusers, such as Matthew Hopkins the East Anglian witch finder, their brutality defined them as outsiders to post-Restoration society: 'part of the dreadfulness of the 1640s and 1650s' (Sharpe 2004). As the witch trials and each of the chapters in Part III demonstrate, agents, identities and actors matter, but their decisions are historically contingent, and it is this that defines an individual's relationship with a particular rubric.

Duncan Sayer is Reader in Archaeology at the University of Central Lancashire, United Kingdom. He is the author of *Ethics and Burial Archaeology* (BCP, 2010) and edited *Mortuary Practice and Social Identity in the Middle Ages* (Liverpool University Press, 2013) and *The Archaeology of Post-medieval Religion* (Boydell, 2011). He is Honorary Treasurer for the Society for Medieval Archaeology and Vice Chair of the Chartered Institute for Archaeology's Advisory Panel. He is a field archaeologist at heart and has directed two significant excavation projects focused on an early Anglo-Saxon cemetery in Oakington, Cambridgeshire, and the post-Roman phases inside the north gate at Ribchester Roman Fort, Lancashire.

References

Geis, G., and I. Bunn. 1997. *A Trial of Witches: A Seventeenth-Century Witchcraft Prosecution*. London: Routledge.
Hasted, R. 1993. *The Pendle Witch Trial 1612*. Lancaster: Lancashire County Books.
Hutton, R. 2000. *The Triumph of the Moon: A History of Modern Pagan Witchcraft*. Oxford: Oxford University Press.
King, C., and D. Sayer. 2011. 'Conflict, Community and Custom: The Material Remains of Post-medieval Religion', in C. King and D. Sayer (eds), *The Archaeology of Post-medieval Religion*. Woodbridge: Boydell, pp. 1–18.
Lenton, D.A. 2015. 'Domestic & Social Practice in Later Medieval Córdoba, Spain', in M. Bourton, J. Hawkes and M. Herman (eds), *The Art, Literature and Material Culture of the Medieval World*. Dublin: Four Courts Press, pp. 42–58.
Pumfrey, S. 2002. 'Potts, Plots and Politics: James I's Daemonologie and the Wonderfull Discoverie of Witches', in R. Poole (ed.), *The Lancashire Witches*. Manchester, Manchester University Press, pp. 22–41.
Sayer, D. 2013. 'Christian Burial Practice in the Early Middle Ages: Rethinking the Anglo-Saxon Funerary Sphere', *History Compass* 11(2): 133–46.
Sharpe, J. 2002. 'The Lancaster Witches in Historical Context', in R. Poole, (ed.), *The Lancashire Witches*. Manchester: Manchester University Press, pp. 1–18.
———. 2004. 'Hopkins, Matthew (d. 1647)', in *Oxford Dictionary of National Biography*. Oxford: Oxford University Press.
Winzeler, R. 2007. *Anthropology and Religion: What We Know, Think, and Question*. Plymouth: Altamira Press.

Chapter 11

Gone to the Dogs?
Negotiating the Human-Animal Boundary in Anglo-Saxon England

Kristopher Poole

Introduction

Attitudes regarding actions and interactions are fundamental to human social life. They may be enforced in a number of ways, including legally sanctioned rules and regulations, religious doctrine, and informal rules and customs. As demonstrated by the other chapters in this volume, these attitudes play a significant role in the creation and maintenance of identity, including religious beliefs, gender and status. Faced with these restrictions, people may follow or defy them, whether intentionally or otherwise. In many cases, emphasis has been on interactions between humans and of human identities. The very notion of humanity is bound up with notions of appropriate behaviour, most commonly determined through comparison with other animate beings, namely animals (Steel 2008), and through interactions in daily life (Poole 2013a, 2015).

This chapter will explore the differing attitudes to human and animal bodies in Anglo-Saxon England (c. 410–1066), through comparison of the early Anglo-Saxon period (c. 410–650) and the mid to late Anglo-Saxon period (c. 650–1066). It focuses on patterns of behaviour, which, through their repetition over time, became entrenched within society. This replication of behaviour may suggest observable patterns in the archaeological record, making it a vital means of understanding the customs that governed human-animal interactions. This is especially important given that much engagement between humans and animals was governed by unconscious thought and therefore has probably gone unremarked within written sources. Nonetheless, legal texts can be used to identify such patterns, although Anglo-Saxon period laws involving animals were preoccupied with the value of animals and the restitution to be paid if they were harmed, or they caused damage to another person or their property. Religious texts also provide insight into the concerns of churchmen regarding humans and animals. However, their influence on quotidian life of most people needs to be assessed utilizing the material world, which is, after all, the context within which meaning was generated.

Throughout this study, consideration is given to domestic animals at a broad level, with a primary focus on dogs. These animals potentially enjoyed a wide range of very different relationships with people, compared with relationships between humans and most other domestic species. However, dogs have enjoyed relatively little direct scholarly attention in Anglo-Saxon research, particularly compared to studies of horses in this period, another species with distinctive relationships with people (e.g. Fern 2005, 2007). This chapter begins by considering the evidence for attitudes to spatial proximity between humans and animals, first in terms of living at settlements, followed by evidence for co-burials of humans and dogs. This is followed by examining aspects of interaction in life, namely human-animal bodily practices, questions of ownership, the value attached to dogs, and the relationships generated between them and humans.

Spatial Proximity

Living Together

Dog bones are regularly identified within Anglo-Saxon period faunal assemblages, in at least three-quarters of sites excavated to date (Table 11.1). Even when physically absent, their presence around settlements is frequently indicated by canine gnawing marks on bones. Dogs would therefore have been a familiar sight on all settlements across the Anglo-Saxon period. Interestingly, their remains make up a larger percentage of bone assemblages on rural and ecclesiastical sites in the middle Anglo-Saxon period and on rural sites in the late Saxon period. This is not to say that dogs were more common in life on these sites; Albarella (2005: 138–39) has suggested that on sites where meat was not regularly eaten, non-food animals will show up in higher frequencies than on sites where meat was more commonly consumed (see below). Regardless of site type, dog bones are found in relatively small numbers when compared to the main domesticates (cattle, sheep/goat and pigs), making up an average of 0.2 to 3.5 per cent of bone assemblages. Although there is not necessarily

Table 11.1 Frequency with which dogs are identified with Anglo-Saxon bone assemblages

Phase	No. of sites	No. with dogs	% of sites with dogs
Early Saxon rural	36	26	72.7
Mid Saxon rural	24	18	75.0
Mid Saxon urban	17	15	88.2
Mid Saxon ecclesiastical	4	3	75.0
Mid Saxon high status	10	8	80.0
Mid Saxon total	**55**	**44**	**80.0**
Late Saxon rural	13	12	92.3
Late Saxon urban	45	37	82.2
Late Saxon ecclesiastical	3	3	100.0
Late Saxon high status	13	10	76.9
Late Saxon total	**74**	**62**	**83.8**

a direct equation between numbers of bone fragments and living animals at a site, dogs were probably present in smaller numbers.

Humans working closely with species such as cattle and sheep may have felt ties of affection towards them (Poole 2013a), although for animals such as dogs, the relationship would have been more one-to-one rather than group/herd based. Moreover, some (though not all) dogs would have been allowed into buildings with humans, in contrast to most other domesticates. Throughout the Anglo-Saxon period, there is no evidence in England of longhouses, structures that housed both animals and humans (Hamerow 2002: 47), so animals seem to have been generally excluded from buildings. Yet dogs are well suited to living closely with people because, more than any other species, they understand how to act towards other dogs, as well as humans, and are more adaptable at doing so (Bradshaw 2013: 101). Zooarchaeological data, particularly metrics, suggest that there were a range of different-sized dogs, from small lapdogs through to large 'wolf-sized' dogs in this period (Harcourt 1974; Clark 1995). Although size and purpose are not necessarily directly correlated, this may have affected the sorts of interactions that dogs had with humans, as discussed below.

Burial Together

The majority of animal bones dating to the Anglo-Saxon period, including dogs, have been excavated in settlements. This contrasts with humans, most of whom were interred in areas of the landscape set aside as cemeteries. However, there are instances, almost all dating to the early Anglo-Saxon period, where animals have been intentionally buried in cemeteries, either accompanying humans or occasionally in grave cuts of their own. It seems likely that they were killed specifically to accompany the deceased, rather than just being animals that happened to die at the same time, but the practice is more commonly related to cremation than inhumation (Williams 2005). Interment of animals in graves could include whole animals, selected portions of animals, as well as single body parts (see Lee 2007). Where evidence is available, dogs and horses appear to have been cremated whole, as were many cattle carcasses (Bond and Worley 2006). This, coupled with the lack of butchery marks on horse and dog bones in cremations (with the exception of Sancton I, where a horse had been decapitated but with all body parts being placed on the pyre) perhaps indicates dogs and horses were status markers for humans in death (McKinley 1994: 96–97). In contrast, sheep and pigs tend to be represented by body parts, suggesting food offerings (Bond and Worley 2006: 92). Wild animals are occasionally present, generally as single bones, possibly from amulets (McKinley 1994: 96).

Cemeteries tend to contain a wider range of species than settlements, with some animals disproportionately represented, including horses and dogs (Bond and Worley 2006). Of seven cremation cemeteries with animal bone that Bond (1996) cites, only Sancton I and Spong Hill had dogs. At Sancton I, 134 cremations contained animal remains, of which three (2.2 per cent) were dogs and at Spong Hill, twenty-six of 645 cremations (4 per cent) with animal bone contained dog remains, in contrast to average dog frequencies on contemporary settlements (0.8 per cent). Notably, in the Spong Hill settlement, no dogs were identified at all, although this might be partly explained by poor preservation. Thus, certain animal types were specifically selected to accompany humans, as were other aspects of the grave equipment, including the urn (Richards 1987).

Although there are some instances of cremated animals being interred in their own vessel ('animal accessory vessels'), alongside another vessel containing cremated human remains (McKinley 1994: 93), the majority of animal remains in cremations have been found mixed with humans. However, apart from being deliberately slaughtered, when apparently whole animals are involved, they may have undergone the same processes as people. We cannot rule out the possibility that some apparently whole animals were butchered before burning. These marks may have been destroyed during cremation, yet the possibility exists that close bonds were being expressed throughout the process.

The provision of whole dogs in cremations and inhumations is paralleled by contemporary cemeteries in continental Europe, including Scandinavia, Germany and the Low Countries, and numbers of dog burials are similarly low (Prummel 1992). In England, for example, dogs inhumed whole appear at Foulden cemetery (Norfolk), where a dog was placed with its head on the knees of a male burial (Meaney 1964: 175) and in a multiple burial at Loveden Hill (Lincolnshire) of a very elderly man with a five-and-a-half-year-old child in his arms and an elderly lame dog at his feet; to reach this age, the dog would likely have had to be retained and cared for by the family (Wilkinson 1980: 229–30). As with the inclusion of dogs in cremations, these burials appear to be articulating close relationships between the humans interred with them (e.g. Morey 2006: 159). Examples of dogs interred in their own grave cuts in cemeteries are also known, such as at Great Chesterford, Essex (Serjeantson 1994), which Sally Crawford (2009: 166–67) interprets as dogs being buried as if they were people. Some of these inhumed dogs in the early Saxon period were possibly pets, but dogs, as with animals of any kind, are almost completely absent from middle to late Anglo-Saxon funerary contexts. Very rare exceptions in some parts of the country were created following the arrival of Scandinavian settlers in the late Anglo-Saxon period (Bond and Worley 2006: 96).

Whatever the origin of the burials described here, as noted above, the vast majority will have been disposed of in and around settlements. As well as the occurrence of their bones as isolated finds, dogs also frequently appear as articulated remains or Associated Bone Groups (ABGs). Morris' (2010) study of ABGs in Wessex found that dogs were the most frequently represented species, making up 37.1 per cent of deposits, although he included the whole Anglo-Saxon period. However, if we focus on the early Anglo-Saxon period, dogs are the most frequent species making up ABGs, at ten out of seventeen examples (58.8 per cent; see Poole 2011). As with cemeteries, these figures are disproportionate to the representation of dogs based on the overall number of identified bones on settlements (Poole 2011). Whilst perhaps partly due to dogs not being eaten (see below), other non-food animals, such as cats, do not appear as ABGs in this period. This indicates that, just as with graves, there was a deliberate selection of particular animals for burial in this manner. In this respect, the early Anglo-Saxon data show similarities with Roman Britain, as well as other contemporary settlements in the Continental North Sea area (Hamerow 2006: 20, 22–26). Whilst it is dangerous to place meta-interpretations onto these finds (Morris and Jervis 2011), a number of these deposits have been argued to be deliberately placed, representing 'termination deposits', given their frequent association with abandoned structures (Hamerow 2006).

On settlement sites, dogs continue to appear as ABGs on sites of middle and late Saxon date, although more often as partial ABGs than complete skeletons. This suggests that their remains were largely disposed of along with other waste, subject to the actions of scavengers, although post-depositional disturbance is also possible. Although the full details of these deposits are not always available, there is potentially a contrast here with the careful placement of some dogs in the early Anglo-Saxon period. At Saddler Street, Durham, a dog was simply dumped on a midden that was probably associated with a house, whilst at Site 1092, Thetford, a dog was crammed into the base of a ditch. The above thus perhaps indicates a shift in attitude to dogs over the course of the Anglo-Saxon period – does the evidence for bodily practice shed light on this?

Bodily Practice – Value – Ownership

Ownership

Dogs owned by people could have been used for a variety of purposes, including for hunting, herding, as guard animals and pest controllers, as well as pets. Determining which roles were played by a dog found in a bone assemblage is difficult. Although a small dog may not have been a particularly terrifying prospect, the noise it might make could have served as deterrent to a person seeking to steal another person's property. Equally, even if a dog was often used for herding, this would not necessarily stop people from feeling ties of affection towards it – the same individual could have been viewed differently, for example, when interacting with it in a household-context (see Poole 2015). It is unclear whether pet-keeping was practised in Anglo-Saxon England. The documentary sources are silent on the issue, whilst pets are difficult to identify in the archaeological record. Even if treated well in life, a pet dog could have simply been dumped along with food waste (Thomas 2005: 95). Some of the lap dog bones recovered from late Saxon deposits, such as from Winchester (Bourdillon 2009) and Lincoln (Dobney, Jaques and Irving 1996), could also have been pets, but might equally have been used as ratting dogs. Contemporary societies were known to keep pets, as illustrated by seventh- to eighth-century law codes in Ireland, where a pet dog was seen as a necessity for high-ranking ladies, and men of status should have hunting hounds (*Corpus Iuris Hibernici*: vol. ii 567.26; vol. iii 783.33 = CG 16.408). Other Irish law codes saw pet dogs and hunting dogs as being of equal value (*Corpus Iuris Hibernici*: iii 806.34; iv 1531.2). Pet-keeping was also well known in the later Middle Ages, where it was frowned upon by the Church, although not forbidden, at least not to the secular world (Thomas 2005). The absence of mentions to the practice for Anglo-Saxon England might indicate that it was not very common or that Church leaders ignored it (and if it was associated with elites at the time, this may have been prudent).

If some dogs were kept as pets, it is possible that they were treated as if they were members of a household and were treated better than some people (Walker-Meikle 2012: 1). However, other dogs may have been less fortunate, as indicated by pathological evidence. One dog found at Lake End Road, Dorney, showed evidence of massive trauma from a sharp implement to the left side of its skull, which it had survived, along with fractures to its spine and an infection on its right tibia (Powell 2002). Whilst one of these injuries on its own might have originated from a variety of events, the amount of damage suffered by one individual may well indicate a series of injuries, deliberately inflicted by a person or persons (Binois et al. 2013). Greater caution is needed when dealing with pathologies exhibited on disarticulated animal bones, where the whole skeleton of the same animal cannot be examined. Nonetheless, human action remains a distinct possibility in such cases, although cases of dog trauma were also noted at the early Anglo-Saxon site of West Stow (Crabtree 1989), so that not all dogs before the mid to late Saxon period were well treated. The ageing data for dogs from this period indicate that a large number of dogs were not reaching maturity in this era. This includes a number from urban sites, which might indicate feral populations, taking advantage of the feeding opportunities on offer (e.g. O'Connor 2013). Such animals were potentially a nuisance and it is possible that at least some were deliberately killed, whilst others may have suffered from poor health. This raises the possibility of a distinctly 'urban' attitude towards at least some dogs, although this may not have exclusively been so. Nonetheless, some part of negative views of dogs perhaps stemmed from their behaviour, including their dietary habits.

Consuming Each Other's Bodies

Cattle, sheep/goats and pigs were clearly sources of food during this period, as indicated by the presence of their bones in rubbish deposits on settlements, butchery marks on their bones and stable isotope studies from human remains (Hull and O'Connell 2011; Poole 2011). Horses were also eaten at this time, but less frequently than cattle, sheep/goats and pigs, and perhaps in special contexts (Poole 2013b). Two species that almost never show evidence of exploitation for food at this time are cats (Poole 2015) and dogs. The only published example of a dog bone with butchery marks for the early Saxon period was found at Shrivenham Road, Ashbury, Oxford (Hall 1998), which likely represents exploitation of its hide, rather than for food. This apparent avoidance of dog flesh was perhaps driven by its reputation as a scavenger, especially given that Sally Crawford (2009) suggests they were seen as enemies of child burials, which were often buried in shallow graves, including around settlements, and so were susceptible to being attacked by dogs or wolves. By contrast, a greater number of examples of dog bones with butchery marks have been identified from the mid to late Saxon period. Understanding the origin of these marks is difficult. Some marks may represent skinning in order to make use of dog hides, such as an example from Bishopstone and some of the bones from Norwich Cathedral Refectory, or might represent bone working (Fishergate, Norwich). Others, including examples from Higham Ferrers, Thetford and Norwich Cathedral Refectory, might represent carcass division, raising the prospect of dogs being consumed by humans (Poole 2011).

As carnivorous animals, known for their scavenging, it seems unlikely that dogs would have been a food of choice. In late Anglo-Saxon sources, for instance, the breakdown of the body after death was almost always expressed entirely in terms of being eaten by animals of some kind (Thompson 2004: 138). As such, dogs may only have been eaten in times of famine. This is suggested by slightly later sources, such as the twelfth-century *Liber Elensis* (lib.II, 104), in which famine in 1069 led to people eating 'horses, dogs and cats, and human flesh'. Eating dogs (amongst other animals) was thus equated with cannibalism, casting further doubt on consumption of canids by humans. A number of these sites were owned by high-status persons, who were presumably better insulated from starvation than those of lower status.

Use of dogs for hunting may instead provide an explanation. In the mid and late Saxon period, hunting was increasingly an activity conducted and led by elites, who used hunting hounds for the purpose (Marvin 2006). Wilson and Edwards (1993) discuss the presence of butchered horse and dog bones in post-medieval deposits at Witney Palace, Oxfordshire, concluding that these probably represent animals slaughtered and butchered for feeding to hunting hounds. Although this is a much later time period, a similar practice may have been followed at some of these mid to late Saxon sites.

Bestiality

Earlier Germanic law codes (unfortunately, none have survived from early Anglo-Saxon England) make no mention of bestiality, either indicating that it was not common (at least not on a large enough scale to warrant a law code) or that it was not seen as a concern in society (Salisbury 1994: 87). In contrast, numerous penitentials from England, Ireland and Northern Europe deal with the act of bestiality. Men who were frequently involved in bestiality had to perform either ten or fifteen years' penance, according to the *Penitential of Theodore* (U, lib. II, cap. XI, §1–2). Egbert of

York's Penitentials (*Poenitentiale Egberti*: cap. V, §20) list a range of penances from different sources. From the mid Saxon period onwards, the animals involved in bestiality were supposed to be killed and not eaten, as they were now 'unclean', but were not held culpable (Meens 1995: 10–11). In most if not all cases of bestiality, it may have been that religious sanctions, as specified in penitential texts, were applied.

There are four notable examples of animals buried in mid to late Anglo-Saxon execution cemeteries that may suggest archaeological evidence of bestiality, including Burial 19 (mid eleventh century) from Stockbridge Down, Hampshire (Reynolds 2009: 154, 172, 236–37). This contained a decapitated male human, accompanied by a decapitated dog. Reynolds (2009: 172) considered the possibility of this representing illegal hunting, but by drawing upon late and post-medieval pan-European accounts, he instead proposed that it represented a punishment for bestiality, with human and dog both being penalized. However, this is far from certain, especially given that the earliest surviving English written law that makes bestiality a capital offence dates from 1534 (Thomas 1996: 39). Nonetheless, it is possible that such acts with some animals may have been seen as worse than with others. Almost no penitential texts distinguish between particular types of animals with regard to bestiality, although the *Poenitentiale Hubertense* (C.XXXIV, C.LVIII), a ninth-century Frankish text, differentiates between bestiality with clean and unclean animals, whilst the *Synod of the Grove of Victory* (conducted in Wales in 569) states that: 'He who sins with a dog or with an animal, two and a half years [penance]' (*Synod*: §7). The Stockbridge Down dog is one of the very few examples of an animal being deliberately interred with a human within a burial context from the mid to late Saxon period. Perhaps some cases of bestiality were therefore considered to require punishment outside the norm? These were, after all, 'deviant' burials, those that appear to have acted, and thus were buried in ways different from other people in society, even allowing for some variation in burial practices (Reynolds 2009). If there were members of local communities present at the burial, the display of the human and dog bodies, both beheaded, could have acted as a warning to avoid the sort of behaviour that led to their execution.

Discussions

Issues Relating to Spatial Proximity

Regardless of the period, it is likely that at least some dogs shared living space with people. This would not have been true for all members of this species; some, particularly feral dogs or those belonging to other people, may have been excluded from dwellings. However, as fellow living beings, dogs were always capable of acting in ways viewed as incompatible with human standards of interaction, including entering spaces they were not supposed to access. Those dogs allowed indoors, however, enjoyed distinct relationships with humans compared to many other domestic animals. Even horses, often also interpreted as companion animals and linked with social status by researchers (Fern 2005), would not have occupied the living space of people. The close bonds that could be enjoyed between humans and dogs are perhaps expressed in their co-burial in early Anglo-Saxon graves. Dogs were more frequent in cremation burials than they were on contemporary settlements, indicating that some form of relationship was being articulated. These likely spanned a range of different forms, with individual dogs playing varying roles in society, meaning that we cannot attribute one cause to the practice of burying dogs in human graves. This is true of all animals at this time, including horses. A number of inhumations containing horses have been interpreted as social expressions of a martial elite (Fern 2005). However, horse bones were more frequent in cremations, with both men and women. Some of these bones have pathological conditions, perhaps indicative of their use as working animals, which represent an important reminder of the varied relationships that different members of the same species could have with humans.

In contrast to the early Saxon period, where interring animals in graves was acceptable, this practice ceased during the mid to late Saxon period (barring the exceptions mentioned above). It is possible that animals were excluded from burials because of perceived links of such practices with pagan beliefs and the implication that they were being devoted to non-Christian gods (Gilhus 2006: 154). However, it may also have been due to differences identified between humans and animals. Various late Anglo-Saxon textual sources portray animals as lacking souls: 'He [God] gave no beast or fish a soul, but their life is their blood and once they are dead they are finished with' (*Homilies of Ælfric*: Sermon I). Actively excluding animals from graves represented one way in which such a distinction was marked out. Given the close links between the spread of Christianity and elites (Carver 2010), it is possible that the influence of lords not being buried with animals also influenced the transition. Nonetheless, dogs are found as ABGs on settlements in both periods. Although this may be due in part to dogs apparently only very rarely being eaten and their bodies therefore not being deliberately dismembered, the greater tendency for dog ABGs in the early Anglo-Saxon period hints at different treatment of their remains than later on. This is especially evident in the apparently more careful deposition of at least some of the early Anglo-Saxon examples, compared to the more haphazard treatment of some of the dogs in later periods. Altogether, these data indicate a culture that emphasized human-animal similarities within funerary contexts in one period, but that made clear distinctions between the treatment of human and animal bodies in death later on. Whilst burial treatments are not necessarily a direct reflection of the deceased's social identity when alive (Hodder 1982: 142–43), they are influenced by societal concerns. In particular, funerary rituals provide occasions for dominant groups to assert their own perspective on the world (Parker Pearson 1982). Did this mean that human–canine relationships were not as close in later periods? In order to answer this question, we must give further consideration to the evidence for bodily practice.

Issues Relating to Bodily Practice – Value – Ownership

As noted above, throughout the Anglo-Saxon period, dogs could have had a variety of relations with humans. This would have been true of other species too, including horses, which enjoyed different roles from the main domesticates. We therefore need to be careful not to impose homogeneity onto human–animal relationships. Some of the roles that dogs had will have led to closer ties with humans than others. For example, a pet dog may have been kept close to their owner most of the time, perhaps even sleeping alongside them, whereas those kept for guarding livestock were perhaps slightly more distant. This would have extended into a dog's youth, since dogs, like humans, need to be socialized into the community in which they live (Birke, Bryld and Lykke 2004). It is by the process of humans and other animals engaging with dogs, in particular ways, that dogs come to have a particular role, or even 'identity', whilst the continuing performance of such tasks serves to reinforce this (see Birke, Bryld and Lykke 2004; Poole 2015). In contrast, many dogs in Anglo-Saxon England would have led a feral existence. Such animals would have had varying degrees of human contact, from those nominally owned by someone but allowed to roam freely to truly feral populations, living around human settlements but existing almost completely on scavenged food (van Kerkhove 2004: 281).

All dogs at a settlement were capable of scavenging food, whether in the form of table scraps, middens or from other sources. This relatively greater freedom over dietary intake and ability to move around a settlement could have marked dogs out as distinct from many other domestic mammals, including horses. Conversely, the potential for dogs to consume matter considered as disgusting, potentially including human flesh, played an important role in the formation of negative views towards them. It is notable that dogs do not appear to have been a normal part of the diet and perhaps were only consumed by humans in times of desperation. In contrast, horses do appear to have been eaten in early Anglo-Saxon England, although possibly only in special contexts. This practice was banned by the Church during the middle to late Anglo-Saxon period, the impact of which is visible in the zooarchaeological record (Poole 2013b). That people in the early Anglo-Saxon period ate horse but not dogs may, in part, be due to the special cultic significance the former held, but also because horses did not eat meat. Other animals known for scavenging and eating meat, namely members of the crow family, could also hold religious significance, but were apparently not eaten (Poole 2011). Therefore, an animal's diet may have been the most significant factor in terms of whether it was consumed. That dogs were potentially being fed to other dogs in the mid to late Saxon period could well have reinforced a perception of dogs as unclean animals. Bestiality with a dog could thus perhaps have been seen as even more abhorrent than with other species.

Conclusions

The differing interactions between humans and various animals in the Anglo-Saxon period would have contributed to ideas regarding humanity and one's place in the world. The majority of animals were treated in ways distinct from the treatment of humans. Nonetheless, people throughout this period often lived closely with animals and close bonds may have formed between them. This was likely more so for dogs than for other species, as they could have enjoyed one-to-one relationships with people and potentially shared their homes. However, ultimately, perceptions of dogs depended upon the types of interactions that took place and the role that the dog was expected to play. Some dogs may have been highly prized and cared for, even treated better than other humans, whereas other dogs were likely to have been considered a nuisance and ill-treated. This diversity seems apparent in the early and mid to late Saxon period but burial evidence perhaps indicates some conceptual differences between eras. Deliberate inclusion of animals, including dogs, with people in the early Saxon period contrasts strongly with later burials. It is not necessarily the case that people saw themselves as completely distinct from animals, but rather that ideologies of elites and Church leaders controlled burial rites, as they did other aspects of everyday existence, through laws and religious doctrine. In this way, the funerary data may misrepresent human–animal relationships in life at this time. For this reason, reconstructing human–animal relationships in past societies necessitates an integrated approach, attempting to gain a holistic perspective on the multiplicity of interactions that existed between humans and individual animals from the same species.

Kristopher Poole works for Trent and Peak Archaeology and is an Honorary Research Fellow at the University of Sheffield, United Kingdom. Prior to this, he was Lecturer in Zooarchaeology at the University of Sheffield and a Post-doctoral Research Associate at the University of Nottingham. His research focuses on human–animal relationships, with particular interest in animals and identity, nature and society, animal introductions and extinctions, and animals and funerary archaeology, with a particular focus on the Anglo-Saxon and medieval periods.

References

Primary Sources

Corpus Iuris Hibernici vol. i–iv, ed./trans. D.A. Binchy. 1978. Dublin: Dublin Institute for Advanced Studies.
Homilies of Ælfric, trans. B. Thorpe. 1844. *The Homilies of the Anglo-Saxon Church: The First Part, Containing the Sermones Catholici, or Homilies of Ælfric*. London: Ælfric Society.
Penitential of Theodore, ed./trans. J.T. McNeill and H.M. Gamer. 1965. *Medieval Handbooks of Penance*. New York: Colombia University Press, pp. 179–215.
Poenitentiale Egberti, ed. H. Wasserschleben. 1851. *Die Bussordnungen der abendländischen Kirche*. Halle: Ch. Graeger, pp. 231–47.
Poenitentiale Hubertense, ed. H.J. Schmitz. 1898. *Die Bussbücher und das kanonische Bussverfahren: Nach handschriftlichen Quellen dargestellt, Vol. II*. Düsseldorf: Schwann, pp. 331–39.
Synod of the Grove of Victory, trans. J.T. McNeill and H.M. Gamer. 1965. *Medieval Handbooks of Penance*. New York: Colombia University Press, pp. 171–72.

Secondary Literature

Albarella, U. 2005. 'Meat Production and Consumption in Town and Country', in K. Giles and C. Dyer (eds), *Town and Country in the Middle Ages*. Leeds: Maney, pp. 131–48.
Binois, A., C. Wardius, P. Rio, A. Bridault and C. Petit. 2013. 'A Dog's Life: Multiple Trauma and Potential Abuse in a Medieval Dog from Guimps (Charente, France)', *International Journal of Paleopathology* 3(1): 39–47.
Birke, L., M. Bryld and N. Lykke. 2004. 'Animal Performances: An Exploration of Intersections between Feminist Science Studies and Studies of Human/Animal Relationships', *Feminist Theory* 5(2): 167–83.
Bond, J.M. 1996. 'Burnt Offerings: Animal Bone in Anglo-Saxon Cremations', *World Archaeology* 28(1): 76–88.

Bond, J.M., and F.L. Worley. 2006. 'Companions in Death: The Roles of Animals in Anglo-Saxon and Viking Cremation Rituals in Britain', in R. Gowland and C. Knüsel (eds), *Social Archaeology of Funerary Remains*. Oxford: Oxbow, pp. 89–98.

Bourdillon, J. 2009. 'Late Saxon Animal Bone from the Northern and Eastern Suburbs and City Defences', in D. Serjeantson and H. Rees (eds), *Food, Craft and Status Saxon and Medieval Winchester*. Winchester: Winchester Museums Service, pp. 55–81.

Bradshaw, J. 2013. *Cat Sense: The Feline Enigma Revealed*. London: Allen Lane.

Carver, M. 2010. 'Agency, Intellect and the Archaeological Agenda', in M. Carver, A. Sanmark and S. Semple (eds), *Signals of Belief in Anglo-Saxon England*. Oxford: Oxbow, pp. 1–20.

Clark, K.M. 1995. 'The Later Prehistoric and Protohistoric Dog: The Emergence of Canine Diversity', *Archaeozoologia* 7(2): 9–32.

Crabtree, P.J. 1989. *West Stow, Suffolk: Early Anglo-Saxon Animal Husbandry*, East Anglian Archaeology 47. Ipswich: Suffolk County Council.

Crawford, S. 2009. *Daily Life in Anglo-Saxon England*. Oxford: Greenwood Publications.

Dobney, K.M., S.D. Jacques and B.G. Irving. 1996. *Of Butchers and Breeds: Report on Vertebrate Remains from Various Sites in the City of Lincoln*, Archaeological Studies 5. Lincoln: City of Lincoln Council.

Fern, C. 2005. 'The Archaeological Evidence for Equestrianism in Early Anglo-Saxon England, c. 450–700', in A. Pluskowski (ed.), *Just Skin and Bones?* BAR British Series 1410. Oxford: Archaeopress, pp. 43–71.

———. 2007. 'Early Anglo-Saxon Horse Burial of the Fifth to Seventh Centuries AD', in S. Semple and H. Williams (eds), *Early Medieval Mortuary Practices*, Anglo-Saxon Studies in Archaeology and History 14. Oxford: Oxford University/School of Archaeology, pp. 92–109.

Gilhus, I.S. 2006. *Animals, Gods and Humans: Changing Attitudes to Animals in Greek, Roman and Early Christian Ideas*. London: Routledge.

Hall, M. 1998. 'The Archaeology of the Ashbury to Bishopstone Pipeline, South Oxfordshire/Wiltshire, 1993', *Oxoniensia* 63: 199–220.

Hamerow, H. 2002. *Early Medieval Settlements: The Archaeology of Rural Communities in Northwest Europe 400–900*. Oxford: Oxford University Press.

———. 2006. 'Special Deposits in Anglo-Saxon Settlements', *Medieval Archaeology* 50: 1–30.

Harcourt, R.A. 1974. 'The Dog in Prehistoric and Early Historic Britain', *Journal of Archaeological Science* 1: 151–75.

Hodder, I. (ed.). 1982. *Symbolic and Structural Archaeology*. Cambridge: Cambridge University Press.

Hull, B., and T.C. O'Connell. 2011, 'Diet: Recent Evidence from Analytical Chemical Techniques', in H. Hamerow, D. Hinton and S. Crawford (eds), *The Oxford Handbook of Anglo-Saxon Archaeology*. Oxford: Oxford University Press, pp. 667–87.

Lee, C. 2007. *Feasting the Dead: Food and Drink in Anglo-Saxon Burial Rituals*. Woodbridge: Boydell.

Marvin, W.P. 2006. *Hunting Law and Ritual in Medieval English Literature*. Cambridge: Brewer.

McKinley, J.I. 1994. *The Anglo-Saxon Cemetery at Spong Hill, North Elmham. Part VIII: the Cremations*, East Anglian Archaeology 69. Gressenhall: Norfolk Museum Service Field Archaeology Division.

Meaney, A.L. 1964. *A Gazetteer of Early Anglo-Saxon Burial Sites*. London: Allen & Unwin.

Meens, R. 1995. 'Pollution in the Early Middle Ages: The Case of the Food Regulations in Penitentials', *Early Medieval Europe* 4(1): 3–19.

Morey, D.F. 2006. 'Burying Key Evidence: The Social Bond between Dogs and People', *Journal of Archaeological Science* 33: 158–75.

Morris, J. 2010. 'The Composition and Interpretation of Associated Bone Groups from Wessex', in D. Campana, P.J. Crabtree, S.D. deFrance, J. Lev-Tov and A. Choyke (eds), *Anthropological Approaches to Zooarchaeology*. Oxford: Oxbow, pp. 257–69.

Morris, J., and B. Jervis. 2011. 'What's So Special? A Reinterpretation of Anglo-Saxon "Special Deposits"', *Medieval Archaeology* 55: 66–81.

O'Connor, T.P. 2013. *Animals as Neighbours: The Past and Present of Commensal Animals*. East Lansing, MI: Michigan State University Press.

Parker Pearson, M. 1982. 'Mortuary Practices, Society and Ideology: An Ethnoarchaeological Study', in I. Hodder (ed.), *Symbolic and Structural Archaeology*. Cambridge: Cambridge University Press, pp. 99–113.

Poole, K. 2011. 'The Nature of Society in England, c. AD 410–1066', Ph.D. dissertation. Nottingham: University of Nottingham.

———. 2013a. 'Engendering Debate: Animals and Identity in Anglo-Saxon England', *Medieval Archaeology* 57(1): 61–82.

———. 2013b. 'Horses for Courses? Religious Change and Dietary Shifts in Anglo-Saxon England', *Oxford Journal of Archaeology* 32(3): 319–33.

———. 2015. 'The Contextual Cat: Human-Animal Relations and Social Meaning in Anglo-Saxon England', *Journal of Archaeological Method and Theory* 22: 857–82.

Powell, A. 2002. 'Animal Bone', in S. Foreman, J. Hiller and D. Petts (eds), *Gathering the People, Settling the Land*. Oxford: Oxford Archaeology, pp. 44–49.

Prummel, W. 1992. 'Early Medieval Dog Burials among the Germanic Tribes', *Helinium* 32(1–2): 132–94.

Reynolds, A. 2009. *Anglo-Saxon Deviant Burial Customs*. Oxford: Oxford University Press.

Richards, J.D. 1987. *The Significance of Form and Decoration of Anglo-Saxon Cremation Urns*, BAR British Series 166. Oxford: Archaeopress.

Salisbury, J.E. 1994. *The Beast Within: Animals in the Middle Ages*. London: Routledge.

Serjeantson, D. 1994. 'The Animal Bones', in V.I. Evison (ed.), *An Anglo-Saxon Cemetery at Great Chesterford, Essex*, Council for British Archaeology Research Report 91. London: CBA, pp. 66–70.

Steel, K. 2008. 'How to Make a Human', *Exemplaria* 20(1): 3–27.

Thomas, K. 1996. *Man and the Natural World: Changing Attitudes in England, 1500–1800*. Oxford: Oxford University Press.

Thomas, R. 2005. 'Perceptions Versus Reality: Changing Attitudes towards Pets in Medieval and Post-medieval England', in A. Pluskowski (ed.), *Just Skin and Bones?*, BAR International Series 1410. Oxford: Archaeopress, pp. 95–105.

Thompson, V. 2004. *Dying and Death in Later Anglo-Saxon England*. Woodbridge: Boydell & Brewer.

Van Kerkhove, W. 2004. 'A Fresh Look at the Wolf-Pack Theory of Companion-Animal Dog Social Behaviour', *Journal of Applied Animal Welfare Science* 7(4): 279–285.

Walker-Meikle, K. 2012. *Medieval Pets*. Woodbridge: Boydell & Brewer.

Williams, H. 2005. 'Animals, Ashes and Ancestors', in A. Pluskowski (ed.), *Just Skin and Bones?*, BAR International Series 1410. Oxford: Archaeopress, pp. 19–40.

Wilkinson, L. 1980. 'Problems of Analysis and Interpretation of Skeletal Remains', in P. Rahtz, T. Dickinson and L. Watts (eds), *Anglo-Saxon Cemeteries 1979*, BAR British Series 82. Oxford: Archaeopress, pp. 221–31.

Wilson, B., and P. Edwards. 1993. 'Butchery of Horse and Dog at Witney Palace, Oxfordshire, and the Knackering and Feeding of Meat to Hounds during the Post-medieval Period', *Post-Medieval Archaeology* 27: 43–56.

Chapter 12

Adherence to Islamic Tradition and the Formation of Iberian Islam in Early Medieval Al-Andalus

Sarah Inskip

Introduction

In archaeology, Islam has been viewed as homogeneous (Insoll 1999). As such, archaeologists have identified Islamic groups through the recognition of specific behaviours or items associated with Islam. Considering the global variation, assuming uniformity in Islamic identity is flawed. Research in anthropology and ethnography has shown that the significant differences in Islamic identity are attributable to the variable interpretation of Islamic tradition in contrasting pre-existing social and political contexts (Marranci 2008). Thus, the malleable nature of rules plays a central part in identity variation; while it is consistent adherence to rules that maintain Islamic identity as new and unexperienced events occur, rules can be changed in order to maintain identity. Such events could include behavioural shifts in the actions of surrounding groups or other changes in social organization. Through rule adaptability, new and different behaviours become either included or excluded and, as a result, identities are redrawn. Without such adaptability, identities become compromised and can be lost (Schöpflin 2001). Accordingly, if archaeologists explore which Islamic rules and traditions were followed, and how their appearance relates to other sociopolitical factors, it might be possible to understand the formation of different Islamic identities in the past and present.

Material Culture, Religious Rules and the Body

Archaeologists can use religious rules to analyse identity because of their critical role in dictating both the form and production of material culture. Important in this respect is the relationship between object production and identity reproduction. Accordingly, changes in the production or form of material culture potentially reflect changes or challenges to rules, and therefore to identity. Even though archaeology has a long history of studying religious material, little research has focused on items that are not overtly religious (Diaz-Andreu et al. 2005). Such a bias likely reflects notions surrounding the division between the sacred and profane, proffered by Durkheim in the twentieth century. Critics of this dichotomy suggest that the impact of religious rules on everyday life is not explored (Insoll 1999), with ethnographic, archaeological and anthropological research clearly indicating that such a separation does not always exist (Brück 1999). Apparently ordinary material culture can also be significantly imbued with religious meaning.

One area of significant potential lies in the field of bioarchaeology and the analysis of the body. In Islam, as strong ideology surrounds both the physical and the metaphorical body, it is an ideal entity with which to explore variation in traditions. Specifically, research has demonstrated how the physical body can be analysed to explore social change in a similar manner to other types of material culture (Sofaer 2006). Bone morphology is not static – it remodels in reaction to physical activity and stress (Shaw and Stock 2009), and can therefore be viewed as a product of social action. In fact, many studies have employed the remodelling properties of bone to explore shifts in human lifeways and a range of bone modifications have been studied to achieve this. Osteoarthritis and bony extensions to joint surfaces have been used to explore limb use (Lieverse et al. 2007). Entheseal (muscle) changes, demonstrated by the addition or destruction of bone at muscle and ligament attachment sites of the skeleton, can also inform us about activity patterns (Villotte and Knüsel 2013). Bone morphology (shape) has been used as an indicator of bone strength and mobility (Shaw and Stock 2009). Additionally, isotopic analysis is now providing valuable complementary evidence on diet and mobility (Montgomery and Evans 2006). In terms of the symbolic body, Islamic ideology surrounding notions of purity and pollution, as well as ideas about the afterlife, also strongly impacts on behaviour during life and at death. These ideals can be made visible through the analysis of material culture using faunal analysis, funerary archaeology and chemical analysis. Despite this, to date, bioarchaeology has not been used to extensively explore religious change. When taken into account, it tends to focus on one aspect, usually burial rites (Gilchrist 1994; Scott 2012) and the physical body itself is largely ignored.

The aim of this chapter is to demonstrate that, by assessing variation in Islamic traditions primarily via analysis of the body, it is possible to explore how and the extent to which people negotiated rules with other social factors. This will include an analysis of gender division of labour, prayer, diet and burial rites in various Islamic and Christian cemetery populations from southern Iberia.

Islamic Iberia

The religious identity of individuals from early medieval Iberia after the eighth-century arrival of Arabs and Berbers has often been debated. While recent research on religious identities has departed from classical notions where Islam was seen as a foreign entity, explorations of social structural changes (e.g. Guichard 1974) have been met with criticism primarily for a lack of insight into how Islam itself impacted on the general inhabitants of the region (Guichard 1992). Even though attempts to understand the process of conversion have been made (Barceló 1993; Bulliet 1994), they still do not inform us as to whether Iberians undertook Islamic practices, or take into consideration potential rural and urban differences. Seeking to address this issue, Boone and Benco (1999) explored the process of Islamization, including the uptake of Islamic diet and styles of dress, ceramic production and architecture. Although recognizing that Iberians were following new religious law, and thus were Islamic, this top-down approach still assumes an extrinsic origin for Islamic identity. It denies the active role that Iberians had in creating identity, even though the importance of agency and regionalization have been realized by other authors (Carvajal 2013). Accordingly, to understand why Iberian Islam emerged and formed the way it did, an exploration of how Muslims followed rules to fit within their own particular social circumstances is required. In this way, Iberian Islam can be seen as unique.

Prior to the eighth century, Iberia was largely Christian (Arian and then Catholic). Beginning in 711, Berbers and Arabs gained the majority control of Iberia in just a few years (Fletcher 2001). Córdoba was quickly made the capital of al-Andalus. Although the first forty years of rule were turbulent (see Kennedy 1996), the instatement of Abd al-Rahman I as Amir in 756 initiated the beginning of the Iberian Umayyad period, the longest and most prosperous period in al-Andalus. Later, in 929, Abd al-Rahman III declared himself Caliph of al-Andalus, severing ties with eastern Islamic rulers, a move that was thought to strengthen his local and interregional power. It was a move that aimed to make al-Andalus the capital of the Islamic world. Christians and Jews were not forced to convert; through paying tax, it was possible that they could continue to practise their own faith (Kennedy 1996). Not only did this mean that Muslims were initially outnumbered by Christians (Fletcher 2001), it also meant that Christians and Jews remained in Iberia during the Islamic period.

Initially, the Syriac school of law (Awza'i) was followed in al-Andalus (Lapidus 2002), but during the reign of Hisham I (788–96), Iberian Muslims followed the Maliki school of teaching. Malikism was established by Abu Abdallah Malik ibn Anas in Medina and traditions, including Malik ibn Anas' most notable work, the *Muwattah* (Imamuddin 1981), arrived in al-Andalus via scholars who travelled east (Marín 1992). As Malik ibn Anas was particularly influenced by the traditions of the Prophet, law extensively covers obligations to Allah and individual behaviour. Accordingly, teaching is strongly related to Qur'anic law (Fierro 1992), tending to be literal in its interpretation (Reilly 1993: 69). By 850, Malikism was established, as the official school of law and historical texts note al-Andalus as a Maliki stronghold (Fierro 1992). Staunch opposition to 'innovators' – individuals and laws considered a threat to established Maliki jurisprudence – existed (Reilly 1993). In the tenth century, when Abd al-Rahman III declared himself Caliph, ruler of all Muslim peoples, he strongly asserted that the Maliki School of teaching was the correct school of thought, a view that continued after his death (Safran 2001).

Numerous revolts led to the collapse of the Umayyad caliphate in the early eleventh century (Reilly 1993). This culminated in the fragmentation of al-Andalus into numerous states run by local princes and leaders. During this period, hostility between the Christian west and Islamic east increased, including the initiation of the Crusades in 1096.

It is clear that there were many significant social factors that could have impacted on the way in which Islamic traditions were used and interpreted in al-Andalus. Accordingly, the following sections will outline some principal Islamic traditions and how they can be observed in the archaeological record in various locations in southern Spain (see Figure 12.1 for the regions covered).

Sex Differences in Physical Activity Patterns and Gender Division of Labour

In Islam, biological sex strongly dictates gender identities. While in the eyes of the Qur'an men and women are spiritually equal, they are differentiated on physical grounds based on their reproductive abilities

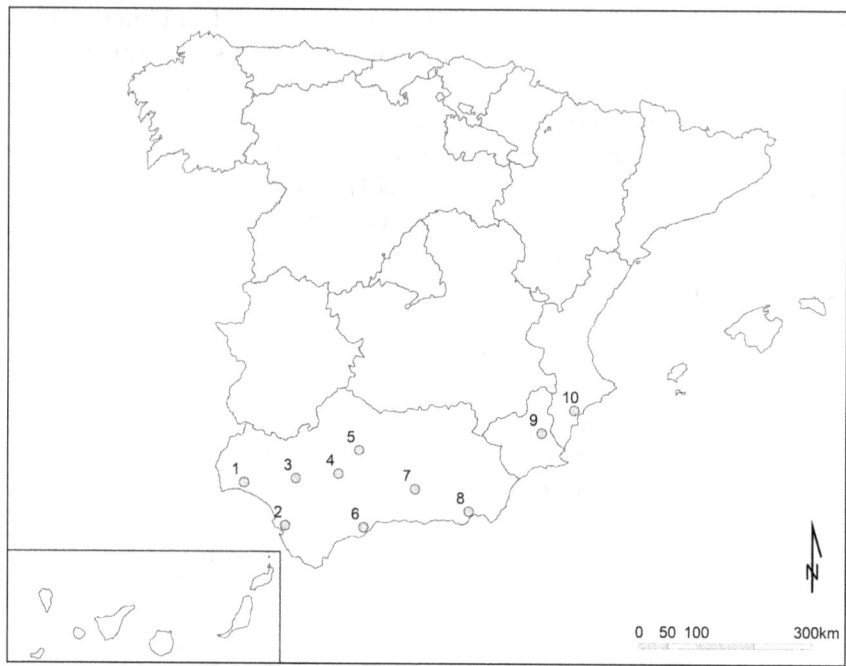

Figure 12.1 Map of Spain with major Islamic sites: 1) Huelva, 2) Cadiz, 3) Seville, 4) Écija, 5) Córdoba, 6) Malaga, 7) Granada, 8) Almeria, 9) Murcia and 10) Alicante (illustration by Barbara Hausmair)

(Minai 1981: 13). It is on the basis of these physical characteristics that males and females are accorded their social roles. Specific behaviours outlined for men and women in order for them to be a good Muslim differ (Marranci 2008). For men, this entails protecting and providing for the family through adherence to Islamic practices. Female Islamic identity is strongly influenced by ideas of chastity and the protection of paternity. While technically nothing in the Islamic faith precludes men or women from any role, in many Islamic societies such ideology has resulted in a clear gender division of labour (Lindsay 2005: 180). While the actual activities this entails vary according to the economic/subsistence strategy of the group, if gender ideology was significant in dictating the activities of men and women in Iberia, a gender division of labour should be observable in the osteoarchaeological record through analysis of activity-related skeletal changes.

Based on the analysis of activity-related skeletal modifications by sex, a number of studies have demonstrated greater differences between Islamic men and women than between the sexes in Christian groups. For example,

Table 12.1 Number of statistically significant sex differences in the Coracho pre-Islamic and Écija Islamic skeletal material (after Inskip 2013a)

Modification type	Coracho	Écija
Entheses	2	10
Joint modifications/extensions	2	5
Osteoarthritis	3	3
Long bone cross-sections	7	9
Total number of individuals analysed	**114**	**204**

comparison of entheseal scores, joint modifications/extensions, patterns of osteoarthritis and long bone cross-sections (Inskip 2013) had more statistically significant sex differences in the eighth- to eleventh-century Muslims from Écija than in fourth- to seventh-century pre-Islamic Christians from Cortijo del Coracho (Lucena) (see Table 12.1). Similar sex differences were observed at many southern Iberian sites, including at eleventh- to thirteenth-century San Nicolás, Murcia (Robles Rodríguez 1997).

The analysis of lower limb cross-sections has also highlighted a difference between the Écijan Islamic sexes. As bone forms in areas of functional demand, it changes shape when forces are applied to it; thus, examination of bone morphology can be informative about activities. According to tibial and femoral cross-sections, males appeared to be comparatively more mobile than females. Although at the time of their research Pomeroy and Zakrzewski (2009) were unable to make a comparison with a suitable Christian sample, subsequent analysis has demonstrated that the sex differences in cross-sections were indeed greater in the Écija group in comparison to the individuals from Cortijo del Coracho (Inskip forthcoming). Interestingly, at Xarea (Vélez-Rubio, Almería) (Sanz 1998) and Écija (Zakrzewski 2010), sex differences in strontium isotope ratios appear between men and women, with females having more homogeneous results. Although it is not entirely clear if this solely relates to mobility, it certainly warrants further investigation. The results thus suggest a shift in the relationship between gender identity and activity with the emergence of Islam.

Interestingly, al-Oumaoui, Jiménez-Brobeil and du Souich's (2004) comparative research on entheseal (muscle attachment) scores in Iberia demonstrated that this difference is also observable in rural communities. The rural Islamic group from La Torrecilla (Granada) had more sex differences in entheseal scores than a ninth- to twelfth-century Christian group from rural Villanueva (Burgos), implying a clearer gender difference in activity within the Islamic community. This also suggests that at rural Islamic sites, males and females may have more closely observed specific physical activities. The stronger Islamic sex differences therefore suggest that demonstrating belief by adhering to gendered patterns of physical activity was important for Muslims, and that it may not have been as essential for Christians, or that gender identity was expressed through ways that are not visible on bone.

Joint Modifications and Ritual Prayer

Ritual prayers (*ṣalāt*) are the second pillar of Islam (Abu-Hamdiyyah 2000: 57). Heiko Henkel (2005) argues that prayer is the most visible and important of the five pillars. *Ṣalāt* patterns vary little between faith denominations, which may be a result of its presence in the Qur'an. Citing various authors, Timothy Insoll (1999: 26) suggests that *ṣalāt* is not just a spiritual action, but one that teaches equality and brotherhood through communal prayer. It would thus strengthen the community, a feature potentially important in the early years of Islam, where in conquered regions Muslims were a minority (Kennedy 1996).

Ṣalāt is highly ritualized and follows a set of actions to be undertaken five times per day (Henkel 2005). The physical movements consist of several steps (for details, see Lindsay 2005), which require kneeling, prostration and hyperdorsiflexion of the ankle and toes. As medical literature has hinted, prayer can impact on the body through improvement of flexibility (Reze, Urakami and Mano 2002), and as habitual posture adoption can change joint surface morphology, there is potential to detect differences in joint structures in individuals who pray. Certainly Ullinger, Guise Sheridan and DeVries (2004) argue that kneeling for prayer in a Christian community from Jerusalem was potentially detectable from the skeletal record. However, as the knees, ankles and toes are also flexed in many other activities, it is important that other evidence for the adoption of prayer, including documentary, is also considered.

Documents from ninth-century Córdoba indicate the importance of prayer in Iberian Muslim life. In particular, judgements surrounding the specific movements and procedure, Imam behaviour and apostasy from prayer testify to the fact that the correct undertaking of the ritual was a concern for local scholars (see Marín 1992; Safran 2001). The prevalence of joint modifications associated with kneeling and ankle hyperdorsiflexion have been analysed in the Écija Islamic and the pre-Islamic Coracho population. These included osteochondritis, tibial imprints, vastus fossa, vastus notches and squatting facets on the tibia and talus. Statistically significant prevalence differences existed between the two groups, and all but tibial imprints, were far more frequent in the Islamic group, particularly tibial and talus squatting facets (see Table 12.2).

Table 12.2 Chi-squared test results on joint modifications in the knee and ankle for pre-Islamic Coracho and Islamic Écija

Modification	Coracho	Écija	P value	No. of observations
Osteochondritis	9%	11%	1	454
Tibial imprints	44%	27%	0.002	442
Vastus fossa	38%	52%	0.068	247
Vastus notch	45%	53%	0.368	217
Lateral tibial squatting facet	26%	93%	≤0.001	255
Talus squatting facets	28%	97%	≤0.001	372

Admittedly, only at Écija and Coracho have all the modifications been recorded. However, the lateral tibial squatting facet has been consistently scored at many other sites (see Table 12.3). The high prevalence of tibial squatting facets noted at Écija was also identified in the urban Islamic assemblage from San Nicolás, Murcia (Robles Rodríguez 1997) and Rossio do Carmo, Mértola, Portugal (Le Bars 2005). While no data for southern Iberian Christian sites exists, the prevalence is much higher than urban Christian groups in northern Spain (Robles Rodríguez 1997). The only Christians with similar prevalence were the pre-Islamic females at Coracho. Interestingly, a comparison of the Écijan and San Nicolás samples with the La Torrecilla (Granada) sample demonstrated that rural Muslims have a lower prevalence of tibial squatting facets (Table 12.3).

Francisco J. Robles Rodríguez (1997) argued that the high prevalence of tibial facets at San Nicolás was related to the adoption of squatting during crafting activities in towns, especially since images depicting this posture exist. However, similar craft activities were undertaken in other parts of Europe and they do not present with such a high prevalence of facets. In fact, in English material (Mays 2007; Waldron 2007), Dutch material (Schats, Kootker and Houchin 2014) and French material (Buchet 1983), rural sites have more squatting facets than urban groups, and females always appear to have more squatting facets than males. It appears that a cultural factor is responsible for the difference, as has been alluded to by Dominique Le Bars (2005). The equal prevalence of tibial facets in both males and females at urban Islamic sites may suggest that prayer, an activity that should be carried out by men and women, could be responsible. However, with the current data, we need to remain cautious, especially considering the problems of associating changes to a specific activity. While it may relate to hyperdorsiflexion as a working and resting position, something documented in African and Arab populations, more

Table 12.3 Prevalence of tibial squatting facets in various Iberian sites. Key: STP=Sant Pere Terressa, UI=Urban Islamic, RI=Rural Islamic, RPI=Rural pre-Islamic, UPI=Urban pre-Islamic, RC=Rural Christian, UC=Urban Christian

Site	Sex	Date	Type	Left %	Right %	Side undetermined %	Source
Écija	Males	8th–11th c.	UI	94.1	91.7		Inskip 2013b
	Females	8th–11th c.	UI	96.1	93.9		Inskip 2013b
San Nicolás	Males	11th–13th c.	UI	88.0	88.0		Robles Rodríguez 1997
	Females	11th–13th c.	UI	89.3	87.5		Robles Rodríguez 1997
Santa Clara	Males	13th–14th c.	RI			63.1	Herrerin López 2004
	Females	13th–14th c.	RI			74.4	López 2004
Coracho	Males	5th–7th c.	RPI	70.0	61.5		Inskip 2013b
	Females	5th–7th c.	RPI	83.3	85.7		Inskip 2013b
La Torrecilla	Males	9th–14th c.	RI	55.0	55.0		López 2004
	Females	9th–14th c.	RI	55.0	68.7		López 2004
Sepulveda	Both	12th–14th c.	RC	37.9	39.6		Bermúdez de Castro 1979
STP1	Males	4th–8th c.	UPI			53.0	Comin 2007
	Females	4th–8th c.	UPI			75.0	Comin 2007
STP2	Males	9th–13th c.	UC			64.3	Comin 2007
	Females	9th–13th c.	UC			40.0	Comin 2007

widespread data on the modifications are needed to either exclude or include prayer as a factor.

Diet

Body purity is important in Islam (Safran 2001). As some food items are considered polluting, rules regarding what can be consumed exist (Insoll 1999). The Qur'an says: 'Partake of what is lawful and good on this Earth' (2: 168; 16: 44). Three categories of food exist in Islamic law; *halal* (lawful), *haram* (prohibited) and *makruh* (reprehensible). Dogs, carrion, excrement, the milk of prohibited animals, alcohol and some types of fish and birds are *haram*. Presence or absence of remains from such foods can inform about variation in traditions. Generally, faunal analysis has focused on pork consumption, which is forbidden by the Qur'an. In Spain, Muñiz et al.'s (2011) multisite evaluation demonstrated that the consumption of pork was low, and mostly absent across Islamic Iberia. Just three out of fourteen Islamic sites had pig remains. Of these, two sites were late (twelfth to thirteenth centuries) and the other was a military settlement. Pig bones were ubiquitous at the fifteen Christian sites where they made up between 6.0 and 29.6 per cent of the mammal remains, with the exception of one site where just 1.7 per cent of the animal remains were pig. This absence was previously noted by Lentacker and Ervynck's (1999) analysis of medieval Huelva. While at present, insufficient information exists to permit a geographical or temporal analysis, this data has demonstrated that a significant potential exists in this area, especially if isotopes were integrated and more scholars studied other taboo animals. At present, it appears that most Iberian Muslims were avoiding pork.

Burial Rites

Through engaging in funerary rituals, burial becomes a critical element in the construction and maintenance of religious identity (Halevi 2007). Cemeteries in the landscape and public involvement in the funerary process act to reinforce community ties. Exploring burial patterns can inform us as to changes in identity. In Islam, a number of instructions for body preparation and position at burial exist, including positioning the bodies facing Mecca and on their right side (see Figure 12.2). The Islamic tradition favours wrapping bodies in shrouds, interment without a coffin and placement in an empty, single-occupancy grave (see Figure 12.2) (Insoll 1999). Grave markers and grave goods are also discouraged. In pre-Islamic Iberia, individuals were usually interred supine and, although not always present, jewellery, coins, ceramic and glass vessels and other items were

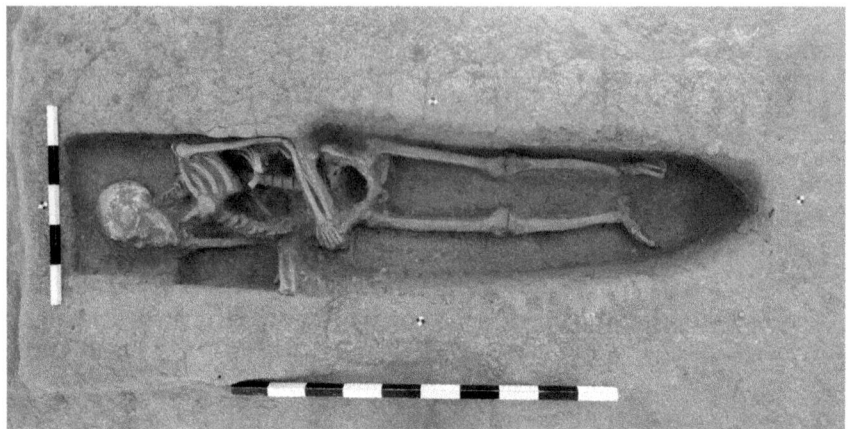

Figure 12.2 Islamic right-side burial at Çatalhöyük with face and body orientated towards Mecca (photograph by Scott D. Haddow/Çatalhöyük Research Project)

placed in the grave (Diéguez-Ramírez 2011). The reuse of graves was also common.

At Écija, where pre-Islamic and Islamic graves were uncovered in the same area, there was a clear difference in the burial practices. The individuals in the pre-Islamic graves were supine, with glass vessels, lamps, coins and jewellery (González et al. 2005). In the Islamic period, nearly all individuals were facing Mecca, with most being positioned on their right side. Very few items were recovered from the graves. A similar shift in burial rites was observed at Murcia (Crespo 2000).

With regard to body position, it is clear that while some individuals were buried according to Christian traditions, such as those at Murcia (Serrano and López 2004), Tossal de les Basses (Laguillo et al. 2009) and possibly at Córdoba (Muñoz 2009), certainly by the ninth century, great uniformity in burial position existed in southern Iberian Islamic cemeteries. The orientation of the face towards Mecca is especially adhered to. Additionally, a strong degree of uniformity in right-side body positioning was recorded at Triana, Seville (Reina and Azogue 2001), San Nicolás (Robles Rodríguez 1997) and Santa Eulalia (Guillamón 2001) in Murcia, Puerta Elvira, Granada (López López et al. 1995), Xarea in Almería (Sanz 1998) and Bab Al-Hanax (Togores n.d.) in Valencia. Perhaps the most common variation is for the individual to be buried supine, akin to pre-Islamic traditions, but the heads are still usually orientated towards Mecca.

As highlighted by Reina and Azogue (2001: 103), it would be wrong to assume homogeneity as some extreme exceptions exist. Occasionally, left-side burials appear: a boy, interred with a woman was found at El Molo (de Miguel Ibáñez et al. 2009) and a woman in the Castillo de Triana, Seville (Reina and Azogue 2001: 103). Men, women and children at the Castillo de Triana (Reina and Azogue 2001: 103) and at Xarea (Sanz 1998) were buried prone. However, these examples are few in number, representing less than 5.0 per cent of all burials. At present, there appears to be no correlation between these unusual burials and demographic attributes. Furthermore, it appears that some burials in Córdoba were orientated south, in accordance with the incorrectly aligned *Qibla* of the mosque at Córdoba (Hillenbrand 1992). Interestingly, this alignment matches that of Damascus, the home of the original Umayyad Caliphate from which the rulers of Islamic Iberia descended. Nevertheless, an overall uniformity in burial position is striking in the southern Iberian region.

In contrast, grave structures show considerable variation. The majority of burials were simple pits; however, the use of tiles, mudbrick, stones and slabs varied significantly both in and between sites, and demonstrates some continuity with previous traditions. At the larger cemeteries, such as Écija, San Nicolás, Santa Eulalia and Puerta Elvira, a temporal trend for increasing grave structure elaboration is observed (García Baena 2006). Like burial position, there still appears to be no correlation between the types of graves and individuals interred. However, in line with ideals, gravegoods were extremely infrequent. Where items were recovered, they were usually jewellery and shroud pins. At the largest Islamic cemeteries, including Écija and San Nicolás, beads and coins were identified. Occasionally, ceramic fragments were found in graves, but in most cases it is not possible to establish whether these were accidental inclusions.

Discussion

Although the evidence presented here is by no means exhaustive and reflects only the initial stages of research, the change in the gender division of labour, dietary taboos, possible adherence to prayer and shifts in funerary rites suggest that, at least in southern Iberia, many Islamic rules were visibly followed. As it is now thought that the majority of Muslims, at least by the ninth and tenth centuries, were indigenous (Barceló 1993; Bulliet 1994), the incorporation of these rules into daily routine supports the notion that Islam became a central aspect of life that was actively recreated by the population. The relative orthodoxy demonstrates that following Islamic rules was important in the region and that these new ideas took precedence over many pre-existing traditions. As other social and political factors impact on how rules and traditions are interpreted, it is important to explore these in order to understand patterns in the archaeological record and why Islamic identity took the form that it did.

Al-Andalus was on the edge of the Islamic world, and Muslims arrived into a region that was primarily Christian, with some Jewish influence. This situation aroused fear in contemporary Islamic judges, who documented their concerns of identity loss (Fierro 2005), particularly given the surrounding Christian influences. One way to prevent the degradation of Islam was to use rules to create social boundaries between groups. Safran (2001) discusses how ideology could have been key in articulating this – for example, notions about pollution could have been used by *ulama* (learned men) to control contact between Muslims and Christians. The examples provided by Safran (2001) focus on the use of water left by Christians, which is deemed to be impure, and also how marriage to a Christian woman could result in impurity. Scholars also stated that Muslims would be judged by the company they kept and the behaviours they followed. This latter concept may be responsible for replicating Muslim behaviour and publicly avoiding Christian practices, which could of course include eating pork, a lack of gender division in activities or being buried in a Christian manner. In relation to this, Fierro (2005) notes that calling a Muslim a Christian in al-Andalus was offensive, and accusations of apostasy and heresy were taken extremely seriously due to the severe consequences. Apostasy from prayer was theoretically punishable by death in al-Andalus (Safran 2001). Thus, publicly displaying Islamic practices was also important in avoiding allegations of heresy. It is clear that adherence to rules was crucial in maintaining the ideological differences that existed between Muslims and Christians, and that these religious concepts may have been used to control social interaction.

A further important related factor is that it was presumably elites who used accusations of heresy as a means to impose social threats and obtain political goals (Judd 2011). Al-Andalus was renowned for being strongly Maliki (Lapidus 2002), a school of Islamic law focusing on Qur'anic teaching and practice, where ideology surrounding the sexes, diet and prayer are found. Critically, historians have identified that ruling elites were strongly opposed to the integration of laws from other schools of teaching (Fierro 2005) and only in the eleventh century did other teachings begin to emerge. It is unclear whether orthodoxy was maintained for religious reasons only, but it is likely that staunch support of Maliki rules made up an important part of ordaining al-Andalus as the centre of the Islamic world. In fact, Abd al-Rahman III was said to be preoccupied with returning followers to the 'true faith', and it is possible that this was part of restoring the Umayyads as the legitimate Caliphs of the Islamic world, following their deposal at the hands of the Abbasids in the eighth century. Indeed, during the Umayyad period and beyond, an increasing number of heresy cases were heard at Córdoban courts (Melville and Ubaydli 1992). Thus, invoking heresy was a means by which to remove opposition to the Caliphate (Safran 2001).

It seems clear that, for multiple reasons, the public expression of Islamic identity through direct adherence to scripture or via conformity to social rules articulated through religious rules was important. However, these factors do not explain the slight variation in the traditions observed through bioarchaeology, particularly the potential rural and urban difference. While it is thought that rural individuals were slower to convert, or did not convert at all (Bulliet 1994), it appears contradictory that some traditions appear clearly in the archaeological record, whereas others do not. Perhaps an alternative hypothesis lies in the distance from large Islamic cities and/or courts. With reduced pressure from peers and authorities, it may have been possible for rules to be reinterpreted in more remote locations, thus permitting some small-scale regionalization to occur and public behaviour to change. Indeed, different rules might be in place for these regions. In relation to this, ethnic differences may also be significant, and it is argued that ethnic stratification was a persistent problem in the region (Kennedy 1996). Some scholars suggest that Arabs tended to settle in towns, while Berbers lived in the country (Imamuddin 1981). If such a hypothesis is true, we should consider that the majority of the samples discussed here were large settlements supposedly dominated by Arabs (Écija, Córdoba and Granada) rather than Berbers. Accordingly, good adherence to Islamic tradition in these areas may reflect Arab influence in the region, and the link between pre-Islamic Arab customs and later Islamic traditions. While it is not entirely clear whether these ethnic differences existed as clearly as we would imagine them, and debate certainly exists, it is these sorts of differences in social context that could alter the way traditions were viewed.

Conclusions

While only the results of preliminary research, the data presented in this chapter suggest that by changing their behaviour and adhering to scripture, the people of southern Iberia created an orthodox Islam in which a number of key Islamic traditions, including dietary taboos, a gender division of labour, burial orientation and possibly prayer, were vital to their identity. While it is never possible to be certain as to why individuals chose to adopt these traditions, examination of anthropological and historical sources demonstrates a number of important social factors that may have played an important role. It appears that the importance attached to physically demonstrating belief through action in Islam and therefore public expression of identity was an important driving mechanism for change for a number of reasons. Politically, ruling elites may have actively used rules as a means of both re-creating and legitimizing the Umayyad Caliphate as the leader of the Islamic world. Socially and economically, publicly displaying Islamic identity would have been important in differentiating oneself from Christians and Jews, and later avoiding heresy charges. It is perhaps this critical public element that may explain rural and urban differences. Where public pressure was reduced or differed (e.g. ethnic priorities), changes in behaviour may have occurred. As a significant amount of data on many sites across al-Andalus exist, an extended, dedicated study of the similarities and variations visible across the region could further explore these patterns and significantly contribute to an understanding of the formation of religious identities. Regardless, this research clearly demonstrates not only the benefits of taking a more holistic approach, which considers multiple types of evidence (including archaeological, historical and anthropological), but also the critical role that rules have in both creating and changing past societies.

Sarah Inskip is Research Associate at the McDonald Institute for Archaeological Research, University of Cambridge, United Kingdom. Previously she was Assistant Professor in Human Osteoarchaeology at Leiden University, the Netherlands. Her research interests include activity-related skeletal modifications, paleopathology and funerary archaeology. She completed undergraduate studies at the University of Lincoln, and undertook M.A. and Ph.D. research at the University of Southampton, United Kingdom. Her doctoral research focused on physical activity patterns and gender division in early medieval Islamic burials from Spain in order to explore development of the Iberian Islamic identity. In her teaching and research positions, she has continued to develop innovative strategies for studying religious identity and variable burial practices across the medieval Islamic world.

References

Abu-Hamdiyyah, M. 2000. *The Qur'an: An Introduction*. London: Routledge.
Al-Oumaoui, I., S. Jiménez-Brobeil, and R. du Souich. 2004. 'Markers of Activity Patterns in Some Populations of the Iberian Peninsula', *International Journal of Osteoarchaeology* 14(5): 343–59.

Barceló, M. 1993. 'Al-Mulk, el verde y el blanco: La vajilla califal omeya de Madinat Al-Zahra', in A. Malpica Cuello (ed.), *La Ceramica Altomedieval en el Sur de al-Andalus*. Granada: Universidad de Granada, pp. 291–99.
Bermúdez de Castro, J,M. 1979. *Estudio antropológico de huesos largos procedentes de una Necrópolis medieval de Sepúlveda (Segovia)*, Memoria de Licenciatura. Madrid: Universidad Complutense de Madrid.
Boone, J., and N.L. Benco. 1999. 'Islamic Settlement in North Africa and the Iberian Peninsula', *Annual Review of Anthropology* 28: 51–71.
Brück, J. 1999. 'Ritual and Rationality: Some Problems of Interpretation in European Archaeology', *European Journal of Archaeology* 2(3): 313–44.
Buchet, L. 1983. 'L'inhumation en basilique funéraire: observations, interprétations et commentaires', in L. Buchet (ed.), *Le matériel anthropologique provenant des édifices religieux*. Paris: CNRS, pp. 69–73.
Bulliet, R.W. 1994. *Islam: The View from the Edge*. New York: Columbia University Press.
Carvajal, J.C. 2013. 'Islamicization or Islamicizations? Expansion of Islam and Social Practice in the Vega of Granada (South-East Spain)', *World Archaeology* 45(1): 109–23.
Crespo, J.Z. 2000. 'Estudio de los restos óseos de la necrópolis de Rinconada de Olivares, Jumilla (Murcia)', *Memorias de Arqueológica de la Región de Murcia* 9: 432–40.
Comin, X.J. 2007. 'Caracterització i evoluvió comunitat medieval catalana: Estudi bioantropològic de les inhumacions de les Esgléies de Sant Pere', Ph.D. dissertation. Barcelona: Universitat Autònoma de Barcelona.
De Miguel Ibáñez, M.P., A.J. Lorrío Alvarado, M.D. Sánchez de Prado and P. de Miguel Ibáñez. 2009. 'Inhumaciones islámicas en El Molón (Camporrobles, Valencia)', in M. Polo Cerdá and E. García-Prósper (eds), *Investigaciones histórico-médicas sobre salud y enfermedad en el Pasado*. Valencia: Grupo Palaeolab, pp. 271–75.
Diaz-Andreu, M., S. Lucy, S. Babic, D.N. Edwards and N. David. 2005. *The Archaeology of Identity*. London: Routledge.
Diéguez-Ramírez, J.P. 2011. 'Estudio bioantropológico comparado de tres necrópolis históricas situadas en el Término Municipal de Lucena (Córdoba)', Ph.D. dissertation. Granada: Universidad de Granada.
Fierro, M.I. 1992. 'Heresy in Al-Andalus', in S.K. Jayyusi (ed.), *The Legacy of al-Andalus*. Leiden: Brill, pp. 895–908.
———. 2005. *Abd-al Rahman III: The First Cordoban Caliph*. London: Oneworld Publications.
Fletcher, R. 2001. 'The Early Middle Ages 700–1250', in R. Carr (ed.), *Spain*. Oxford: Oxford University Press, pp. 63–89.
García Baena, A. 2006. *Écija Musulmana, Ulemas y Familias*. Écija: Talleres Graficos Codair.
Gilchrist, R. 1994. *Gender and Material Culture: The Archaeology of Religious Women*. London: Routledge.
González, J., S. García-Dils de la Vega, S.A. Ordóñez, M. Magariño and I. López. 2005. 'La tumba Visigoda de "Sapatio"', *SPAL* 14: 259–80.

Guichard, P. 1974. 'Les arabes ont bien envahi l'Espagne: les structures sociales de l'Espagne musulmane', *Annales Économies, Sociétés, Civilisations* 29: 483–513.

———. 1992. 'The Social History of Muslim Spain', in S.K. Jayyusi (ed.), *The Legacy of al-Anadlus*. Leiden: Brill, pp. 697–708.

Guillamón, M.B. 2001. 'Casas y cementerios Islamicos en Murcia : El Solar No 1–3 de la Plaza De Santa Eulalia', *Memorias de Arqueologíca de la Región de Murcia* 10: 573–94.

Halevi, L. 2007. *Muhammad's Grave: Death Rites and the Making of Islamic Society*. New York: Columbia University Press.

Henkel, H. 2005. 'Between Belief and Unbelief Lies the Performance of Salāt: Meaning and Efficacy of a Muslim Ritual', *Journal of the Royal Anthropological Institute* 11(3): 487–507.

Herrerin López, J. 2004. *La Maqbara de Santa Clara: Estudio de una Necróplis Musulmana en Cuéllar*. Segovia: Caja Segovia.

Hillenbrand, R. 1992. 'The Ornament of the World: Medieval Cordoba as a Cultural Centre', in S.K. Jayyusi (ed.), *The Legacy of al-Anadlus*. Leiden: Brill, pp. 112–35.

Imamuddin, S.M. 1981. *Muslim Spain 711–1492 A.D.: A Sociological Study*. Leiden: Brill.

Insoll, T. 1999. *The Archaeology of Islam*. Oxford: Blackwell.

Inskip, S.A. 2013a. 'Islam in Iberia or Iberian Islam: Sociobioarchaeology and the Analysis of Emerging Islamic Identity in Early Medieval Iberia', Ph.D. dissertation. Southampton: University of Southampton.

———. 2013b. 'Islam in Iberia or Iberian Islam: Bioarchaeology and the Analysis of Emerging Islamic Identity in Early Medieval Iberia', *Post Classical Archaeologies* 3: 63–93.

———. Forthcoming. *Metric Analysis of Long Bone Cross Sections in Pre-Islamic and Islamic Spain*.

Judd, S. 2011. 'Muslim Persecution of Heretics during the Marwanid Period (64–132/684–750)', *Al-Masaq* 23: 1–14.

Kennedy, H. 1996. *Muslim Spain and Portugal: A Political History of al-Andulus*. London: Longman.

Laguillo, O., A. Nuñez, X. Jordana, P. Rosser and A. Malgosa. 2009. 'Caracterización bioantropológica de una poblacion islámica en Alicante: los enterramientos de época alto-medieval del Tossal de les Basses', *Sociedad Española de Antropología Física* 30: 51–74.

Lapidus, I.M. 2002. *A History of Islamic Societies*. Cambridge: Cambridge University Press.

Le Bars, D. 2005. 'Étude archéo-anthropologique de la nécropole musulmane de Rossio do Carmo, Mértola: bilan des fouilles anciennes (1981–1990)', *Arqueologia Medieval* 9: 223–57.

Lentacker, A.N., and A. Ervynck. 1999. 'The Archaeofauna of the Late Medieval, Islamic Harbour Town of Saltes (Huelva, Spain)', *Archaeofauna* 8: 141–57.

Lindsay, J.E. 2005. *Daily Life in the Medieval Islamic World*. Indianapolis, IN: Hackett.

Lieverse, A.R., A.W. Weber, V.I. Bazaliiskiy, O.I. Goriunova and N.A. Savel'ev. 2007. 'Osteoarthritis in Siberia's Cis-Baikal: Skeletal Indicators of Hunter-

Gatherer Adaptation and Cultural Change', *American Journal of Physical Anthropology* 132: 1–16.
López López, M., E. Fresneda Padilla, I. Toro Moyano, J.M. Peña Rodríguez and E. Arroyo Perez. 1995. 'La Necrópolis Musulmana de Puerta Elvira (Granada)', in M. Acién Almansa and M.P. Torre Palomo (eds), *Estudios sobre cementerios islamicos andalusíes*. Málaga: Universidad de Málaga, pp. 137–55.
Marín, M. 1992. 'Muslim Religious Practices in al-Andalus ($2^{nd}/8^{th}$–$4^{th}/10^{th}$ Centuries)', in S.K. Jayyusi (ed.), *The Legacy of al-Anadlus*. Leiden: Brill, pp. 878–94.
Marranci, G. 2008. *The Anthropology of Islam*. Oxford: Berg.
Mays, S. 2007. 'The Human Remains', in S. Mays, C. Harding and C. Heighway (eds), *The Churchyard, Wharram XI*. York: York University, pp. 77–192.
Melville, C., and A. Ubaydli. 1992. *Christians and Moors in Spain, Vol. III: Arabic Sources (711–1501)*. Warminster: Aris & Phillips.
Minai, N. 1981. *Women in Islam: Tradition and Transition in the Middle East*. London: HarperCollins.
Montgomery, J., and J.A. Evans. 2004. 'Immigrants on the Isle of Lewis: Combining Traditional Funerary and Modern Isotope Evidence to Investigate Social Differentiation, Migration and Dietary Change in the Outer Hebrides of Scotland', in R. Gowland and C. Knüsel (eds), *The Social Archaeology of Funerary Remains*. Oxford: Oxbow, pp. 122–42.
Muñiz, A.M., M. Moreno García, E.R. Izquierdo, L.L. Rodríguez and D.M. Morales Muñiz. 2011. '711 AD: El origen de una disyunción alimentaria?', *Zona Arqueologica* 1/2011: 303–19.
Muñoz, A.L. 2009. '¡Hombres! la promesa de Dios en verdadera ... El mundo funerario islámico en Córdoba (siglos VIII–XIII)', *Arquelogia Medieval* 4–5: 24–49.
Pomeroy, E., and S.R. Zakrzewski. 2009. 'Sexual Dimorphism in Diaphyseal Cross-sectional Shape in the Medieval Muslim Population of Écija, Spain and Anglo-Saxon Great Chesterford, UK', *International Journal of Osteoarchaeology* 19(1): 50–65.
Reilly, B.F. 1993. *The Contest of Christian and Muslim Spain: 1031–1157*. Oxford: Blackwell.
Reina, M.V., and A.R. Azogue. 2001. *Triana en la Baja Edad Media: El cementerio musulmán*. Seville: Ayuntamiento de Sevilla.
Reze, M.F., Y. Urakami and Y. Mano. 2002. 'Evaluation of a New Physical Exercise Taken from Salat (Prayer) as a Short-Duration and Frequent Physical Activity in Rehabilitation of Geriatric and Disabled Patients', *Annals of Saudi Medicine* 22: 177–80.
Robles Rodríguez, F.J. 1997. 'Caracteristicas biológicas de la población hispanomusulmana de San Nicolás (Murcia, sXI–XIII)', Ph.D. dissertation. Madrid: Universidad Autónoma de Madrid.
Safran, J. 2001. 'Identity and Differentiation in Ninth-Century al-Andalus', *Speculum* 76(3): 183–98.
Sanz, B.R. 1998. 'Dieta, indicadores de salud y caracterización biométrica de la población medieval musulmana de Xarea (Vélez Rubio, Almería)', Ph.D. dissertation. Madrid: Universidad Complutense of Madrid.

Schats, R., L. Kootker and R. Houchin. 2014. 'De menselyke skeletten', in A. Hakvoort, A. Griffioen, R. Schats and P. Bitter (eds), *Graven en begraven bij de Minderbroeders*. Alkmaar: Alkmaar, pp. 147–206.

Schöpflin, G. 2001. 'The Construction of Identity', *Österreichischer Wissenschaftstag Conference 2001*. Vienna: Österreichische Forschungsgemeinschaft. Retrieved 25 May 2017 from http://www.oefg.at/legacy/text/veranstaltungen/wissenschaftstag/wissenschaftstag01/Beitrag_Schopflin.pdf.

Scott, R. 2012. 'Religious Identity and Mortuary Practice: The Significance of Christian Burial in Early Medieval Ireland', in A. Baadsgard, A.T. Boutin and J.E. Buikstra (eds), *Breathing New Life into the Evidence of Death*. Santa Fe, NM: SAR Press, pp. 55–78.

Serrano, J.B., and J.A.M. López. 2004. 'Aportación al estudio de la maqbara islámica de Alhama de Murcia: excavación en la calle Fulgencio Cerón Cava, nº 2', *Memorias de Arqueología de la Región de Murcia* 13: 313–34.

Shaw, C.N., and J.T. Stock. 2009. 'Habitual Throwing and Swimming Correspond with Upper Limb Diaphyseal Strength and Shape in Modern Human Athletes', *American Journal of Physical Anthropology* 140(1): 160–72.

Sofaer, J.R. 2006. *The Body as Material Culture: A Theoretical Osteoarchaeology*. Cambridge: Cambridge University Press.

Togores, C.R. n.d. 'Analisis antropológico de los restos óseos del cementerio islámico Bab al-Hanax (Valencia)', *Asociación Española de Paleopatología Congresos 2006*. Retrieved 25 May 2017 from http://pendientedemigracion.ucm.es/info/aep/boletin/actas/47.pdf.

Ullinger, J., S. Guise Sheridan and B. DeVries. 2004. '"Fall on Your Knees": Squatting Faces in a Byzantine Monastery', *American Journal of Physical Anthropology* 123(Supplement 38): 198.

Villotte, S., and C. Knüsel. 2013. 'Understanding Entheseal Changes: Definition and Life Course Changes', *International Journal of Osteoarchaeology* 23(2): 135–46.

Waldron, T. 2007. *St Peter's Barton-upon-Humbar: A Parish Church and its Community. Volume 2. The Human Remains*. Oxford: Oxbow.

Zakrzewski, S.R. 2010. 'Population Migration, Variation and Identity: An Islamic Population in Iberia', in S.C. Agarwal and B.A. Glencross (eds), *Social Bioarchaeology*. Oxford: Wiley-Blackwell, pp. 183–210.

Chapter 13

Break a Rule But Save a Soul
Unbaptized Children and Medieval Burial Regulation

Barbara Hausmair

Introduction

The social order in medieval Europe was permeated by Christian ontology and metaphysics. Not only did the teachings of the Church determine daily life and practices, but the ecclesiastic elites also claimed the sole authority over conceptions of the afterlife, its ontological and spatial structure, and the conditions to be met in order to qualify for redemption after death (Gurevič 1994). By the twelfth century – following a cross-generational, theological debate over what constituted the afterlife – Christian scholars had developed a complex and hierarchical picture of the world, divided into several spheres including heaven, hell, purgatory and earth (Le Goff 1990). However, the highest aspiration of Christian faith – to be bodily resurrected on Doomsday, enter heaven and see God – was not meant for everyone. A vast compendium of rules and conditions that had emerged from theological considerations and political agendas of the religious elite determined who was to hope for salvation and who was not. While purgatory was believed to be a place where every remorseful Christian was awaiting resurrection in devoted repentance and thus could escape eternal condemnation through purifying one's soul, the prospects for those who died before becoming members of the Christian community were, mildly speaking, unfortunate (Swanson 2010: 355–56). Theological scholars in the twelfth and thirteenth centuries suggested that children who died without baptism would have to reside eternally in a special place at the margins of hell where they would be deprived from salvation, the so-called *limbus puerorum*.

Written sources from this period (e.g. *Summa Theologica*: III-supp., q. 69, a. 6; q. 71, a. 7; *Von sehs mordaeren*; *Rationale*: lib. I, cap. 5, 14 and 16) largely reflect the theological discourse and burial regulations that were established by the ecclesiastical authorities and that denied unbaptized children a funeral in consecrated ground. By contrast, very little is transmitted in the written record about how those teachings and regulations influenced actual burial practices and whether they were accepted, rejected or even challenged by the lay population.

On the other hand, archaeological remains of past mortuary ritual offer insights into practices and beliefs in lay culture and how theological concepts of the world's structure were transcribed onto the religious and social landscape. In order to explore popular attitudes towards infants who died unbaptized and related burial regulations, it is therefore vital to assess the spatial factors of medieval infant burials (Hausmair 2017). As this chapter will show, such an approach permits discussions surrounding the relationship between institutional rules resulting from theological considerations and their handling by the lay population through social practices enacted in the material environment.

Limbus Puerorum and Related Burial Regulations

Discussions about the destiny of children who died without baptism reached an initial peak in the fifth century in connection with disputes about the nature of Original Sin and the necessity of baptism (Walsh 2011: 138–39). In Christian thought, humans were (and in Catholic thought still are) considered to be born in a state of Original Sin, which derived from Adam and Eve's disobedience in paradise and led to the distortion of human nature. The impact of Original Sin on the possibility of salvation became a central issue in eschatological debates. In an attempt to oppose 'heretic' teachings on the nature of Original Sin and to reinforce the necessity of baptism for the soul's purification, Augustine of Hippo declared the remission of all sins as indispensable for resurrection: 'God does not remit sins but to the baptized. The very sins which He remits first, He remits not but to the baptized' (*De Symbolo*: col. 636, cap. VIII-16).

Those who died without baptism, including children, would consequently be excluded from Beatific Vision and consigned to hell for all eternity. Augustine's teachings remained dominant in theological discourse throughout the centuries until the Middle Ages, when scholastics started challenging his teachings on the nature of Original Sin and hence its influence on a person's whereabouts in the afterlife. Scholars such as Thomas Aquinas, Anselm or Abelard understood Original Sin as an unavoidable natural human condition rather than actual guilt or a genuine corruption of the soul (Schwarz 2006). Since unbaptized children were thought to be free of personal guilt, their condemnation to hell was revoked and replaced by the concept of *limbus puerorum* in the twelfth century (O'Connor 1991: 17–19), marking a crucial change in theological thought.

The *limbus* was believed to be a place located at the margins of hell, as described in a thirteenth-century sermon of Berthold of Regensburg:

> All the children of Christians who die without holy baptism: all of them were at one place that is called limbo and is [located] in front of hell ... the harm is that they will never see God's face. They will have no other agony: neither will they freeze nor will they starve nor will they be thirsty and they will have no pain, it is not too small nor too big, they are neither too hot nor too cold. (*Von sehs mordaeren*: p. 126, lin. 23–38)

Translocating unbaptized infants from the depths of hell, where Augustine had referred them to in the fifth century, to a place where they at least would not be tormented constituted a definite improvement from a theological perspective. Nevertheless, the *limbus* represented an environment where such children were deprived of salvation.

Although limbo never became an official dogma of the Church, it did not remain an exclusively theological issue either. Pedobaptism – the baptism of children – was an early agenda in the Church. However, the practice of christening children soon after birth only developed in the High Middle Ages. Before, baptisms usually took place only twice a year at Easter and Pentecost (Walsh 2011: 89). The propagation of unbaptized children's exclusion from heaven supported the acceptance of pedobaptism outside the traditional feast periods and eventually led to the acknowledgement of emergency baptisms through midwives by the Church (York 2012: 96; see also Taglia 2001; Hausmair 2017: 4–5). Conveying the *limbus* concept directly to the population through sermons such as Berthold's one indirectly promoted pedobaptism at an early stage after birth. The prediction of unbaptized children's exclusion from the Christian community in the afterlife pressured parents into ensuring an early Christening of their newborns and further strengthened the Church's position as the dominant power of social order.

However, parents were not only confronted with an unpleasant outlook for their offspring's position in the afterlife and its supposedly unchangeable fate. Burial regulations were introduced that prohibited the interment of unbaptized children in consecrated ground and denied them a Christian funeral. The influential French canonist Guillaume Durand de Mende (1230–96), for instance, stated in his liturgical treatise *Rationale Divinorum Officiorum* that 'only a baptized Christian ought to be buried in a Christian cemetery' (*Rationale*: lib. I, cap. 15, 14), thus indicating that unbaptized children must not be buried in consecrated ground. Instead, unbaptized infants should be disposed of together with suicides and criminals in the fields or buried outside the cemetery walls (Grabmayer 1999: 72). It should be noted that the denial of an ecclesiastical burial for unbaptized children officially remained part of Catholic Canon Laws until 1983 (compare *Codex Iuris Canonici* 1917: can. 1239, par. 1; and *Codex Iuris Canonici* 1983: can. 1183, §2). Durand's *Rationale* (lib. I, cap. 15, 16) also states that in the event of a woman's death during pregnancy, the foetus should be excised from the mother's womb and buried outside the cemetery, since the unbaptized corpse would corrupt the mother's body as well.

Children's Extended Life Course and Medieval Space

Limbus theory and related burial regulations carried considerable potential for conflict between the religious elites and the people who were actually affected by these teachings – parents and families. While from a theological point of view the *limbus* constituted a safe haven for children separated from hell, for the parents it embodied the denial of their children's salvation (Boswell 1998: 398), a notion that was further enforced by the prohibition of a Christian burial. The Church's insistence on the immutability of unbaptized children's post-mortal fates constituted an especially stringent problem.

Jenny Hockey and Janet Draper (2005) have pointed out that social identities do not necessarily have to coincide with the actual presence of a living body, but can be sustained beyond death (or acquired before birth), thus empowering the dead to remain agents in social networks and even change their social position or status long after their biological lifespan has ended. Their proposed concept of the extended life course offers a valuable perspective on the position of unbaptized children in medieval society. Roberta Gilchrist characterizes the medieval life course 'as a continuum which spanned life, death and the afterlife' (Gilchrist 2012: 19). Purgatory was only an intermediate stage in the Christian soul's journey after death, which ideally would result in bodily resurrection on Doomsday. For those who died as baptized Christians, the medieval extended life course proceeded into a long period of repentance followed by the soul's reunification with the carnal body and eventually its elevation into heaven. For those who died without baptism, on the other hand, their position in the afterlife became immutable and final, thus contradicting the ideal model of a continuous post-mortal existence with a progressive improvement of one's situation. The early biological death that prevented infants from being christened denied them the necessary progression to a stage in their life course where they would be considered members of the Christian community (Hausmair 2017).

Limbus teachings and related burial regulations thus stigmatized unbaptized children in the afterlife and ostracized them from the Christian community. The prohibition against burying unbaptized children within Christian cemeteries was both a possibility to construct their status in relation to the Christian community and also a means of leverage to threaten people and force them to baptize their children as soon as possible in order to prevent them from an eternity in limbo and visible exclusion from the community.

Both the theological concepts and the legal measures are characterized by deliberate spatial configurations that demonstrated the social position of the infants: the *limbus* was conceived as a confined place that, although not identical to hell, was still located beneath the earth, which formed a visible and impenetrable border between the children and the heavenly kingdom. The denial of a funeral in Christian cemeteries transcribed the metaphysical exclusion into a physical one that spatially separated the unbaptized children from the Christian community, making their unfavourable status visible to everyone (Hausmair 2015: 43). Especially in the Middle Ages, the social and metaphysical order of the world was inscribed in the structuring and connotation of both profane and sacred spaces. The celestial kingdom was imagined quite literally and the divine geography of the world was connected to empirical observations of the natural world (Hausmair 2017). Heaven was considered to lie just above the atmospheric sky, while volcanoes or caves represented entrances to the fires of hell burning beneath the earth (Keller 2011: 161).

Space and the material world are an essential part of human life and social structure (Lefebvre 1991). The material environment does not constitute a static physical entity in which agents communicate with each other, detached from their surroundings. Social structures and ontologies are established, reinforced but also challenged through exclusion and inclusion of humans and objects in the material world, thus creating spatial atmospheres of social order (Löw 2008). Therefore, spatial structure is not only a reflection or a result of ideological viewpoints of different agents, but also an integrative part of social processes and meaningful action through which ontologies and social orders are created, mediated or reinforced (Bourdieu 1989). At the same time, space plays a key role when conflicts between different social groups arise and social connotations of physical places are employed to transgress boundaries and to challenge existing concepts (Dartmann and Füssel 2004).

Heinrich Härke has stressed the importance of cemeteries as 'fields of discourse' (Härke 2001: 13). Here, social structures and power relations are deliberately displayed, negotiated or challenged by employing internal spatial structures and the actual location of burial grounds as material expressions of social relationships. Härke pointed out that in the medieval period, mortuary rituals were deliberately controlled by priests who mediated the burial processes as ritual specialists. As liminal spaces between the living and the dead, cemeteries themselves became powerful places that were woven into Christian cosmology. The deliberate placing of the dead, both inside an enclosed graveyard and in relation to the surrounding landscape, was tightly bound to mental topographies of the divine world order and materialized social structure. Including or excluding certain social groups in/from the cemetery space therefore constituted a powerful statement in relation to social relationships (Härke 2001: 17–19).

An Archaeology of Unbaptized Children

Since the denial of a Christian burial presumably required the parents to take care of their children's funeral without priestly support, it can be assumed that archaeological remains of unbaptized children provide an insight into the lay population's handling of official regulations and religious teachings. It has been pointed out above how strongly medieval life was shaped by projecting 'divine' concepts of space onto society and its material environment. When scrutinizing remains of unbaptized infants' burials, the spatial dimensions incorporated in *limbus* theory and related burial regulation have to be considered. This allows us to explore how the non-clerical population interpreted religious concepts, along with their possible reactions to enforced rules and teachings. It is thus suggested here that the spatial positioning of presumably unbaptized infants can be conceptualized as a material legacy of people's ideas about the fate of children in the afterlife.

Problems arise, however, when trying to convincingly identify graves of unbaptized children in the archaeological record. While it is justified to assume that in general, burials of newborns or very young infants are prime candidates for the category of unbaptized children, it would be imprudent to assume that burials of early deceased infants in a regular Christian cemetery would per se represent 'illegal' burials of unbaptized children. Numerous archaeological excavations in parish cemeteries of the high and late medieval period have shown that burials of these age groups increase significantly from around 1000 onwards (Ulrich-Bochsler 1997). It thus seems more reasonable to assume that most of these burials represent the graves of baptized individuals and probably reflect an increase in pedobaptism shortly after birth. However, anthropological analyses have shown that premature and presumably stillborn children were also occasionally buried in regular cemeteries (e.g. in Walkringen, Switzerland; see Ulrich-Bochsler 1997: Figure 83, 76), leaving room for speculation about whether such findings could point towards unauthorized burial practices. Modern Swiss folk stories, for instance, inform about the Protestant practice of burying unbaptized children in parish cemeteries directly beneath church roofs. It was believed that rainwater dripping down from the roof onto the graves would provide a kind of post-mortal baptism (Ulrich-Bochsler 1997). However, it has to be kept in mind that in Protestant areas, ecclesiastic burials for unbaptized children were no longer prohibited, since reformed theologies from the sixteenth century onwards rejected the *limbus* concept (Herzog 2006: 125).

The interpretation of infant burials within regular cemeteries of the medieval period is thus very problematic and the identification of unbaptized children is difficult. These circumstances require further scrutiny both from archaeological and historical perspectives (Hausmair 2017: 2–4). However, for the purposes of this chapter, I will shift my focus to another type of infant inhumation, which provides a more solid basis for the issues discussed above. There is some evidence for medieval cemeteries that consisted almost exclusively of child burials, among them often foetuses and neonates, e.g. in Irlbach, Germany (Scherbaum 2005), at Michelberg/Haslbach, Austria (Lauermann et al. 2014), or Göttweig, Austria (Hausmair and Urban 2010, 2011; Hausmair 2017). The latter site will now form part of a more detailed discussion.

The Infant Cemetery of St George/Göttweig

From 2005 to 2010 the University of Vienna and the Austrian Cultural Heritage Office (BDA) conducted excavations at the medieval church of St George (in German *St Georg*) on Mount Göttweig, Lower Austria. During the final two years of excavation an infant cemetery was discovered that consisted almost exclusively of premature and newborn children (see Hausmair and Urban 2010, 2011; Hausmair 2017). The only exception was the single grave of an adult male individual (Hausmair 2017).

Mount Göttweig is a landscape-dominating hill on the south side of the River Danube. On its northern plateau is situated the Benedictine Abbey of Göttweig, which was founded in the eleventh century and has been maintained up to the present day. The church of St George is located 700 m south of the abbey on the highest elevation of Mount Göttweig. Several villages, situated at the foot of the hill, have been continuously occupied since the Middle Ages, e.g. Furth bei Göttweig, Klein Wien and Paudorf (Figure 13.1).

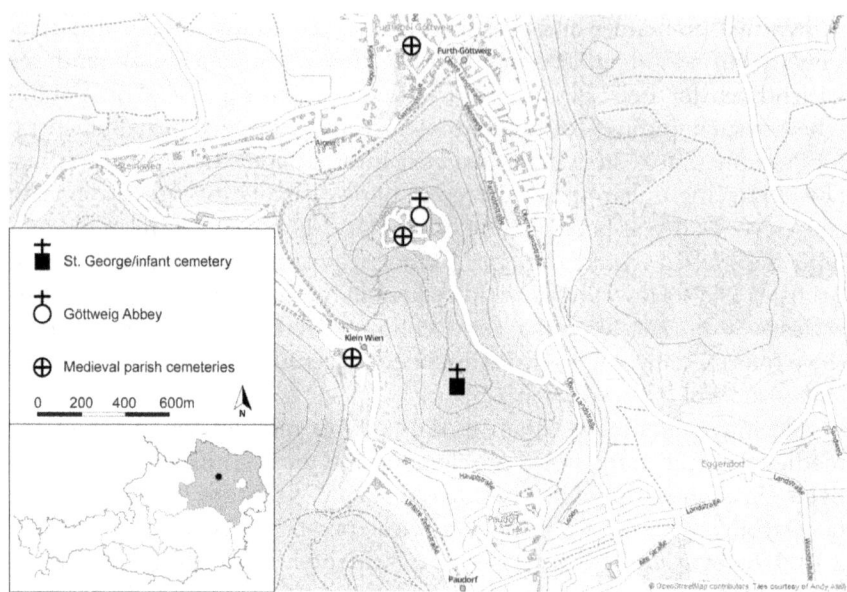

Figure 13.1 Map of Mount Göttweig (background map © OpenStreetMap contributors; tiles courtesy of Andy Allan)

St George's prominent location offers a view over the entire valley to the south, west and southeast of the hill, as well as a direct sight connection to the abbey in the north. In correlation with written sources, the church itself can be dated from the late eleventh century to the early sixteenth century, when it was presumably destroyed in the course of the Ottoman invasions in 1529. During its use, it was maintained by the clergy from the Benedictine Abbey, but it did not serve as parish church for any of the surrounding villages and supposedly it did not have burial privileges (Fischer 2002; for burial privileges in general, see Schimmelpfennig 1980: col. 1807–8).

Around the church, an infant cemetery was discovered that can be roughly dated from the thirteenth century to the sixteenth century due to its stratigraphic relationships with the church's different occupation and destruction layers. This suggests that the cemetery's usage ended together with that of the church. Forty-one sub-adult individuals were uncovered, although at the request of the local clergy and Christian community of the present-day Göttweig region, not all skeletons were collected after documentation and a further unknown number of burials remained undisturbed in a ditch north of the church. Over twenty-five of the excavated burials were located in ditches running parallel directly along the longitudinal walls and the presbytery of the church. Since the foundations of the presbytery were completely demolished, its original outline could only be reconstructed from the infant burials that outlined the previous dimensions of the building. Another thirteen graves were recorded south of the building (Figure 13.3). The recently completed analysis of the skeletal remains (Wimmer 2016: Table 1; age-estimations from photogrammetric images of non-collected individuals kindly provided by Michaela Binder)[1] determined twenty-one individuals who died between the fifth and tenth lunar month, seventeen neonates (maximum two months of age) and only one infant who was not older than three months (Figure 13.2). For a further two individuals, an accurate determination was not possible and they can only be classed as 'infants definitely not older than one month of age'. Except for two S-N-oriented bodies, the burials were positioned along the W-E axis, which corresponds to the regular orientation of Christian burials. There was no material evidence to suggest the use of coffins, where the dense position of several infant bodies – especially in the ditches along the church building – would also seem to negate the use of wooden containers in these cases. However, the rather constricted positions of the limbs could indicate that some children were wrapped in some kind of cloth or shroud. Iron pins found with some of the burials could have been

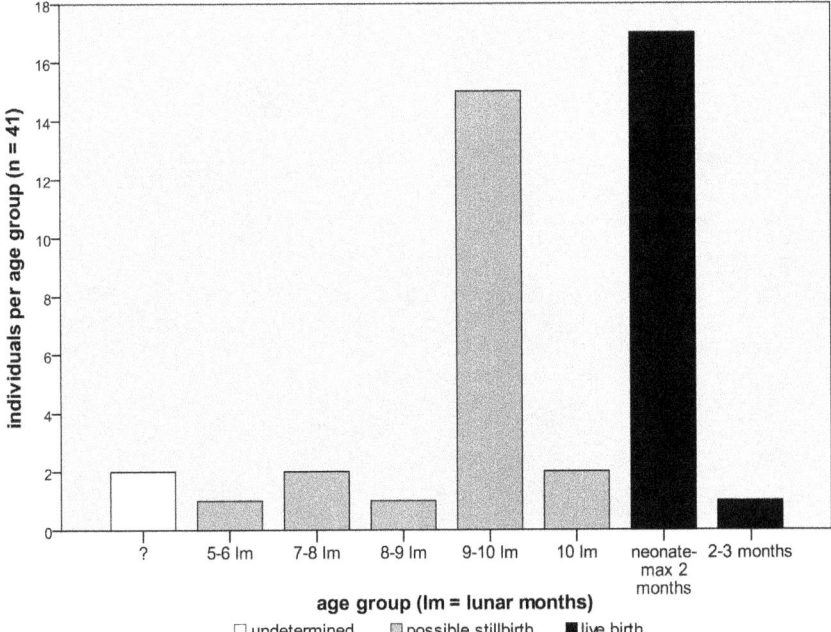

Figure 13.2 Age distribution within the sample of infant inhumations from the church of St George

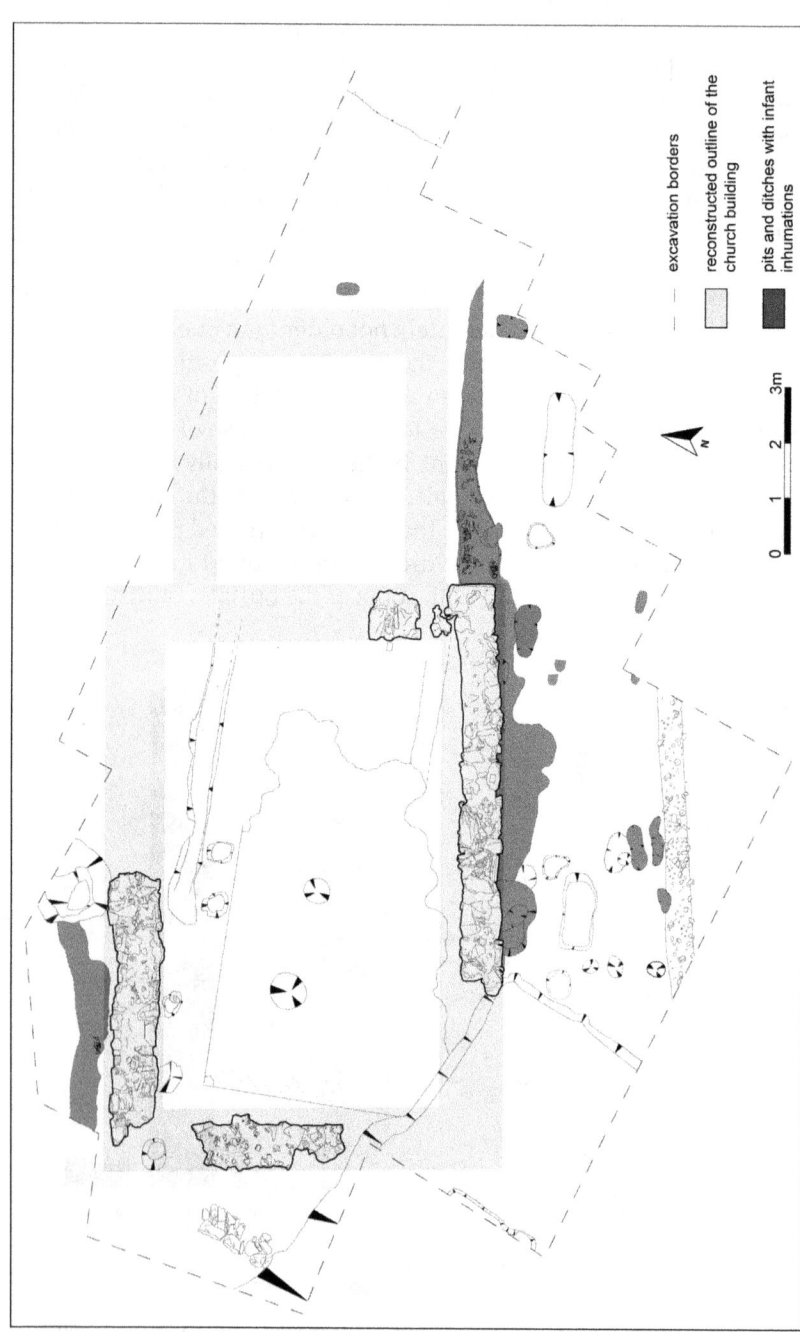

Figure 13.3 Excavation plan of the church of St George and the surrounding infant cemetery (illustrations by Barbara Hausmair)

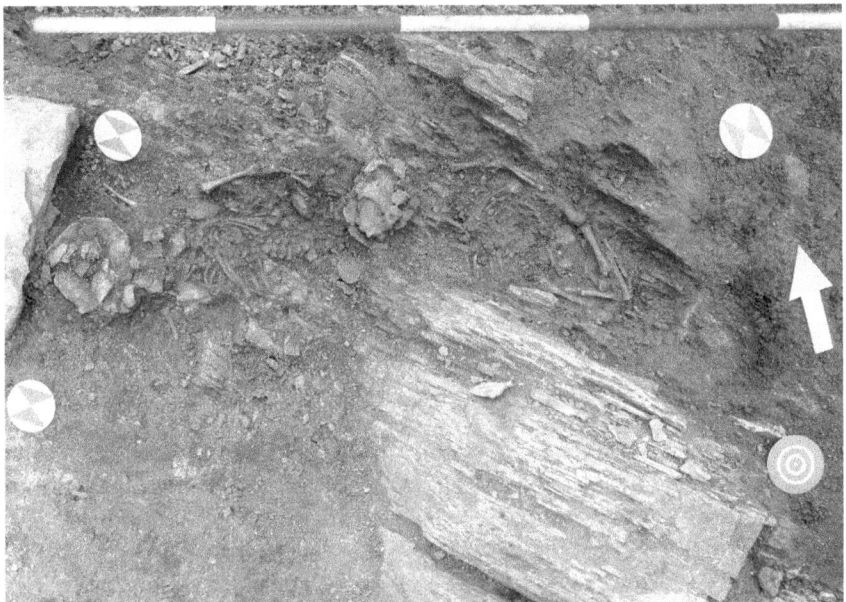

Figure 13.4 Overlapping infant burials in the southern area of the cemetery (photograph by Barbara Hausmair)

used to fix them. The frequently occurring disturbances of older burials by younger ones suggest that above-ground grave markers were not used and hence the graves were not always visible when a newly deceased infant was buried (Figure 13.4).

Even though there is a strong likelihood that many of the prematurely born infants were actually stillbirths, the neonates and infant of maximum three months of age clearly show that children who survived birth were also buried at St George. The exclusively young age of the recorded individuals and the context of the site thus make it highly likely that the cemetery was a special burial ground for unbaptized children. In the following I will discuss how these burials and their spatial settings may enhance our understanding of the relationships of parents, local parishes and the Church in relation to the handling of theological concepts and official rules.

The Göttweig Infants, Religious Space and Lay Concepts of the Extended Life Course

When exploring the location of the infant cemetery at St George, it becomes clear that the place embodies multiple and ambivalent meanings in relation to medieval ontology and social structure.

Figure 13.5 Mount Göttweig with the Benedictine Abbey on its northern plateau. St George is located on its southern peak, visible in the left part of the photo (photograph by Barbara Hausmair)

The lines-of-sight from St George to its surrounding environment must have been extensive in the medieval period, considering that Mount Göttweig was at least partly deforested during that period (Fischer 2002). Even today, the highest plateau of the hill is visible from kilometres away (Figure 13.5). A newly erected flagpole next to the excavation dominates the scenery when entering the valley south of Mount Göttweig. When the forest is bare in winter, it allows the church's position to be seen from the abbey, 700 m away. In the Middle Ages, the church would have been a highly visible monument for the areas to the south, west and east of the hill, and a permanently dominant feature in the landscape (for an analyses of lines-of-sight between St George and the local surroundings see Hausmair 2017). At the same time, St George was an isolated place; no other buildings or areas for social activity existed in its immediate proximity and access to the hilltop required extensive walking. Although the building itself was prominently placed, the cemetery occupied a more or less concealed space that was not directly neighboured by any areas of daily social activity, thus creating an ambivalent atmosphere of openness and seclusion (compare Löw 2008).

The same ambivalence can be traced when connecting the spatial settings to the medieval religious landscape and topographies. Being located on the highest elevation of Mount Göttweig, St George and the unbaptized children occupied a position that was physically closer to the sky than any other place in the surrounding area. Translated into the medieval image of the world, the children were deliberately buried in a place that was obviously closer to the heavens than it was to hell, almost touching the sky when viewed from below. On the other hand, the considerable distance between St George, the villages in the valley and the abbey spatially separated the children from the Christian communities in a way that would have been obvious to everyone.

It is also worth mentioning that the preserved account books of the abbey from the early sixteenth century reveal that the highest amount of donations for the liturgical year took place on *Georgitag*, the feast day of St George. The saint around whose church the locals buried their deceased children received more donations than any other saint with a patrocinium in the area (Fischer 2002). This fact may reflect the special meaning that the church held for the population. Alternatively, the considerable donations may also denote a more practical reason, such as paying money for the redemption of the children's souls. The patrocinium probably also influenced the choice of St George as a resting place for the dead children. Ranked among the 'Martyrs of Indestructible Life', St George was a powerful saint when it came to matters of death. Hubertus Halbfas (2002) has also argued that the main message contained in the legends of St George centres on the importance of baptism. After St George had killed the dragon (a metaphor for Satan), the King and people of Silene were christened, thus defeating the Devil. Burying unbaptized children in sacred space that was guarded by a saint whose characterization was so closely connected to the rescue of souls suggests that people trusted in the power of this patron and hoped for his positive influence on the infants' fate in the afterlife.

These ambivalences and different connotations of the infant cemetery's place in the medieval landscape characterize the population's situation and provide a possibility to explore their attitudes towards the authorities' directives and teachings. For the sake of their infants, community members were willing to go to considerable lengths by walking up from the villages to the highest elevation of Mount Göttweig (approximately 200–250 m difference in altitude). Moreover, digging a grave often went hand in hand with disturbing or even touching older burials. The visual and haptic, maybe even olfactory sensations during this process and the active engagement with both the child that had just died and the dead bodies of already buried children would have created an intense engagement with the dead infants. These observations indicate a high degree of concern and devotion for such a problematic social group, reflecting a dissymmetry between the concepts and rules promoted by the Church and the ideas that were active in lay culture.

Reconsidering Social Relationships and Burial Regulations

The ambivalences surrounding St George as a burial place for unbaptized infants raise questions about whether these archaeologically traceable practices should be read as evidence for the lay population's obedience in relation to the official teachings or whether they should be interpreted as deliberate violation of burial rules. These questions require a broader look at funerary evidence from the Göttweig area.

During excavations of the medieval cemetery at the parish church of Klein Wien, the closest village to Mount Göttweig (Figure 13.1), almost no infant remains were found, except in contexts with two adult females, who presumably died during pregnancy (unpublished excavation report kindly provided by P. Udo Fischer). In such cases, the *Rationale* (lib. I, cap. 15, 16) requests the extraction of the unbaptized foetus from the mother's womb in order for her body to qualify for a Christian burial. While this directive was obviously not consequently followed in Klein Wien, the absence of any single burials of prematurely deceased children suggests that the local population, as well as the clergy, respected the official directives at least partially by excluding born but not yet baptized infants from the parish cemetery. On the other hand, choosing the secluded church of St George as a burial ground also breached ecclesiastical regulations. Although the church of St George did not seem to have had burial privileges attached to its status as an external building of the abbey, the definition of consecrated ground was not bound to burial privileges alone. In the Council of Rome in 1058, the span of the reliquary and the altar that transformed the surroundings of a church into sacred space was officially set to 60 ft (Kenzler 2011: 12), thus also transforming St George's immediate surroundings into consecrated ground. Despite respecting the burial prohibition in the parish cemeteries, Göttweig's population still tried to bury their deceased children in sacred soil.

Physically separating infants from the regular cemeteries could be seen as a materialization of the local communities' understanding of the children as a problematic social group, thus expressing at least a partial acknowledgement of the Church's authority in these matters. However, this very same spatial configuration possibly also embodies hope for the rescue of the infants' souls and a flexible concept of the extended life course where their identities in death could still be influenced.

Burying the unbaptized children in a particularly Christian manner – next to a church in W-E orientation – almost seems like an attempt to bypass the institutional Church and bring the matter directly in front of the highest authority, God and his saints. People thus contested the teachings and disobeyed the regulations in a deliberate way. On the other hand, the remote location of the cemetery also embodies a notion of an unauthorized custom that, if not totally secret, still needed to be concealed to some extent as it opposed the Church's regulations. Although probably exercised in a hidden manner, this kind of insubordination could suggest that the idea of limbo and the Church's denial of children's salvation were deeply rejected by the population, if not at the very least mistrusted.

Whether or not the local clergy of both the parishes and the abbey were aware of what was going on next to the secluded church on the hilltop must remain an unsolved question. There is not one written account in the rich archive of the abbey that refers to a burial place at St George, even though the church itself is frequently mentioned in written documents. However, considering the large number of children buried around St George, it is very likely that the clergy was aware of the custom, as a repeated opening of the ground would certainly have been recognizable on the surface. The number of burials also suggests that the cemetery was used for quite some time, thus implying that the local authorities did not try to put a stop to this practice. Although it can only be speculated as to whether or not the clergy was actively involved in the actual burial process, the fact that the custom was seemingly tolerated also shows a degree of disobedience on the part of the local clergy in relation to the official teachings.

Conclusion

Exploring the archaeology of unbaptized children reveals an ambivalent relationship between the medieval lay population, the local clergy, and the official Church and its regulations. One crucial point underlying this conflict can surely be seen in varying concepts of the extended life course and also the different goals that were being sought by those involved. While the Church certainly pursued the establishment of early pedobaptism and further enhancement of its power over the lay population and social processes in medieval society, parents and families acted out of desperation, employing any possible means to change their children's destiny. Through examining the archaeological record, it is possible to trace these concepts through the spatial relationships being created by the burial community. The fear of children's doomed fate in the afterlife was a collective trauma for the medieval population that deeply undermined their trust in the Church. This can be seen by the continuity of practices similar to those presented in this chapter. Miracle baptisms of already-deceased children that emerged in the late medieval period continued in some Central European areas until the early twentieth century (Gélis 2006). Even in communities of reformed/Protestant faith where the resurrection of unbaptized children was no longer a theological obstacle, special treatment of this group can be traced until recently (Ulrich-Bochsler 1997). Drawing on these observations, it has to be concluded that burials like the ones from St George are not a picturesque reflection of a superstitious folk custom; they are materializations of an ambivalent relationship between the ecclesiastic authorities, their local representatives and the actual population.

Acknowledgements

I sincerely thank Otto H. Urban, Jakob Maurer and Judith Klieber (University of Vienna), Christoph Blesl (Austrian Cultural Heritage Office) and P. Udo Fischer (Paudorf Parish/Göttweig) for the excellent team work during our excavation; Göttweig Abbey and the members of Paudorf Parish for greatly supporting our fieldwork; Maria Teschler-Nicola and Katharina Wimmer (Natural History Museum Vienna) and Michaela Binder (Austrian Archaeological Institute) for kindly providing age determinations of the infant remains; and Susi Ulrich-Bochsler (University of Bern) and Gabriela Signori (University of Konstanz) for helpful discussions. This research was kindly supported by the EU FP7 Marie Curie Zukunftskolleg Incoming Fellowship Programme, University of Konstanz (grant no. 291784).

Barbara Hausmair is a post-doctoral researcher at the Freie Universität Berlin, Germany and previously held a Marie-Skłodowska-Curie-Fellowship at the Zukunftskolleg, University of Konstanz, Germany. As research associate and site supervisor at the University of Vienna, Austria, she was involved in excavation projects in France, Austria and Italy. She is the author of *Am Rande des Grabs* (Sidestone Press, 2015), co-editor of *Spruch von den sibnen* (Thorbecke, 2016) and has published on medieval mortuary practices as well as the archaeology of Nazi terror.

Note

1. Preliminary results of age determination published in Hausmair 2017 slightly divert from these data.

References

Primary Sources

Codex Iuris Canonici. 1917. In *Acta Apostolicae Sedis* 9(2): 11–521.
———. 1983. In *Acta Apostolicae Sedis* 75(2): 1–320.
De Symbolo Sermo ad Catechumenos, Augustine of Hippo, ed. J.-P. Migne. 1865. Patrologia Latina, Vol. 40. Paris: Petit-Montrouge, col. 627–68.
Rationale Divinorum Officiorum, Guillaume Durand de Mende, ed. J.-P. Buysson. 1592. Lyon: Junta.

Summa Theologica, Thomas Aquinas, trans. Fathers of the English Dominican Province. 1947. New York: Benziger Bros.
Von sehs mordaeren, Berthold of Regensburg, ed. F. Pfeiffer. 1862. *Berthold von Regensburg: Vollständige Ausgabe seiner Predigten Vol. 1*. Vienna: W. Braumüller, pp. 124–39.

Secondary Literature

Boswell, J. 1998. *The Kindness of Strangers: The Abandonment of Children in Western Europe from Late Antiquity to the Renaissance*. Chicago, IL: University of Chicago Press.
Bourdieu, P. 1989. 'Social Space and Symbolic Power', *Sociological Theory* 7(1): 14–25.
Dartmann, C., and M. Füssel. 2004. 'Einleitung', in C. Dartmann, M. Füssel and S. Rüther (eds), *Raum und Konflikt*, Symbolische Kommunikation und gesellschaftliche Wertesysteme 5. Münster: Rhema, pp. 9–18.
Fischer, U. 2002. *Atlas der Pfarre Paudorf-Göttweig*. Paudorf: Pfarrgemeinderat der Pfarre Paudorf-Göttweig.
Gélis, J. 2006. *Les Enfants des Limbes*. Paris: Audibert.
Gilchrist, R. 2012. *Medieval Life: Archaeology and the Life Course*. Woodbridge: Boydell.
Grabmayer, J. 1999. *Zwischen Diesseits und Jenseits: Oberrheinische Chroniken als Quellen zur Kulturgeschichte des späten Mittelalters*. Cologne: Böhlau.
Gurevič, A.J. 1994. *Das Individuum im europäischen Mittelalter*, trans. E. Glier. Munich: Beck.
Halbfas, H. 2002. 'Die Wahrheit der Legende', in E. Volgger (ed.), *Sankt Georg und sein Bilderzyklus in Neuhaus, Böhmen (Jindřichův Hradec)*, Quellen und Studien zur Geschichte des Deutschen Ordens 57. Marburg: Elwert, pp. 137–52.
Härke, H. 2001. 'Cemeteries as Places of Power', in M. de Jong and F. Theuws (eds), *Topographies of Power in the Early Middle Ages*, Transformation of the Roman World 6. Leiden: Brill, pp. 9–30.
Hausmair, B. 2015. *Am Rande des Grabs: Todeskonzepte und Bestattungsritual in der frühmittelalterlichen Alamannia*. Leiden: Sidestone Press.
———. 2017. 'Topographies of the Afterlife: Reconsidering Infant burials in Medieval Mortuary Space', *Journal of Social Archaeology* 17(2): 210–36.
Hausmair, B., and O.H. Urban. 2010. 'KG Göttweig, MG Furth bei Göttweig, VB Krems', *Fundberichte aus Österreich* 48(2009): 473.
———. 2011. 'KG Göttweig, MG Furth bei Göttweig, VB Krems', *Fundberichte aus Österreich* 49(2010): 275–76.
Herzog, M. 2006. 'Strafleidenstheorie – Anthropologie – Kosmologie – Soteriologie. Kontroversen in der Höllenfahrttheologie der Reformation des 16. Jahrhunderts', in M. Herzog (ed.), *Höllen-Fahrten*. Stuttgart: Kohlhammer, pp. 109–30.
Hockey, J., and J. Draper. 2005. 'Beyond the Womb and the Tomb: Identity, (Dis) embodiment and the Life Course', *Body and Society* 11(2): 41–57.
Keller, S.B. 2011. 'Picturing the Inaccessible: Gazing under the Earth's Surface between Empiricism and Speculation', in J. Häcki and M. Volmert (eds), *Vom Objekt zum Bild*. Berlin: Akademie-Verlag, pp. 157–88.

Kenzler, H. 2011. 'Totenbrauchtum und Reformation, Wandel und Kontinuität', *Mitteilungen der deutschen Gesellschaft für Archäologie des Mittelalters und der Neuzeit* 23: 9–34.
Lauermann, E., P. Mitchell, and E. Rammer. 2014. 'Der Michelberg und seine Kirchen', *Beiträge zur Mittelalterarchäologie in Österreich* 30: 7–22.
Le Goff, J. 1990. *The Birth of Purgatory*. Aldershot: Scolar Press.
Lefebvre, H. 1991. *The Production of Space*, trans. D. Nicholson-Smith. Oxford: Wiley & Blackwell.
Löw, M. 2008. 'The Constitution of Space', *European Journal of Social Theory* 11(1): 25–49.
O'Connor, A. 1991. *Child Murderess and Dead Child Traditions: A Comparative Study*, FF Communications 249. Helsinki: Suomalainen Tiedeakatemia.
Scherbaum, J. 2005. 'Die Grabung in der Pfarrkirche Maria Himmelfahrt in Irlbach/Lkr. Regensburg', *Beiträge zur Archäologie in der Oberpfalz und in Regensburg* 7: 223–47.
Schimmelpfennig, B. 1980. 'Begräbnis, Begräbnisrecht. C. Kirchliches Begräbnisrecht', in *Lexikon des Mittelalters Vol. 1*. Munich: Artemis & Winkler Verlag, col. 1807–8.
Schwarz, J.M. 2006. *Zwischen Limbus und Gottesschau: Das Schicksal ungetauft sterbender Kinder in der theologischen Diskussion des zwanzigsten Jahrhunderts. Ein theologiegeschichtliches Panorama*. Kißlegg: fe-medienverlag.
Swanson, R.N. 2010. 'The Burdens of Purgatory', in D.E. Bornstein (ed.), *Medieval Christianity*, People's History of Christianity 4. Minneapolis: Augsburg Fortress, pp. 353–80.
Taglia, K. 2001. 'Delivering a Christian Identity: Midwives in Northern French Synodal Legislation, c. 1220–1500', in P. Biller and J. Ziegler J (eds), *Religion and Medicine in the Middle Ages*, York: York Medieval Press, pp. 77–90.
Ulrich-Bochsler, S. 1997. *Anthropologische Befunde zur Stellung von Frau und Kind in Mittelalter und Neuzeit: Soziobiologische und soziokulturelle Aspekte im Lichte der Archäologie, Geschichte, Volkskunde und Medizingeschichte*. Bern: Berner Lehrmittel- und Medienverlag.
Walsh, L.G. 2011. *Sacraments of Initiation: A Theology of Rite, Word, and Life*. Chicago: Hillenbrand Books.
Wimmer, K. 2016. 'Die Anthropologie der Göttweiger Traufkinder', M.A. dissertation. Vienna: University of Vienna.
York, W.H. 2012. *Health and Wellness in Antiquity through the Middle Ages*. Santa Barbara, CA: Greenwood.

Chapter 14

Medieval Monastic Text and the Treatment of the Dead
An Archaeothanatological Perspective on Adherence to the Cluniac Customaries

Eleanor Williams

Introduction

The sixth-century Rule of Saint Benedict (*Benedicti Regula*) became the principal guide to monastic living in the medieval period. Its seventy-three chapters define the requirements for daily life of the individual and governance of the monastic community. The degree of specificity on matters of life can be greatly contrasted to the almost complete absence of guidance relating to matters of death and burial. As Veronique Gazeau (2004: 13) writes, the Rule of Saint Benedict presents the dead as both God's punishment and a source of redemption, but at no point does it envisage treatment, or commemoration, of the dead. Prompted by the absence of formal guidance, individual monastic communities were thus required to provide their own structured solutions to the physical and spiritual care and management of the dying and deceased, for which the eleventh-century Cluniac Customaries constitute some of the most detailed and influential examples. These texts specify how the dying monk, his dead body and memory were to be physically and spiritually treated. Although various prescribed actions are archaeologically untraceable, including the complex sequences of prayers and many of the bodily gestures performed by the community, others offer the potential to be materially explored, particularly through the study of osteological remains. One such element discussed herein is the prescribed method of pre-interment body preparation.

This chapter considers evidence from comprehensively recorded funerary contexts for two eleventh-century Cluniac foundations, Bermondsey

Abbey (London, England) and Notre Dame, La Charité-sur-Loire (Burgundy, France). It explores how detailed taphonomic archaeothanatological approaches can be used post-excavation to provide greater insight into specific elements of medieval monastic funerary practice, thus addressing the dynamic relationship between Cluniac and, more generally, monastic text and practice. In so doing, it considers both the opportunities and difficulties encountered in attempting to trace monastic responses to regulatory texts through the archaeological record. Gazeau (2004: 15) has suggested crossing the instructions deriving from monastic customaries, which she describes as highly theoretical prescriptions, with the practice. Thus, the convergence of these different strands of material and documentary evidence also offers new perspectives on the nature of these texts, in terms of their creation, purpose and use; in short, how 'theoretical' were they for specific elements of Cluniac practice and how far can archaeology contribute to our understanding of them?

The Cluniacs and Their Customaries

The founding of the Burgundian house Cluny in c. 910 marked the start of a new form of monasticism. Breaking with the previous tradition of independent monasteries, a network of dependencies was established; to varying degrees, these houses were governed either directly or indirectly by Cluny itself. By the end of the eleventh century, many hundreds of houses had been established, with the foundation of Lewes Priory (Sussex, England) in c. 1081 instigating Cluniac monasticism across the Channel. These geographically dispersed houses of varying size and status required cohesiveness and conformity of practice, for as Abbot Hugh V's statute in 1200 proclaimed: 'Since we are of one congregation and order we should conform in everything' (quoted in Constable 2010: 268). The later eleventh-century Cluniac Customaries, which came to form 'the institutional basis for life at Cluny, her dependencies and affiliates' (Paxton 1993: 1), were arguably compiled in part to promote this. Gert Melville has described these texts as 'repositories of norms' that were transferable in time and space (Melville 2005: 83), which, although at first descriptive, could become prescriptive upon adoption in another monastery (Krüger 2005: 194). Although Cluny's heads would undoubtedly have been desirous of the dependencies adopting the customs, the documents themselves were not binding; a degree of fluidity in their uptake and regulatory power thus existed. Houses may only have borrowed from them in part, or adapted them, thus preserving local traditions (Palazzo 1998: 217; see also Boynton 2006). Many twelfth-century reformed houses had no customaries; statutes, decrees of General Chapters and increasingly visitations helped to ensure uniformity (Constable 1998: 173). However, as the visitation records of English Cluniac foundations evidence, these 'inspections' could be few and far between. Inevitably, regulatory focus was directed towards the more readily observable aspects of everyday life rather than on practical matters of death and burial (see Duckett 1890). Adherence to specific funerary practices in accordance with the Cluniac Customaries was thus arguably left more in the control of the individual houses.

The Cluniac Customaries discussed herein were compiled in the eleventh century: the early to mid eleventh-century *Liber Tramitis* (*LT*), and the roughly contemporaneous *Customary of Ulrich* (*Antiquiores Consuetudines Cluniacensis Monasterii*/*Ulr*) and the *Customary of Bernard* (*Ordo Cluniacensis*/ *Bern*). Both dated c. 1080, the *Ulr* is based primarily on experiences at Cluny in the early 1060s, with the *Bern* depicting Cluny in the late 1070s and early 1080s (Boynton 2005: 110). These texts provide significant detail on the ante-mortem and post-mortem rites to be performed on the death of a brother. Their degree of specificity and complexity, particularly the *Ulr* and the *Bern*, are likely, in part, to be a product of the time in which they were composed; by the late eleventh century, as Cochelin (2000: 30) notes, the Cluniac quest to construct a perfect community had placed increasing importance on the customs. Many houses sought to imitate Cluny's practices – a factor prompting the creation of Ulrich's text for Abbot William of Hirsau. In the case of the *Bern* at least, written principally for Cluny's novices (Boynton 2005: 110), change was an important stimulus in its creation. Saurette (2005: 85) writes that anxieties over the loss of community memory led to the validity of the customs being questioned, thus motivating Bernard's commissioning to preserve contemporary norms in the Cluniac way of life. This is clearly expressed within his preface. The death of an abbot, or possibly even the frequent movement of senior monks between houses (see Knowles, Brooke and London 2001) could have been a source of concern, but fear of change could also have been a crucial agent for the codification of practice. The rapid increase in geographically dispersed Cluniac establishments during this period was possibly a key factor prompting the desire for more formal, transferable instructions. The two later customaries were written under Hugh's Abbacy (1049–1109), during which, for instance, requests were made for monks to be sent from Cluny to found a priory at Lewes; concerns over their isolation and governability delayed Hugh's decision (Lyne 1997: 5–6). The possibility of transmitting copies of these newly compiled customaries, or at least elements of them, may have contributed to some degree in assuaging fears over distance.

Although it is unknown exactly how long the Cluniac Customaries in their various forms were in active use within each institution, evidence does suggest a relatively long duration in certain contexts. The *Bern*, for instance, was copied into the late Middle Ages in monasteries once associated with the Cluniac sphere of influence (Saurette 2005: 87).

The Cluniac Customaries and the Treatment of the Dead

Particularly since the 1990s, the death and burial rites within the *LT*, the *Ulr* and the *Bern* have been the focus of a growing body of historical, anthropological and thanatological research (e.g. Paxton 1993, 2005, 2013; Boynton 2006). In particular, Paxton's (1993, 2013) translations and commentaries of the *Ulr* and the *Bern* have demonstrated their potential for exploring how the dying and deceased may have been perceived, but also practically managed by, at the very least, Cluny's later eleventh-century community. Although the Cluniac Customaries have incited significant interest, particularly amongst historians (see the papers in Boynton and Cochelin 2005; Constable 2010), their consideration within archaeological research remains minimal. This is despite their significant influence on the development of funerary rites across Western monasticism and the exceptional level of detail contained within.

From deathbed to the grave and beyond, the *Ulr* and the *Bern* prescribe a protracted and communal ceremonial programme. They convey a highly ritualized and intimate approach to the body, structured by the interplay of repetitive symbolic actions combined with the practical requirements of treating and disposing of a cadaver. One element afforded considerable attention within these texts is the process for pre-interment body preparation.

Both written by monks of Cluny, the *Ulr* and the *Bern* specify, for the most part, a comparable sequence of actions. The following summarizes the principal steps for preparing the body of a brother; the abbot, instead, is to be dressed in his priestly vestments (*Bern*: cap. XXV, p. 199; see also Paxton 1993, 2013). After death, the monk is laid on a table in the infirmary. Once the body has been washed, it is dressed in a wool shirt, cowl, sudary and night shoes (*caligis nocturnalibus*), which are closed at the ends. The cowl is drawn over the face and sewn down on both sides. The hands are folded together over the chest, and the cowl is brought together and sewn so that none of its parts are loose. The night shoes are also sewn together. The body is laid within a shroud (*stragula*) (*Bern*: cap. XXIV, p. 194). This procedure is markedly different from that provided within the earlier *LT*. Here, certain actions are not prescribed, such as the sewing together of garments. Burial in a cowl is specified, with drawers/breeches (*femoralia*) and shoes (*calciamenta*) (*LT*: cap. XXXIII, p. 273). Paxton (2005: 298) has suggested that the *Regularis Concordia* (*RC*), a customary written in c. 970 for use in all monasteries in the English kingdom, may have influenced the *LT*; the method of body preparation at least is certainly comparable (see *RC*: cap. XII, p. 65). Customary practice could thus develop substantially over a relatively short time span. This inevitably introduces a strong degree of complexity when examining adherence to specific regulatory texts archaeologically. Materially exploring subtle intrasite or intersite differences or changes in practice, directly or indirectly influenced by written regulations, requires sufficiently detailed analytical approaches. For a study of this nature, these approaches are strongly dependent on preservational factors and the quality of the excavation documentation. This can be particularly problematic for the analysis of medieval burial grounds, where both contemporary and modern grave disturbance has left many funerary contexts incomplete. Nevertheless, use of the appropriate analytical techniques can substantially enrich our enquiries.

It is proposed that uptake of the highly specific body preparation method detailed within the later eleventh-century Cluniac Customaries could be explored to some extent within the archaeological record. Theoretically, if adherence was strict and enduring, a distinct and fairly uniform skeletal patterning could be expected for a large proportion of examined individuals deriving from Cluniac burial grounds. For instance, the forearms or hands would be folded or joined together over the trunk (arguably demonstrating a strong degree of symmetry), the feet would be positioned together in close proximity, and the overall skeletal profile could exhibit constrictions along the body consistent with a wrapping (tightly sewn robes and a shroud). An archaeothanatological 'body-focused' approach to human burials provides the ideal analytical framework for a high-resolution study into specific pre-interment gestures supposedly performed to, and for, the deceased's body by the Cluniac community.

Archaeothanatology and Cluniac Pre-interment Body Preparation

Since the 1990s in particular, there has been a surge of research focused on taphonomic approaches to mortuary contexts. This interest grew out of the development in the 1970s of detailed recording methods specific to human burials in the field, prompting the birth of *l'anthropologie de terrain* (field anthropology) as a formal approach to burial contexts. Pioneered by the French osteologist Henri Duday (see in particular Duday 2009), this approach to excavation forms one element of the broader *archaeothanatology* (the archaeology of the biological and social components of death). The aim is to reconstruct the original burial context through detailed in situ recording of the spatial relationships between individual bones, as well as to all other elements of the grave. It is based on 'an understanding of the dynamics involved in the disarticulation of the skeleton and the creation and subsequent infilling of empty spaces resulting from the decomposition of soft tissue' (Nilsson Stutz 2006a: 38–39). This allows for a separation of natural processes impacting upon the body and the overall grave context, from traces of mortuary practices. The latter can include preburial treatment of the corpse (e.g. use of wrappings), original body positioning on interment, the volume in which the body decomposed (e.g. in a filled space or a void), the mode of burial (e.g. directly in the ground and covered with earth, under a cover or in a container) and disturbance of the body during or after decomposition (e.g. Nilsson Stutz 2003, 2006a, 2006b; Duday 2009; Willis and Tayles 2009). As demonstrated below, this approach thus permits an examination of funerary contexts beyond the more readily observable and commonly recorded overall body placement (e.g. supine or prone), upper limb positioning, and remains of nonperishable grave structures and inclusions, to consider more intricate actions surrounding short- and longer-term management of the dead body.

Although detailed taphonomic analyses should ideally begin in the field, relatively recent work, notably on prehistoric burial contexts, has demonstrated the potential for using documentation (e.g. photographs, burial plans and field notes) to reconstruct specific funerary practices post-excavation, even in the absence of any direct archaeological indicators, such as the remains of nails, wood and burial dress. In particular, Nilsson Stutz (2006b) and Willis and Tayles (2009) have explored evidence for wrappings from prehistoric skeletal remains. Buquet-Marcon, Pecqueur and Detante's (2009) and Fossurier's (2009) work has further refined the study for medieval contexts, examining skeletal indicators for interment within specific forms of clothing or wrappings. A brief study of observed skeletal patterning in individuals from Bermondsey and La Charité, demonstrates how this approach can be applied to an examination of Cluniac practice, considered in relation to the later eleventh-century customaries.

As the body decomposes, the bones destabilize and move; eventually, they are re-stabilized by sediment filling the spaces around them. Burial directly under earth can result in a more rapid infilling, where even the most labile articulations (those that break down the most rapidly, such as the hand and distal foot bones) are maintained, and bones rest in positions of instability above the grave floor (see Duday 2009: 25–27). Shifting of elements is more pronounced where decomposition occurs within a void and can include significant movements outside of the initial volume of the body (Nilsson Stutz 2003: 154). Various forms of body preparation can also influence how skeletal elements move and their resultant spatial patterning. The method for wrapping stipulated in the *Bern*, for instance, could produce distinct osteological patterns.

Figure 14.1 to Figure 14.4 present six individuals from La Charité's internal gallery and cemetery, which arguably exhibit some evidence for

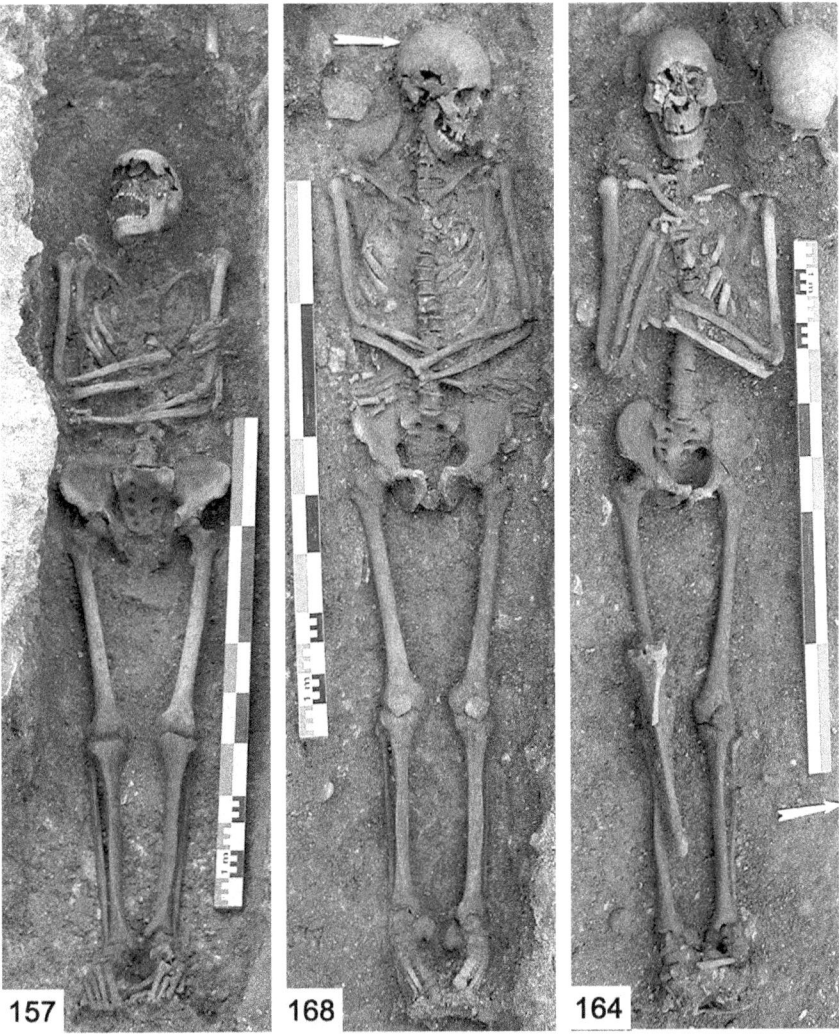

Figure 14.1–14.3 Individuals from La Charité's thirteenth-century gallery possibly exhibiting skeletal evidence for preparation in line with the *Bern* (photographs by David Billoin/©INRAP)

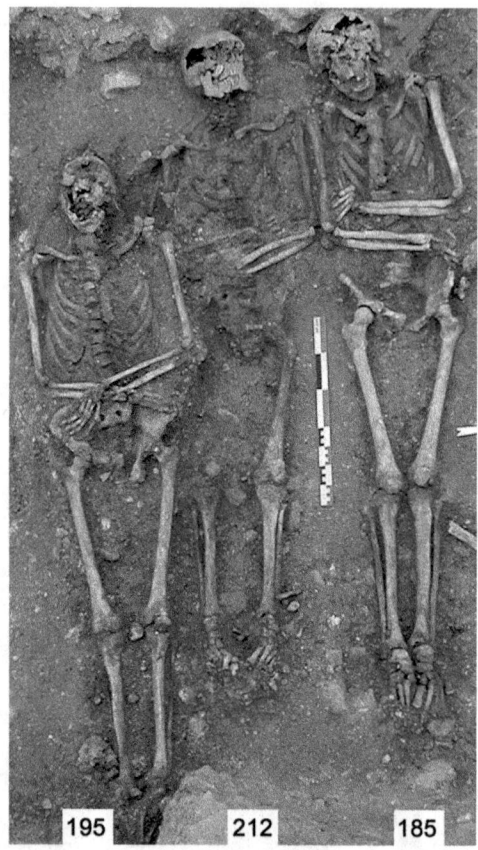

Figure 14.4 Individuals from pre-gallery cemetery possibly exhibiting skeletal evidence for preparation in line with the *Bern* (photograph by David Billoin/©INRAP)

pre-interment body preparation in line with the *Bern*. It should be noted that a marked degree of uniformity is apparent across these individuals, where the forearms are predominantly resting together (crossed or parallel) over the trunk, the lower limbs are extended and the feet are positioned together or close.

Constrictions evident within various regions of the bodies could indicate that some form of constrictive wrapping was used. Considering burial 157 (Figure 14.1), the individual exhibits a bilateral pressure at the shoulders, which has resulted in the clavicles moving into more oblique positions. The shoulders are projected upwards and forwards, and demonstrate a 'wall effect'; this, as Nilsson Stutz (2006b: 220) explains, is the impression that the bones are leaning on an invisible obstruction, which if not there would cause them to roll outwards to obtain a position of equilibrium. Luc Staniaszek's (2005: 99–100) field notes indicate that in this instance, the left shoulder was away from the cut wall (the right is less clear), and given that decomposition took place in a filled space (note the maintenance of hand and foot bones in positions of instability above the grave floor), walls of a durable burial container are unlikely to have caused this spatial arrangement. A constrictive wrapping could instead be proposed. Similar reasoning could also be applied to burial 185 (Figure 14.4). Constrictions are apparent along the individual's body; there is a bilateral pressure evident at the shoulders (away from the cut wall on the left), there is a tight convergence at the knees and ankles, and the feet are in a close union. Except in the case of burial 157, where the evidence is more ambiguous, the foot bones in each of the remaining examples exhibit a spatial patterning possibly indicative of a constrictive wrapping within this region. Burials 168 and 212 (Figure 14.2 and 14.4) include individuals with a pronounced symmetrical plantarflexion of the feet (away from the grave walls); although to some extent pressure from the surrounding soil could have contributed to this distinct spatial patterning, it could also indicate the former presence of a perishable element of constraint. Buquet-Marcon, Pecqueur and Detante (2009: 72) argue that a union of the feet, one towards or on top of the other, could suggest a flexible element encompassing both; this is opposed to a clothed burial, where the feet can be distinctly apart, or the bones move in opposing ways (see, for example, individual 168; Figure 14.5).

Figures 14.5 to 14.7 present three burials from Bermondsey exhibiting a markedly different spatial patterning of skeletal elements from those presented above. The upper limbs are not resting together over the chest region as the *Ulr* and the *Bern* prescribe; they are positioned alongside the body. Considering individual 123, no constrictions are evident across the skeleton, and the lower limbs are asymmetrically positioned and distinctly apart; a tight wrapping is not in evidence. As this individual decomposed in a 'filled space' (note, for example, numerous bones have remained in highly unstable positions), significant post-depositional movement within a void cannot account for this positioning. The thoracic cage of individual 49 appears strongly constricted, with a distinct separation from the humeri. Its rectangular profile is comparable to examples recorded by Buquet-Marcon, Pecqueur and Detante (2009: 68) and Fossurier (2009: 22); here, clothing incorporating a constrictive bust with independent sleeves was proposed. Overall, these particular individuals demonstrate few skeletal characteristics for body preparation in strict accordance with the late eleventh-century Cluniac Customaries for the treatment of a brother. As will now be shown, intersite patterns can offer

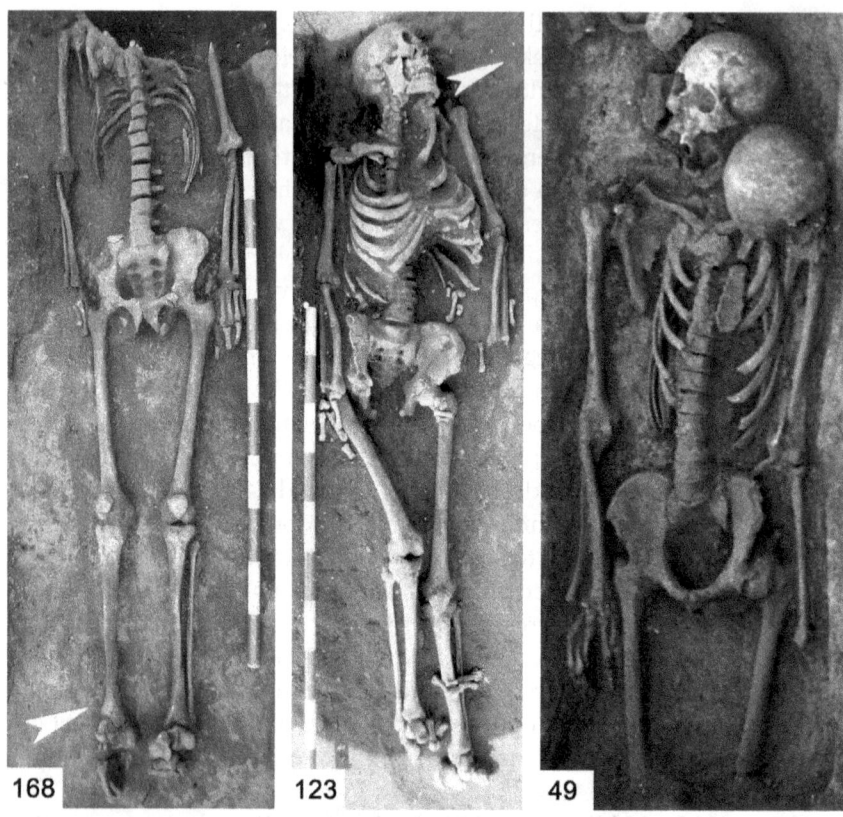

Figure 14.5–14.7 Individuals from Bermondsey Abbey exhibiting no clear skeletal evidence for preparation in line with the *Bern* (photographs courtesy LAARC/Museum of London)

further insight into the nature and use of these documents within these two monastic communities.

Notre Dame, La Charité-sur-Loire and Bermondsey Abbey: The Burials

Established entirely from new under Hugh's abbacy (1049–1109), Notre Dame, La Charité-sur-Loire and its daughterhouse, Bermondsey Abbey (founded c. 1059 and c. 1089, respectively) were two of Cluny's larger and more important dependencies. As Cluniac visitation records show (see Duckett 1890), both enjoyed considerable status within the network (particularly La Charité), possessing their own dependencies and acquiring authority over monitoring conformity of practice within other Cluniac houses, directly subordinate or otherwise. It is thus not unreasonable to propose that relatively close adherence to Cluny's customaries may have been both strongly encouraged and actively sought within these two establishments.

Excavations at Bermondsey Abbey were conducted by the Department of Greater London Archaeology/Museum of London (1984–88). A total of 202 individuals were recorded from discrete graves dating from roughly 1100 to 1430. They derived predominantly from a cemetery area south of the priory church, where Brian Connell and William White (2011) identified 137 males and possible males, eight females and possible females, and only one individual aged fifteen or under. Based on the age and sex profiles, it has been proposed that the cemetery zone could have catered for the interment of Bermondsey's adult male monastic community (Dyson et al. 2011: 131). Although the rare inclusion of females and possible females indicates that this zone cannot have been used exclusively for Bermondsey's male monastic population, arguably the demographic profile appears to be fairly representative of the house's living community.

In 2003, David Billoin (INRAP) directed the excavation of forty-six Cluniac-period burials from La Charité-sur-Loire. Thirty-seven derived from a cemetery area to the east of the priory church (dated to the mid eleventh to early thirteenth centuries) and nine were recorded from within a later gallery built directly over this cemetery zone in the early thirteenth century. This structure connected the main priory church with the annex church of Saint Laurent (Billoin 2005: 39–40). Osteologist Luc Staniaszek identified twenty-four males and possible males from the discrete graves. When including all disturbed skeletal remains, there were over one hundred individuals; no females and only two individuals under the age of sixteen were recorded. This predominately adult male composition does not reflect a regular population and, similarly to Bermondsey, fits with the monastic nature of the site (Billoin 2005: 77).

A broad intersite assessment of individuals in discrete graves from both sites revealed, overall, a marked variation in the spatial arrangement of skeletal elements, possibly in part indicative of differences in pre-interment body preparation. It should be noted that a taphonomic study was undertaken of each individual from La Charité and Bermondsey (Williams 2015). For the former, this built on the detailed assessment conducted by Staniaszek (2005). Where the original position of skeletal elements could not be confidently ascertained due to post-depositional disturbance (e.g. by animals, water action, grave intercutting or during excavation) or from significant movement during decomposition (particularly when it occurred within a void), these individuals were not considered.

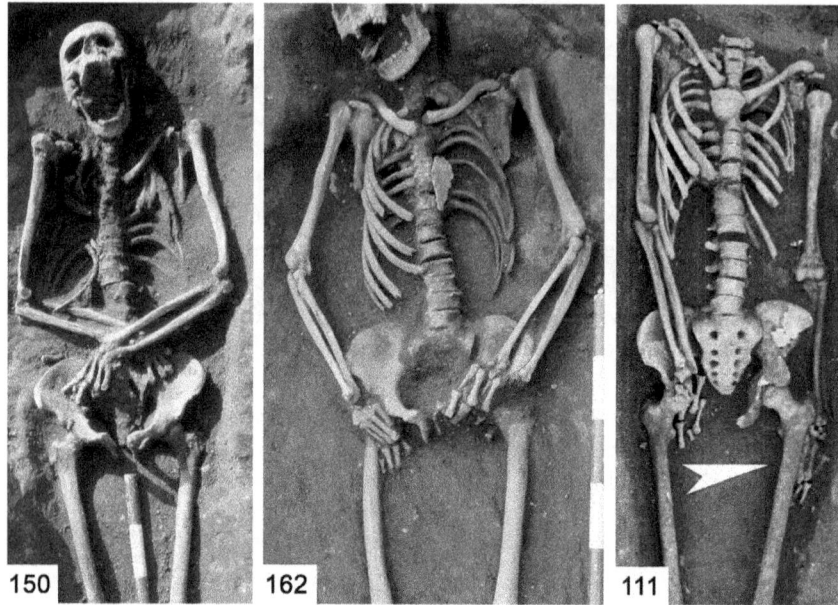

Figures 14.8–14.10 Individuals from Bermondsey Abbey exhibiting varied forearm positions (photographs courtesy LAARC/Museum of London)

A much stronger degree of uniformity in forearm and lower limb positioning was recorded in those from La Charité. Here, for the twenty-four individuals where the position of both forearms could be assessed, all were arranged over the body; only four exhibited a distinct asymmetry between the left and right. Fourteen had their forearms positioned together at roughly right angles across the upper body (see, for example, burial 157; Figure 14.1). Those from Bermondsey exhibited a greater degree of variation. Of 107 assessed individuals, 23 per cent (n=25) exhibited a clear asymmetry between sides, where a joining of upper limbs together during the preparatory rites could not be convincingly supported. Furthermore, 20 per cent (n=21) had one or both positioned alongside the body, in clear contravention of all three later Cluniac Customaries. For the vast majority of the remainder, there was a greater extension at the elbows, where the forearms were either crossed or uncrossed, with the hands positioned over the pelvic region (Figure 14.8–14.10).

Proximity of the lower limbs was assessed to gauge the extent to which the *Bern*'s prescription for the cowl to be sewn so that no part is loose, the body shrouded and for the night slippers to be joined together may have been adhered to. Taking ≤ 5 cm apart at the knees and ankles as a measure

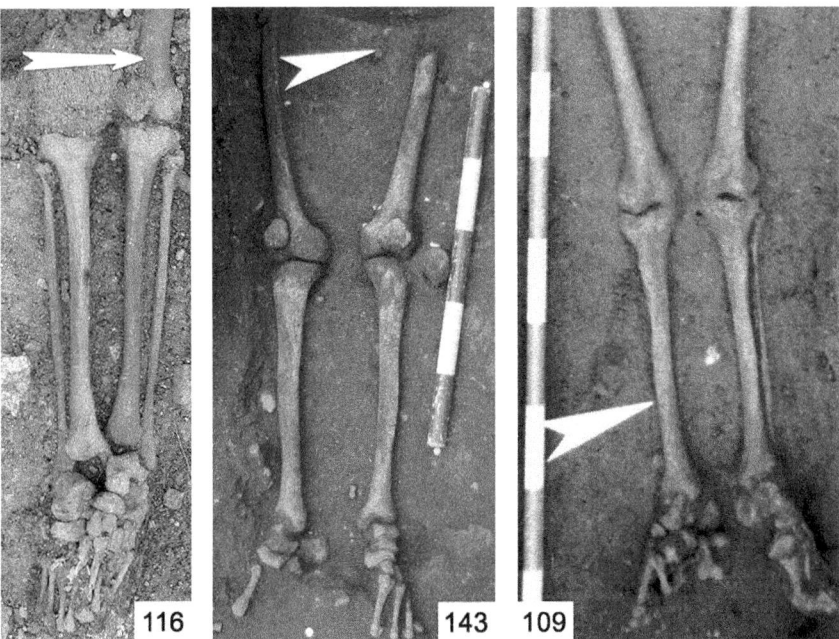

Figures 14.11–14.13 Examples of lower limb positioning in individuals from La Charité (116; photograph by David Billoin/©INRAP) and Bermondsey Abbey (143, 109; photographs courtesy LAARC/Museum of London)

for convergence (see Buquet-Marcon, Pecqueur and Detante 2009), inter-site differences appeared marked. Of the thirty-two individuals from La Charité who could be assessed, 66 per cent (n=21) exhibited a convergence (≤ 5 cm apart) at both the knees and ankles. The feet were in strict contact (often with a comingling of bones in a clearly delineated space) or the majority of foot bones were positioned close (≤ 5 cm apart; Figures 14.4 and 14.11). Those from Bermondsey exhibited more varied positions. Of eighty-three assessed individuals, 24 per cent (n=20) demonstrated a clear convergence, where the feet were also together or close. Knees and ankles in 31 per cent (n=26) of individuals were distinctly separate, often significantly more than 5 cm apart and the feet had clearly decomposed independently (Figures 14.6, 14.12 and 14.13). A total of 19 per cent (n=16) demonstrated a convergence at the knees and ankles, but the feet were clearly out-turned; a sewing together of night shoes and an additional wrapping could not be convincingly supported.

Considering evidence for wrappings, as presented above, of the thirty-one individuals from La Charité who could be assessed for overall body preparation, 61 per cent (n=19) exhibited evidence for bone constrictions possibly deriving from a wrapping. Those from Bermondsey exhibited skeletal profiles more markedly at odds with the *Bern*'s prescriptions, where a distinct lack of uniformity across the sample was noted. Of the ninety-nine assessed individuals, only 17 per cent (n=17) demonstrated osteological evidence for some form of constrictive wrapping.

Between Cluniac Text and Practice: A Discussion

Overall, interments from La Charité exhibited greater osteological evidence for closer adherence to the *Bern*'s method of pre-interment body preparation for a brother. Relative proximity to the motherhouse, Cluny, could have enabled, and resulted in, a more direct, frequent and potentially monitored transfer of practical knowledge. The desire for La Charité to mirror Cluny's splendour is evident in the architectural developments (see Barnoud 2010); closer adherence to Cluny's highly esteemed funerary customs may therefore also have been more actively sought or imposed. Given that La Charité was one of Cluny's five principal daughters, its brethren could also have been expected to set an example to resident and visiting monastics of 'correct' practice in accordance with Cluny's desires.

For Bermondsey's 'monastic cemetery', the stronger degree of variability in limb positioning together with limited evidence for wrappings as prescribed within the later eleventh-century Cluniac Customaries are undoubtedly the result of many interrelated factors. However, it should be stressed that these customaries were compiled based on practice within a significantly larger, more elite establishment. Wollasch (1990: 52) has estimated that by the early twelfth century, between three hundred and four hundred monks resided at Cluny. The prescribed death and burial rites involved the whole community of monks and were greatly protracted and elaborate. Undoubtedly under great scrutiny and required to 'set the standard' for its many dependencies and admirers, transmitting an image of spiritual grandeur and practical perfection was clearly essential to Cluny. This could also be argued for La Charité. Such concerns may not have been afforded equal weight within other, lower-status foundations, therefore potentially resulting in greater adaptation or curtailment of the funerary procedure to suit the individual community's requirements. As the documentary evidence demonstrates, Bermondsey's community was significantly smaller, with the house suffering numerous and sustained periods of crippling debt, flooding and political uncertainty (see Duckett 1890; Dyson et al. 2011). Less focus overall may have been placed on exacting Cluny's customs at all times.

In exploring the relationship between monastic text and practice, as seen through the archaeological evidence, the establishment's individual circumstances should therefore be considered, regardless of whether they belonged to the same order. No two houses were the same, for which the documentary record offers invaluable insights. In considering the meaning of texts and the multiplicity of ways in which they may have been understood, the specific contexts in which they were created and used, and by whom they were read, are critical (see Moreland 2001). The degree and nature of adherence to regulatory texts is equally context-specific. For instance, heads of Cluniac communities were frequently moved between houses (see Knowles, Brooke and London 2001), thus potentially prompting impartation of new interpretations on customary practice acquired from previous houses (Cluniac or non-Cluniac) or based on personal readings of the texts. The individual agency of senior monastics in effecting varied responses to the customaries' prescriptions should therefore be considered.

The customaries have been described as 'living texts' where their prescribed practices could be adapted to suit the community's needs (Kerr 2007: 14–15). If Paxton (2005) is correct and the *RC* influenced the *LT*, the former must have remained an influential force within English monasticism for a number of years. It states that a monk should be buried in clean clothes, including a shirt, cowl, stockings and shoes, no matter what his rank (*RC*: cap. XII, p. 65); no mention is made of upper limb positioning, for instance. The *RC*'s influence on funerary practice at Bermondsey cannot be proven, but the possibility that such pre-existing regulatory texts were afforded some authority within a newly founded Cluniac establishment cannot be dismissed. The status of 'foreign house' was at times a major hindrance to Cluniac foundations in England (see Dyson et al. 2011: 73–78); under certain circumstances, an association with established English monastic customs or explicitly non-Cluniac practice may thus have been keenly sought. The specific spatial and temporal contexts within which these texts were being circulated are thus crucial to consider, where in this case, the changing political environment may have variably influenced adherence to them on an individual site basis.

Considering both sites overall, slight or significant variability in body preparation between individuals is to be expected, even where rigid adherence to the Cluniac Customaries was actively pursued. These texts clearly outline the ideal death and burial. The *Bern* (cap. XXIV, p. 191), for instance, states that death should not come unexpectedly, but in reality this would frequently have been unavoidable. Death from an infectious disease, for example, may have necessitated rapid burial with limited bodily interaction, certainly not to the degree required by the *Bern*. This could, for instance, explain the unusual and seemingly haphazard body positioning recorded for Bermondsey burial 123 (Figure 14.6). Harvey (1993: 113) reports on the obituary records from Christ Church Cathedral Priory, Canterbury, demonstrating that funeral rites of plague victims had to be curtailed, even to the extent that interment took place at night. Nilsson Stutz (2008) reminds us that as archaeologists, we should not forget the 'biological reality' of the dead body, yet it is often overlooked in our enquiries. The *Bern* specifies highly regimented funerary procedures, but a fresh cadaver is not so easily regulated. In reality, processes such as *rigor mortis*, which sets in around two to four hours (but can sometimes be instantaneous) and can last for up to thirty-six hours (Nilsson Stutz 2003: 143), may have necessitated advancing, delaying or adapting the customary rites. Other monastic customaries were cognizant of practical issues and regulated for them; Ælfric's eleventh-century letter to the Monks of Eynsham, for instance, specifies that a stole should be placed over the cowl, but only if resources permit (Jones 1998: 143). These examples demonstrate the complex relationship that existed between the ideal scenarios laid down in monastic customaries and the practicalities of realizing them, for which texts, individuals, objects, the biological (and at times unpredictable) realities of death and broader social, political and economic circumstances were all intimately entwined.

Conclusions

The discussed texts, as Cochelin (2000: 22) writes, offer a 'selective snapshot' of Cluniac customs, where they 'strove to outline everything considered worthy of admiration in Cluny's activities'. They may thus have been in part intended as a 'public declaration of how it did things and a monument to collective pride' (Constable 1998: 173). In this respect, the Cluniac Customaries should not simply be seen as oppressive vehicles through which spiritual and practical control was sought over the dependencies. Rather, these shared documents could also positively reinforce community ties, uniting the order's far-flung congregation in common practice (or at the very least an understanding of what it should be) and a shared sense of identity and pride, regardless of how rigidly the customs were actually followed. These malleable documents thus played a central role in structuring monastic relationships and were in turn structured by them.

An ideal depiction of Cluniac practice they may thus have been to a degree, but Bernard (like Ælfric) was also realistic in the extent to which certain elements of practice could be regulated. His text explicitly permitted the custom of burial to be changed if required by a reasonable cause (*Bern*: cap. XXIV, p. 196); what constituted 'reasonable' would undoubtedly have been variously interpreted. This deliberate ambiguity in the textual record has therefore left the door wide open for individual responses, which are diversely manifested in the archaeological record. There is thus meaning in what is included in texts, but also in what is purposefully omitted or left ambiguous. Our archaeological enquiries should take into account these intricacies in the textual record, alongside the diverse range of factors influencing individual and group responses to rules and regulation, if we are to develop a more nuanced approach to the relationship between text and practice.

Paxton (2005: 304–5) has proposed that Bernard could have been an *armarius* (liturgical director). As such, he would have had close involvement in the funerary rites and would thus have been acutely aware of death's inherent unpredictability and the resulting difficulties of practically regulating its biological reality. Charged with important administrative duties at Cluny itself and writing at a time of rapid expansion, Bernard must also have been conscious of the diversity of houses in existence and of the difficulties in imposing and regulating such rigid and protracted funerary procedures. An ideal scenario was thus knowingly presented within the Cluniac Customaries and, as such, fluidity in adherence was arguably more likely to be tolerated. Interestingly, Cluniac visitation records document how rigorously certain practices related to daily life were regulated and managed when abuses crept in. The Prior of Horton was given strict injunctions never to ride without leggings or a crupper for his saddle, or for the brothers to eat meat in the presence of secular persons (Duckett 1890: 16). These publicly observable activities were clearly of particular concern. Cluny was undoubtedly intent on promulgating an image of perfection to monastics and laity alike. During the funeral of a monk, however, the *Bern* (cap. XXIV, p. 192) specifies that the monastery should be shut away from the outside world; the monks were not permitted to leave. Access may also have been limited or denied for the laity. Behind closed doors, away from the public gaze, deviations in practice from the Cluniac Customaries could thus also have been more readily accepted. These documents thus acquired meaning and significance not simply through being read and used, but also through the process of witnessing (or not) the enactment of their prescribed practices by the various religious or lay audiences. The degree of observation and by whom were also therefore key factors underlying the extent to, and manner in which, these texts could be adapted and, more generally, the extent to which elements of prescribed monastic practice were more stringently imposed.

Acknowledgements

I would like to express my sincerest gratitude to David Billoin (INRAP), the Museum of London, Museum of London Archaeology,and the London Archaeological Archive and Research Centre (LAARC) for their assistance with site documentation. I would also like to thank my co-editors and reviewers for all their valuable comments.

Eleanor Williams is Lecturer in Archaeology at Canterbury Christ Church University, United Kingdom, specializing in human osteology, zooarchaeology and medieval archaeology. She gained her Ph.D. from the University of Southampton, United Kingdom, on burial practices in Cluniac monasteries in England and France, with a particular focus on the relationship between practice and the Cluniac customaries. She has presented and published on different aspects of her research, including with the Centre d'Archéologie et d'Histoire Médiévales des Etablissements Religieux. She is currently collaborating at CCCU on the HLF sponsored community project 'Finding Eanswythe: The Life and Afterlife of an Anglo-Saxon Saint'.

References

Primary Sources

Antiquiores Consuetudines Cluniacensis Monasterii, Ulrich of Cluny, ed. J.-P. Migne. 1853. *Patrologia Latina, Vol. 149*. Paris: Petit-Montrouge, col. 635–778.
Benedicti Regula, Benedict of Nursia, ed. R. Hanslik. 1960. *Corpus Scriptorum Ecclesiasticorum Latinorum 75*. Vienna: Hölder-Pichler-Tempsky.
Liber Tramitis Aevi Odilonis Abbatis, ed. P. Dinter. 1980. *Corpus Consuetudinum Monasticarum 10*. Sieburg: Franz Schmitt.
Ordo Cluniacensis, Bernard of Cluny, ed. M. Herrgott. 1726. *Vetus Disciplina Monastica*. Paris: Osmont, pp. 133–364.
Regularis Concordia, Æthelwold of Winchester, ed./trans. T. Symons. 1953. *Regularis Concordia: The Monastic Agreement of the Monks and Nuns of the English Nation*. New York: Oxford University Press.

Secondary Literature

Barnoud, P. 2010. 'La Charité-sur-Loire, un monastère dans la ville', *Bulletin du Centre d'Études Médiévales d'Auxerre* 3: 2–12.
Billoin, D. 2005. *La Charité-sur-Loire: Square des Bénédictins*. Dijon: Inrap GES.

Boynton, S. 2005. 'The Customaries of Bernard and Ulrich as Liturgical Sources', in S. Boynton and I. Cochelin (eds), *From Dead of Night to End of Day: The Medieval Customs of Cluny*. Leiden: Brepols, pp. 109–22.

———. 2006. *Shaping a Monastic Identity: Liturgy and History at the Imperial Abbey of Farfa 1000–1125*. New York: Cornell University Press.

Boynton, S., and I. Cochelin (eds). 2005. *From Dead of Night to End of Day: The Medieval Customs of Cluny*. Leiden: Brepols.

Buquet-Marcon, C., L. Pecqueur and M. Detante. 2009. 'Parés d'habits invisibles', in B. Bizot and M. Signoli (eds), *Rencontres autour des Sépultures Habillées*. Gap: Editions des Hautes-Alpes, pp. 65–75.

Cochelin, I. 2000. 'Besides the Book: Using the Body to Mould the Mind – Cluny in the Tenth and Eleventh Centuries', in G. Ferzoco and C. Muessig (eds), *Medieval Monastic Education*. Leicester: Leicester University Press, pp. 21–34.

Connell, B., and W. White. 2011. 'Human Remains', in T. Dyson, M. Samuel, A. Steele and S.M. Wright (eds), *The Cluniac Priory and Abbey of St Saviour Bermondsey, Surrey: Excavations 1984–95*, MOLA Monograph 50. London: Museum of London Archaeology, pp. 263–74.

Constable, G. 1998. *The Reformation of the Twelfth Century*. Cambridge: Cambridge University Press.

———. 2010. *The Abbey of Cluny: A Collection of Essays to Mark the Eleven-Hundredth Anniversary of its Foundation*. Berlin: Lit Verlag.

Duckett, G.F. 1890. *Visitations of English Cluniac Foundations*. London: Kegan Paul, Trench, Trübner & Co.

Duday, H. 2009. *The Archaeology of the Dead: Lectures in Archaeothanatology*. Oxford: Oxbow.

Dyson, T., M. Samuel, A. Steele and S.M. Wright (eds). 2011. *The Cluniac Priory and Abbey of St Saviour Bermondsey, Surrey. Excavations 1984–95*, MOLA Monograph 50. London: Museum of London Archaeology.

Fossurier, C. 2009. 'Le site de Chanteloup-en-Brie (Ile de France): études de cas et difficultés d'analyse taphonomique', in B. Bizot and M. Signoli (eds), *Rencontres autour des Sépultures Habillées*. Gap: Editions des Hautes-Alpes, pp. 21–27.

Gazeau, V. 2004. 'La mort des moines: sources textuelles et méthodologie (XIe–XIIe siècles)', in A. Alduc-Le Bagousse (ed.), *Inhumations et Édifices Religieux au Moyen Âge entre Loire et Seine*. Caen: CRAHM, pp. 13–21.

Harvey, B. 1993. *Living and Dying in England 1100–1540: The Monastic Experience*. Oxford: Oxford University Press.

Jones, C.A. 1998. *Ælfric's Letter to the Monks of Eynsham*. Cambridge: Cambridge University Press.

Kerr, J. 2007. *Monastic Hospitality. The Benedictines in England, c. 1070–c. 1250*. Woodbridge: Boydell Press.

Knowles, D., C.N.L. Brooke and V.C.M London (eds). 2001. *The Heads of Religious Houses: England & Wales, I. 940–1216*. Cambridge: Cambridge University Press.

Krüger, K. 2005. 'Monastic Customs and Liturgy in the Light of the Architectural Evidence: A Case Study on Processions (Eleventh–Twelfth Centuries)', in S. Boynton and I. Cochelin (eds), *From Dead of Night to End of Day: The Medieval Customs of Cluny*. Leiden: Brepols, pp. 191–220.

Lyne, M. 1997. *Lewes Priory: Excavations by Richard Lewis 1962–82*. Lewes: Lewes Priory Trust.
Melville, G. 2005. 'Action, Text, and Validity: On Re-examining Cluny's Consuetudines and Statutes', in S. Boynton and I. Cochelin (eds), *From Dead of Night to End of Day: The Medieval Customs of Cluny*. Leiden: Brepols, pp. 67–83.
Moreland, J. 2001. *Archaeology and Text*. London: Duckworth.
Nilsson Stutz, L. 2003. *Embodied Rituals and Ritualized Bodies: Tracing Ritual Practices in Late Mesolithic Burials*. Stockholm: Almqvist & Wiksell International.
———. 2006a. 'Setting it Straight. A Re-analysis of the Mesolithic Barum Burial According to the Principles of Anthropologie de Terrain', *Lund Archaeological Review* 11–12: 37–46.
———. 2006b, 'Unwrapping the Dead: Searching for Evidence of Mortuary Practices at Zvenjnieke', in L. Larsson and I. Zagorska, (eds), *Back to the Origin*. Stockholm: Almqvist & Wiksell, pp. 217–33.
———. 2008. 'More than a Metaphor: Approaching the Human Cadaver in Archaeology', in F. Fahlander and T. Oestigaard (eds), *The Materiality of Death: Bodies, Burials and Beliefs*, British Archaeological Reports International Series 1768. Oxford: Archaeopress, pp. 19–28.
Palazzo, E. 1998. *A History of Liturgical Books from the Beginning to the Thirteenth Century*. Minnesota: Order of St. Benedict, Inc.
Paxton, F.S. 1993. *A Medieval Latin Death Ritual: The Monastic Customaries of Bernard and Ulrich of Cluny*. Missoula, MT: St Dunstan's Press.
———. 2005. 'Death by Customary at Eleventh-Century Cluny', in S. Boynton and I. Cochelin (eds), *From Dead of Night to End of Day: The Medieval Customs of Cluny*. Leiden: Brepols, pp. 297–314.
———. 2013. *The Death Ritual at Cluny in the Central Middle Ages*. Leiden: Brepols.
Saurette, M. 2005. 'Excavating and Renovating Ancient Texts: Seventeenth- and Eighteenth-Century Editions of Bernard of Cluny's Consuetudines and Early-Modern Monastic Scholarship', in S. Boynton and I. Cochelin (eds), *From Dead of Night to End of Day: The Medieval Customs of Cluny*. Leiden: Brepols, pp. 85–107.
Staniaszek, L. 2005, 'V. Catalogue des sépultures', in Billoin, D. (ed.), *La Charité-sur-Loire*, Dijon: Inrap GES, 81–180.
Williams, E. 2015. 'Fresh Cadaver to Skeletal Matter: Text, Practice and the Cluniac Death-Course', Ph.D. dissertation. Southampton: University of Southampton.
Willis, A., and N. Tayles. 2009. 'Field Anthropology: Application to Burial Contexts in Prehistoric Southeast Asia', *Journal of Archaeological Science* 36: 547–54.
Wollasch, J. 1990. 'Les moines et la mémoire des morts', in D. Iogna-Prat and J.-C. Picard (eds), *Religion et Culture autour de l'An Mil*. Paris: Picard, pp. 47–54.

Chapter 15

'With as Much Secresy and Delicacy as Possible'
Nineteenth-Century Burial Practices at the London Hospital

Louise Fowler and Natasha Powers

Introduction

The Royal London Hospital was founded as the London Infirmary in 1740. It soon became known as the London Hospital (the 'Royal' suffix was given on its 250th anniversary in 1990) and moved from the eastern outskirts of the City of London to a new purpose-built hospital about a mile further to the east, in rural Whitechapel. When the new building first opened its doors to patients in 1757, the hospital was surrounded by farmland, although it was easily reached from the City. During the nineteenth century, the area became rapidly urbanized (Fowler and Powers 2012: 13–20).

'The London', as it is affectionately known, was one of the first charitable hospitals founded across London and in many English counties throughout the eighteenth century. Its patients were largely the working poor – those who might be prevented from working through illness or injury. They received treatment so that they were able to return to work without becoming a burden on parish funds (Rivett 1986; Lane 2001: 44–57). As such, the incurable were often excluded.

Patients were admitted via two main routes. Some were recommended for treatment by one of the hospital's many governors, who subscribed funds to the charity, either annually or for life. Prospective patients attended one of the weekly meetings of the House Committee with a letter of recommendation. If admitted, they were not charged fees (unlike some other London institutions). From its inception, the London admitted 'extra cases necessary for the preservation of life' (as they were described in the hospital records), in addition to those recommended by the governors. Often these were cases arising from accidents, but they also included those suffering from acute medical conditions (Fowler and Powers 2012: 95).

The London was the first hospital in England with an attached medical school: the London Hospital Medical College was founded by Sir William Blizard and Dr James Maddocks in 1785. Blizard believed passionately that better care and treatment would result from the opportunity to learn both principles and practice in the same institution. Initially the hospital governors were wary of this new development and the college was run independently of the hospital, without access to the funds of the charity and on the promise that hospital patients were not to be used for demonstrations (Clark-Kennedy 1962: 166; Ellis 1986: 5–9).

In common with other hospitals, the London had to deal with the problem presented by patients who died within its walls leaving no friends or relatives who were able to take the body away for burial. Some hospitals charged patients a returnable 'burial fee' on admission to cover the costs if they died during treatment. The London buried its dead patients within its own grounds and from its own funds (Fowler and Powers 2012: 23). From c. 1800 to 1841, the hospital burial ground was conveniently located to the east of the east wing of the hospital, directly behind the medical college (Fowler and Powers 2012: 24–27).

In advance of the construction of a new hospital building, Museum of London Archaeology (MOLA) was funded by SKANSKA Barts and the London to undertake a programme of archaeological work at the site. The main phase of excavation took place in 2006, when archaeologists excavated a group of inhumations from a portion of the burial ground which was in use from c. 1825 to 1841, the period immediately prior to and following the passing of the Anatomy Act of 1832 (2 & 3.Will.4.c.75). Attempts to identify archaeological and documentary evidence for this important change in the law led us to the realization that the excavated burials are the product of many complex relationships between rule creators, rule enforcers and rule breakers. Here we consider how those who produced the archaeological record were both affected by rules and involved in their creation: the Governors of the hospital who prescribed rules to be followed; the students and their lecturers in the dissecting room; the House Governor Reverend Valentine, who read the funeral services over the deceased; the hospital staff and porters who interred, disinterred and re-interred remains to supply the medical college, and the public, who were not always silent in their observations.

The Anatomy Act of 1832

From the eighteenth century onwards, anatomical dissection had become increasingly important as a means of medical teaching, but before 1832 the only way of legally acquiring a 'subject' for dissection was to obtain the remains of an executed criminal (Richardson 2001: 32–37). Supply did not meet the demand from the growing number of medical schools, and disregard for the law was widespread. The medical profession turned to the services of the 'resurrection men' who acquired bodies (frequently but not always through grave-robbing or 'resurrecting') at a price. Often dismissed as opportunistic criminals, there was in fact a core group of established professionals operating in London at the beginning of the nineteenth century, and they were able to hold the medical profession to ransom somewhat. Sometimes resurrection men were prosecuted and jailed, but the punishment was not heavy; as a dead body could not be 'owned', charges involved the stealing of clothes or belongings on the corpse (Richardson 2001: 54–71). In 1823 William Millard and Cornelius Bryant were sentenced to six months at the treadmill under the terms of the recently passed Vagrancy Act (3 Geo. IV c.40, 1822) for being unable to give a good account of what they were doing in the London Hospital burial ground at one o'clock in the morning (Fowler and Powers 2012: 201–2). Millard was more educated than most resurrection men, having previously been employed as superintendent of the dissecting room at St Thomas' Hospital. The medical profession largely supported men like Millard and Bryant when they found themselves on the wrong side of the law, providing security for bail and assisting them financially whilst they were serving jail sentences (Richardson 2001: 86). Sir Astley Cooper, in a letter to Robert Peel requesting clemency for the unfortunate Millard, by then in a state of ill health, claimed that without such offences as that for which Millard was in reality incarcerated being committed, 'science must perish' (Agnew 1963: 176). Clearly in Cooper's mind, the crime of resurrection was a lesser evil than that of hindering medical progress, and he was not alone in this view.

The Anatomy Act of 1832 (2 & 3.Will.4.c.75) was intended to break the stranglehold of the resurrection men and effectively permitted institutions such as hospitals, prisons and workhouses to give up to anatomists the 'unclaimed' bodies of deceased inmates.

Many viewed the prospect of dissection as punishment for poverty, and with good reason, since this fate was one that had previously been reserved for the worst of criminals, the purpose to specifically deny the corpse a proper burial (Richardson 2001: 35–37). Uncertainty in the teachings of the Church regarding the status of the physical corpse and the soul after death, including beliefs in the physical resurrection of the body on the Day of Judgement, also contributed to fear of dissection amongst the general public (Richardson 2001: 15–17, 77; Cherryson 2010: 141). A partial attempt to assuage this fear was provided in Section 13 of the Anatomy Act, which was concerned with the 'decent' burial of dissected remains:

> Provided always, and be it enacted, That every such Body so removed as aforesaid for the Purpose of Examination shall, before such Removal, be placed in a decent Coffin or Shell, and be removed therein; and that the Party removing the same, or causing the same to be removed as aforesaid, shall make Provision that such Body, after undergoing Anatomical Examination, be decently interred in consecrated Ground, or in some public Burial Ground in use for Persons of that religious Persuasion to which the Person whose Body was so removed belonged; and that a Certificate of the Interment of such Body shall be transmitted to the Inspector of the District within Six Weeks after the Day on which such Body was received as aforesaid. (2 & 3. Will.4.c.75: sec. 13)

Any initial clarity soon gives way to deliberate obfuscation and ambiguity; reference is made to 'anatomical examination' rather than dissection (Richardson 1987: 128, 204; Hurren 2012: 28–29), putting in mind a less destructive practice more in common with autopsy or a post-mortem examination. Dissection usually involved the complete dismembering of the body, leaving little but fragments of flesh and bone (Richardson 2001: 128; Cherryson 2010). Those without direct experience of the practice of dissection were left to draw their own conclusions about exactly what the practice of 'anatomical examination' entailed.

Similarly, the Anatomy Act did not provide guidance as to what constituted a 'decent burial'. There was widespread noncompliance with this section of the Act, and the Inspector of Anatomy often encountered problems including bodies being kept for longer than six weeks, and the absence or even falsification of Certificates for Interment (Richardson 2001: 243). This was the only section of the Act to be amended later in the nineteenth century, to permit bodies to be kept for up to six months and eventually for up to two years (Richardson 2001: 255; Hurren 2012: 31). Elizabeth Hurren (2012: 30) notes potential divergence between a 'decent' burial and a dignified one: a 'decent' burial was the best possible under the circumstances, while a dignified one respected cultural expectations, whatever the financial implications.

The Act was controversial and its administration was shrouded in secrecy, with considerable effort spent on hiding its full workings from the general public. Evidence for wrongdoing and noncompliance was often suppressed; crimes went unpunished out of fear of the social unrest and cessation of supply that bad publicity might bring (Richardson 2001: 240–58). Later in the nineteenth century, the administration of the Act fell under the Official Secrets Act of 1889 (Hurren 2012: 71). There appears to have been a concerted attempt to hide from the public the full reality of an 'anatomy burial'.

Deception, falsification and the persistent use of euphemism in the historical literature cloud the reality of how a 'pauper funeral' differed from an 'anatomy burial'. Hurren writes that 'for many, the latter was too awful to write down or speak out loud' (Hurren 2012: 71). George J. Guthrie (Professor of Anatomy and Surgery at the Royal College of Surgeons), writing in 1829 (before the Anatomy Act was passed), claimed that it was impossible to give dissected remains a decent burial, as it simply was not possible to store up all the separated parts of a body dissected over a long period of time (Wise 2004: 250). Archaeological evidence for the burial of anatomized remains is therefore particularly important in understanding how the letter of the Act translated into practice.

Archaeological excavations in Britain have uncovered relatively little evidence for the burial of dissected human remains. However, the discovery of individuals who underwent autopsy to understand cause of death, which became increasingly common during the eighteenth and nineteenth centuries, is not unusual (Cherryson 2010: 143; Fowler and Powers 2010: 4). There are a small number of groups of dissected remains thought to have been curated for a time before burial: a deposit of dissected human and animal remains from Surgeon's Square, Edinburgh (Henderson, Collard and Johnston 1996), a group of dissected and disarticulated human and animal remains interpreted as a discarded teaching collection buried during construction work in the late eighteenth century in Oxford (Hull 2003), and in London, a group of eighteenth-century dissected remains given an informal burial in the basement of Benjamin Franklin's House, Craven Street (Hillson et al. 1999; Kausmally 2010). Dissected remains have also been found associated with charitable hospitals at Newcastle Infirmary, Worcester Royal Infirmary and the Radcliffe Infirmary, Oxford (Boulter, Robertson and Start 1998; Western and Kausmally 2014; L. Loe pers. comm.). Within the excavated burial ground at Newcastle, there were a small number of formal burials of dissected material, with further evidence coming from four large charnel pits (Boulter, Robertson and Start 1998). At Worcester, dissected remains were amongst the disarticulated material found within two large pits and a disturbed layer (Western and Kausmally 2014).

The London Hospital Burial Ground

The excavated section of the London Hospital burial ground contained the remains of at least 259 individuals within regularly spaced graves, each containing up to eight burials (coffins). The practice of stacking coffins within graves is well known from other excavated post-medieval burial grounds in London. However, the site is particularly unusual in that many coffins contained the partially articulated remains of several people interred together and seventy-five graves also contained the remains of animals. All of the primary inhumations (largely complete individuals who were considered to be the principal occupant of each coffin and were found throughout the cemetery) were extended and supine, aligned east-west and, in all but two cases, lay with the head to the west. The burials of partially articulated remains followed a similar pattern, so that where the remains were within a standard kite-shaped coffin, the 'head' lay to the west.

The remains were buried in simple wooden coffins of the same specification as those supplied to the Whitechapel Union for the burial of parish paupers (Fowler and Powers 2012: 33), though the coffins had largely decayed. A finger ring on the hand of a female skeleton is the sole find that might be taken to be a personal possession. The decay of the coffins made it difficult or impossible to ascertain precisely how many burials were placed within each grave, but it is worth noting that the estimated number of 262 burials is close to the minimum number of individuals represented by the skeletal remains. Unfortunately, no burial registers for this period have survived within the hospital records, so it is not possible to determine the size of the excavated burials as a proportion of the buried population.

Three distinct groups of burials were identified (Figure 15.1). The first (group 20) consisted of fifty-two regularly spaced graves in up to six rows – a total of 118 burials. These graves lay within a wall that is shown on a reconstructed plan of the hospital in c. 1830 (Figure 15.2) and therefore represent the earliest group. To the east of the cemetery wall shown on the plan was a further group of sixteen graves containing seventy-four burials (group 21). The graves were also regularly spaced but deeper, with six unusual graves dug end to end. The more densely packed burials in this group, and the use of an area outside the original confines of the burial ground, suggest an increasing pressure for space and indicate that these burials are later in date. A final group of burials was identified to the south of this. Group 22 consisted of seventy tightly packed burials, which had been stacked up to five deep on a contemporary ground surface and covered with rubble. It is almost certain that these burials were moved in

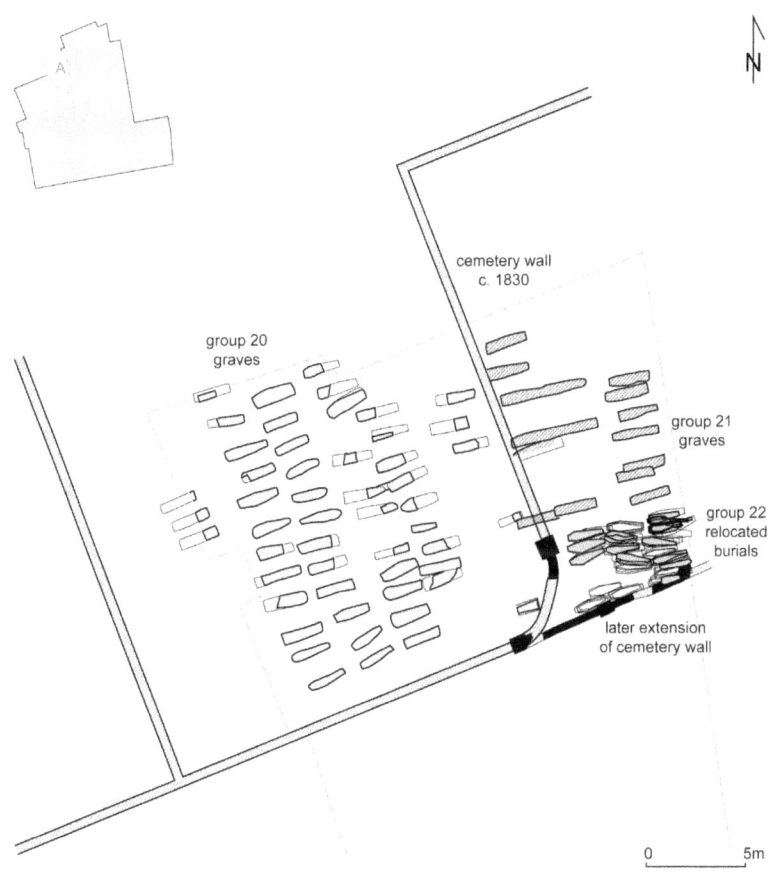

Figure 15.1 Plan of the excavated burial ground (illustration by Carlos Lemos/©MOLA)

c. 1841, when an extension to the east wing of the hospital was built across a portion of the burial ground. The burials lay up against the foundation of a wall for the new burial ground, which was constructed to the south at the same time. Some of the remains within this final group did not appear to have been buried within standard coffins, but it is unclear whether the material was originally interred in this way or was disturbed during relocation. A large deposit of disarticulated bone (containing the remains of a minimum of thirty-six individuals) is thought to derive from the reburial of remains disturbed during later construction work and it is highly probable that all human remains were originally buried within formal graves (Fowler and Powers 2012: 28–33).

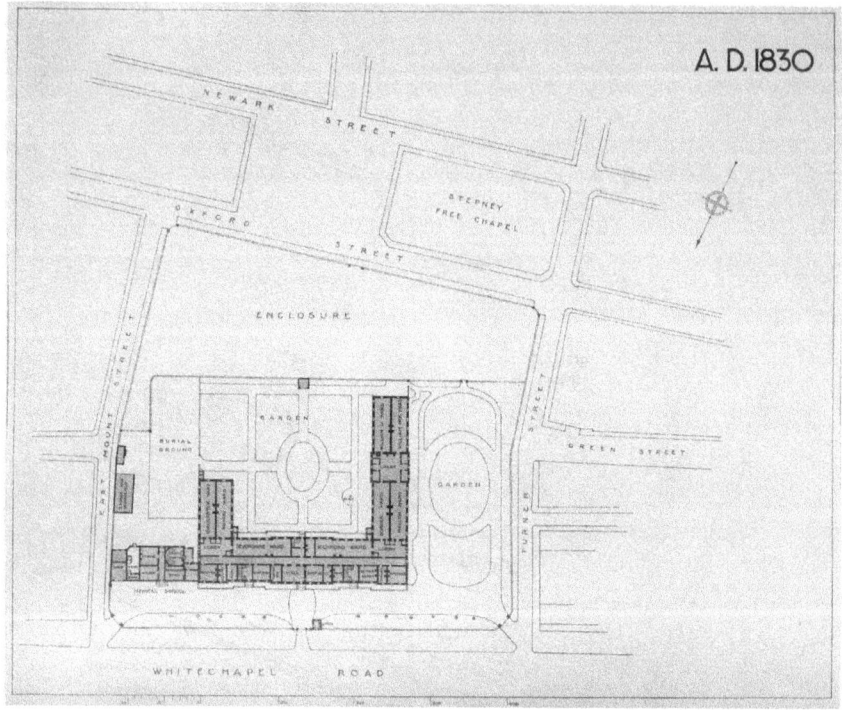

Figure 15.2 J.G. Oatley's (?1907) reconstructed plan of the hospital buildings in c. 1830 (scale is in feet) (LH/S/1/21)

The burials are likely to be the unclaimed remains of patients who had died during treatment. Male [124] is likely to have been admitted as an 'extra case'. He had a fractured femur (thigh bone), the result of a fall or high-impact collision, in which the initial stages of healing could be observed, suggesting that he had died within three weeks of receiving his injury (Fowler and Powers 2012: 66). Male [242] provided the best evidence of a patient who did not survive surgery. His left hand had been amputated and although it was not clear whether this had occurred before or after death, he also had a healing fracture to the rib, possibly indicating an accident that had also caused an injury to his hand (Fowler and Powers 2012: 136). Evidence for autopsy (limited post-mortem investigation, with the opening of the thoracic cavity and/or cranium and a maximum of one further investigation, e.g. sawing through the pubis or posterior spine) was observed in 27.7 per cent of the primary inhumations (48/173; Fowler and Powers 2012: 194).

The burials of partially articulated remains probably included surgical waste from amputations; it is virtually impossible to differentiate between

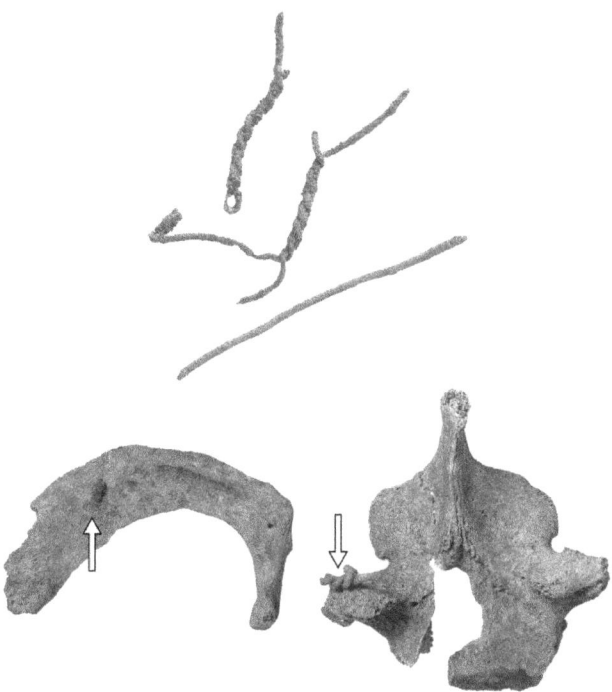

Figure 15.3 Copper-alloy wire <86> and a rib and vertebra with drilled holes from [23401], found in association (photograph by Andy Chopping/©MOLA)

surgical waste and material derived from surgical teaching, during which students practised such operations on cadavers. Nonetheless, much of the partially articulated material is certainly derived from the dissecting room of the medical school. In addition, the remains included material used in teaching; bones that had been perforated by small holes to allow suspension and articulation with copper alloy wire and iron pins (Figure 15.3) (Fowler and Powers 2012: 189–91). A numbered bone label found with one burial may derive from a prosection (prepared teaching specimen) used in the medical school. This indicates that some remains were curated for a time before burial. There was also evidence for activity with no apparent medical benefit or educational purpose: a section of femur appeared to have been worked on a lathe and another had been filed, both probably with the intention of turning the bone into artefacts (Fowler and Powers 2012: 186–87).

Bodies used for dissection may also have come from other sources: the convicted murderer Elizabeth Ross was conveyed to the London Hospital for dissection following her execution in January 1832 (Dobson 1951: 120), and 'subjects' may also have been supplied by the resurrection men or even by the staff of other hospitals. After the Anatomy Act, the hospital is known to have supplemented its own supply with bodies received from workhouses (Richardson 2001: 243). Remains buried after coroners' inquests may also have been interred within the hospital burial ground (Fowler and Powers 2012: 194). Given that admissions procedures at the London excluded young children and pregnant women, a portion of foetal remains with staining that indicated their preparation as a specimen may well have been a teaching aid, which had been specifically bought in from elsewhere.

It can be inferred that the regular spacing of the rows of graves indicates that they were dug and filled in sequence. Although the precise sequence could not be determined, some areas of the burial ground would have been in use before 1832, whilst the burials in other areas (e.g. group 21) post-dated the passing of the Anatomy Act. Groups 20 and 21 were examined to look for possible changes in practice that might be related to the introduction of the Act, including the proportion of dissected remains, the inclusion of dissected animal remains and the presence of burials of remains that had been reunited for burial. No evidence for change could be discerned (Fowler and Powers 2012).

A 'Decent' Burial

Although Section 13 of the Anatomy Act (2 & 3.Will.4.c.75: sec. 13) specified that the body had to be removed from the place of death to the anatomy school in a 'decent Coffin or Shell', it did not specify that the dissected remains should be buried in the same. With no definition of a 'decent' burial, there was potential for differing interpretations. Detailed study of historical accounts has allowed us to gain some understanding of the relationship between rules and practice at the London.

Prior to 1832, one individual had undertaken a personal battle to ensure a degree of respect for those who were dissected within the medical school. In 1818, the House Committee of Governors decided to unite the previously separate roles of Superintendent and Chaplain into one post. They appointed the Reverend William Valentine as House Governor, responsible for the day-to-day running of the hospital as well as its spiritual wellbeing. He remained in this role until 1840. His religious background and lack of medical experience often brought him into conflict with the medical staff (Fowler and Powers 2012: 111–14). Although little mention is made of the illegal practices within the hospital and its medical school, an insight is provided when, in 1823, the body of a young woman was stolen from the dead house. During the following investigations into whether staff of the hospital had been receiving money to supply bodies to the students, Valentine reported back to the committee that: 'The subject was brought, incidentally, before the Committee in November [1822], + several present expressed their opinion that the Bodies of Patients unclaimed by their friends, should be devoted to the school; at that time I dissented from that opinion.' By the following year, he 'could scarcely make up [his] mind between the claims of professional science, + the feelings of regret that such proceedings should be necessary' (LH/A/17/3: 75–77).

Valentine, perhaps more than any other individual, was responsible for the burial of the remains in the excavated burial ground. He was in post throughout its use and he conducted the funeral services. When the Anatomy Act was passed in 1832, he expressed concern to the House Committee: 'Whether the Burial Service can with propriety be performed at the interment of the remains of such bodies of Patients as may have been submitted to Anatomical examination; and if so what possible provisions may be made, with a view of precluding such a performance from being a desecrating of that most solemn and affecting service of the Church' (LH/A/5/19: 339). This statement highlights his fears about whether Section 13 of the Act truly provided for a 'decent' burial in the eyes of the Church. A little illumination is provided by contemporary accounts, which suggest that prior to the 1832 Act, Valentine had negotiated a way in which he could bring the practices of the medical school more in line with his Christian beliefs. Ann Millard, the widow of one of the men arrested in the hospital burial ground in 1823, noted that patients who had died in the hospital were interred in the burial ground 'for the sake of appearances' before being transferred to the dissecting room (Millard 1825: 25). The account is supported by Valentine's own report to the House Committee:

> I have had an opportunity of conferring with Mr Headington [Surgeon and Lecturer in the Medical College], who informed me, that during the winter months, in which dissections and Lectures are given, the School is supplied with subjects chiefly from the Burying Ground of the Hospital, + that He himself pays the Theatre + Surgery Beadle for their trouble in procuring them from the Ground with as much secresy and delicacy as possible; that this is the practice of other Hospitals , + has been of this, ever since there have been Lectures and dissections here, + no obstacles have been thrown in the way by the House Committee, but they had always calculated on their conviction of its necessity, + therefore on their affording every facility, except their public concurrence. (LH/A/17/3: 78)

This may explain Valentine's later concerns about the provisions of the Anatomy Act and the way in which he had come to accommodate the practices of the medical school. If a Christian funeral service had been properly performed prior to dissection, then to some extent a 'decent' burial had been performed and the soul of the deceased had been safeguarded. Millard also wryly noted that Valentine was 'a strenuous advocate for the rights of the Church, and the strict observance of decency, seldom permitting a deceased patient to be dissected before burial' (Millard 1825: 27). However, the Anatomy Act only provided for the funeral service to be performed after dissection. This created a particular problem, and Valentine attempted to negotiate changes to the hospital's own practice and standing orders to maintain a practice of 'decent' burial. The House Committee resolved to draw the attention of all the medical staff to Section 13 of the Act, and informed them that only anatomical examination consistent with that section was to be permitted, and that the remains of each body were to be 'kept separate and distinct' for burial (LH/A/5/19: 339).

Evidence from the burial ground suggests that reuniting of remains for burial was not universal: there were eighteen burials with evidence for the practice from group 20 (18/118, 15 per cent), twenty from group 21 (12/74, 16 per cent) and four from group 22 (4/70, 6 per cent) (Fowler and Powers 2012: 197). The practice could be identified during the osteological examination by visually and metrically matching paired elements and/or by directly reuniting articulated elements from within the same coffin, but that had clearly been separated from each other by saw and knife and no longer lay in anything resembling anatomical association – for example, the right and left hip and the upper leg, bisected along the midline of the body, or paired dissected knee joints. Most notable were the jumbled, portioned limbs of one individual placed within the same coffin and an adult mandible sawn into three parts, all found within different areas of the grave. Although there are a slightly higher number of examples of the practice from group 21, instances appear to be spread spatially throughout the burial ground. This suggests that the reuniting of remains was carried out throughout the time in which the burial ground was in use and was neither a response to nor prevented by the introduction of the Act. The lack of reunited burials from group 22 might be a product of the movement of the remains from their original burial context, or may indicate that they came from a part of the burial ground in use when the practice was not common. The practicalities of reuniting remains for burial were difficult: a shortage in supply and the problems created by a lack of refrigeration meant that cadavers were often shared between several students and that dissection might take place over several weeks. In all cases, although parts had been reunited, the body was not complete. For example, the limbs of one body were interred together in spite of multiple saw cuts portioning them into 'standard' sections, but the lower left leg, torso and head were absent (Figure 15.4). In burial [166] the left leg had been sawn through above the knee and portions of femoral shaft from two other adults had been placed within the grave as if to make up for the absence of the lower leg (Fowler and Powers 2012: 197). This is particularly intriguing since the substitution would have been immediately

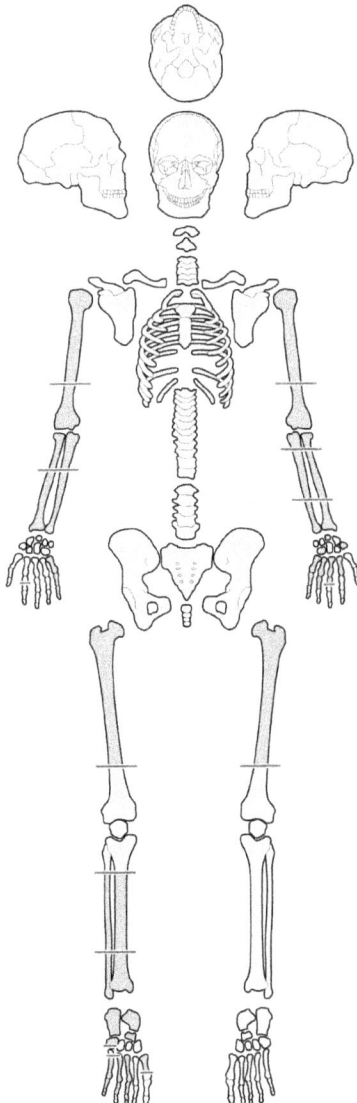

Figure 15.4 Context [52203] showing standardized portions reunited for burial (illustration by Judit Peresztegi/©MOLA)

obvious to even the lay person, supposing the coffin were to be open and inspected – though perhaps the additional weight provided by the intrusive legs would have prevented awkward questions when lifting a closed casket. It is equally plausible that the burial of the unfortunate subject of an unsuccessful amputation simply provided a convenient location to dispose of other medical waste, whilst the offending limb itself was retained for further study. Perhaps the reuniting of remains for burial was an ideal to which those preparing them for interment aspired and endeavoured to achieve, but that it was not always practical to attain.

Some of the dissected remains may not have received a formal burial at all: the cranium was underrepresented amongst the remains and there were eight instances of burials where the head and neck appeared to have been retained. This may indicate the subsequent further dissection of the head, resulting in the creation of numerous disarticulated fragments, which could not be recognized as associated with any particular individual. Alternatively, and perhaps more likely, it may demonstrate the retention or sale of head and neck specimens (Fowler and Powers 2012: 180). The section of femur, which had been worked on a lathe, was a 'waste' piece, so presumably the remainder of the bone was worked into a finished artefact and that was retained (Fowler and Powers 2012: 186). Retention of dissected remains was not explicitly permitted by the Anatomy Act, but nor was it prohibited (Richardson 2001: 244–45).

Valentine's report to the House Committee indicates that although members of the House Committee (perhaps not all) were aware that practices within the hospital and medical school violated the law, they effectively 'turned a blind eye' so long as those practices were not brought to the attention of the public. The events of 1823 provided unwelcome attention; the House Committee strongly pursued the conviction of Millard and Bryant, and directed that a notice be displayed on the walls of the burial ground stating that trespassers would be prosecuted 'with the utmost severity of the Law' (LH/A/5/17: 263). During the subsequent trial and appeal, Blizard told Millard that 'we shall be very happy to accommodate any lecturer who may be in want of our assistance, but we must not have things taken away by force' (Millard 1825: 31). Valentine implies that in acting with 'secresy and delicacy' in their own proceedings, the servants of the school had observed a sense of decency that was violated by the intruders in the burial ground. The need for 'secresy and delicacy' is also seen in an unwillingness to properly minute relevant sections of the House Committee meetings, presumably because these were documents that might be consulted by others. Much of the detail provided to the House Committee by Valentine survives only in his own notebooks. Indeed, Valentine himself claimed to have been discouraged by

Committee members from bringing the question of what best to do about dissection before the House Committee, being told that it was 'better to abstain from bringing it into discussion' (*LH/A/17/3*: 77).

It should also be noted that the burial ground at this time lay directly below the windows of several wards in the east wing of the hospital, and it was the patients and members of staff who raised the alarm after noticing intruders in the burial ground. The patients' view of what constituted a 'decent' burial may have varied from that of the governors and staff. To the latter, a 'decent' burial was one that did not draw attention. In that sense, 'decency' was equated with 'secresy and delicacy'. In this deception the fully dissected contents of many of the coffins were effectively hidden from the gaze of the patients.

The coffin itself is a powerful symbol, evoking the presence of one individual within it, and few observers might have questioned whether this was in fact the case. The suggestion that burying the remains within coffins was in part motivated by these practicalities, rather than an overriding sense of respect for the dead, may also help to explain the presence of dissected animal remains amongst the burials. Perhaps it was simply convenient to dispose of all the remains from the school in the same way. Alternatively, perhaps 'hiding' the dissected animal remains reduced the likelihood of patients becoming concerned about the goings on within the medical school.

Conclusions: Law Breaking at the London

The gap between practice and the written laws, bye-laws and standing orders intended to govern actions within the hospital can perhaps be understood by observing how individuals and groups attempted to rationalize their actions.

The motives of the governors and the hospital chaplain (to cure as many patients as possible as quickly as possible) at first seem incompatible with those of the teaching staff of the medical school (to further medical science), but the reality was not simply a conflict and ensuing struggle for power. The most influential staff of the London at this time claimed to have a genuine wish to cure and to relieve the suffering of the sick, and this was backed up by their actions. Richard Headington lectured his students that 'an unfeeling heart, harshness of character, or insensibility to human suffering, should form no part of a surgeon's composition' (Headington 1824: 35–36) and that 'anatomy is studied with a view to perfect education ... the happiness of many is to be confined to our care', though 'there are prejudices to surmount, and difficulties to overcome of a peculiar nature, but which even the anatomist would not wish to have entirely removed' (Headington 1825: 63–64). Sir William Blizard espoused similar views and in 1791 established a Samaritan Society, to which many of the medical staff subscribed funds, to provide relief for patients who had been discharged from the hospital, but who needed financial assistance or items such as glasses or artificial limbs. Before the society was founded, Blizard had been using his own money for this purpose (Clark-Kennedy 1962: 182). Valentine acted as almoner for the society. His changing views regarding the necessity of anatomical dissection clearly spring from discussions with the medical staff and a new conviction that furthering medical science would reduce the suffering that must have been all too apparent to a man so embroiled in the daily functioning of the London. This longer-term view provided a framework, which united governors and staff, and meant that some transgressions of rules could be tolerated as long as 'secresy and delicacy' were maintained.

It is particularly interesting to note that the method of supplying subjects for dissection at the London prior to 1832 was legitimized by the Anatomy Act. In 1823 Sir Astley Cooper asked a number of prominent anatomists about potential alternatives to the reliance on the resurrection men. Only two of the nine men suggested the 'unclaimed' dead from hospitals as a potential supply, although four were in favour of using the 'unclaimed' dead from workhouses (Richardson 2001: 163). After conversing with 'many Governors of Hospitals', the Home Secretary Robert Peel found that 'without the existence of any legislative authority for it, a pretty free use is made of the bodies of those who die in public Hospitals' (*Bentham/XI/184*, cited in Richardson 2001: 111).

It is possible that by the time that the Anatomy Act was introduced, the practices in use at the London and seen at other hospitals (including those on the continent) had provided evidence for an effective alternative model that would enable the supply of corpses to medical schools and break the hold of the resurrection men.

Louise Fowler is Post-Excavation Manager at MOLA (Museum of London Archaeology), United Kingdom. Since receiving an M.Phil. in Archaeology from the University of Cambridge in 2005, she has been working on commercial projects in London both in the field and in the office, and is particularly interested in the deeply stratified and multiperiod urban sites of the City and Westminster. She is co-author with Natasha Powers of *Doctors, Dissection and Resurrection Men* (2012), the monograph that reported on the excavation of the early nineteenth-century burial ground associated with the London Hospital in Whitechapel.

Natasha Powers is Senior Manager at Allen Archaeology Ltd, based in Lincoln. An archaeologist and osteologist, she has analysed everything from prehistoric cremation burials to nineteenth-century inhumations and has published widely on a variety of related subjects. She is currently working with the Humboldt-Universität zu Berlin, Germany, researching the origins of the medieval population of the city. Her research interests lie in the integration of osteological information with other strands of archaeological evidence to provide a holistic picture of our past. She is an honorary research fellow at the University of Bradford and previously held the same position at the University of Birmingham.

References

Primary Sources

2 & 3.Will.4.c.75. Parliament of the United Kingdom.1832. Anatomy Act – An Act for Regulating Schools of Anatomy.

3.Geo.4.c.40. Parliament of the United Kingdom. 1822. Vagrancy Act – An Act for Consolidating into One Act and Amending the Laws Relating to Idle and Disorderly Persons, Rogues, and Vagabonds, Incorrigible Rogues and Other Vagrants.

Bentham/XI/184. University College London Special Collection, London, UK (letter of Sir Robert Peel to Jeremy Bentham, 1826).

LH/A/5/17. Royal London Hospital Archives & Museum, London, UK (herein after RLH) (minute book of the meetings of the House Committee; commencing 2 January 1821).

LH/A/5/19. RLH (minute book of the meetings of the House Committee, commencing 6 January 1831).

LH/A/17/3. RLH (*House Governor's Report Book,* 20 August 1822 to 7 December 1824).

LH/S/1/21. RLH (J.G. Oatley's (1907?) reconstructed plan of the hospital buildings in c. 1830).

Secondary Literature

Agnew, L.R.C. 1963. 'Sir Astley Cooper and William Millard – A Vindication', *Journal of the History of Medicine and Allied Sciences* 18(2): 176–78.

Boulter, S., D. Robertson and H. Start. 1998. *The Newcastle Infirmary at the Forth, Newcastle upon Tyne, Volume II. The Osteology: People, Disease and Surgery.* Sheffield: ARCUS.

Cherryson, A. 2010. 'In the Pursuit of Knowledge: Dissection, Post-mortem Surgery and the Retention of Body Parts in 18th- and 19th-Century Britain', in K. Rebay-Salisbury, M.L.S. Sørensen and J. Hughes (eds), *Body Parts and Bodies Whole*. Oxford: Oxbow, pp. 135–48.

Clark-Kennedy, A.E. 1962. *The London: A Study in the Voluntary Hospital System Vol. 1, 1740–1840*. London: Pitman Medical Publishing Co.

Cooper, B.B. 1843. *The Life of Sir Astley Cooper, Bart (Volume 1)*. London: John W Parker.

Dobson, J. 1951. 'The "Anatomizing" of Criminals', *Annals of the Royal College of Surgeons of England* 9(2): 112–20.

Ellis, J. 1986. *LHMC 1785–1985: The Story of the London Hospital Medical College*. London: London Hospital Medical Club.

Fowler, L., and N. Powers. 2012. *Doctors, Dissection and Resurrection Men: Excavations in the 19th Century Burial Ground of the London Hospital, 2006*, MOLA Monograph 62. London: Museum of London Archaeology.

Headington, R. 1824. 'No Title', *The Lancet* 3(54, 9 October 1824): 33–37.

———. 1825. 'No Title', *The Lancet* 5(109, 8 October 1825): 61–64.

Henderson, D., M. Collard and D.A. Johnston. 1996. 'Archaeological Evidence for 18th Century Medical Practice in the Old Town of Edinburgh: Excavations at 13 Infirmary Street and Surgeons' Square', *Proceedings of the Society of Antiquaries of Scotland* 126: 929–41.

Hillson, S., T. Waldron, B. Owen-Smith and L. Martin. 1999. 'Benjamin Franklin, William Hewson and the Craven Street Bones', *Archaeology International* 2: 14–17.

Hull, G. 2003. 'The Excavation and Analysis of an 18th-Century Deposit of Anatomical Remains and Chemical Apparatus from the Rear of the First Ashmolean Museum (Now the Museum of the History of Science), Broad Street, Oxford', *Post-Medieval Archaeology* 37(1): 1–28.

Hurren, E.T. 2012. *Dying for Victorian Medicine: English Anatomy and its Trade in the Dead Poor, c.1834–1929*. Basingstoke: Palgrave Macmillan.

Kausmally, T. 2010. 'William Hewson and the Craven Street Anatomy School', *American Journal of Physical Anthropology* 141(Supplement 50): 140.

Lane, J. 2001. *A Social History of Medicine: Health, Healing and Disease in England 1750–1950*. London: Routledge.

Millard, A. 1825. *An Account of the Circumstances Attending the Imprisonment and Death of the Late William Millard*. London: Ann Millard.

Richardson, R. 2001. *Death, Dissection and the Destitute*, 2nd edn. Chicago, IL: University of Chicago Press.

Rivett, G. 1986. *The Development of the London Hospital System, 1823–1982*. Oxford: Oxford University Press.

Western, A.G., and T. Kausmally. 2014. *Osteological Analysis of Human Remains from the Worcester Royal Infirmary, Castle Street, Worcester*. Worcester Archaeology Research Report no 3. Worcester: Worcestershire County Council

Wise, S. 2004. *The Italian Boy: Murder and Grave-Robbery in 1830s London*. London: Pimlico.

The Archaeology of Rules and Regulation
Closing Remarks

Duncan H. Brown

Very few societies operate without hierarchies and the degree of their immutability is surely what gives rise to the creation and enforcement of various systems of governance. The 'rules' presented and discussed in this collection do not necessarily represent the setting of high level laws, but just as there are social hierarchies, so it is possible to perceive distinctions between them. There are rules that are adhered to implicitly and could therefore be characterized as custom; those that are understood to be a common responsibility; those that are seen to protect; those that symbolize accepted, shared behaviours. Indeed, rules and regulations may be founded in notions of cultural custom, responsibility, security and continuity. As such, those that follow them accept regulation as a sort of glue that binds and in some way defines their 'civilization'. Those who live by no rules are therefore regarded as more primitive in almost every sense. If it is understood that civilization means to enforce an identity in ways that are social, economic, geographical and political, then it is possible to see regulation as operating at those levels too. Some rules, in fact, must have developed out of responses to external forces, such as the environment, natural resources and human relations, progressing from habit, to custom, to undeniable law. This may be why rules provide the means to settle disputes, because they have formalized what everyone should know and understand. There are also, however, rules that are imposed and have no origin in a mutual framework of practice or necessity. These sharpen the tensions inherent within hierarchies, especially between the 'doers' and the 'done to', and can prompt change. This will often be formulated in opposition, which can also occur on a number of levels, including ambivalence, adaptation, unpredictability or defiance. Rules may change simply because nobody takes any notice of them or nobody is seriously enforcing them; alternatively, whole social systems may change, or be reborn, due to openly hostile opposition. If archaeology is, in part at least, the observation of change and a search for reasons for it, then it has to be important to understand what systems of regulation defined human behaviour. The chapters collected here address this in a variety of ways, across many chronological periods, but they all aspire to evaluate and elucidate changes that stem from rule-making.

In examining regulation using a multidisciplinary approach, certain fundamental questions arise: what did rules do; who were rules for; how did rules work? The chapters collected here offer answers from various perspectives, but may be unified in their consideration of those fundamental issues. In cases of defiance, it is temptingly easy to characterize rule-makers and rule-breakers as diametrically opposed, but even then, there are surely nuances that the study of material culture can illuminate. As archaeologists know, the remnants of human actions can reveal much more than chronological or technical progression and they also do much more than enhance the written record. Discarded animal remains, buried humans, the artefacts of imprisonment and changes in building form can all provide insights into how rules and hierarchies were established, enforced and countered, simply by reflecting how diverse people can be. Here, therefore, it is possible to look at how the effects of rules are manifested in physical evidence, and where they vary from written accounts. Archaeology can add a further dimension and it is therefore worth thinking about how archaeological methods might be developed specifically to examine issues of regulation. The same should also apply to archaeological theory, as is shown in Chapter 1 on Southampton. Indeed, throughout this collection, theory provides an essential backdrop to these case studies, giving rise to further questions, such as what conformity would look like archaeologically and how far variance can go before it becomes counteraction. Uniformity among transatlantic Swedish settlers, for instance, reflected the opposite of acquiescence, but how easy is it to recognize that from the archaeological evidence alone? A major strength here is the willingness to use documentary and archaeological sources as codependant; casting light not only on rules in the past but also on our own conventions and procedures. In so doing, we bring to the surface an understanding of subconscious rule-following and this too should be recalled as we examine the evidence of the past. If we are defined by inherent behaviour or accepted norms, then are we also defining the construct that is habitus? How close can archaeology and history bring us to human thought as well as action? It is noteworthy that all these contributions are based in historical periods and a next step should surely be to take interpretations of observed phenomena into the undocumented past. As is shown here, there are various ways of responding to regulation, each resulting in archaeological patterns that, without knowledge of the rules that gave rise to them, could be understood in different ways. It also seems to be the case that it is variance from the regulated norm that is most frequently offered and more easily understood, and archaeologists are generally no strangers to nonconformity. The underlying theme is that of relationships: within and between hierarchies; among those who set rules and those who either follow them or do not; between physical and written sources; and among archaeological disciplines. If rules are guidelines for the establishment and preservation of relationships, then the analysis presented here is a good first step in developing new connections and opening more lines of enquiry.

Duncan H. Brown is Head of Archaeological Archives for Historic England, having previously been Curator of Archaeology at Southampton Museum. He is a specialist in medieval archaeology and particularly the study of pottery, being the author of *Pottery in Medieval Southampton c. 1066–1510* (CBA, 2002) and a former president of the Medieval Pottery Research Group.

Index

A
Abd al Rahman III, 256–57, 266
afterlife, 255, 273–78, 285, 287
al-Andalus, 6, 256–57, 266, 268
alcohol: class and, 185–87; Islam and, 263; military culture and, 107, 171–73, 186–87; in New Sweden, 87, 93; prohibition of, 94–96, 98–99, 169–173, 185–87, 263; trade and, 94–96, 98–99
alcohol bottles, 176–78, 181, 183, 186
Anatomy Act of 1832, 5, 7, 235, 313–15, 320–22
animals: bone handicraft and, 54; bones of, 53–54, 66–68, 70–71; in Diepensee, 66–67; disposal of, 70–71, 74–75, 77; as non-food animals, 67, 244–45, 248–49, 263; use of bone in pavement in, 53. *See also* cattle; dogs; horses; meat; sheep/goats
Anselm, 274–75
anthropologie de terrain, 295
archaeology: active role of material culture and, 9–10; critique of, 25; documentary records and, 1–2, 12–14, 21–23, 25, 31, 105–6, 214, 227–28, 330–31; human-animal relations in, 238; of legal culture, 2, 14; ontologies and, 9–12; patterns of behaviour in, 238; pork in, 47, 53–55, 67, 239, 241, 244, 263; social theory and, 1; of spaces, 150
archaeothanatology, 295–96
architecture: boundaries and, 113; communality and, 105–6; emigration and, 88–91; as familiar, 88–91; identity and, 36; importance of, 7; meaning of, 7; mercantile class houses and, 36; in New Sweden, 88–91. *See also* asylums; castles; churches; institutions; longhouses; prisons; theatres
Armagh Asylum (County Armagh, Northern Ireland), 203
asylums: advancements in, 195–96; architecture of, 192; churches and, 192–94, 197–98, 201, 203–6; gender and, 204–5; history of, 195–96; hygiene in, 201; increased use of, 195; Irish system of, 194–98, 201, 203–4; layout of, 204–5; marginalization of patients of, 207–8; material culture of, 192; moral management of, 195–96, 200; non-restraint system and, 200, 208; open-plan wards of, 201; overcrowding

asylums (*cont.*)
of, 200; for paupers, 193; prisons and, 192; regulation of space in, 107, 204–5; religion and, 192–94, 196–98, 201; as a total institution, 206; urban growth and, 195; workhouses and, 192
Aquinas, Thomas, 274–75
Augustine of Hippo, 274

B
Bab Al-Hanax, 264
bakers, 29, 35
Bankside (London, England), 151
baptisms: of children, 275, 278–79; emergency, 275; miracle, 287; post-mortal, 287; St George and, 285
Behan, Brendan, 213
Belfast Agreement of 1998, 216
Belfast District Lunatic Asylum (Belfast, Northern Ireland), 197
Benedictine Abbey (Göttweig, Austria), 234, 279–280, 284
Bermondsey Abbey (London, England), 291–92, 296, 299–305
bestiality, 245–46, 249
Berthold of Regensburg, 46, 275
Binckson, John, 92
biographies: of bodies, 7; of material culture, 8, 14; of places, 6; rules and, 8–9; of things, 6, 63, 215, 217; of waste, 8
'black boxes', 11, 32
Blizard, William, 312, 326
bone morphology: bone strength and, 255; diet and, 255; entheseal changes and, 255; gender division of labour and, 257–260; hyperdorsiflexion and, 260–63; Islam and, 255–56, 260–63, 267–68; limb use and, 255; mobility and, 255, 259; prayers and, 6, 260–63; rural versus urban and, 260; *salāt* and, 260–63; tibial facets and, 260–63
Boot Cotton Mills (Massachusetts, United States), 187
borough court (portmote), 131
boundaries, 111–14, 116–19, 120–22

Bourdieu, Pierre, 3, 21, 62, 65, 78
Breiter Markt (Tulln an der Donau, Austria): archaeology of, 48, 52, 55–56; butcher stalls of, 52; description of, 48; map of, *49*; meat production and, 52; rubbish management and, 50; selling of meat in, 52; use of bone in pavement in, 53; uses of, 48; wells of, 52
buildings, cultural memory and, 3
burh, 128
burial mounds, 112–13
butchers: bone handicraft and, 54; hygiene and, 29, 51; rubbish management and, 55–56; slaughterhouses and, 51; of Southampton, 29; use of bone in pavement in, 53
Butchers' Guild: Christianity and, 46, 50–51; competition and, 43, 45; hygiene and, 45; Jewish meat trade and, 45–46; Judaism and, 50–51; marketplace and, 47–50; market-related regulations and, 48; meat distribution and, 46, 56; meat prices and, 45, 56; meat production and, 46; moral standards of, 46; punishment, 45; rubbish management and, 55–56; rules of, 43–44, 52, 55–56; trade and, 43, 45, 48
byres, 106, 116–18

C
cadaver pits, 67–68, 70, 74–75
Carlow Asylum (County Carlow, Ireland), 203, 207
castellum (castle), 128–29, 131–32, 141–42
Castillo de Triana (Seville, Spain), 264–65
Castle Acre (Norfolk, England), 128–29
Castle Park (Cheshire, England): archaeological study of, 138; cartographic research of, 134–35; earthworks of, *136*; magnetometry geophysics surveys for, 135, 137–39;

moated enclosures of, 136, 138; mound in, 136, 138; Tithe Map of, 134–5, 139
castles: construction of, 139–140; definition of, 7, 11, 127–29, 139–142; galleries of, 162–63; great chambers of, 163; hall screens of, 161; internal porches of, 161; legal status of, 7; meaning of, 141–42; phases of, 139–140; power of, 7, 127–28, 141–42; privacy and, 161, 163–64; private rooms of, 161; promenading in, 162–63; seating in, 162–63; significance of, 7; theatres and, 160–63; vertical planes of, 160–64
castrum (castle), 128
Catholic Canon Laws, 276
Catholic Emancipation Act of 1829, 204
cattle, 45, 47, 53–55, 67, 90, 239–41, 244
cats, 242, 244
cemeteries: disinterment from, 320–21; as fields of discourse, 277–78; of the Royal London Hospital, 316–320; social relationships and, 277–78. *See also* child burials; St George infant cemetery
chaîne éliminatoire, 8, 62–65
chaîne opératoire, 6
charters, 26–27, 34, 38–39, 195
child burials: afterlife and, 276–77; archaeology of, 278–79; cemeteries for, 279; Christianity and, 273–77; in consecrated ground, 10, 273–77; dogs and, 244–45; of foetuses, 276; grave markers and, 283; grave orientation, 281, 286; heaven and, 284; identity and, 276–77, 283–84; *limbus puerorum* and, 10, 276, 279; pedobaptisms and, 275–76, 278–79; shroud burials, 281; spatial structure surrounding, 277–78, 283–85; for stillborn children, 276, 278–79, 286; Swiss folk stories and, 279
Christianity: afterlife and, 273, 276–77, 287; attitudes toward, 285–87; baptism and, 274; Butchers' Guild and, 50–51; child burials and, 273–77; dogs and, 235–36, 243, 247, 249; dominant power of, 275, 277, 285, 287; emergency baptisms, 275; heaven and, 277, 284; Iberia and, 256; Islam and, 257–58, 266, 268; *limbus puerorum* and, 273–75; as an ontology, 10; Original Sin and, 274–75; pedobaptisms and, 275, 287; rules and, 285–87; struggles within, 234; symbology of, 50–51; unbaptized children and, 273–77
churches: altars and, 158; communality of, 158–160; effigies in, 159; exclusive spaces of, 158–160; funerary monuments of, 159–160; hierarchies and, 159–160; interments and, 159–160; intervisibility in, 106, 159–160; privacy and, 158–160, 163–64; promenading in, 162–63; seating in, 162–63; theatres and, 149; vertical planes of, 158–59, 163–64. *See also* asylums
Clonmel Asylum (County Tipperary, Ireland), 203
clothing, 224–25, 256
Cluniac Customaries: adherence to, 234, 295, 298–300, 302–7; community ties and, 293, 306; dates of, 293; fluidity of, 5, 292–93, 295, 304–7; importance of, 293; material evidence of, 12–13, 292; monastic funerary rights and, 294–95; pre-interment body preparations and, 291, 294–95, 299–300, 305–6; regulation by, 293, 295
Cluniac monasticism, 292
Cluny (Saône-et-Loire, France), 292–94, 300, 304, 307
Cock, Per, 95
coffins, 314, 316–17, 322
commodification, 45–46
Common Book of Prayer, 158
communality: architecture and, 105–6; Cluniac Customaries and, 293, 306; guilds and, 32; resistance and, 38; rules and, 36
Conolly, John, 196, 200–1

conscriptions, 86
Conseil d'Etat, 31
conspicuous consumption, 39, 45
consumer research, 45–46
consumption, 8, 45–47, 55–56
copper, 84
Córdoba (Spain), 256, 260, 265
corpses: Anatomy Act of 1832 and, 313–15; interment of, 314; medical need for, 313; medical study of, 11; resurrection men and, 313; rules and, 11; supply of, 326. *See also* child burials; interments
Cortijo de Coracho (Córdoba, Spain), 259–261
Council of Rome in 1058, 286
County Asylums Act of 1808, 195–96
County Asylums Act of 1845, 197
Court Leet (Southampton, England), 28
Crusades, 257
The Curtain (London, England), 148–49, 151–52
Customary of Bernard (*Ordo Cluniacensis/Bern*), 293–94, 297–99, 304–5, 307
Customary of Ulrich (*Antiquiores Consuetudines Cluniacensis Monasterii/Ulr*), 293–94, 299

D
death: biology of, 296, 305, 307, 315, 318; and burial, 248, 291, 293, 304; conceptions of 5, 245, 255, 273, 276, 285, 305–6, 314; identity and, 6–7, 241, 276, 286, 306; during pregnancy, 276; place of, 320; St George and, 285; and ritual, 293–94, 304; violence and, 96;
death penalty, 94–95, 112, 119, 266
de Blundeville, Ranulf, 131–33, 139–140
deildegasten, 112
Delamere Forest (Cheshire, England), 132–33
Delaware River, 84, 86, 90, 92, 95–96
Derby Asylum (Derbyshire, England), 200–1

deserters, 86, 97, 171
Diepensee (Brandenburg, Germany): animal bones and, 66–68, 70–71; archaeology of, 70–74; assemblage of, 65–68, 70; ceramics of, 68, 70, 75; dating of, 65–66, 68–71; description of, 65–66; excavation plan of, *69*; fire of, 75–76; human remains and, 66
Diplock Courts, 216
diseases, 74–75, 305–6
documentary records: active nature of, 12; archaeology and, 1–2, 12–14, 21–23, 25, 31, 48, 105–6, 330–31; growth of, 22; legal status of, 2, 31; as material culture, 32; medieval mind and, 61; monasteries and, 61; regulatory, 2
dogs: as Associated Bone Groups (ABGs), 242, 247; bestiality and, 245–46, 249; bones of, 67, 71; cemetery burials of, 240–42; child burials and, 244–45; Christianity and, 235–36, 243, 247, 249; co-burials with humans, 235–36, 239–243, 246–47; cremation of, 240–42; different sizes of, 240; in early Anglo-Saxon England, 235–36, 241–43, 247–48; feral populations of, 244, 248; frequency of bones of, 239–241; in Germany, 241; hunting and, 243–46; individual burials of, 241–42, 246–48; in Ireland, 243; in late Anglo-Saxon England, 242–43, 245, 247–48; living conditions of, 240; in the Low Countries, 241; in middle Anglo-Saxon England, 242–43, 245, 247–48; as non-food animals, 67, 244–45, 248–49, 263; as a nuisance, 244, 249; ownership of, 243–44; perceptions of, 11–12, 235–36, 244–45, 247–49; as pets, 243–44; purposes of, 240, 243–44, 247–49; relationship with humans of, 240, 246–47; in Sancton I, 241; in Scandinavia, 241; as scavengers, 244, 248–49; in Spong Hill, 241; as status

Index

markers, 241; treatment of, 244, 247–49; value of, 239
Domesday Book, 128, 132–33
domus defensibilis (fortified house), 128
Doomsday, 276
Durand de Mende, Guillaume, 275

E

Ecclesiologist Movement, 198
Écija (Spain), 259–261, 264–65
El Molo (Spain), 264–65
emigration, 4, 87–88, 97–99
English Civil War, 235

F

famine, 208, 245
Fleischbänke, 52
Fleischhauerordnung, 43–44
Fleischmarkt, 52
folklore, 13, 112–13, 118, 120, 279
Forest Eyre of the Justiciar of Chester, 131–33
Forsa rune ring, 110, 119
Fort Christina (Delaware, United States), 84
Fort Hoskins (Oregon, United States), 186
The Fortune (London, England), 148, 151, 155–57
Fort Yamhill (Oregon, United States): alcohol-related artefacts of, 176–185; archaeological study of, 174–76; history of, 173; kitchen artefact assemblage from, 180–83; layout of, 10, 173–74, 179–180, 185–87; location of, 173–74; map of, 175; military culture and, 185–87; Native Americans and, 173; officers' quarters of, 174, 180; parade grounds of, 179; purpose of, 173; tobacco-related artefacts of, 177–185
Foucault, Michel, 212–13
Foulden cemetery (Norfolk, England), 241–42
Fourth Lateran Council of 1215, 56
Frey Haverstick Site (Pennsylvania, United States), 95–96

Frodsham Castle (Cheshire, England): archaeological study of, 139–140; boroughs of, 131; cartographic research for, 134–35; as a *castellum* (castle), 131–32; construction of, 129, 138–141; courts of, 131; defensive structures of, 139; description of, 131; evidence for, 129, 131, 133–34, 139–141; Goltho and, 139; the great chamber of, 131; hunting and, 132–33; importance of, 132; King Edward the Confessor and, 129; location of, 129–*130*, 138; magnetometry geophysics surveys for, 135; as manor house, 131–32; mound and, 139; oriel window of, 131–32; phases of, 139; port of, 131; Ranulf de Blundeville and, 131–33, 139–140; renovations to, 131–32; royal power and, 132–33; Sulgrave and, 139; value of, 131; water mill of, 131–34
funerary monuments, 113

G

garðr, 111
gender roles: bone morphology and, 257–260; food and, 46; Islam and, 256–260, 265, 267–68
Georgitag, 285
globalization, 45–46
The Globe (London, England), 148–49, 151–53, 155–56
gluttony, 46
Goltho (Lincolnshire, England), 136, 138–39
Göttingen (Niedersachsen, Germany), 76
Guild Merchant: administration of, 28, 38; bread prices and, 29; as charitable, 28; concerns of, 26–27; duties of, 28; history of, 38; hygiene and, 29; literacy and, 30; meat prices and, 29; membership of, 30; mercantile elite and, 30; municipal authority and, 27; night watches and, 28; power of, 27, 39; purposes

Guild Merchant (*cont.*)
of, 38; rubbish management and, 29; rules of, 28–29; of Southampton, 26–27, 29–30, 34, 38; trust and, 27, 30, 32, 34, 38; welfare and, 28

guilds: accumulation of wealth, 35–36, 39; community and, 32; as continuity, 32; credit and, 26; description of, 26; economic relationships and, 27; feasts of, 36, 40n4; king and, 26–27; meat prices and, 29, 45; membership of, 26, 40n2, 40n3; mercantile identity and, 35–36; moral standards of, 46; motives behind, 26; municipal authority and, 27; ordinances of, 10, 32; origins of, 26; power of, 27, 32; purposes of, 26–28, 32; as security, 32; trade and, 26–27, 32, 34–35; trust and, 27, 30, 32, 34, 38. *See also* Butchers' Guild; Guild Merchant

gunflints, 95–96

H

habitus, 3–5, 21, 65, 77–78

halal (lawful), 263

Hälsingland (Sweden), 110

Hanwell Asylum (Middlesex, England), 196

haram (prohibited), 263

haugbúi, 112

H Blocks, 107, 215, 217, 219–220, 222–23

Hisham I, 257

The Hope (London, England), 148–49, 151, 155, 161

horses, 54, 66–67, 90, 239, 241, 244–45, 247–49

hospitality, 106, 114

humoral theory, 75, 78

hunger strikes, 216–17

hunting, 132–33, 243–44

hygiene: animal bones and, 74–75; food consumption and, 21; food waste and, 74–75; Guild Merchant and, 29; meat and, 77; of medieval towns, 76–77; rubbish management and, 21, 29, 65, 74–75; smell and, 75–76; soil and, 75, 77

hyperdorsiflexion, 260–63

I

Iberia: Christianity and, 257, 266, 268; history of, 256; Islam and, 256–57; Judaism and, 257, 266; rural versus urban and, 267; Umayyad period of, 256–57, 266–67

identity: communality and, 105–6; formation of, 39, 254; institutions and, 169; Islamic, 254, 256, 267–68; material culture and, 255; mercantile, 35–36; *Oak Book* and, 38; rules and, 39, 254–55; spatial rules and, 148–49; theatres and, 152–53

indulgence items, 168–69

institutions, 106–7, 168–69, 192–94

interments: of abbots, 294; archaeothanatology and, 296; body positioning and, 263–64, 294–96; body preparations for, 291–92; Christian rules governing, 285–87; churches and, 159–160; clothing in, 294–96; co-burials of humans and dogs, 239–243; coffins and, 314, 316–17, 322, 324–25; decomposition and, 296–97; diseases and, 305–6; disturbances of, 296–97; exhumations of, 6–7; feet positions in, 294–96, 298–99; grave goods, 263–64; grave markers and, 263–64; grave structure and, 296; hand positions in, 294–96, 298–99; hierarchies and, 159–160; identity and, 263; Islam and, 256; Islamic burial rites and, 263–65; meaning and, 5; meanings and, 11; Mecca and, 264; of medical cadavers, 313–14, 320–25; monastic funerary rights and, 294–95; of monks, 294–95; of plague victims, 306; pre-interment body preparations and, 294–97; reburials, 5; regulations and, 5; specialist employment and, 7, 313;

uniformity of, 5; wrappings and, 263, 294–96, 298–99. *See also* child burials
intervisibility: in churches, 106, 159–160; St George infant cemetery and, 284; in theatres, 150, 158
Irish Lunatic Asylums for the Poor Act of 1817, 195, 200
Islam: adherence to, 265–68; architecture of, 256; bone morphology and, 255–56, 260–63, 267–68; burial rites of, 263–65, 267–68; ceramics of, 256, 265; Christianity and, 257–58; conversion to, 256–57, 266–68; diet and, 255, 263, 265; entheseal changes and, 259; gender division of labour and, 256–260, 265, 267–68; gender roles and, 257–58; heresy and, 234, 265–67; ideology of, 255, 265–68; interments and, 256; material culture of, 255–56; pork and, 263; prayer and, 6–7, 256; purity and, 255; rural versus urban and, 260, 267; *salāt* and, 260–63

J
Johnston, Francis, 194, 199
Judaism, 45–56, 50–51, 54–56, 257

K
Kilkenny District Lunatic Asylum (County Kilkenny, Ireland), 202–3, 205
King Edward the Confessor, 129
Kingsley (Cheshire, England), 133
Klein Wien (Göttweig, Austria), 286

L
La Charité-sur-Loire (Nièvre, France): body positioning and, 301; burials within, 301; burial uniformity of, 302–4; *Customary of Bernard* (*Ordo Cluniacensis/Bern*) and, 304; feet positions in, 303; hand positions in, 302; location of, 301; pre-interment body preparations and, 298, 301; wrappings and, 303–4

Lakehurst Shops (New Jersey, United States), 187
Landnámabók, 111
Latour, Bruno, 10, 21, 31–32
latrines, 50, 55, 76–77
lawyers, 32
Lewes Priory (Sussex, England), 292–93
Liber Elensis, 245
Liber Tramitis (*LT*), 293–95, 305
limbus puerorum, 273–79, 286–87
Lindeström, Per, 94
literacy, 22, 30
Long Finn Rebellion, 92, 98
longhouses: archaeology of, 116–17; artefact assemblage from, 117; boundaries of, 114, 116–17; byres of, 117–18, 121–22; dates of, 116; description of, 116–17; in England, 240; entrances of, 114, 119; feasting and, 116; gold foils and, 117; habitus and, 3; hall buildings and, 114, 116; hearths of, 117–18; history of, 109–10; hospitality and, 114; human behaviour and, 109; importance of, 110; internal boundaries of, 116–19; layouts of, 116; ontologies and, 11; origins of, 109–10; rituals and, 116; sanctity and, 114, 118; status and, 106; uses of, 116
Long Kesh/Maze (Lisburn, Northern Ireland): artefact assemblage from, 217–18, 220, 223–28; cellular structure of, 222–23; communal nature of, 222–23; complying prisoners of, 8, 107, 217, 219–220, 223; documentary evidence of, 227–28; documentary records of, 213–14, 223–24; escapes from, 216, 220, 222; H Blocks of, 215, 217, 223; hunger strikes of, 216–17, 225; as an internment camp, 216; legality of, 216; material culture of, 8, 214–15; noncomplying prisoners of, 8, 107, 217, 219–220, 223–26; oral histories of, 107, 220, 223; peace agreements and, 216; Perspex windows of,

Long Kesh/Maze (*cont.*)
225–26; prison art of, 219–220; prisoner agency and, 220, 224–28; prisoner clothing and, 224–25; prisoner communication methods within, 223; prisoner memories of, 214–15; prisoner political status in, 214–15, 223–25; prison guards of, 226–27; protests in, 8, 220, 224–26

Lübeck (Schleswig-Holstein, Germany), 52–53

Lunacy Acts of 1845, 195, 201

Lutheranism, 84, 86–87, 92, 98

M

Maddocks, James, 312

Magnus Lagabøte's Law, 112

makruh (reprehensible), 263

Malik ibn Anas, Aub Abdallah, 257

Malikism, 257, 266

manor court (halmote), 131

Maryborough District Lunatic Asylum (County Laoise, Ireland): chapels of, 193–94, 201–2, 204–5, 207–8; construction of, 198; farms of, 207; gender and, 204–5; layout of, 199, 204–5; local churches near, 205–6; location of, 198–99; marginalization of patients of, 207–8; material culture of, 207; moral management of, 200; non-restraint system and, 200, 208; overcrowding of, 200; patient recreation and, 199–201; regulation of space in, 204–5; religion and, 198–200, 207–8; renovations to, 207. *See also* St. Fintan's Hospital

material culture: agency of, 32; identity and, 255; religion and, 255

McKeown, Laurence, 225

meat: animal bones and, 66–68, 70–71; bone handicraft and, 54; class and, 47; consumption of, 45–47, 51, 54; dairy products and, 54; disposal of, 55–56; distribution of, 46; fasting and, 46; hygiene and, 45, 51, 77; pork, 50, 263; prices of, 29, 45; production of, 46, 52; rubbish management and, 55–56; slaughterhouses and, 51; use of bone in pavement in, 53

medieval towns: administration of, 26; charters for, 26; Cheshire and, 140; consumption in, 45–49, 51–52, 54–55; description of, 25; documentary records and, 61; food and, 45–49; hygiene of, 76–77; religion and, 50–51; trade and, 56. *See also* al-Andalus; rubbish management; Tulln an der Donau

memory: bodily, 97; collective, 38; communal, 38, 293; continuation of, 291; cultural, 3; identity and, 108; of Long Kesh/Maze, 218; oral histories and, 218; role of, 215; social, 110, 112

miasmas, 75, 78

military culture: alcohol and, 10–11, 107, 169–173; identity and, 169; layout of forts and, 170; parade grounds and, 170; social performance within, 10, 107, 186–87; tobacco use and, 107, 170–73

monasteries, 50–51, 61

monasticism, 292

Mount Göttweig (Göttweig, Austria), 279–280, 284–86

Murray, William, 194, 199

Muwattah, 257

N

Native Americans: Fort Yamhill and, 173; New Sweden and, 86, 94–96, 98; trade with, 94–96, 98

New Castle (Delaware, United States), 92

New Sweden: alcohol, 93; alcohol and, 87; archaeology of, 94; architecture of, 88–91; artefact assemblage from, 90–91; community and, 87–91, 97–99; crime in, 93, 97–99; date of, 84; Dutch takeover of, 84, 86–87, 97–99; emigration to, 87, 97–99; food and, 91; furnishings of, 91; governors of, 87–88; hierarchies and, 87; investors of, 84; location of, 84–85, 88–91;

loyalty to, 87; Lutheranism and, 84, 86–87, 92, 98; Native Americans and, 86–87, 94–96, 98; Peter Stuyvesant and, 92; punishment and, 92–93, 99; punishments and, 86; reasons for, 84–85; religion and, 84; resistance within, 86, 91–94, 96–99; rules and, 87–88; settlers to, 84–85, 97–99; Swedish language and, 87, 91, 98
Newington Butts playhouse (London, England), 148, 151
night watches, 28
Nissen huts of Compound, 215, 219
Notre Dame (Nièvre, France), *See* La Charité-sur-Loire
Northampton General Lunatic Asylum (Northampton, England), 197
Northern Irish Troubles, 216–17

O
Oak Book, 27–29, 32, 34–36, 38–39
óðalsmaðr, 112
Odin, 113
ontologies, 9–12
Original Sin, 274–75

P
parade grounds, 170
pauper asylums, 193
'Paxbread', 28
pedobaptisms, 275, 278–79, 287
Penitential of Theodore, 245–46
Penn, William, 87, 94
pet-keeping, 243–44
pigs, 47, 53–55, 67, 239, 241, 244, 263
Pinel, Philippe, 195
Poenitentiale Egberti, 245–46
Poenitentiale Hubertense, 246
prayers: adherence to rules and, 265–66; corpse preparation and, 291; morphology and, 6, 256, 260–63; *Common Book of Prayer*, 158; identity and, 267; as an iterative process, 6
Prestwich Asylum (Lancashire, England), 204
Printz, Johan, 84, 86–88, 92–95

prisons: art of, 219–220; asylums and, 192; dichotomous study of, 212; escapes from, 216; identity and, 214; material culture of, 214–15; power structures of, 8; prison art and, 219–220; prisoner agency and, 213–14; stills and, 220, 222; weapons and, 220
privacy, 105–6, 122, 161
prostitution, 205
Protestant Reformation, 94, 153, 158, 197, 200, 234, 279, 287
Puerta Elvira (Granada, Spain), 264–65
Pugin, Augustus, 198
punishment, 28, 34–35, 45, 86, 169–70, 246, 266, 291, 313, 315; administration of, 32; exile and, 119; for poverty, 313; for trespassing, 119
purgatory, 273, 276
puritanism, 151, 234

Q
Quakers, 196
Qur'an, 257, 263

R
Rationale Divinorum Officiorum, 275–76, 286
The Red Lion (Middlesex, England), 148, 151
Regularis Concordia, 295, 305
religion, 45, 112–13, 193, 196–97, 204, 206–7, 255
The Retreat (York, England), 196
Rhuddlan, 129
Richmond Asylum (Dublin, Ireland), 206
Risingh, Johan, 84, 87–88
River Danube, 44, 48, 51, 279
River Mersey, 134, 138
River Thames, 151
River Weaver, 131, 135
Roberts Site (Pennsylvania, United States), 95–96
The Rose (London, England), 148–49, 151–56

Ross Female Factory (Tasmania, Australia), 214
Rossio do Carmo (Portugal), 261
Royal London Hospital (London, England): archaeological study of, 312, 316–320; cemetery of, 316–320; cost of treatment in, 311–12; deceased patients of, 312–14; founding of, 311; history of, 311–12; location of, 311; medical school of, 311–12, 325–26; patients of, 311–12; treatment in, 311–12
rubbish management: animal bones and, 70–71, 74–75; *Breiter Markt* and, 50; categories of waste and, 4, 10, 63–65; consumption and, 8, 47; contamination and, 74–75; definitions of rubbish and, 62, 64–65; disposal problems, 78; fluid disposal and, 76; food waste and, 74–75; Guild Merchant and, 29; habitus and, 3–4, 65; hygiene and, 29, 65, 74–75; large objects and, 75–76; latrines and, 77; material culture and, 21; *Oak Book* and, 29; power and, 8; privately organized, 75–76; purity and, 76; quick disposal and, 67; refuse and, 63; religion and, 8; rules and, 63–64; rules on, 36–37; smell and, 75–76; in South, 31; in Southampton, 31; urbanization and, 78
rules: action and, 5; agency of, 30–33; archaeological study of, 1–2, 330–31; behaviour and, 6; biographies and, 8–9; bone morphology and, 6; classification and, 64; community and, 32, 36; continuity and, 4–5, 32, 83, 87–88, 329; as cultural customs, 1, 14, 87–88, 107–8, 233, 235, 329; defiance and, 1–2, 4–5, 22–23, 107, 330; development of, 5; disputes and, 233–34, 329; of engagement, 83; fluidity of, 32; habitus and, 4–5; hierarchies and, 107–8, 329; the human experience and, 1, 6–7; imposed, 5, 107–8, 234–36, 329; individual guilt and, 234; as material culture, 13–14; mistrust and, 233–36; *Oak Book* and, 29; ontologies and, 10; physical impact of, 6; punishment and, 1; rejection of, 1–2, 4–5, 235–36; relationships and, 25; renegotiation of, 234–35; as responsibilities, 234, 329; rubbish management and, 36–37, 63–64; as security, 32, 329; social context of, 25; spatial, 150–51; tensions and, 1, 329; as text, 6; transitions of, 6; writing down of, 13, 27, 35–36. *See also* Cluniac Customaries; *Oak Book*
Rule of Saint Benedict (*Benedicti Regula*), 291
rural communities, 4, 13, 43, 45, 47, 77–78, 233–4, 239, 256, 259, 261, 267–8, 311

S

Sancton I (Yorkshire, England), 241
Santa Eulalia (Murcia, Spain), 264–65
San Nicolás (Murcia, Spain), 261, 264–65
settlements, 25–6, 50, 52, 54, 67, 68, 99, 106, 10911, 131, 133–34, 141, 239–42, 245, 247–8, 263, 267; boundaries and, 11, 111, 114, 116, 118–21; colonialism and, 83–4; and Native Americans, 95–6; waste and 8, 61
sheep/goat, 45, 53–54, 66–67, 86, 90, 239–41, 244
Sligo Asylum (County Sligo, Ireland), 201, 206–7
social theory, 1–2, 21, 29
soil, 75, 77, 112, 286
Southampton (Hampshire, England): administration of, 29–30; charter for, 26, 34; craft guild of, 40n1; Guild Merchant of, 26, 29–30, 34, 38; mercantile elite and, 30; port of, 29–30, 34; pottery of, 35–36; as a royal town, 29–30, 34, 38; rubbish management of, 31; trade and, 26–27, 35–36

spark caps, 177
Spong Hill (Norfolk, England), 241
Stanley Royd Hospital Church (Wakefield, England), 193. *See also* Wakefield Asylum
St Augustine's Soliloquies, 131
St Fintan's Hospital (County Laoise, Ireland), 195. *See also* Maryborough District Lunatic Asylum
St George (Göttweig, Austria), 285
St George infant cemetery (Göttweig, Austria): age of infants within, 281, 283; Benedictine Abbey and, 280; burials within, 279–280; Church teachings and, 285–87; continued use of, 287; dating of, 280; documentary evidence of, 280; elevation of, 284; *Georgitag* and, 285; grave disturbances within, 283; grave markers and, 283; grave orientation, 281, 286; heaven and, 284; identity and, 283–84; isolation of, 284; Klein Wien and, 286; layout of, 282; lines of sight of, 284; location of, 279–280, 284; meaning of, 283–85; Mount Göttweig and, 284; shroud burials, 281; spatial structure surrounding, 283–85; stillborn children and, 286
stills, 96, 220
Stockbridge Down (Hampshire, England), 246
Strickler Site (Pennsylvania, United States), 95–96
Stuyvesant, Peter, 92, 94–95
Sumptuary Laws, 152–53
Susquehannocks, 95
The Swan (London, England), 148, 151, 155, 156, 162
synagogues, 50
Synod of the Grove of Victory, 246

T
tableware, 177, 181, 183
The Theatre (London, England), 148–49, 153

theatres: active zones of, 162–63; alternative activities in, 152, 162–63; backstage of, 155; brothels and, 151; churches and, 149, 158–160; city officials and, 150–51; class and, 149; communality of, 161; construction of, 148; costumes of, 158; crime in, 152; cross dressing and, 152; design of, 156; elite residences and, 149; exclusive spaces of, 149, 152, 157–160; galleries of, 155, 157, 162–63; gentlemen's rooms of, 152, 157; hierarchies and, 149; identity and, 152–53; as immoral, 151; intervisibility in, 150, 158; layout of, 157; layouts of, 155; locations of, 151; Lord's Room of, 152, 157; marginal locations of, 4; perceptions of, 151, 158; prices of, 152, 154, 157–58, 161–62; privacy and, 161; private rooms of, 152; promenading in, 162–63; reconstruction of, 150; remodelling of, 154–55; seating in, 162–63; shapes of, 148, 156; size of, 154; social segregation of, 157; spatial rules and, 150; spatial rules of, 148–49, 157, 161–64; stages of, 158; stairs in, 155–56; studies of, 149–150; Sumptuary Laws and, 152–53, 158; tiring rooms of, 155, 157; as transgressive spaces, 4, 150; unlicensed actors and, 151; vertical planes of, 149, 157, 160–64
tibial facets, 260–63
toasting, 172, 177
tobacco: artefacts of, 177–185; pipes, 177–78, 183; trade of, 84; use of, 107, 170–73
total institutions, 194, 198, 206
trade: alcohol and, 94–96, 98–99; of beaver pelts, 84; guilds and, 26–27, 32, 34–35; prohibited items in, 94–96, 98; tobacco, 84; Tulln an der Donau and, 43, 48; weapons and, 94–96, 98–99
trust, 27, 30, 32, 34, 38, 47, 287
Tuke, Samuel, 195–96

Tulln an der Donau (Austria): *Breiter Markt* of, 48; church of, 50–51; city wall of, 43; description of, 43; history of, 43; location of, 43; map of, 44; marketplace of, 43, 47–50; markets of, 49–50; rubbish management and, 47, 55–56; 'Schranne' of, 51–52; trade and, 43, 48

U

Umayyad Caliphate, 234, 256–57, 266–67
urban, 13, 38, 47, 54, 56, 61, 74, 77–78, 195, 244, 256, 261, 267–8
US Army Regulations (USWD), 169

V

Vagrancy Act of 1822, 151, 313
Valentine, William, 312, 320–22, 324, 326

W

Wakefield Asylum (Yorkshire, England), 192, 204
Weeting Castle (Norfolk, England), 129
West Riding Asylum (Yorkshire, England), 196
Wilde, Oscar, 213
witchcraft, 93–94
witch trials, 94, 233–36
workhouses, 169, 192, 313, 320, 326

X

Xarea (Almería, Spain), 264

Y

York Asylum (Yorkshire, England), 196, 206

www.ingramcontent.com/pod-product-compliance
Lightning Source LLC
Chambersburg PA
CBHW070802040426
42333CB00061B/1780